MACMILLAN'S TRAVEL SERIES

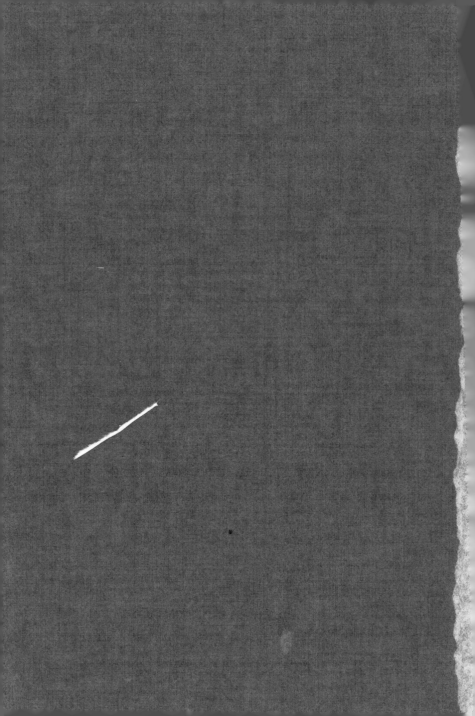

CHARLESTON

St. Michael's Church

CHARLESTON

THE PLACE AND THE PEOPLE

BY

MRS. ST. JULIEN RAVENEL

MACMILLAN'S
TRAVEL SERIES

THE MACMILLAN COMPANY

New York 1912

LONDON: MACMILLAN & CO. LIMITED

Norwood Press:
J. S. Cushing Co. — Berwick & Smith Co.
Norwood, Mass., U.S.A.

PREFACE

THIS book has not the slightest pretension to be the continuous history of the City of Charleston.

The writer has simply chosen from the story of its two hundred and fifty years such events as seem to her to have had most to do in shaping the fortunes of the men who made the town, or best to illustrate the character of their children who have lived in it.

What that fortune and character were, it is to be hoped the book may show. The writer has made no attempt to judge her people; has only tried to draw them as they appeared to themselves and to their contemporaries.

With this view she has used, wherever possible, the accounts of the actors in the drama, or of those who knew them best, — the earliest histories and memoirs to be found, especially the publications of the Hon. William A. Courtenay, and of the Historical Society of South Carolina, the "Shaftesbury Papers," and others.

She is under great obligations to friends who have assisted her with letters or information in their possession, — to Mrs. Julius Heyward of Middleton Place; to Mrs. John Kinloch (daughter of the historian and novelist of Carolina, W. Gilmore Simms); to Miss Pringle, Miss Alston and Miss Conner; to the Hon. James Simons, Vice President-General of the Cincinnati; to Captain Thomas and Captain C. C. Pinckney; to Dr. Henry Middleton Fisher; of Philadelphia; to D. Huger Bacot, Esq.; to Professor

v

Yates Snowden, University of South Carolina; and to Theodore D. Jervey, Esq. Also to Miss R. M. Pringle, Miss R. P. Ravenel, and others who have recalled to her the tales and legends of bygone days. These latter, when resting on tradition only, are introduced by "there was a story" or "the legend was."

It is hardly necessary to mention the extraordinary obligation which every student of the Annals of Carolina must be under to her chief historian, the late General Edward McCrady.

For the chapter entitled " Confederate Charleston," the authorities are the " Life of General Beauregard," by Alfred Roman, papers published in the " Year Books of Charleston," and the " Defence of Charleston Harbour," by John Johnson, engineer in charge, — now rector of St. Philip's.

For the reminiscent tone which has crept into the last chapters, the writer apologizes. She could not write otherwise.

HARRIOTT HORRŸ (RUTLEDGE) RAVENEL.

CHARLESTON, SOUTH CAROLINA,
June 20, 1906.

CONTENTS

CHAPTER XIX

CHAPTER XX

CHAPTER XXI

ILLUSTRATIONS

CHARLESTON

CHAPTER I

HIS MOST SACRED MAJESTY. THE LORDS PROPRIETORS

IN the year of our Lord 1679 the Lords Proprietors of the Province of Carolina on the Continent of North America ordered the Governor of their said province to remove his "Towne of Trade" (a small settlement on the west bank of the Ashley River) to the peninsula opposite, lying between what we call the Ashley and the Cooper rivers, but which were known to the Indians as the Kiawah and the Wando.

The Lords Proprietors were certain nobles and gentlemen to whom his Most Sacred Majesty King Charles II. had, in gratitude for services rendered to his father and himself, given all that territory "situate between the southernmost parts of Virginia, and the river San Mathias," the northern boundary of the Spanish dominions.

These gentlemen were: Lord Clarendon, the great historian; the Duke of Albemarle, who, as General Monk, had brought back the King from exile to "enjoy his own again"; the sagacious statesman, Sir Anthony Ashley Cooper, Lord Ashley (afterward Earl of Shaftesbury); Lord Craven, the *preux chevalier* of the age, who, like a knight of old, had vowed life and fortune to the service of the beautiful Elizabeth Stuart, Queen of Bohemia — and of Hearts; Lord Berkeley; Sir George Carteret; Sir John Colleton; and Sir William Berkeley, — all gallant and loyal cavaliers.

All these had done and suffered much in the service of the two Charleses, and to allow them, at their own expense, to secure and settle a province was an easy way to pay a debt of gratitude. Moreover, the King expressly stated in the charter, or patent, which he granted them, that he did so, finding that they " were incited by a laudable and pious design of propagating the Christian religion and the enlargement of the English empire and dominion," — matters which the Merry Monarch was suspected of not having deeply at heart.

The territory which he gave had not always been claimed by England; indeed, its very name " Carolina " had been given a hundred years before, by a luckless band of French Huguenots sent by the great Admiral Coligny to find a refuge for "men of the religion" in the New World. They, led by the Sieur Jean Ribault, had landed at the "fair entrance " to which they gave the name of Port Royal. Delighted with the beauty and fertility of the country, they claimed and named it for their king, Charles IX. of France; built a fort and raised the French flag. But misfortune overtaking them, they abandoned the place, only to be done to death by the Spaniards at St. Augustine, — dying for their faith and scorning to abjure.

In the reign of Charles II. a ruined fort, a broken column carved with the *fleur-de-lys*, and the names " Carolina " and " Port Royal " alone remained to tell the tale.

The country had, for nearly a century, " lain like a derelict " to be taken by the first comer, so England stepped in and claimed it for her own. There were many difficulties and delays, but the Proprietors sent exploring expeditions, on one of which a bold captain, Robert Sandford, coasting along from the Cape Fear to Port Royal, landed and " took seizin by turffe and twigge " of the territory in the name of the King and realm of England.

Three years later the first settlement was made by a

colony sent from England *via* Barbadoes and Bermuda, commanded by Captain William Sayle. Sayle, after ex-

OLD TOWN PLANTATION

Site of the first Charleston. The present city lies across the Ashley River, in the distance.

amining St. Helena Island and Port Royal, decided upon going northward to what the Spaniards called St. George's Bay, but which Sandford, in honour of the Proprietor who had taken the chief interest in the matter, had named the "River Ashley."

Here they landed and built a little town and called it "Albemarle Point," afterwards "Charles Town," a small place of nine acres, with the river on one side, a creek on the other, and a little ditch and palisade between it and the boundless forest at the back, — the forest in which were terrible beasts and yet more terrible men — the men of the "shaven head and the painted face," who had laid St. Helen's waste only a year before. In this little company of one hundred and sixty souls were several women. Surely the women of those days must have been heroic creatures! What did they think and feel, those mothers of Carolina, as they looked from their low bluff upon the wilderness around? Had they the prophetic vision of comfort and plenty and happy homes for their children, or did the trials and privations of the present fill their hearts? However they may have felt, no word of fear escaped them; the letters tell of suffering, but never of despondency.

At Albemarle Point they endured all the first horrors of colonization. Want, hunger, sickness, danger from Indians, and so on. Their food was for a time reduced to one pint of "damnified peas " a day, and but for the help of the friendly Indians they might have starved. These were their neighbours, and their friendship was gained chiefly by the wisdom of one man, a "brave chirurgeon," Mr. Henry Woodward, who, having accompanied Sandford on his exploring expedition, had offered to remain for a whole year alone among the savages, to learn their language and interpret for his people when they should return. The nephew of the chief, "the Cassique of Kiawah," had taken his place on Sandford's ship in order to learn English, and had great influence in deciding the choice of Ashley River as the place of settlement.

Woodward had gained the favour of his Indian hosts and was thus enabled to avert dangers which would have overwhelmed the little band.

For the government of their colony the Proprietors had prepared a singular code of laws. By their charter from the King, which granted them all the territory now comprised in the states of North and South Carolina and Georgia, with an indefinite extension westward "to the South Seas," they were *enjoined* to establish the Church of England, and *permitted* to grant liberty of conscience. They might make laws, but only with the consent of the "greater part" of the people (a most unusual provision for those days) ; they were to establish a nobility, but not to give the nobles English titles; and place and people were ever to remain "of His Majesty's allegiance."

The Province was to be created a County Palatine, and the Proprietors, the oldest of whom, for the time being, was to be the Palatine, were authorized to build forts, castles, towns, etc., to appoint governors and officers, to make laws, levy taxes and customs, establish the Church of England, wage war, pursue their enemies, put down rebellion, tumult, and sedition. All these powers they were "to have, use and enjoy in as ample a manner as any Bishop of Durham in our kingdom of England ever heretofore held, used, or enjoyed."

A "County Palatine" is a frontier province where, for the prompt action needful when enemies are close at hand, the King delegates the supreme power to a "Palatine," who can exercise for the time all regal functions. Such had been the English counties of Chester, Lancashire, and Durham, in the days when the Welsh threatened the west country, and the Cathedral of Durham was "half Church of God, half tower against the Scot." Of the three, in the reign of Charles II., Durham alone kept its ancient privilege ; and so the powers of that feudal potentate, the Lord Bishop, were cited as the model for those of the Proprietors of Carolina.

This charter was for a long time as dear to the people of Carolina as is Magna Carta to the English. In addition Lord Ashley (not yet Lord Shaftesbury), calling to his aid the great philosopher John Locke, prepared the "Fundamental Constitution," which enlarged and added to the statutes of His Majesty. Among other things it arranged for the proposed "nobility," "in order to avoid a too numerous democracy." This nobility was little more than a plutocracy, depending upon the amount of land owned by a man, which might be bought by him, without regard to birth or breeding, or service to the State. The titles passed by purchase as well as by descent.

As land was held at a penny an acre, it did not require a large fortune to become a "baron" with twelve thousand acres, a cassique with twenty-four thousand, or even a landgrave (these were the titles chosen) with forty-eight thousand. The estates were called "baronies," and there were many which long kept the name, as the "Wadboo," the "Broughton," the "Colleton," the "Fairlawn Barony," but no one was addressed as "baron" or "cassique," and the landgraves, who were generally given the title to qualify them as governors (there were some exceptions), simply prefixed the title to their surnames. No man was landgrave of Edisto or of Accabee, but Landgrave Morton or Landgrave Smith. Neither did any "lord of the manor" exercise manorial rights over white leetmen or negro slaves. Furnished with this constitution and with some more practical "Temporary Laws," the colony began its career.

A contemporaneous, *facsimile* copy of this constitution (commonly called "Locke's") is among the treasures of the Charleston Library, and may be seen by the curious.

Governor Sayle had brought with him only one hundred and sixty persons, but the number of inhabitants was rapidly increased by subsequent immigration. Especially was this the case when Governor Sir John Yeamans came from Barbadoes, bringing with him negroes accustomed to the agriculture of the islands and to labour under tropical suns. By so doing he decided the institutions and conditions of Carolina for all future time.

Yeamans was the son of an alderman of Bristol who had suffered death for his fidelity to the crown. He himself had warmly supported the royal cause in Barbadoes, already a thriving colony. For so doing and for prospective services in colonization he, Sir Peter Colleton, and some other gentlemen of like principles, had been made baronets ; — the old people used to refer to them as "only-badian Baronets." He had provoked the colonists by not accompanying them on their voyage and they vainly protested against his appointment now. In many respects he made a bad Governor, oppressing the people by his exactions, and offending the Proprietors by demands for buildings and fortifications, which although needed they had no mind to give.

Still, he had the advantage of understanding the needs and resources of a new colony, putting the place into a tolerable state of defence, and pointing out the agriculture suited to the climate. He also showed the resources of the forests, cutting and sending to Lord Ashley twelve great logs of cedarwood, as the first-fruits of his new possession. From that time the demand for cedar was as constant and eager as was that of Solomon upon Hiram, King of Tyre.

A still more important service was, that by his advice

and influence many rich planters from Barbadoes and other West Indian Islands came to the Province, bringing their negroes with them. They settled themselves chiefly on a small affluent of the Cooper, called, from the fancied

ALONG GOOSE CREEK

resemblance of its winding course to the curving neck of the goose, " Goose-creek. " Thence, they and their friends on the Ashley and Cooper were known as the " Goose-creek men."

They differed from the " plain people " — mostly dissenters — who had come out with Sayle, in being generally of a higher class, wealthy, and members of the Church of England. Thus began — and not from the fanciful nobility — that untitled class of landed gentry which, perfectly well understood and accepted during the colonial period, survived the Revolution and formed a distinct and influential element of Charleston society down to 1865.

Long after Yeamans had been removed this movement continued, and gentlemen of wealth and position arrived from England and the Islands to the great benefit of the Province.

It was during Sir John's term of office that the question of removing the first town was mooted, and Mr. Dalton, secretary to the "Grand Council," wrote the following letter to Lord Ashley, who had proposed a new "Towne of Trade" in January, 1671.

" We cannot reasonably believe that the world is now asleep, or that the Spaniard has forgot his sullenness, therefore as it has been the practice of the most skilful settlers, soe it will become us, to erect townes of safety as well as of Trade, to which purpose there is a place — between Ashley and Wando rivers, about six hundred acres left vacant for a towne and Fort, by the direction of the old Governor Coll. Sayle, for that it commands both the Rivers. It is not a mile over between River and river, with a bold landing free from any marsh, soe as many shipps as can may ride before the Towne at once, and as many shipps as can come into the River under the protection of the fort, if one should be there.

" It is as it were a Key to open and shut this settlement into safety or danger ; Charles Towne [their first town] indeed can very well defend itself, and that's all ; but that like an iron gate shutts up all the Townes that are or may be in these rivers ; besides it has a full view of the sea, being but a league or a few miles from the mouth of the river and noe shipp can come upon the Coast but may be seen from thence and may receive the benefit of a Pilott from that Towne."

"The settlements being thick about it, it cannot be surprised [he probably means by Indians] it is likewise the most convenient for building and launching of shipps as large as can come into this harbour. It must of necessity be very healthy, being free from any noxious vapors, and all the summer long being refreshed with continual cool breathings from the sea, which up in the country men are not soe fully sensible of."

No better description of the site of Charleston and of its harbour could be written to-day. Its inhabitants are still "all the summer long refreshed with cool breathings from the sea"; and for its strength, the fleets of France and Spain, of England, and of the United States, have all tried to force the iron gate, — and failed.

In September of the same year Lord Ashley wrote to Sir John, "Above all things let me recommend to you the making of a Port Town upon the River Ashley," etc.

Sir John was evidently of the same mind as his old predecessor, and took the first steps by negotiating with the persons who had taken up the land between the two rivers. Accordingly in February, 1672, Mr. Henry Hughes and "John Coming and Affra his wife" appeared before the Grand Council and surrendered their land, "nere a place upon Ashley River known as Oyster Point to be imployed in and towards enlarging of a Towne and Common of Pasture there intended to be erected."

"Mr. John Coming and Affra his wife" are perhaps the most interesting people of that early time, because it is impossible not to suspect a romance concerning them.

For why should "Mistress Affra Harleston of Mollyns, daughter of John Harleston Gent., of a family long seated at South Ockenden Essex, and having estates in Ireland," come out to America as servant to Mr. Owens, but for a sentimental reason? Her father's house, as described in the inventory, contained "seller, parlour, kitchen, larder, great chamber, painted chamber, nurserie, butterie, gallerie to the garretts," etc. Why, having everything thus handsome about her, did she leave it all, if it were not to marry John Coming, first mate of the *Carolina*, and afterward captain of the good ships *Edisto* and *Blessing?* Coming was a hardy Devonshire sailor of the race of Drake and Raleigh and Kingsley's heroes. The family tradition says, that having lost a ship some time before he had been accused of cowardice, whereupon he had with his own hands built and rigged a longboat, in which he had crossed the Atlantic. He must have been a man of means, for on first arrival he settled a place on Ashley River and afterward one on the Cooper. His name lives in "Comings Point," the southern cape of Charleston Harbour, charted by him in 1671, and in the fine plantation "Coming-tee," now in possession of his collateral descendants, the Balls.

This *may* have been the first runaway match in South Carolina!

Mrs. Affra has kept the town waiting, but in fact it waited long. Sir John Yeamans fell into disgrace with the Proprietors, as before said, and was superseded before anything more was done. He withdrew to Barbadoes "with much estate but small esteem." His wife, "Dame Margaret," had been known in a right womanly way while in the Province. Two unfortunate men had been condemned to death for desertion, but were pardoned "on account of the warmest sollicitations of Margaret Lady Yeamans and the rest of the ladyes and gentlewomen of this Province." Her daughter married James Moore, afterward Governor, and has left numerous descendants in Carolina.

It was probably owing to this and other troubles that it

was not until '79 that Lord Ashley wrote authoritatively to Governor West, " We let you know that Oyster Point is the place we do appoint for the New Towne, of which you are to take notice and call it Charles Town."

West appointed a commission to carry out these orders, and in the course of the next year the move was made. The first settlement, gradually abandoned, and despoiled even of its name, became at length a plantation, still known as " Old Town Plantation," and the new Charles Town arose in its stead, the capital of the " Colony of Ashley River."

CHAPTER II

GOVERNOR WEST was a grave and sober-minded man, and can but have been amused at the magnificent directions which Lord Ashley sent for the building of the chief town of a province which had at that time only twelve hundred inhabitants.   It should, His Lordship said, have at least sixscore squares each of three hundred feet and " it is necessary that you lay out the great Port Town into regular streets, for be the buildings never soe meane and thin at first, yet as the town increases in riches and people, the voyde spaces will be filled up and the buildings will grow more beautyfull.   Your great street cannot be less than one hundred or six score broad, your lesser streets none under 60, your alleys 8 or ten feet.   A Pallisado round the Towne with a small ditch is a sufficient Fortification against the Indians. . There is a necessity that you leave a Common round the Towne soe that noe Enclosure may come nearer than the 3rd part of a mile to the Pallisado," etc.

For the carrying out of these directions West had the assistance of his committee of Council.   Surveyor-general Culpepper had already drawn a plan and Stephen Bull (afterward surveyor-general) took an active part. Stephen Bull was, next to West and Woodward, the most important of all the emigrants who came with Governor Sayle.   He came bringing many servants, and at once took up a large body of land on Ashley River and named it " Ashley Hall."   He was Lord Ashley's deputy, a member of Council, master of ordnance, and held a dozen other important offices. Of most consequence to the colony was the fact that as an explorer among the Indians he became so friendly with them that they chose him for their Cassique, and he thus was enabled to make an advantageous treaty with them in 1696. A small one-story brick house built by him at Ashley Hall is still standing,

ASHLEY HALL PLANTATION

Remains of the steps of Ashley Hall in the foreground.

— the oldest on the river. The estate remained in the possession of the family for over two hundred years, and in all those years there was hardly a time in which one of the name did not go out to take part in the government of South Carolina.

The committee does not seem to have attempted to execute Lord Ashley's plan in full. Everything, however, is comparative, and the wide streets of that day are the narrow ones of this. Not even the most devoted Charlestonian would now call Tradd, Elliott, and Church streets

" broad," but Mr. Thomas Ashe, clerk of the ship *Richmond*, writing in 1682 says, " The town is regularly laid out into broad and capacious streets "!

It really was a narrow parallelogram about four squares long by three wide. The first street fronted on the Cooper River, extending on the south from a creek (Vander Horst's), which ran where Water Street is now, to another on the north over which the City Market now stands. On the west the present Meeting Street was bounded by a wall in which was a half moon, with a gate and drawbridge giving access to the country without. The wall also extended along the three sides of water front, and had bastions and small forts at the corners. Of course all this was not constructed at once, but it was as described in a very few years. From the river front projected wharves, and soon " sixteen merchant vessels sometimes rode at once in the harbour." There was a place reserved, Ashe says, for a church and a Town Hall and a parade ground for the militia. The streets running north and south were Bay Street, Church, and Meeting; east and west were Tradd, so named in honour of the first male white child born in the town, Elliott, Broad, and Dock, now Queen. The early maps show these only extending from the Bay to Meeting Street, but in 1700 they are said to reach from river to river. Some persons lived outside of the walls on little farms, and the Council ordered that the peninsula should be cleared of all trees and bushes that might conceal a lurking enemy. There was a court of guard, and watch was kept, both there and upon Sullivan's Island, for " Topsayle Vessels " and other suspicious craft.

In the years from 1679 to 1689 colonists were continually arriving. The accession of James II. quickened the emigration from England. Five hundred dissenters, led by Morton and Axtell, who were made Landgraves for

their services, came out in a single month.   Mr. Benjamin
Blake was an important person in this connection.

The Barbadians continued to come, and gentlemen from
the other West Indian Islands and from England also.
Thomas Drayton, William and Arthur Middleton, and Robert Daniel, all names of note in Carolina, came in 1679.
Moore, Ladson, Grimball, Cantey, Boone, Thomas Smith,
Schenking, and Izard appear soon after.   All of these took
up lands; many of the original grants still remain, and
the Council Journals show the extent, as " Lands granted
on Goose Creek to Edward Middleton, Gent., one of the
honourable persons of this Province."   This land became
afterward the beautiful plantation " Crowfield," long considered the handsomest landscape garden in the Province.
Another grant of a thousand acres to the same person
was the " Oaks," the stately avenue of which still remains.

Mr. Thomas Amy is to have twelve thousand acres
(a barony) " In consideration of his great services " (in encouraging emigration), and John Gibbs, Esq., kinsman of
the Duke of Albemarle, is to " have every attention paid to
him, and three thousand acres *rent free.*"   This last is a
very rare order; the quit-rent, which made much trouble,
was generally to be paid.   But although the chief residences of these gentlemen were on their plantations, they
were likewise important citizens; in fact the country for a
radius of twenty miles around was but a greater Charles
Town.   Most of the chief planters in those early days
were merchants as well ; the Indian trade was long the
chief source of wealth.   "Charles Town trades for 1000
miles into the continent," one old writer says.   The Proprietors tried to restrict the fur trade to within one hundred miles of the town, reserving all beyond to themselves;
but although they appointed Indian agents to enforce
the law, it was continually eluded.   In troublous times

some of these agents became persons of great importance. Besides the furs, they had for exports, as has been already said, the products of the forest, lumber of all sorts, tar, pitch, and turpentine. To these, in defiance of the objections of the Proprietors, there was added salt-beef and bacon. What was a man whose estate numbered thousands of acres to do but to graze it ? The cattle throve and multiplied enormously in a climate where food was plentiful all the year, and a bracken bush could keep the cow in the severest weather. Wolves prevented the increase of sheep as worthless dogs do now, but most planters protected a small flock, to supply the family with mutton and with wool for the ever whirling wheels. Swine could take care of themselves; they fattened on the acorns of the oak groves, and soon became an important article of export, while as yet crops were small and inadequate.

These sources of prosperity had so increased the well-being of the little community that when Thomas Ashe, clerk of the ship *Richmond*, came out in 1680 with the first Huguenot colony, he declared in the " View of Carolina " which he published on his return to England, that there was no longer any suffering or want of food to be apprehended ; that the settlers were well established, had all sorts of European grains and fruits and " twenty sorts of pulse not known in England, all of them good for food." It would be interesting to learn what they were. Most families kept an Indian, who for a mere trifle would supply a household of twenty people with an ample quantity of game, venison, turkeys, ducks, etc. This custom lasted down to the Revolution, and in some cases still later.

In the town the work of building went on. It seems extraordinary that the colony should have been founded for fourteen years before any attempt was made to erect a church. The uncertainty of occupation of Albemarle

c

Point was probably the cause of this delay, or perhaps the small number of churchmen among the original settlers. Old Governor Sayle had indeed selected and laid out a graveyard, adjoining the old town, of eighty acres (surely a liberal provision), in which we may presume that he himself was interred, but not until 1682 was St. Philip's begun.

It was placed where St. Michael's now stands, at the corner of Broad and Meeting streets just opposite the half moon and drawbridge, and was built of the black cypress which Mr. Maurice Mathews, correspondent of Lord Shaftesbury, had strongly commended ten years before. "The black cypress is wonderful large and tall and smoothe, of a delicate graine, and smells. It will hereafter be a good commodity to ye prying planter who looks abroad." Its value as a building material was now known. The foundation was of brick, and this mode of building, namely a cypress house on a brick foundation, was long esteemed and continued in the colony. For lime they burnt the old Indian heaps of oyster shells, which Sandford had described as piled thick along the river banks near the coast, where are many still to be seen. This lime makes the strongest possible mortar. Walls and whole buildings were often made of a concrete, called "tappy," or "pisé," — composed of these shells mixed with the lime which becomes hard as stone. The only building now standing in Charleston *known* to have been erected in the seventeenth century, the old Powder Magazine in Cumberland Street, which was attached to the small fort at Carteret Bastion at the northwest corner of the old wall, is built of this "tappy."

St. Philip's was said to be "large and stately" and to have a neat palisade around it. It shows the good feeling between the sects that Mrs. Blake (sometimes, as the wife of a Landgrave and Proprietor, called "Lady Blake"), who was the daughter of Landgrave Axtell, should have contributed liberally to the adornment and completion of

GLEBE HOUSE

St. Philip's, although herself a Baptist. It was endowed by the piety of that true daughter of the Church, Mrs.

Affra Coming, who in 1698 "for love and duty" bestowed upon it seventeen acres of land just outside the walls. This land, now covered by the "Middle Western" part of the city, has, as Glebe land, been of great value. Glebe Street and Coming Street keep the memory of the gift and the donor. A large old-fashioned brick house on the east side of the former street was, until a comparatively recent period, the Rectory of St. Philip's, and was always known as the "Glebe House."

The other denominations soon housed themselves also. In Meeting Street, near the north wall, the Presbyterians or Independents built in 1685 their "White Meeting House," to which Governor Blake ten years later gave a thousand pounds sterling. This gave the name to Meeting Street.

The Huguenot emigrants, who only arrived in 1680 to 1686, began their "French Church" about 1687 in the upper part of Church Street on land conveyed by Ralph Izard and Mary his wife (a Miss Middleton) for that purpose. Isaac Mazÿck, one of the earliest and wealthiest emigrants of their race, gave generously to its erection and support. At the other end of Church Street were the Baptists, on land given by William Elliott, and the Quakers had a "Friends' Meeting House" outside the walls, near to the present King Street.

Thus in ten years from the founding of Charles Town there was no lack of places of worship; it is remarkable that although no one of the original buildings remains churches still stand upon each of these sites, belonging to the same organizations and denominations. The "Friends'" is the only exception to this. The building was destroyed by fire, and there being no Quakers now in the city it was never rebuilt ; but the lot is kept sacred, and is still owned by the society.

So far the people of all these various denominations were, with the exception of a few Dutch, from Nova-Belgia,

natives of Great Britain, subjects of the King; but now
from 1680 to 1688 came the French Huguenots, strangers
and aliens, into this English community. So much im-

THE HUGUENOT CHURCH

portance has been attached to this people that it strikes
us strangely to find that they amounted, all told, only to
about four hundred and fifty persons. A small number
for which to claim the amount of influence often attributed

to them, until we remember that there were at that time
but twenty-five hundred white people in the colony.
Thus the arrival of a compact and very individual body of
foreigners, one-sixth of their whole number, might easily
create some uneasiness. At first nothing of this appeared.
Some few, wisely fleeing the wrath to come, had left France
before the severity of persecution began, carrying with
them much of their property, as the Mazÿcks, St. Juliens,
and others.

Those who remained until after the Revocation of the
Edict of Nantes were happy if they escaped with life and
unbroken families.

The stories of the flight are pathetic, but do not properly belong here. Well treated in England, highly commended by the Archbishop of Canterbury, and protected
by the King, the colony who came in the *Richmond* sailed
under royal patronage, sent by King Charles himself, to
cultivate wine, oil, and silk; in all of which they absolutely failed. The Proprietors recommended them
strongly to the Governor, and they were kindly received.
The merchants and artisans, of whom there were many,
both in this and succeeding migrations, settled generally
in the town. The others took up land on the lower part
of the Santee River, thence called " French Santee," and
on the Cooper, in what was then known as " Orange
Quarter," now the parishes of St. Denis and St. John's
Berkeley. The greater number who came to Carolina
were people of humble station, yet there were among them
some of superior rank; "*Sieurs*"; "*Marchands d'outremer*";
clergymen and physicians; but all came for one cause,
all had made the same sacrifice, all were bound in one
brotherhood of kindliness.

Inspired by a faith as strong, a morality as pure, as the
most rigid Puritanism could demand, they escaped its
harsher and grimmer features, and dwelt more on the

mercy of the Father than on the vengeance of the Judge.
This strikes one in the entries in the few family Bibles of
the emigrants still preserved, in which thanks for preservation are strangely unmixed with denunciations of their
relentless persecutors.

The emigrant Daniel Huger writes : —

"Oh Lord in Christ our blessed Redeemer, I here acknowledge with all humility that thy chastisement hath
been mixed with wonderful mercies. Thou hast preserved us from the persecutors of Thy blessed Gospel, and
hast brought us into this remote part of the World, where
Thou hast guided us and blessed us here in a wonderful
manner, and we now enjoy the benefits of Thy dear
Gospel in peace and quietness through Our dear Lord
Jesus Christ. Amen."

They cast no longing backward glances as men who
had left home under happier fortunes would have done,
and grateful to the country which sheltered them became
her devoted children. It has been supposed that lands
were *given* to these emigrants, but this is shown to be a
mistake, as only two free grants are on record. They
bought on the same terms as other settlers, and some took
up large estates — The de Chastaigners, Seigneurs de
Cramaché et de Lisle, three thousand acres, Goulard de
Vervant twelve thousand, etc. Neither of these families
survives in Carolina except in the female line.

The last emigrants who came in a body to Charles Town
and its vicinity arrived in 1695, from Dorchester, Massachusetts. They established themselves about twenty miles
from the town on the Ashley River, and called the place
Dorchester for their old home. Here they built a meeting
house and lived for sixty years "keeping much to themselves." At the end of that time they removed to Middle
Georgia in search of a better climate. Some few of the
congregation remained, and the name of "Ioor," known in

the Revolution, still survives "as an appendage to another."

The account of this last emigration has been given out

CONGREGATIONAL CHURCH, DORCHESTER

Second building, 1700.
From painting in South Carolina Historical Society rooms.

of due chronological sequence, in order to complete the tale of those who were to make the people of Charles Town. Large companies of Germans and Swiss did indeed come later into the Province, but they were settled in the middle country and did not materially affect the seaboard population. Emigrants of course continued to arrive, and were often of the first importance, — as Trott and Rhett in 1694 and 1698; but they came as individuals or families; there were no large groups of newcomers to be reckoned with after 1695.

Even so the elements were strangely different. In most of the other Provinces there was a certain homogeneity. Roughly speaking, it may be said that New England was settled by Puritans, Pennsylvania by Quakers, Maryland by Catholics, and Virginia by loyal Cavaliers. In Carolina, on the contrary, was infinite variety. There were English churchmen, influential and proud, but numerically weak; there were English, Scotch, and Irish dissenters of every shade of creed, who claimed in 1706 to be two-thirds of the population. There were some Dutch, a few Swiss and Belgians, some Quakers, and the French Huguenots. From these various sources sprang, under the imperial genius of the English race, and the wise government of the English law, applied to the grave responsibility of his own industrial system, the well-marked characteristics of the Carolinian of "the parishes." At the outbreak of the Revolution there was no community more absolutely one, more absolutely devoted to the old country, than this, Charles Town and its dependencies.

CHAPTER III

THE MURDER OF THE SCOTS.   INTOLERANCE

BEFORE the Huguenot immigration was complete
Charles Town was startled and shocked by a tragedy which, though not precisely within her borders,
touched her nearly.

She had not been too well pleased when in 1682 the
Lords Proprietors had informed Mr. Joseph Morton, then
Governor, that they intended sending out a Scotch colony
to be planted to the southward, somewhere near Port
Royal, which was to be independent, or nearly so, of the
existing authorities on Ashley River.   This colony grew
out of the troubled condition of Scotland.   Times were
hard for the Covenanters then; the easy-going Charles
was still upon the throne, but the persecutions which followed the " Rising in the West," so pathetically told in
song and story, were going on, and the Whigs knew well
that the scourge which fell upon them now would become
a scorpion in the hand of James.   Therefore, turning
their eyes to Carolina, as " to a place of refuge and safe
retreat from arbitrary government," several lords and
gentlemen proposed to the Proprietors to carry a colony
of ten thousand people to their Province.

The Lords were gracious; they gave the right, insisting
only that the " Fundamental Constitution " should be
most strictly observed, and they also gave a sort of co-
ordinate authority to the Governors of the old and the
new colonies, an arrangement which could hardly fail to
breed dissension.   In an unhappy hour Henry, Lord Car-

dross, of the noble houses of Mar and Buchan, came with a small following to Port Royal. The number is not definitely known, some saying that only ten families accompanied him, others giving more. On arriving, Cardross notified Morton of his coming, and his claims. Morton doubted his authority and summoned the Scotch lord to appear before him as his superior officer. They could not agree upon their relative positions, Morton even ordering the arrest of some of the Scotch as disobedient to his commands. Cardross, in a very manly letter, explained his position.

"STUART'S TOWN ON PORT ROYALL ye 25th March, 1684.

"HONOURED SIR, — The Bearer hereof, Mr. Dunlop, one of our number having some occasions att Charles Towne, we have laid it upon him to give you an account of the state of our affairs, that noe mistakes may arise betwixt you and us. [He alludes to jealousies of jurisdiction etc.] We nothing doubt but that you all know the contracts and treaties that have been made between the Lords Proprietors and us and other of our countrymen. We have the ties of living under the same Royall King, and of having the same Lords Proprietors, soe that it will never be the true interest of any of us to lett Jealousies arise among us, especially att this tyme when we have ground to apprehend the invasion of the Forraigner. We expected to have heard what your resolves were, after the perusall of the Spanish Letter we sent you, but as yett have not ; " he reports Spanish Indians intriguing against them and concludes : —

"We desire you cause delivir to the bearer those six Gunns the Lords Proprietors appoynted for us, we will trouble you no further, but remitt all to the bearer by whom we expect a return from you."

No satisfaction was received and the petty dispute went

on. Morton was removed from office, and a Colonel Quarry was acting Governor in his stead, when Cardross, who appears to have known this gentleman, and to have hoped something from that circumstance, wrote again : —

"I have heard what the Resolucions of the Grand Council were concerning mee and that the Council continue in the apprehencion that I have committed some high misdemeanour and look upon my not appearing as a great contempt of their authoritye. Sir, I doe not look upon myself as an English lawyer and therefore shall not be positive in every notion I have taken of it." He speaks of former communications and says that what he has done is to sustain the authority of the government at Charles Town, speaks of illness (fever and ague) by reason " of these heats which I have not been acquainted with," and concludes : —

"I hope what I now write will satisfye you and the rest of the gentlemen of the Grand Council that they will not further trouble themselves by sending for one who is very willing to take the first opportunity to come.

"I crave pardon for the tedious lyne in writing, whereof I am forced to make use of anothers hand, but I have presumed on the small acquaintance I have with you, and on the character which you now beare in the Government of which I wish you much joy, etc., etc.

"CARDROSSE."

His hopes were vain ; Quarry was no more responsive than Morton had been, and at last worn out by illness and mortification, Cardross resigned his office and returned to Scotland. It had been well if his companions had gone with him, for in 1686, the Spaniards, well informed of the conditions by the " trusty Indians," made a descent upon the coast, landing at Edisto. Fortunately for themselves, Morton (then again Governor) and Mr. Paul Grimball, Secretary of the Province (first of the name in Carolina), were not on their plantations. The Spaniards sacked and burnt their houses, carried off money, plate, and negroes, killed the brother-in-law of the Governor, and then fell upon Port Royal. Here were only twenty-five fever-stricken men to oppose them. They killed some, whipped and tortured others, and carried the rest captive to St. Augustine; only two or three escaped to bring the news to Charles Town.

Great was the horror and rage when the tale was told, — rage it may be supposed not unmixed with self-reproach. They could not hold themselves guiltless toward the Scotch, and Edisto was of their own government, not more than forty miles away. A political quarrel was going on at the moment and parties were bitterly opposed, but under this calamity such differences were forgotten, and all felt and acted as Englishmen. They sent a dispatch to the Proprietors asking aid from them, and from the King; but not waiting for help which must needs be slow, they assessed themselves; armed two vessels and four hundred men, and resolved to beard the lion in his den by attacking St. Augustine itself, as became a County Palatine with all its rights of pursuing enemies, waging war, etc.

Unhappily before the expedition could start there arrived James Colleton, a Landgrave, brother to the Proprietor Sir John, and to Sir Peter who had acted as agent for the colony at Barbadoes. Colleton brought with him his commission as Governor, and the people were glad, nothing doubting that a man of his soldierly race would prove a gallant commander. To their anger and disgust he ordered immediate disarmament of vessels and men, and absolutely forbade the expedition. The people appealed to the Proprietors, but they entirely supported Colleton. The reason was not far to seek. James II.,

who was on the throne, was the sworn foe to Proprietary
governments and a friend of his most Catholic Majesty.
The Proprietors trembled for their charter — nothing
would endanger it so much as a quarrel with Spain. So
they ordered the most humiliating submission, told Morton and the proposed commander, Captain Godfrey, that
they " might well have been hung " had they made war upon
his Majesty's friends ; equivocated shamefully about the
rights of a County Palatine, and ordered that a " polite
letter " should be addressed to the Governor of St. Augustine asking by what authority he acted. Seldom if ever
have Englishmen been so abused ! The furious colonists,
not understanding that their honour was being sacrificed
to policy, attributed an even baser motive to the hated
Governor, the instrument of their disgrace. He desired,
they said, to monopolize the Indian trade, it being " supposed on rational grounds that he hath a partner in London," and of truckling to Spain for the same avaricious
reasons. They wrote : —

" We have often received letters from the Spanish
Governor at St. Augustine which we use to answer with
courage and we hope with prudence ; but the Spaniards
did invade us in the year 1686, destroying severall plantations and much stock, and most barbarously burned alive
one of our people and caryed others away into captivity,
and ye whole country did resolve by fresh pursuite to be
revenged upon them, but the late Governor arriving here,
did forbid it att that time, and afterwards when a new
Governor at St. Augustine did send a Fryar and a lieutenant to treat with the Governor here about all differences,
the Governor (Landgrave Colleton) did not advise with
the commoners of the Council about the matter, (unlesse
once when he desired the Spanish Messengers should by
their consent be maintained out of the publick Treasury),
but did, contrary to the Honour of the English Nation,

pass by all the bloody Insolencys the Spaniards had committed against this Collony, and did with others enter
into a contract of Trade with the Fryar, and sent goods
with him. We are of opinion we ought not to be
angry att a trade with the Spaniards, but as Englishmen
who wanted not courage to do themselves honourable
satisfaction, we could not admire that soe execrable a
barbarity committed upon the person of an Englishman,
and the great desolation that was made in the Southern
part of this Settlement " (Port Royal) " should be buryed
in silence for the hope of a little filthy lucre, which, however, was missed of, for the Fryar never sent the retournes
promised," etc.

There was some evident satisfaction in the last two
lines!

If this book were a history, which it is far from
assuming to be, it would have to relate the endless
quarrels between the people and Landgrave Colleton.
Oldmixon, writing eighteen years later, says of him, " Had
he had as much honour and capacity as his brother, we
should have had no reason to excuse ourselves for keeping
to the truth of history in his behalf."

The simple truth seems to have been that he tried according to his lights to represent the Proprietors. Unluckily he only succeeded in making them so odious, that
the dissatisfaction which ended in the overthrow of the
Proprietary Government in 1719 may be said to have
begun then. He used in his little province the methods
which in the Mother Country lost the Stuart crown ;
denying the rights of the Commons, proroguing Parlia-
ments, dismissing officers illegally, attempting to establish
martial law, etc. At last after four years of misrule,
which had almost resulted in anarchy, the colonists
became so indignant that they pronounced sentence of
banishment upon him and those of his council who had

supported him. " A fate," says Oldmixon, " which few
Governors of Colonies were so unfortunate as to meet
with." Fortunately for the people there was a new rule
at home. William and Mary " filled the Stuarts' throne,"
and the Proprietors, who dreaded above all things an appeal to the crown, abandoned him to his fate, — especially
disappointed, since they had " hoped much from his
nobility." He left reluctantly the beautiful home which
he had built for himself and his family, on the west bank
of the Ashley near Wappoo, on a large tract of land known
as the " Waheewah Barony," and withdrew to Barbadoes,
whence he had come intending to settle permanently, four
years before.

The disputes went on, greatly aggravated by the feeling
which had arisen against the Huguenot settlers. They
lived chiefly in Craven County, which had never before
been allowed a representation like that of Colleton, which
was the stronghold of the dissenters, or Berkeley, the first
and most populous of the three. But at the election
ordered by Governor Ludwell, who had been sent to pacify
the discords raised by Colleton, six out of the twenty representatives who formed the Parliament were Huguenots
from Craven County. The English " especially," says
Hewat, " the common sort " were enraged. " Shall the
French who cannot even speak our language make our
laws?" they demanded. The feeling was not unreasonable, and was so strong that Ludwell and Landgrave
Smith, who succeeded him in office, were compelled to tell
the Proprietors that in order not to alienate the affections of
the people it was necessary to exclude the French from all
participation in the government. This is perhaps easily
comprehensible, but the proceedings against them were in
other respects unjustifiable. Hewat explains by saying that
they were not accused of any wrong-doing, but that their
prosperity aroused the jealousy of their neighbours.

" Many of the refugees, being possessed of considerable property in France, had sold it and brought the money to England. Having purchased large tracts of land with this money, they set down in more advantageous circumstances than the poorer sort of the English emigrants. Having clergymen of their own persuasion for whom they entertained the highest respect and admiration, they were disposed to encourage them as far as their narrow circumstances would permit." The two pastors who had accompanied their flock were the Reverend Elias Prioleau of the church of Pons in Saintonge, whose grandfather, a member of the ducal house of Priuli of Venice, had surrendered rank and fortune for the Protestant faith sixty years before; and the Reverend Florente Philippe Trouillard. M. Prioleau was dead (his monument may be seen in the French Protestant church of Charleston), but M. Trouillard and his "*ancien*" or elder, M. Boutelle, petitioned the Proprietors on the injustice done to their people.

The Proprietors in reply sent the following very worthy answer to the Governor and Council in 1693 : —

" The French have complained to us that they are threatened to have their estates taken from their children after their death because they are aliens. Now many of them have bought the land they enjoy of us, and if their estates are forfeited they escheat to us, and God forbid that we should take advantage of the forfeiture, nor do we so intend and therefore have sent our declaration under our hands and seals to that purpose, which we will shall be registered that it may remain upon record in Carolina, and be obliging to our heirs, successors and assigns."

They order that the French shall not be obliged to begin their Divine worship at an hour inconvenient to the tide (they came to church by water), that the validity of

D

their marriages and legitimacy of their children shall be recognized, "although their ministers are not ordained by some bishop." "We have power by our patent to grant liberty of conscience in Carolina, and it is granted by an act of Parliament here." "We desire that these things may be remedied and that their complaints of all kinds may be heard with favour, and that they have equal justice with Englishmen and enjoy the same privileges; it being for their Majesties' service to have as many of them as we can in Carolina."

Notwithstanding this august recommendation the desired liberties were not yet granted. Governors Ludwell, Smith, and Archdale all found it an impossible task; the latter, a peace-loving and well-meaning Quaker, being congratulated at the close of his administration that "every one was happy *except* the French." Still, "Time and the hour win through the longest day," and five years later Governor Blake, the first Governor of Carolinian birth, procured them the wished-for boon. He recommended that the Huguenots should apply for naturalization, and thus losing the quality of aliens, be less objectionable to the English. This was done by the great majority of them accordingly, and an act was passed in 1697 "making aliens free of this part of the Province, and granting liberty of conscience to all *protestants*." There is a long preamble to this act which states, among other things, that these aliens "had given good testimony of their duty and loyalty to his Majesty and the Crown of England, of their fidelity to the Lords Proprietors, of their good affection to the inhabitants, and by their industry, diligence, and trade, had very much enriched and advanced the settlement." Thereafter these long-suffering people were free to work out their own prosperity with no let or hindrance.

All this was accomplished in Mr. Blake's administra-

tion of four years, the most beneficent in the annals of
Charles Town, although the two last were marked by
calamities as dire as those proverbially attributed to the
fin-de-siècle. In 1697 and 1698 smallpox ravaged the
town and country; earthquake and fire added their horrors
to the scene. Mrs. Affra Coming wrote to postpone her
sister's visit, describing the conditions and telling of the
burning of one-third of the town, " which they say was
of equal value with what remains ! "

In 1699 a frightful epidemic which must certainly from
the description have been yellow fever, although they
called it the plague, smote the place. Numbers of people
died, among them some prominent men who had only
lately arrived. Edmund Bohun, the chief justice, a gentleman of ancient English family ; Mr. Marshall, rector of
St. Philip's ; Mr. Ely, receiver-general ; were among its
victims. These gentlemen had been sent out only two
years before with the highest encomiums of the Proprietors as to their capacity and usefulness in law and
divinity. Mr. Jonathan Amory, speaker of the Commons,
and many others also died. Dr. Dalcho, in his "Church
History," says, "the town was thinned to a very few persons." It was especially mentioned by the Council that
the disease did not extend into the country, and that
persons contracting it in town and returning to die on
their plantations did not communicate the infection to
their families. This has always been the case in Carolina;
presumably the yellow fever mosquito has never penetrated
beyond the seaboard.

While the epidemic was still raging, in September of
the same year a tremendous hurricane struck the town.
The water rose to the second stories of the houses, wharves
were swept away, vessels driven ashore, etc. But few
lives were lost in the town; but the combination of storm,
inundation, and fever, which again occurred in 1854,

created a misery and distress which can hardly be imagined. Outside of the bar the ship *Rising Sun*, which had on board the survivors of the unhappy Scotch colony of Darien, was lying at anchor. She was on her way from the Isthmus to Scotland and had stopped for water and provisions. The congregation of the "White Meeting House," hearing that the Rev. Archibald Stobo was among the passengers, sent down to invite him to come up and preach for them on Sunday. He came, bringing his wife with him. They and the boat's crew which had brought them were therefore in Charles Town when the storm arose, and were the sole survivors of the wreck. The bodies of their unfortunate companions strewed the beach of James Island.

It need hardly be said that the congregation of the "White Meeting House" were obedient to the finger of Providence. Mr. Stobo was "called" to the church and proved himself an excellent and influential minister, leaving many descendants in the Province.

And thus closed the twentieth year of the town.

CHAPTER IV

CHURCH ACTS. THE COUNTRY FOR THE QUEEN

SUCH calamities as those narrated in the last chapter were enough to have caused " great discouragement " to any people, but the Charlestonians rallied quickly, and, with the assistance of an architect sent out by the Proprietors, began to rebuild their waste places and improve their town. There were in the colony by this time many men of ambition and talent, all of whom had, with varying characteristics, that force and energy of mind, which more than any other quality, influences for weal or woe, individuals and communities. Four of these now came prominently forward. They were James Moore, William Rhett, Nicholas Trott, and Sir Nathaniel Johnson. Rhett, Trott, and Johnson were newcomers, and the three former differed from the gentlemen planters of Goose Creek and the rivers, in that they were constantly " place men," leaders of the people, or what we now call " politicians," first, and planters afterward, whereas Blake, Johnson, Middleton, Izard, and their like, were country gentlemen, who left their plantations when needed to serve the state.

Moore, the first to come to the colony, was a hot-headed Irishman, said to be the son of the Irish chieftain Roger More, who had been a leader in the great revolt after the death of Strafford. He was the type of his countrymen, the type also of the " gentleman adventurer " who had sailed with Drake and Raleigh two generations before. He had come from Barbadoes, where he had married the daughter of Sir John Yeamans, had led a bold and adventurous life, had penetrated the wilderness, traded and fought with the Indians, crossed the Appalachians and found traces of gold there. With small encouragement he would have found both the mines and the Mississippi, but the Lords of Trade, although advised by the Collector Randolph, would not give ear to him, being still of the same mind as Shaftesbury, when years before he had written to Woodward, the earliest explorer : —

" If those inland countryes have given you any knowledge or conjecture of mines there, I earnestly entreat you not to give the least hint of it to anybody whatsoever ; for fear our people being tempted by the hope of present gain should forsake their plantations. If it should be convenient, as perhaps it may be, to give mee some hint of it in letters to mee, pray call Gold always ' Antimony,' and silver ' iron,' by the which I shall always be able to understand you, without any danger if your letters should fall into other hands."

Not having thought of this ingenious way of suppressing discoveries, the Lords severely snubbed Moore, and the mines remained unknown. He returned to trouble the government, succeeded in being elected to the Assembly, and although only a few years before he had been banished with Colleton, the Council, upon the death of Governor Blake, chose him Governor. Why they should have done so remains a mystery. He might, had he been permitted, have been a Lewis or a Clark, but a more unfit man for any civil position did not exist. Possibly it was upon the principle of the famous answer, " If all Ireland cannot govern this Earl, then this Earl shall govern all Ireland." Things went badly. His fortunes were in a desperate condition, and he tried desperate ways of redeeming them. The Parliament was unmanageable and he prorogued and then dismissed it. Another was elected of very doubtful legality, and then the amazed people

The Avenue of Oaks at "The Oaks," Goose Creek

heard that the doors of the House being closed " Captain Moore, Governor, proposed his mind to the Assembly, who condescending thereunto " had granted him men and money to march forthwith upon St. Augustine!

It was really a master-stroke on Moore's part. The people were still sore from the massacres of Edisto and Port Royal, and also from more recent attacks of the Spaniards upon their frontiers. Nothing could have been more popular with the greater number of them than an attempt to wipe out the disgrace, and although the dissenters of Colleton County opposed the measure, alleging that the governor only wanted to capture Indians and sell them to the West Indies, the public supported him. The Assembly had voted two thousand pounds. Six hundred young men volunteered, a like number of friendly Indians were engaged, and ten little vessels were assembled at Port Royal to convey the Governor and his force. A part of the small army commanded by Colonel Daniel was to make its way overland and take the town from the rear. Colonel Daniel was a gallant soldier, who had been in the colony for some years, had worked against Colleton, and had been, with Moore, specially legislated against by the Proprietors. Now he was second in command, and all that was done to save the unhappy expedition from failure was done by him.

It seems inconceivable that such an enterprise could have been planned and put in motion all in the same month of September, 1702, but so the authorities assure us. It proved, as might have been expected, " Raw haste half sister to delay." When Colonel Daniel, having marched all across South Carolina and Georgia (presently speaking), and carrying his men by boat through the creeks and waterways which connect the mouth of the St. John's with the Matanzas River, had taken the wretched little town of St. Augustine, there was nothing more to

do. The Spaniards had withdrawn into their fortress —
the moat was full — the drawbridge raised. They were
provisioned for four months and the Carolinians had no
ammunition for the cannon which Moore brought on his
vessels !

It was an absurd predicament, for they must have
known the strength of the fort. To get the bombs was
the only possible way out of it, and Colonel Daniel,
" being hearty in the design," " the life of the action," was
sent to Jamaica to bring them. He went and returned
with all possible haste, but in the meanwhile two Spanish
vessels (which were afterward found to have been incon-
siderable) appeared off the bar. They were supposed to
be men-of-war, and " Colonel Moore retreated with no
great honour homewards." The Indian king when told
by him "to hasten" said, " No, though your Honour
leaves me, I will not go till my men have gone before
me."

Unrebuked by these words, Moore made no arrangement for warning Colonel Daniel, who on his return with
the ammunition was chased and nearly captured by the
Spaniards. A reluctant vote of thanks was wrung from
the Assembly for the Governor, but Colonel Daniel was
warmly praised.

The story is curious, for Moore was undoubtedly a brave
man. The historians belonged to the opposite party,
which fact should be taken into consideration. Years
after, when a cooler head, Sir Nathaniel Johnson, was
Governor, Moore planned and successfully carried out an
expedition against the Appalachian Indians, who, living
northwest of St. Augustine, were not only the allies and
pupils, but the food purveyors of the Spaniards. This
little war was brilliantly executed. With fifty white men
and some Indians, Moore marched against and stormed
seven well-made Spanish-Indian forts, securing many

prisoners and considerable booty ("ten horses loaded with provisions, the church plate of the Spanish chapel, and fourteen hundred Indians"). Three men of names well known were killed, gallantly fighting: Francis Plowden, Thomas Dale, and John Bellinger — the last probably the son of the Landgrave. Moore was able to make a triumphant report.

" The Indians have now a mighty respect for the whites. Appalatchia is now reduced to so feeble and low a condition that it can neither support St. Augustine with provisions nor distract, endanger or frighten us."

The Committee of Inquiry add with satisfaction, " This important service was effected without putting this Government to the *least expence.*"

Moore's reputation as a soldier was restored, but the people neither forgot nor forgave the dishonour and the debt of six thousand pounds which the ill-starred expedition to St. Augustine had brought upon them and from which the province long suffered.

These events had a more important effect upon the future of the colony than at first appeared. It cannot be doubted that they did much to increase the dissatisfaction of the colonists with the Proprietary Government. They found themselves sorely embarrassed by the consequences of a military expedition of which they were forced to bear the whole cost. Although the frontier province, and fighting against the declared enemies of England, no assistance was given them even now when Queen Anne's War was raging.

They thought of their slaughtered brethren of Cardross's time, to avenge whom they had vainly asked assistance, and of their own humiliated men and empty coffers ; and looked with envy upon the Royal Provinces which had only to appeal to the Sovereign to have ships and regiments sent for their defence. An appeal to the Crown was now constantly in their thoughts, and henceforward in every emergency they endeavoured to use their right of petition to the highest authority. It was the principle which soon overthrew the Proprietary, and afterward the Royal Government.

The appointment in 1702 of Sir Nathaniel Johnson as Governor was deservedly popular. Sir Nathaniel was a stout old soldier, a stern and unbending Tory, who, as a stanch adherent of the Stuarts, had been coldly looked upon by the Proprietors in the reign of William and Mary. His government of the Leeward Isles had then been taken from him, because, like his noble old Palatine, Lord Craven, he had refused to abandon his King. On his coming to Charles Town, Governor Colleton had been specially warned against him by the Lords, as the "worst of the Goose Creek Men." But now times were changed: Queen Anne was on the throne, the Tories were in power, and toasts were drunk to "The King — over the water." Moreover France and Spain were leagued against England, and military experience was too valuable to neglect.

All congratulated themselves upon having a good soldier for their chief, and none apparently apprehended any trouble from his well-known High Church principles.

Sir Nathaniel was unfortunately as earnest for the Church as for the sword, and in fact was approved by Lord Granville, the Palatine of the day, chiefly for that reason. Lord Granville was an absolute bigot, and was indignant at the liberty which the non-conformists had enjoyed in the previous reign in England ; and at the remarkably large share in the government of the colony of Ashley River, which they had exercised from its very beginning. At first this had seemed natural, for the dissenters were among the best of the people and there had been no religious animosity. But as has been shown there had lately been disputes, and the dissenters, especially those of Colleton County, had acted as such, as a party.

Lord Granville determined that in his little dominion at least such presumption should be stopped, and he found a zealous agent in Governor Johnson.

By the Royal Charter the Church of England had been expressly established ; and in the Fundamental Constitution, there was a clause which, never disputed, might be said to have been in abeyance. It was : —

" As the country comes to be sufficiently planted and distributed into fit divisions, it shall belong to the Parliament to take care for the building of churches and the public maintenance of divines, to be employed in the exercise of religion, according to the church of England ; which being the true and orthodox, and the only national religion, of all the king's dominions, is so also of Carolina, and therefore it alone shall be allowed to receive public maintenance by grant of Parliament."

If this clause had been held to enjoin merely the building of churches and paying of parsons, there would have been little discontent, but Lord Granville had a terribly logical mind, and his argument was, " If a man holds a false and illegal religion, he cannot be fit to sit in Parliament and legislate for people who know the truth." Therefore he resolved to stop the procession of members, deputies, counsellors, and governors of this reprehensible sort, who had too long ruled in the colony ! It was an extraordinary position to take, considering that two of his present co-Proprietors — Archdale and Blake — were, one a Quaker, the other an Independent. Not considering this weak point in his armour, Granville ordered Johnson to execute his plan. Sir Nathaniel was nothing loath, for he honestly believed the Palatine to be right, and besides, being a soldier he obeyed his commanding officer. He was accused by the opposite party of other motives. He was a friend of Moore's, and the vexation at, and inquiry into, his failure being still on foot it was said : —

"Sir Nathaniel Johnson by a chymical wit, zeal and art transmuted or changed this civil difference into a religious controversy, and so setting up a standard for those called High Church, ventured all to exclude the Dissenters out of the Assembly, as being those chiefly that were for a strict examination into the miscarriage of the Augustine expedition." Johnson summoned a Parliament, which was declared by the dissenters to be as illegal as Moore's had been. They declared that " Jews, strangers, sailors, servants, negroes, and almost every *Frenchman* in Craven and Berkeley Counties came down to vote, and their votes were taken. The persons by them voted for, were returned by the Sheriff."

The real sting in this accusation was in the "*Frenchman.*" The French had been naturalized some years before and had now the right to vote, but to the great provocation of the non-conformists it appeared that, Calvinism notwithstanding, the sympathies of the Huguenots were with the churchmen, who had been kind and generous to them in their days of trial. In any division their votes would be given to them, and the numerical majority of the dissenting party be lost. Opposition was brewing when like a thunderbolt came a resolution introduced by Colonel Risbee, May 4, 1704, requiring that all members of the Assembly must " take the oaths and conform to the religious worship of the Church of England, and receive the Sacrament of the Lord's Supper according to the rites of the said church." The preamble to the act also stated that the admitting of persons of different persuasions to sit in the Commons House had obstructed the public business and that the above act was according to the laws and usage of England in regard to members of Parliament. This last statement was not true, for members of Parliament were not then obliged to receive the Sacrament. The indignation was instant and violent, but the bill was passed with all due forms with suspicious rapidity, being signed at once by the Governor and five members of his Council. Landgrave Morton wished, but was not permitted, to record his protest. In the House it only passed by a majority of *one;* still it was law. The dissenters were very naturally enraged, and the churchmen greatly divided. The Governor had on his side the majority of his Council and many prominent gentlemen, especially Colonel William Rhett, and Chief Justice Trott — the most accomplished soldier, and the most brilliant lawyer of the colony ; but others were much disturbed. Hitherto the clause in the Constitution had been interpreted that St. Philip's predominated all other places of worship, and that the salary of its Rector, the good and amiable Dr. Marshall, who had died in 1699, 'the year of the sickness,' should be paid from the public treasury! None grumbled at this, all were alike proud of the handsome edifice and fond of the good rector, to whose widow the colonists had been so generous as to win the praise of the Proprietors. Now all was hate and contention, and moderate men reflected sadly that they had long lived in peace and amity with their nonconformist brethren, and some were old enough to remember the evils of attaching religious tests to political rights.

All were amazed, however, when the leader of the opposition was found to be, not some justly indignant Presbyterian or Baptist, but the new rector of St. Philip's, the Reverend Mr. Marston. Mr. Marston had been sent out to take charge of the only Episcopal Church then existing outside of Charles Town ; a little building thirty feet square, erected only the year before by Sir Nathaniel Johnson himself, on Cooper River in the neigh-

bourhood of his place " Silk Hope." It was built, curiously
enough, on land belonging to Pierre de St. Julien, a
Huguenot emigrant, " Pompion Hill Plantation," and
shows the friendly relations already existing between
the French and their Anglican neighbours. Whether the
transference from this little chapel to the importance of
St. Philip's (a transference caused by the death of Mr.
Marshall, and there being no other clergyman in the colony to take his place) had got into Mr. Marston's head,
or whether he had really experienced a change of heart,
we have no means of judging. Certain it is that having
been an ultra-Jacobite whose practice it was " for many
years almost every Lord's Day to preach against the Dissenters whom he treated with so much roughness and
severity that they had wholly deserted the Church, and
were become very great enemys to his person and ministry, and were wont to speak of him in very indecent terms
of disrespect," he now became an ultra-liberal ; took the
field in defence of those whom he had reviled and preached
the most furious sermons against Sir Nathaniel and the
Assembly, making trying comparisons to Korah, Abijah,
etc. His astonished parishioners tried in vain to restrain
him, and the insulted Assembly commanded him to " lay
his sermons before the House " ; but he, declaring himself
independent of " all authority save Christ's," defied Governor and Parliament and continued his diatribes. The
Assembly tried the " pocket pinch." It expressly dis-
claimed all intention of interfering with matters belonging to his " Ecclesiastical Governors and Ordinary," but it
deprived him of " his emoluments, good brick house and
plantation, two negro slaves, cattle, one hundred and fifty
pounds annually, besides fees for marriages, christenings,
etc." Mr. Marston rose superior to such considerations,
and did not change his tone, thereby earning the respect
due to disinterested if mistaken conduct.

The ultimate defeat of the Church Act was, although in a very indirect way, partly due to Mr. Marston's turbulence. His behaviour so rankled in the minds of his opponents, that when Mr. Ralph Izard offered the very commendable bill "An act for the establishment of religious worship in this Province, according to the Church of England, and for the erecting churches for the public worship of God, and also for the maintenance of ministers and the building of convenient houses for them," another bill was enacted, appointing a commission of twenty laymen who should have authority on their discretion to remove from his benefice any clergyman of whom his parishioners should complain — a measure unheard of in the Church of England. This act was directly inspired by the conduct of Mr. Marston, and certainly usurped the powers of the "Ecclesiastical Superiors and Ordinary."

In the meanwhile, very early in the affair, the dissenters had despatched an agent, Mr. Thomas Ash, to England with an appeal to the Lords Proprietors. Lord Granville, as might have been expected, received it with haughty contempt, but Mr. Archdale stood up for the rights of the people. Mr. Ash died, and Mr. Boone, a merchant and planter, son-in-law to Landgrave Axtell, was sent to replace him. With the help of the London merchants he succeeded in bringing a petition before the House of Lords. Had the Tories still held office, his success would have been more than doubtful, but the Whigs were again in power and resented the denial of the suffrage to the non-conformists. Boone (a fervent dissenter) interested the bishops, and especially the Society for the Propagation of the Gospel, against the clause of the lay commission, and finally the peers presented the matter to the Queen herself, asking that she "who had shown so great a concern for all her subjects, would extend her compassion to her distressed people who had the misfortune to be at so great a distance from her Royal person, and not so immediately under her gentle administration."

Her Majesty referred the case to the great law officers of the Crown, and the attorney and solicitor-general decided "That the acts not being consonant to reason, and being repugnant to the laws of England, were not warranted by the Charter and were without sufficient authority from the Crown, and therefore did not bind the inhabitants of the Colony. Her Majesty might therefore lawfully declare these laws null and void, and require the Proprietors and Assembly of the Province to abrogate them." This her Majesty promptly did, and the decision was despatched to Charles Town. There was nothing to be done but to obey. One can imagine Sir Nathaniel's astonishment at such a blow from his Queen, and the joy of the opposition. The bill had been carried originally by *one* vote, and in a subsequent session an attempt had been made to repeal it, which had only failed because the wrathful Governor had sent the members about their business, reproaching them as "unsteady." Now (how reluctantly we may easily suppose), the Parliament being convened March, 1706, he sent them a message reciting the events in England. How their acts had given offence, and that "in order to give full satisfaction to the Lords, the Bishops, and the S. P. G. he proposed that all the said acts be repealed and another 'for the security of the Church' be enacted." The provisions then proposed were excellent, and the law so wrongfully begun ended (the political feature being entirely eliminated) as a blessing to the country.

Ten well-defined parishes were laid out, in which churches were soon built, the ministers being supplied by the generous society. The colony provided the parsonages, and the benefit to the people cannot be overestimated. Mr. Marston, declared to be "the pest of the country, a common incendiary," was removed from his benefice, and peace was restored.

In one respect the fears of the dissenters were realized. The Huguenots outside of the town cast in their lot with the Church. The settlement of St. James Santee, where there were about one hundred families, the people of which were (says Oldmixon) religious and industrious, in the year 1706 petitioned the Governor to "have their settlement made into a Parish, and signified their extream desire to be united to the Church of England, whose doctrine and discipline they did most highly esteam."

Accordingly their church became the parish church of St. James Santee. This congregation, together with those of St. Denis and Orange Quarter, were allowed to use, until they should acquire the English tongue, a French translation of the prayer-book, made by particular direction of his Majesty, King Charles II., and approved by the bishop of London. The Huguenot Church of Charles Town, having ample endowment, kept its own independent organization, which it preserves to this day.

Sir Nathaniel Johnson was more successful in his own profession than in his civic and ecclesiastical experiments. From the moment of his appointment he had laboured to get the town into a condition of defence; had strengthened the bastions, mounted guns, built a little fort on "Windmill Point," the seaward extremity of James Island, had stationed a guard on Sullivan's Island opposite, and reorganized the militia of the Province.

Only four months after the settlement of the late differences the French and Spanish alliance became threatening, and the Governor sent a fast-sailing privateer to cruise in the neighbourhood of Havana and bring word of any gathering of ships in that direction. On the 24th of August the privateer came to harbour under press of sail, having been chased by five French vessels, with both

E

French and Spanish soldiers on board. Sir Nathaniel was at the moment at Silk Hope, sixty miles away, but Colonel William Rhett, who, after the fashion of those days, was, like Prince Rupert, both soldier and sailor, and bore the title of vice-admiral, took command. He sent despatches for the Governor and for the county militia and summoned all citizens to arms by beat of drum. Yellow fever was again raging in the town. Among its victims was the late Governor James Moore, thus prevented from taking what might have been a gallant part in the defence.

The fever greatly increased the trouble, for the country troops were especially liable to it.

The Governor arrived next day, his presence greatly encouraging the people. The militia came hurrying in, and were sent to encamp a mile without the walls to avoid the pest.

To a Carolinian it is interesting to observe the first appearance in arms, of names well known in later wars and still identified with the same localities. Captain (afterward Governor) Logan came down from Goose Creek with a troop of horse (called "the gentlemen of Colonel Logan's troop"), and Major Broughton of Mulberry led two companies from Cooper River. "Mulberry Castle," the pride of the river, was not yet built, but the place already had its name, a part of the "Broughton Barony." A Seabrook came as captain from Edisto, the centre of the late dissent; and Captain Longbois marched sixty Frenchmen from South Santee to fight for their new country. Captain Cantey commanded a body of friendly Indians. Johnson and Hyrne came from James Island.

In the town itself were Colonel William Rhett, first of the name in Carolina, Captain John Barnwell, a gallant Irishman, who was soon to win fame in a desperate campaign, and many others. Colonel Daniel was not there, he had been sent as lieutenant-governor to North Carolina.

Before all were assembled "five separate smokes" appeared on the extremity of Sullivan's Island, the signal by which the watchman was to give notice of the approach and number of the enemy. The drums beat to quarters and the men stood ready, but instead of a rapid advance, the ships — a frigate and four armed sloops — stopped to sound the South Bar — the channel which the Proprietors had warned the Council to "mind," many years before. Then crossing, they came on with a fair wind and sails set for the town. Seeing, however, the forts prepared and flags flying, they turned back to anchor off Sullivan's Island for the night, and the next day sent in a flag of truce. The officer was received by Captain Evans, the commander of Granville Bastion (the foundations of which may still be seen at the head of the East Battery), and led blindfold into the fort. Here he was asked to wait until the Governor could receive him; then after being led around and about and made to believe that the force was much greater than it was, he was presented to the Governor who asked his errand. It was to demand for Monsieur de Féboure, Admiral, in the name of the Kings of France and Spain, "the surrender of the town and country, and of their persons as prisoners of war, — allowing one hour for the answer." Sir Nathaniel answered: "There was no occasion for one minute to answer that message — he held the town and country for the Queen of England, and could trust his men who would rather die than surrender. The place should be defended to the last drop of blood, he (the messenger) might go when he pleased and acquaint Monsieur de Féboure with the answer."

The men applauded and prepared for action. The French, instead of attacking, sent marauding parties into the neighbourhood. On James Island the Indians rushed screaming through the woods and quickly put them to flight, but on " Wando Neck," behind Sullivan's Island, a large party who had plundered the adjacent plantations were feasting merrily on the cattle and pigs which they had carried off, when Captain Cantey with "a hundred picked men" fell suddenly upon them, killed and captured some and chased the others to their boats. In the meanwhile the Governor had hastily armed a few small vessels, and with these Colonel Rhett sailed down to attack the fleet. The French, seeing him coming, weighed anchor, and stood out to sea with all speed. The next night word was brought that "a ship of Force" was in Sewee Bay, a few miles north of Charles Town. Again Colonel Rhett sailed forth, and Captain Fenwicke went by land to the attack. The capture was made with but slight loss, the Frenchmen never firing a shot. Monsieur Arbuset, chief in command of the military part of the expedition, was on board, and, together with the "sea officers," offered a ransom of ten thousand pieces of eight. In all, three out of eight hundred men were killed or taken prisoners, and the invasion was repelled, practically putting an end to the Spanish claim that Carolina was a part of Florida. The joy was great. The people felt their honour restored, the Governor thanked them for their spirited conduct, and the Proprietors granted him a large tract of land with many flattering commendations. The historians do not tell us if they repaid the expenses of the defence which Sir Nathaniel had borne entirely.

This all took place immediately after the obnoxious Church Act had been repealed, and that which was to carry Christianity and enlightenment into the wilds substituted for it. It might be supposed that the brave old knight would have been left in peace to wind his silk and enjoy his laurels, but religious animosity dies hard and he was removed two years later, in consequence of the false and factious representations to the Proprietors of the same

Mr. Boone who had so skilfully fought the battle of the non-conformists in Parliament. The old man made a brave defence to the Assembly, vindicating his honour and defying his accuser, "when had he conspired with the French and what Indians had he abused?" Mr. Boone fled the town rather than be brought to the bar of the House to maintain his accusations, and the Assembly replied in terms of the utmost veneration and respect to their old Belisarius, "a man almost worn out with sickness and old age." They also petitioned the Proprietors in his behalf, but the mischief was done, the superseding appointment had been already made, and he withdrew into retirement.

This account of Governor Johnson's administration has been given thus minutely because two points of great importance were then settled.

The Province was delivered from the fear of Spain, and the union of Church and State, hitherto theoretic, became actual. Church and State do not sound well to American ears, and the dissenters did certainly resent the payment of the salaries of "church parsons" out of the public treasury. On the other hand it must be remembered that the non-conformist leaders, all men of education and intelligence, knew perfectly well what a "church colony" meant, and had not crossed the ocean without learning the provisions of the Royal Charter and of the Fundamental Constitution. They had no right to resent the laws of a land to which they had come of their own free will, no man constraining them. The dissatisfaction arose from the fact that the law had not been observed for the first thirty years of the colony's existence ; now the dissatisfaction gradually died out, and when sixteen years later Mr. Peter Pury, of Neufchatel, proposed to bring a number of his countrymen to Carolina, he could truthfully say, " what is of the greatest importance of all is, that there is an entire liberty of conscience and commerce for all that come hither, without paying anything for it, Justice is duly administrated to all, and everybody can say that what he possesses belongs to him in full Propriety."

The " parish system " thus established, upon which life in the low country of Carolina hinged, continued unchanged to the Revolution, and with necessary modifications down to 1865. Its influence was wide ; in early times much of the ordinary magistrate's business was, as in England, administered by the vestries ; in the country parishes the church became the centre for the too widely scattered plantations; schools were begun, bequests being made for their support, the bond of neighbourhood became a power, each parish forming a little world of its own.

The parishes were divisions of the counties from the sea-coast to about one hundred miles inland, the most fertile portion of the province where were all the large plantations. Above that the undivided counties were inhabited chiefly by farmers with fewer people and smaller holdings.

The "gentlemen of Carolina," Lawson says, had always had tutors for their sons ; but now the necessity for more general education was felt, and after much discussion a free school was established, of which Mr. John Douglas was to be master, "by the name and stile of Preceptor or Teacher of Grammar, and the other Arts and Sciences to be taught at the New School at Charles Town for the Province of South Carolina." It was required that the master should be able to " teach the Latin and Greek tongues and to catechise and instruct the youth in the principles of the Christian religion as proposed by the Church of England." A public library had been established as early as 1708 through the efforts of Dr. Bray, commissary of the bishop of London. It was called the Provincial Library and kept in the parsonage of St.

Philip's, the rector being librarian. The citizens had a proper respect for books, for three years later they passed an act " because several of the books had been lost and others damnified," giving the librarian discretionary power to refuse the volumes to persons " that he shall think will not take care of the same." Also they paid Mr. Mosely five pounds, fifteen shillings for cataloguing them, quite a sum in those days.

Another act of the same period " for the better observation of the Lord's Day, commonly called Sunday," which, it is to be feared, was much needed, may have been induced by the representations of the Reverend Mr. Thomas, a most worthy man, who having been sent out by the S. P. G., became the minister of the little country church which had been left by Mr. Marston for St. Philip's. Mr. Thomas's letters are amusing. He had been sent especially to convert the noble savage so much " compassionated " in Charles II.'s time. The noble savage was better known now, and less enthusiasm felt for his evangelization, — at least in the colony. Nevertheless Mr. Thomas came with a store of prayer-books and " ten pounds worth of cloth to cloath ye wilde Indians." On his arrival he found that his intended converts, the Yemassees, had gone upon the war-path, and were too much occupied with the taking of scalps to listen to him. Also some painful considerations were presented.

" Persons who knew those Indians assured me that a missionary could not, in this time of war, reside among them without the utmost hazard of his life, it being common for the Spanish Indians to steal upon them in the night, and kill some and take others prisoners, and those Prisoners are some of them burnt alive, and others sold to the Spaniards for slaves; *this was one great discouragement to my settlement among them during this war.*" Another " discouragement " was, that the Indians did " not understand

English, and their language is barbarous and savage " —
which seems to have been a great surprise to him! " A gentleman who had long traded among them and was a complete master of their tongue " had translated the Lord's
Prayer, and instead of " Our Father which art in Heaven "
was, as the nearest possible version, compelled to say " Our
Father which art on top " and for " Thy Kingdom come "
" Thy great towne come " " which I conceive are very im-
proper expressions to convey to them the genuine sense of
this most divine prayer."

Mr. Thomas although not desirous of martyrdom, and
without the spirit of an Eliot or a Xavier, was truly
anxious to do good, and being invited by Sir Nathaniel to
take charge of his Pompion Hill Chapel, and minister to
his neighbours, was glad to do so. There were, he says,
between that chapel and Charles Towne, in a distance of
sixty miles, hundreds of English people who had never
enjoyed a settled minister, the Sacraments were never administered to them, their children were unbaptized and
growing up in ignorance, they themselves had in some instances forgot that they were Christians by name. They
were, however, eager for help. "My poor labours were
very acceptable to them, and did excite in them a vehement thirst for God's ordinances ministerially dispensed."
Very properly the poor gentleman thought that he would
be better employed here than among the Yemassees or
Tuscaroras; especially as he says " there are here one thousand negro slaves, eight hundred of whom can speak English tolerably well, and are capable of religious instruction,
many of them desirous of Christian knowledge," so he
accepted Sir Nathaniel's offer, preached, prayed, cate-
chised, and administered indefatigably, established a school,
" taught five poor children free of charge," secured a fund
for the purpose, and seems to have been an excellent parish
priest. But to his dismay the same troublesome Mr.

Marston fell upon him, accused him of deserting his mission, driving a fellow-clergyman "distracted," and so on. The animus of course being that Mr. Thomas was the Governor's friend and chaplain. Mr. Thomas defended himself in the "Report to the Society," from which these extracts are given, and described Mr. Marston's character and mode of preaching as before quoted. His remarks sometimes are of value, as when in answer to "what is the character of the people?" he says "in every parish are many proposing Christianity, and many heathens; among the English inhabitants are many of considerable learning, good judgment and acute parts, and many very ignorant; again there are some truly religious and conscientious, and others haters of religion and practical godliness."

In other words, the people of the Province were like other men, of various sorts; but he censured them forcibly for neglect of Sunday and for making their people work on that day. He declares that his ministry has been successful, speaks of "the religious care of our excellent Governor Sir Nathaniel Johnson," and adds "there is a debt of gratitude which I owe to the people of Carolina, and it is this ; to affirm that Mrs. Marshall, the widow of that Reverend Mr. Marshall, sometime of . . . . in Suffolk, and myself, are living testimonies of their civilities and kindnesses to the ministers of the Church of England, who demean themselves well and as becomes their sacred function."

Unfortunately this sensible and useful man died while on a visit to England, where he had been sent by the Province to procure additional service for the Church. These long extracts have been given because at nearly the same time the Reverend Gideon Johnson affectionately described his flock as, "the vilest race of men upon the earth," etc. The reverend gentleman wrote thus upon first arrival, having been nearly drowned in crossing the bar; so

may have written under "some discouragement." He
remained for eight years as rector of St. Philip's, well
treated, his salary increased on account of his large family, — and well liked.　His terrible indictment of his
people was never known to them, and it is to be hoped
that his opinion became modified in that time.　By an odd
stroke of fortune he was actually drowned on the bar just
where he had nearly experienced the same fate so long
before.

It is certainly to the discredit of the English Church,
that its members, the men of wealth of the colony, should
have let so many years go by without providing more places
of worship outside of the town.　There were in 1702 several non-conformist and three Huguenot churches.　It may
be that the English demanded something more costly for
their solemn ritual than did the dissenters or the "Church
of the Wilderness," to whom any shelter was sufficient for
the expression of "The simple faith that asks no more
than that the heart be warm."

Probably this religious indifference in the higher and
ignorance in the lower class, were reasons for the influence
which the more God-fearing and sober-living independents
had exercised.　When the parish churches were built, they
were small but worthy of their use.　The oldest of all, St.
James's, Goose Creek, sixteen miles from Charles Town, is
yet standing.　The Royal Arms still shine in red and gold
above the chancel, and the "hatchment" of Ralph Izard
still hangs upon the wall, a memory of the English rule-

GOOSE CREEK CHURCH

CHAPTER V

TUSCARORAS AND YEMASSEES

THERE now occurred a curious little episode, what might almost be called a family quarrel, between two highly respectable gentlemen, in a contest for the Governorship.

The law ran that if any Governor should die in office, the deputies of the Proprietors should choose one of themselves to act until their Lordships' pleasure could be known. It so happened that Colonel Tynte, who had superseded Sir Nathaniel, died after a few months' incumbency when there were only three deputies in the Province. They were Colonel Thomas Broughton, Governor Johnson's son-in-law, Mr. Robert Gibbes (both "Goose Creek men"); and Mr. Fortescue Turbeville, a late arrival. There were two sessions on the same day for the election; practically Turbeville was the sole elector. At the second (afternoon) session, he gave his vote for Gibbes, who was proclaimed Governor. Turbeville was then struck by apoplexy and died. It was discovered that in the morning he had voted for Broughton, had been bribed during the recess, had changed his vote accordingly, and had then met his fate. It reminds one of Earl Godwin choking on the consecrated wafer, and Earl Godwin was thought to have been smitten by the vengeance of the Lord.

Thereupon Colonel Broughton claimed the office as having received the honest, unbought (morning) vote of the dead man. The quarrel was sharp and threatened to be bloody. Colonel Broughton came down with armed men from Mulberry to support his claim. Governor Gibbes, being in possession, closed the gates and raised the drawbridge. Broughton's friends within the walls attempted to lower the bridge, and after some scuffling succeeded in doing so. Gibbes wisely forbade his men to fire, and Broughton and his party entered the town. There was much riding to and fro — many speeches and proclamations drowned by the shouts of the mob, some flourishing of swords and a few shots which did no harm, and then — mediators interfered, calmer counsels prevailed, and it was resolved to leave the decision to the Proprietors. Their Lordships unhesitatingly rejected *both* gentlemen and appointed the Honourable Edward Craven, grandson of the old Palatine, but Mr. Gibbes held the office for about a year, until Mr. Craven arrived, with ability and credit.

The chief scene of this riding and rioting was the square at the foot of Broad Street in front of the watch house — now the old post-office and the half moon opposite old St. Philip's, now St. Michael's. The affair is called in old stories of Carolina " Broughton's Rebellion."

Governor Gibbes was still in office when news came from North Carolina that the Tuscarora Indians had fallen upon the white settlers along the Neuse River, and that every atrocity had been committed.

The Governor at once convened the Assembly which promptly voted men and money and offered the command to Colonel John Barnwell, who had already distinguished himself in Le Féboure's invasion. Colonel Barnwell accepted immediately and, as soon as a force, chiefly of Indians, could be collected, set out, and marching through woods and swamps, joined Governor Hyde near Newbern, North Carolina. Here the Indians had a strong fort and intrenchments, but they were soon completely routed. The fort unfortunately could not be stormed, for it was filled with white captives, who screamed to the assailants that they would be murdered at the first attack. Terms were therefore granted and the prisoners liberated.

Colonel Barnwell, ever after known as "Tuscarora Jack," who was severely wounded, returned with his men to Charles Town, with the warmest thanks of the North Carolinians who afterward named a fort in his honour. Enough Indians remained to renew hostilities next year, but he was not sufficiently recovered to take the field again, and James Moore, son of the former Governor, went in command of the force then sent, which finally subdued the savages.

Four years later the war cloud burst upon South Carolina herself. There had long been plantations in the neighbourhood of Port Royal (one of them belonging to Colonel Barnwell), but since Cardross's time, there had been no attempt at an extensive settlement. In 1710, however, the Proprietors ordered that a town should be laid out to be called " Beaufort Town," after the Proprietor of that name, lands surveyed, and settlers invited. All this in the near neighbourhood of the Yemassees, a tribe in close communication with the Spaniards, of which Sir Nathaniel in his farewell report had said "they have five hundred fighting men and are grown great warriors." The Indian will always fight for his lands, and St. Augustine was close behind with arms and encouragement. There were signs of discontent and unrest, but the first real alarm came when a canoe was paddled up to the town by John Fraser, a Scotch trader from the southward, flying with his wife and child from the trouble to come. His story was, that two days before, Sanute, a Yemassee chief, who had become much attached to him and his family, had warned them that in a few days, " as soon as the bloody stick should be sent," the Creeks and Cherokees would join his people and that they would together fall upon the whites and leave not one alive. Fraser had refused to believe the story, but the chief had repeated it, with every solemn sign of sincerity that an Indian could give, and had ended by promising that if they insisted upon remaining, he would, when the time came, kill them with his own hands to save them from tortures worse than death.

Mrs. Fraser, terrified, insisted upon flight, and Sanute lent them his own canoe for the voyage. There was some incredulity, but Governor Craven despatched Captain Nairne, the "agent for Indian affairs," and some other gentlemen to visit the chief near Pocotaligo, about sixty miles south of Charles Town, inquire into the dissatisfaction, and offer redress for all grievances.

Captain Nairne was a Scotch gentleman, who had, a few years earlier, been accused of complicity in the plot to put the Pretender on the throne when Queen Anne should die, — in which the famous " Henry Esmond " was so deeply concerned. He had been imprisoned on the charge, but had vindicated his loyalty, and was now a person of confidence. It was hardly judicious to send a handful of unarmed men to confer with a tribe of infuriated savages, but such has always been the English custom, a result of that splendid audacity which rules the world. It is not so many years since Sir Louis Cavagnari and his escort were done to death in Afghanistan.

The confidence on this occasion was so great that one man took his wife and children with him to the conference ! Cordially received, they went to rest. At break of day the war-whoop sounded and all but one were murdered. That one, a strong young man, Captain Burroughs, broke from his captors, and springing into the river swam across, and ran through the woods to Port Royal, rousing the country as he went. By this warning about three hundred inhabitants of that neighbourhood and of St.

Helena were saved. A merchant ship lying in the entrance took them on board.

The country was ablaze. The " bloody stick," the equivalent of the Highlanders' fiery cross, had done its work. The savages swept the country for fifty miles, killing and burning. The people fled before them, but with scant means of transportation, few escaped. About one hundred and ninety were killed between the Combahee and Stono rivers, a distance of fifty miles. The Stono is but ten miles from Charles Town. The light of the burning houses, the old people used to say, could be seen from the walls.

In all haste the Governor assembled the militia and marched to meet the enemy. They fell back to the Combahee and then attacked his camp. After a hard fight he put them to flight, leaving many of their chief warriors dead on the field. Routing an Indian army is like scattering a swarm of bees, — from the nearest tree they start out and sting again. It was impossible for Craven to stay to follow up his victory, and leaving Captains Mackay and Palmer to complete the work, he hastened back to Charles Town. He came none too soon, for another large body of Indians was approaching from the northward, murdering as they came.

They laid waste the frontier parishes and defeated a troop of cavalry commanded by Captain Barker who was killed, but when within sixteen miles of Charles Town, they were met by Captain Chicken with the Goose Creek militia, and repulsed with great loss. The town was saved for the time being, but the danger remained. The situation looked well-nigh desperate. There were in the colony but fifteen hundred men capable of bearing arms; and there were nine hundred and sixty white women, and seventeen hundred children to be defended! The Indian warriors were counted at from eight to ten thousand, and their leaders had fought under Barnwell, Moore, and Cantey.

The danger of the outlying plantations was great. The parish of St. John's at the head of Cooper River was the outskirt of the settled country. On three plantations within supporting distance there were small forts. At "Wantoot," Mr. Daniel Ravenel's; "Schinkins," Mr.

MULBERRY CASTLE, "BROUGHTON'S FORT," ON COOPER RIVER

Izard's, and "Mulberry," Colonel Broughton's. "Mulberry," but recently built, was the strongest house in the country, and the refuge of the neighbouring women and children when danger threatened. It stands on a high bluff above Cooper River, and is an imposing structure. The brick walls, several feet thick, are pierced for musketry in the lower story. At the four corners are small, square, semidetached buildings with pointed roofs surmounted by ironwork vanes, six feet high, each having the date 1714. Under each of these a trap-door leads to a deep stone-paved cellar for the storage of ammunition, and a few years since two small cannon (date unknown) were ploughed up in an adjacent field. These buildings are called " flankers," but give the impression of turrets. Hence the place was always called " Mulberry Castle." It was built after the picture of "Seaton," the English home of the Broughtons, which may be seen engraved on their family tree.

The forts at Wantoot and Schinkins were probably stockades. Unhappily the garrison at the latter place kept careless guard and made merry. While they were feasting, an Indian, supposed to be a " friendly," persuaded them to admit him. As soon as all were asleep he opened the gate for the entrance of his comrades. All the white men were murdered, many while still asleep; only one negro boy leapt the stockade, and running through the woods all the way to Wantoot gave the alarm. Major Hyrne, commanding the garrison there, immediately marched to Schinkins, and finding the Indians in turn overcome with liquor, put them all to the sword.

The Governor acted with vigour and discretion. He ordered the women and children brought into the town, and all provisions collected and stored in safe places. In addition to the militia he armed two hundred trusty ne-groes. The negroes hated and dreaded the Indians, and no treachery or desertion was to be feared. He sent envoys to the Governors of North Carolina and Virginia, asking aid; and having seized all goods readily convert-ible into money for the benefit of the public, sent M. de la Conseillière to New England to purchase arms. He also wrote an admirable letter, not to the Proprietors of whom his brother was one, but to the Secretary of State, detailing the situation and the measures he has taken to relieve it;

F

says that Carolina now exports so great a quantity of rice, peas, pitch, tar, and other naval stores as to be of great consequence to Great Britain; that the need for help is absolute, and "regrets that so fine a colony should be lost for want of men and arms" — "if once we are driven from hence the French from Moville (Mobile) or from Canada, or from old France will step in here if not prevented, and will be able to march against all or any colony on the main and threaten the whole British settlements." He says, "I trust his Majesty for everything." Neither King nor Proprietors did anything. The rebellion, "the fifteen," was in progress and his Majesty (George I) had work at home for all his soldiers. The Proprietors were suddenly smitten with legal doubts as to how far they could go in assisting their Province, and despite the despairing protests of the colonists who sent agent after agent to reason and implore, they thought it safest (for themselves) to do nothing.

North Carolina returned her obligations freely and promptly, sending a body of men under Maurice Moore, who had remained in that Province after the Tuscarora War. Mr. Arthur Middleton, the envoy to Virginia, found Governor Spotswood ready to furnish powder and shot, but most unwilling to part with men. With much difficulty and at high wages he was only able to get one hundred and fifty, and with these and the small force from her kindly neighbour, the Province fought out her fight. It lasted over a year. By that time, after another desperate battle near Stono, the power of the tribes was broken, most of the chiefs were killed, the numbers greatly reduced, and the spirit subdued.

The Yemassees, the leaders in the conspiracy, which is known as "the Yemassee War," departed to St. Augustine, carrying their spoils and captives with them. They were received as conquerors, with honour and acclamation as having slain heretics and heathens. The other tribes were more thoroughly intimidated, and the power of the Province to guard itself was so well impressed upon them, that no *concerted* action was ever again attempted. The Yemassees from Spanish territory still made occasional descents upon isolated and exposed plantations. The danger on these outlying places long continued. Fortunately the names of many of the "Indian fighters" became such symbols of terror to the savages, as was the "Melek Rik" to the Saracens or the Black Douglas to the English, and protection to their homes. Such was that of Maurice Moore, who had driven the tribes across the Savannah even to the Hiawassee River. "He will run you like Maury Mo" became a proverb. The wife of another of these heroes, James McPherson, was sitting alone outside of her door, her husband having gone hunting, when suddenly from the wood quite near appeared three Indians. The lady was terrified, but had presence of mind enough to conceal it, and to gaze quietly at them. Two sprang forward to seize her, but the third interposed, "No, no touch, she Jimmy Squaw!" She was the grandmother of Colonel McPherson of the Revolution.

There were darker stories than these, stories of women captured and children tortured.

On the family tree of the Bulls, opposite to the name of John, youngest son of the emigrant Stephen, stands "1st wife carried off by Indians 1715." They lived at Bulls, now Coosaw Island, just above St. Helena, and were in the very track of the storm. He too became an "Indian fighter." Another woman, Mrs. Burrows, was taken by a "scalping party" and carried with her child to St. Augustine. The child cried and was instantly killed, and she was ordered, under pain of death, not to weep for him! After being kept a prisoner several years, she was allowed to return to Charles Town, where she told the

Governor that the "Huspah King" who had captured her had told her that his orders from Spain were to kill every white man and bring every negro alive to St. Augustine, and that rewards were given for such services.

The Province was saved, but at fearful cost; great loss of life and greater of property. Every plantation above twenty miles from, and some much nearer to, Charles Town was laid waste. Buildings and fences were burnt, animals killed or carried off. The terrified negroes fled to the woods, but many were taken to St. Augustine for the reward. The labour of years was lost and life was to begin again. In the town trade had come to a dead stop. The debts were terrible. It was declared that the "country was ruined." It is, however, hard to ruin a country in which the natural elements of prosperity are great and the people industrious and courageous. Nothing daunted they set to work again, and this was the last attack upon the good town for sixty years.

She had now, however, to part with her gallant Governor whom the people loved and trusted absolutely. He had had permission to return for some time past on account of the death of his father, but had refused to go until peace was restored. He had been brave in the field and wise in the council and for once honour was given where honour was due, the citizens agreeing most heartily in the report of the Lords of Trade to the Crown,

"That the Honourable Charles Craven had behaved as a man of his quality ought, with the utmost bravery, and to his conduct it was owing that the country was not taken by the enemy."

CHAPTER VI

THE CONQUEST OF THE PIRATES

THE invention of the steam-engine, beneficent in many ways, has in none been more blessed than in one but little thought of nowadays. It has abolished the Pirate.

"The Pirate" was a name written large in the minds of our forefathers, — now known only to us in romance and story. Not all the combined fleets of his Majesty annihilated him so completely as that gigantic kettle, the steam-boiler. So long as sharp lines, spread of sail, bold seamanship, and utter recklessness could enable the fast schooner or brigantine to "show her heels" to the slow-sailing frigate or sloop of war, so long did rover after rover infest the seas. But when the long, black, steady steamer took the field, independent of wind and tide, tracking surely the robber to his den, then — unable to use steam himself, because he could get no coal — gradually the Pirate vanished from the waters, except in some remote South Asian Archipelago. Our fathers had no steam, and were for long at the mercy of these ruffians.

Unhappily the colonies did not in their first years show a proper sense of their iniquity. The pirates did not in the beginning molest them (they were hardly worth molesting), but kept up an incessant warfare upon the Spaniard, — a proceeding well liked by his English neighbours. King Charles himself, who, in 1683, had "heard of the harbouring of pyrates and ordered such persons brought to justice," ended by knighting Morgan, the chief of buccaneers, and making him Governor of Jamaica. So while the plundering was confined to Spanish galleons, the colonies looked on complacently, allowed the " gentlemen rovers" to swagger about the streets, spend freely their Mexican doubloons, and sell for a trifle the silks and wines taken from the ships outward bound.   Smuggling, or illicit trading, as it was more elegantly termed, was common and was frequently carried on by the pirates.   Edward Randolph, " Collector of King's Customs," furious at the injury to the revenue, charges men in high places with complicity in these practices.   Even the Governors do not escape him.   He says of Archdale that " he permitts Pyrates to land and bring their money quietly ashore, for which favour he was well paid by them."   Randolph was hasty and prejudiced, but, exaggeration granted, there was probably some truth in his charges.   Customs were heavy, the stolen goods cheap, and spoils taken from the Egyptians could not be held accursed.   When, however, the colonies increased in wealth, and their own trade became important, the pirates no longer showed this nice discrimination.   Booty was booty whether it came from New York or Charles Town instead of St. Augustine or Havana, and a vessel flying the English flag was no safer than if she showed the red and gold of Spain.

An incredible number of ships were taken along the coast, and it was impossible to undertake even the shortest voyage without being in danger from these desperadoes.

The Cape Fear River to the north and the island of New Providence to the south were their strongholds, from which they preyed upon the commerce and sometimes threatened the towns themselves.

Things had come to a dreadful pass, when, in 1718, Robert Johnson, son of Sir Nathaniel, being Governor, a long-boat pulled audaciously up to the Charles Town wharf, sent with a message by a notorious pirate, one Thatch, or Blackbeard.

The message was peculiar. Blackbeard informed Governor Johnson that his crew was in want of medicines, and that unless the list of drugs forwarded was immediately sent by his boat, the heads of Mr. Samuel Wragg, of his little son, and of some other citizens should be presented to the Council. Mr. Wragg, a prominent merchant, and the others had sailed for England recently, and their ship was one of nine vessels which had been taken near the bar within a few days.

The excitement may be imagined. The Governor, a fearless and resolute man, was furious at the insult ; the Council was divided in opinion. How could they submit to such an indignity ? How sacrifice so good a man ? But the friends and family of Mr. Wragg were unanimous. Should the life of so valued a citizen be weighed in the balance with so useless a scruple ? An eminent merchant put to death for a few drugs ? The situation was horrible; the responsibility rested with Johnson, and he met it manfully. He reminded the people that the Proprietors and the Board of Trade had been repeatedly but vainly urged to send a frigate to protect the commerce, — it was his duty to protect the lives of the citizens. The medicines should be sent, and then — measures *must* be taken.

Meanwhile poor Mr. Wragg and his fellow-passengers had been in great terror. The boat had got aground and so been delayed. Blackbeard had been impatient and had shown so great a desire for their heads that they, with good reason, trembled for their lives.

The drugs appearing, he plundered them of everything which they possessed, securing, it is said, $6000 in specie from Mr. Wragg alone, and sent them on shore almost naked. He then sailed away, carrying the spoils of the many vessels he had captured ; but sailed not so far but that other outrages were to be feared.

In this emergency, of which Johnson wrote instantly to London, Colonel Rhett came to his Excellency's assistance. Rhett was no friend to Johnson, or indeed to any Governor ; his proud, imperious temper found it hard to accept a superior. He had been long in the colony and felt himself a master, so that more than once the Proprietors had to rebuke, and on one occasion to suspend him from office, until he could bend his haughty spirit to apologize to the Governor ; a man calmer and more judicious, but brave and determined as himself. When, however, it was a question of battle, the soldierly vice-admiral came to the front, and proposed that a couple of merchant vessels should be hastily armed, and that he himself should go out and meet the rovers. Johnson was glad to accept the offer, and in a very few days the sloops *Henry* and *Sea Nymph* were fitted with eight guns and about seventy men apiece, and made ready. Rhett put to sea hardly knowing where to find his enemy, who had been cruising along the coast from Cape Race to Florida, plundering as he went ; but hearing that he was near the Cape Fear, determined to seek him there.

On arriving they saw, across the bend of the river, the pirate vessel well up the stream and sheltered from attack. But the Pirate had seen them, and early next morning his great vessel, the *Royal James*, came flying down the river with sails set, the "Jolly Rover" at the masthead and guns cleared for action. She swept down, evidently trying to pass the sloops and gain the open sea. Rhett, in order to interrupt her, closed his vessels in and drove her from the channel so that she stuck hard and fast aground on a sand shoal.

In another moment the sloops were aground also, — the *Henry* within pistol shot of the *James*, the *Sea Nymph* considerably lower downstream.

The tide was on the ebb, there was no hope of release

for hours; both had listed the same way, and lay almost in line, so that the hull of the Pirate was turned toward the Carolinian, while the deck of the latter was exposed to him.

In this absurd position, more like two small forts exchanging shots than ships engaging, Rhett, undaunted, opened fire. The enemy instantly returned a broadside which, on account of the position, swept the deck of the *Henry* with deadly effect. It was death to man the guns, but the Charles Town men stood to their posts, and also kept up a musketry fire upon the pirate crew.

The rover, seeing their losses and his own advantage, expected an easy victory. "Made a wiff with their bloody flag and waved to us with their hats to come aboard and surrender." This being answered with cheers and derision, the fight went on for five hours ; then the tide turned, and the chance of victory with it. The *Henry* floated first. As soon as she righted, Rhett prepared to grapple and board, but terror now possessed the pirates. They saw that the *Sea Nymph* had floated also and was coming to the help of her consort and mutinied against their captain who would have fought to the last. He threatened to shoot them with his own hands, but they overpowered him, threw down their arms, and gave up the ship.

To his amazement Rhett found that he had captured not Thatch, but Stede Bonnet, one of the most remarkable of the many remarkable characters of that time. He was a gentleman by birth and education, of excellent manners and fair estate, had been a major in the army, and afterward a citizen of Bridgetown. There seemed no reason why he should have suddenly taken to piracy ; but having done so, he became one of the fiercest of his dreadful trade. Once he apparently repented, made submission, and took the King's pardon then offered, but immediately returned to his villainy.

A day or two were spent in repairing the damaged sloops, and then Colonel Rhett returned in triumph with the *Royal James* as a prize and Bonnet and thirty of his crew in irons "To the great joy of the whole Province." Eighteen Carolinians were killed and many more wounded.

There was difficulty in finding safekeeping for so many prisoners for there was no jail, but the men were locked up in the watch house, while Bonnet and two others were given in charge to the marshal who was to keep them under guard in his own house.

The trial of these men was remarkable. Chief Justice Trott, commissioned by the King as well as by the Lords, was to hold a Court of Admiralty and try them by an old statute of King Henry VIII., somewhat revised to suit the circumstances. It may have been originally enacted for that " bold rover that lyes on the seas and robs us of our merchant ware, Sir Andrew Barton, Knight." Ten assistant judges were to sit with Trott, and there was a grand jury. A manuscript book preserved in the Charleston Library contains the charge of the chief justice, which is said to be " a most able exposition of the law of the case." To the uninitiated it is an extraordinary production, bristling with Latin and Greek, and expounding to the jury the origin and authority of the court, of which it probably had no doubt whatsoever.

The jury was more likely to be decided by the list of *thirty-eight* vessels taken by Bonnet and Thatch in the last six months, which was displayed by the attorney-general, Richard Allein. The question was, were all of these men aiding in and consenting to the piracies ?

It is extraordinary and shocking to us now that, wicked as they might be, they were not allowed the assistance of counsel.

Imagine the poor wretches, badgered by two clever lawyers, frowned upon by eleven clever judges, confronted by a jury, every man of whom must have wished them hung, and trying to patch up some miserable defence for themselves!

Such was the law in criminal trials then and for many years later. Sydney Smith claims with pride that the "honest boldness of the *Edinburgh Review*" had much to do in the alteration of this abuse. Counsel was not granted until 1836. On this occasion the testimony was that of one caitiff who turned State's evidence. Four of the prisoners were acquitted; the rest condemned to be hung.

Stede Bonnet was not tried at this time. The too careless guard of the marshal had enabled him to make friends in the town, and he had escaped in woman's dress with one of his companions, in a boat with an Indian and a negro.

This evasion was made in the hope of reaching the vessels of another pirate named (it was supposed) Moody, who had appeared off the bar a day or two before, with a large ship of fifty guns and two hundred men; and two others, also armed, captured by him on their way from New England to Charles Town.

These insolent rovers sailed close in shore or lay in the offing waiting for outgoing ships, so that their sails could be seen from the wharves. No help had come from England, and once more Robert Johnson called Council and Assembly and told them that they must rely upon themselves alone. They immediately passed an act to impress and arm the best vessels in port, and called for volunteers. Naturally they expected Colonel Rhett to take command, but he, in consequence it is said of some affront at Johnson, refused. It must have gone hard with him to do so, for he dearly loved a fight. Thereupon the Governor announced that he himself would be Admiral (glad perhaps of an opportunity to show himself a commander), and the people were delighted. Four vessels were mounted with guns, the *Royal James* being one, and three hundred men volunteered. They were nearly ready to sail when Bonnet and his sailing master were found to have escaped. Word was brought to the town that they had gone down to the bar, but finding that Moody was cruising elsewhere that day, they had put back and were on Sullivan's Island. Colonel Rhett offered to head a party for the recovery of his captive. The search was long and difficult, for the sandhills were covered with a dense growth of stunted live-oak and myrtle, and lay close and confusedly together. Nothing was easier than to lose one's way. At last the fugitives were seen. Rhett's men fired and the sailor fell dead. Bonnet was captured and carried back to prison. Sixty years ago a little nook in the hills near the back beach used to be called "the Pirate's cave" (it was not a cave but a hollow in the hills). This adventure of Bonnet's may have given the name. The myrtle has been cut away now and the hills, which were only held together by their roots, have vanished with them.

Whether the pirates intended to make an attack upon the town is not known, but they shortly reappeared, came inside the bar, and rode quietly at anchor. Johnson sailed down at night to the fort named for his father, and waited. Early next morning, the masters of the other vessels having their instructions, he and his consorts crossed the bar quietly, having their guns under cover and no sign of war about them. The pirate, supposing them to be merchantmen, let them pass out, and then closing in behind them to intercept their expected retreat, ran up the black flag and called for surrender. The Governor, having by this stratagem got them between himself and the town, hoisted the royal ensign, threw open his ports, and poured a broadside into the nearest ship. The astonished rover endeavoured to make the open sea, and by skilful handling succeeded in doing so. Johnson followed in hot pursuit, signalling the *Sea Nymph* and the *Royal James* to look after the sloop. Then ensued a desperate fight, the vessels yard-arm to yard-arm.

The pirates at last were driven from their guns. The Carolinians boarded; all the men on deck were killed fighting gallantly; those who had taken refuge in the hold surrendered; the sloop and the survivors of the crew were carried up to the town, where the people had been listening to the guns.

Meanwhile the Governor was pursuing the pirate ship. A stern chase is proverbially a long chase, and the rover threw over boats and cannon in the effort to lighten his vessel, but the Charles Town ship was the faster sailer and overhauled her at last. A surprise awaited the captors. When the hatches were lifted, the hold was found to be full of *women!* "

The vessel was the *Eagle*, carrying convicts and " indentured servants " from England to Virginia. Thirty-six were women.

The Pirate had captured her some time before, changed her name, and taken her for his own. Again the identity of the commander had been mistaken ; not Moody but one still more dreaded, Richard Worley, was the captain. He had been killed on the sloop in the desperate fight off the bar.

The victory was great, but where was Moody ! There was daily apprehension of his appearance. At last after weeks of anxiety it was discovered, that having learned the preparations made to receive him in Charles Town, he had gone to Jamaica, there to avail himself of " the King's pardon " which Admiral Sir Woodes Rogers was authorized to grant to all who should submit themselves voluntarily before the first of the following January.

It remained to punish the prisoners. They were tried

by the court already described ; but interest was aroused for Bonnet, whose gentlemanly appearance and manners, apparent contrition, and protestations of devotion and loyalty, touched many hearts. His appeal, in which the most sacred texts of Scripture were dexterously woven into a petition for life, provoked, however, the ire of Trott, who told him in language as pedantically pious as his own : —

" You being a Gentleman and a Man of letters I believe it will be needless for me to explain to you the nature of Repentance and faith in Christ ;" " considering the course of your life and actions, I have just reason to fear that the principles of Religion that had been instilled into you by your *Education*, have been at least corrupted if not entirely defaced by the *scepticism* and *infidelity* of this wicked Age." " For *had your delight* been in the *Law* of the *Lord* and had you meditated thereon *Day* and *night*, you would have found that God's word was a *Lamp* to your feet and a light to your path," etc.

Pity was shown in an unexpected quarter. The sword is often gentler than the gown, and the good fight he had fought may have appealed to the soldier. Colonel Rhett offered to take Bonnet to London himself to plead for pardon. Johnson knew his duty too well. Bonnet's offences were too flagrant, his hypocrisy too apparent. He had already taken the oath of repentance and had returned at once to his evil ways. His appeal was as the Devil quoting Scripture. He was hanged, as were the other prisoners, forty in all. They were buried on White Point shoal, just above low-water mark. The place has been filled up and is now the Battery Garden, the favourite pleasure ground of Charleston.

About the same time Thatch (or Blackbeard) was taken by an expedition sent out by Governor Spotswood of Virginia, but commanded by officers of the Royal Navy. The Carolinians had fought their fight alone and unaided, the Lords Proprietors having refused to hearken to their calling.

Just at this juncture when the people were angry at their neglect, and at the heavy debt which the expense of the defence left upon them, the Governor alone being " one thousand pounds out of pocket," their Lordships saw fit to

A CORNER OF THE BATTERY GARDEN

enact certain laws and regulations which bore heavily on their trade, and endangered their lands. The colonists saw clearly that their only safety lay in escaping this short-sighted and selfish rule; but how was that to be done? The Proprietors legally owned the whole country as one great estate. Mr. Maurice Ashley, grandson of the great

Lord Shaftesbury, spoke the simple truth when he said " No man has a just title to anything if the Proprietors have not a title to Carolina." The soil thus bound, how could the inhabitants be free? 'Twere long to tell and *dull* to trace the negotiations, the plots and counterplots, the petitions, addresses, memorials, etc., which followed those ill-advised measures. The colony sent agent after agent to urge their claims: Mr. Boone, Mr. Francis Yonge, Colonel John Barnwell. The Proprietors were "deaf as Ailsa Craig," but the " Board of Trade and Plantations " had, ever since seventeen hundred, been prepared by the representations of the Collector Edmund Randolph, for such a condition of things. It strongly advised the Crown to take the Province into its own keeping. A petition signed by over five hundred of the best people of the country (more than half the male inhabitants) could not be called the doings " of a faction or a party," as their Lordships said. The situation was complicated by the double dealing of Judge Trott who kept up a correspondence secretly inciting the Proprietors to resist.

It was proposed to compel them to resign their charter and sell their Province to the King, and this was eventually done, but the territorial right existed for some time after the sovereignty had passed.

While these legal proceedings were dragging their slow length in England, the colonists were taking things into their own hands at home. In December, 1719, the Assembly informed Mr. Johnson that it would not meet the Council just appointed by the Lords or acknowledge its authority.

Governor Johnson remonstrated, and the Assembly stood firm. The people were in a curious predicament. They hated the Government but loved the Governor ; and Johnson, though no man could feel their wrongs more keenly, was too straightforward and honest to allow the distinction. There were several communications all to this purpose and then the Assembly resolved itself into a convention of the people and presented the love letter from which this extract is taken.

" May it please your Honour

" It is with no small concern that we find ourselves obliged to address your Honour in a matter which nothing but the absolute Necessity of Self-Preservation could at this juncture have prevailed on us to do. The reasons are already made known to your Honour and the World, therefore we forebear to rehearse them, but proceed to take Leave to assure you. That it is the greatest satisfaction to us, to find throughout the whole Country that universal Affection, Deference and Respect the inhabitants bear to your Honour's person, and with what passionate Desire they wish for a continuance of your gentle and good Administration; and since we who are intrusted with, and are the Asserters of their Rights and Liberties, are unanimously of opinion That no Person is fitter to Govern so Loyal and Obedient a People to his Sacred Majesty King George, we most earnestly desire and entreat your Honour to take upon you the Government of this Province in his Majesty's name until his pleasure shall be known."

They remind him of how bound they are to him by his " tender regard for it " (the country) " on all Occasions, and particularly in Hazarding your own person in an Expedition against the Pirates, for its Defence, an Example seldom found in Governors," and conclude by assuring him if he will but accept their offer,

" That we will in the most Dutiful Manner Address His Most Sacred Majesty King George, for the continuance of your Government over us, under whom we doubt not to be a Happy People."

No man could receive such an address unmoved, but Johnson stood out. He reminded them that he held his commission from the Proprietors, and that they had no legal right to depose them, and vainly tried by speaking of an expected Spanish invasion to turn them from their purpose. This he did, says Francis Yonge, because he thought their demands " inconsistent with his Honour and the Trust reposed in him by the Lords Proprietors." Colonel Rhett and Mr. Trott did not support the Governor, but " Left their Masters in the Lurch," and his resistance was vain.

He had still some hope of delaying proceedings, but on coming into town on the 21st of December he found the militia drawn up in arms and preparing by beat of drum to proclaim James Moore Governor " for the King." He argued, protested, and ordered, but not even the recently appointed Council stood by him. One member, Mr. Lloyd, accompanied him throughout the day — lest, it was afterward explained, he should lose his temper and be betrayed into some rash act. But although all those men loved him, all felt that the issues at stake were too great for private feeling to be indulged. There was one possible resource. Two men-of-war (sent at last in answer to his appeals) were in the harbour and their captains acknowledged his authority. He ordered the guns run out and proclaimed that he would lay the town in ashes if the people did not submit. The people " being in a Town regularly Fortifyed and 70 Cannon mounted on their Ramparts and near 500 men within " " were not to be so terryfied," and he was obliged to desist.

" Thus the Government became the King's, to the great joy of the People of that Province."

This whole Revolution (for such it was) is as a forecast of that great one of '76. But more than fifty years were to pass before the boys who now shouted for King George were, as old men, to recognize that they had but exchanged the misrule of the Lords Proprietors for that of " his Majesty's Ministers."

CHAPTER VII

THE KING AGAINST THE LORDS.   THE BUILDING OF ST.
PHILIP'S

IT must be confessed that in these times Carolinians were
much of the faith of the Vicar of Bray. Absorbed
in their own affairs, changes of King or of dynasty were
little to them. They had wept for Charles and shouted
for James the Second, had hailed William and Mary as
bulwarks of the Protestant faith (they were all Protestants), Queen Anne had been their Lady and Mother, and
now George was the desire of an adoring people, with
never a longing, lingering look behind for the unhappy
Stuarts. If any little leaven of Jacobitism ever had crept
in, it had been severely repressed. Mr. Nairne had been
imprisoned, as already said, on the charge, but had successfully vindicated himself, only to die at the hands of
the Indians. The turbulent Mr. Marston, the quarrelling
rector of St. Philip's, had cast it off so completely as to
become the champion of the dissenters; and if Colonel
Rhett was suspected, no one durst whisper it above his
breath. There is a hint to this effect in a letter (given
in the Shaftesbury papers) to "A Merchant of Bristol,"
the writer's name being suppressed; which mentions that
a Mr. K., bred up, as he is informed, at St. Germains, as he
supposes with Colonel Rhett, used to pay great respect to
the picture of Sacheverell in the Colonel's hall, but as he
"is afraid of *Stewartizing* this letter will conclude." Possibly this timidly hinted attachment —if such there were

— to the ancient line, may explain the persistent opposition of Trott and Rhett to the change of rule. They probably did not wish their colony to give itself so absolutely to the House of Hanover, for years after when they were both holding office under the Crown, they maintained a correspondence with the last Palatine, Lord Carteret, which would have been esteemed little less than treasonable had it been discovered.

The colony was now (1720) sixty years old and could no longer be called "an infant," however much its growth may have been stunted by the events already related. Charles Town was a thriving little place, sole port, sole law-giver, and seat of government for the whole Province. Her worst troubles were now — for fifty years — over ; safe behind the royal shield she was free to enter the race for wealth and prosperity with small fear from outward foes.

John Lawson, surveyor general of North Carolina, writing in 1709, had said : " The town has very regular and fair Streets, in which are good buildings of Brick or Wood, and since my coming thence " (eight years before) " has had great additions of beautiful large Brick buildings, besides a strong Fort, and regular Fortifications to defend the Town. The inhabitants by their wise management and Industry have much improved the country which is in as thriving condition at this time as any Colony on the Continent of English America." " The Colony was at first planted by a genteel sort of people that were well acquainted with Trade, and had either Money or Parts to make a good use of the Advantages that offered." " They have a considerable Trade with both Europe and the West Indies, whereby they become rich and are supply'd with all Things necessary for Trade and genteel Living, which several other places fall short of. Their co-habiting in a town has drawn to them ingenious People of most Sciences, whereby they have Tutors amongst them that educate their Youth *a-la-mode*."

" Their roads with great Industry are made very good and pleasant. Near the Town is built a fair Parsonage with necessary offices." " They have a well disciplined Militia, their Horse are most Gentlemen " (viz. " the Gentlemen of Captain Logan's troop ") "and well mounted, the best in America, and may equalize any in other parts. Their Officers, both Infantry and Cavalry, generally appear in scarlet Mountings, and as rich as in most Regiments belonging to the Crown, which shows the Richness and Grandeur of this colony." " This place is more plentiful in Money than most or indeed any of the plantations on the Continent." " The merchants are fair, frank traders. The Gentlemen seated in the country, are very courteous, live very nobly in their houses, and give very genteel entertainment to Strangers and others that come to visit them."

Lawson wrote just after the defeat of the French, of whom he says "their Admiral Moville was glad to run away and leave the Enterprise after he had suffered all the loss and disgrace he was capable of." Within five years occurred the frightful disaster of the Yemassee War, and after that the fights with the pirates and the political disturbances.

It is not likely that in such a perturbed time there would be much growth or improvement, but by 1720 the north and west walls had been partially dismantled (Oldmixon sarcastically says they were for beauty, not for use) and houses were built beyond the original precincts. Among the private houses he mentions "some very handsome buildings, as Mr. Landgrave Smith's house on the Key with a drawbridge and wharf before it, Colonel Rhett's is on the Key; also Mr. Boone's, Mr. Logan's, Mr. Schinking's and ten or twelve more which deserve to be taken notice of."

In all these early descriptions of the country there is no mention of flowers. Trees and fruits are repeatedly enumerated, but whether or no these "fair houses" had gardens among them at this early time we know not. The only mention of anything ornamental is Governor Archdale's of what is now called the State Road, but which was long known as "The Path," the old Indian trail, the continuation of the present King Street.

"the land is mixed with blackish mould, it is beautified with odoriferous and fragrant woods, pleasantly green all the year as the Pine, Cedar and Cypress, insomuch that out of Charles Town for three or four miles called the Broadway, is so delightful a Road and walk of a great breadth, so pleasantly green that I believe no Prince in Europe with all their Art, can make so pleasant a sight for the whole year." But not a word of the yellow jessamine, the magnolia, the sweet bay, or the gay catalpa trees which must have filled the woods with odour and colour then, as they do to-day.

In this growing place living was inexpensive. Then, as for generations to come, the plantation furnished the town house with most of the necessaries of life. Transportation was easy, for the settlements clung to the rivers which were the common highways. The expression for making a settlement was "seating a river," as, "I understand two new rivers are about seating"; "they have the advantage of seating a new river" (Archdale). Every planter had his canoe, such as Lawson describes seeing among the Huguenots on the Santee, made of "vast cypress trees that will carry fifty or sixty Barrels" *i.e.* of rice. "After the tree is moulded and dug they saw it in two pieces and so put a plank between and a small Keel to preserve them from the Oyster Banks." Such canoes were still in use fifty years ago, especially among the planters of the islands to the southward, who used to bring their "long staple cotton" piled high in bow and stern. Ten or twelve negroes in the waist plied their long oars, keeping perfect time to the songs or "spirituals," which they chanted incessantly during the row of thirty or forty miles. Sometimes instead of cotton the planter's family came down in these craft, comfortably enough, sleeping at some friend's house on the way, and sheltered by a tarpaulin in case of rain. From the plantations came rice, corn, ground for hominy or bread, potatoes, peas, ham, bacon, salt meat, and poultry. In cold weather a beef could safely come, or a deer, or wild turkeys, which Archdale says an Indian will sell the first for sixpence, the second of forty pounds for twopence of English money! The close trade with the West Indies supplied them with turtle, sugar, coffee, and pepper at low rates, and as they sent much rice to Portugal, it was easy to bring back Port or even Madeira wine. It is no wonder that they "lived well and handsomely entertained their friends."

It is hard at this distance of time to say positively who were the men who had thus already conquered the wilderness and laid the foundations of a state which their children should rule. In a community there are always persons who take no prominent part in public affairs, yet by character and position exercise much influence over their course. Such is the "silent body of country gentlemen who sit but don't speak in the House of Commons." Such was the same class in the little colony of Carolina. But the names most frequently mentioned at that time are first, undoubtedly, Trott and Rhett who overtop all others; Robert Johnson, the displaced Governor, and James Moore, who succeeded him provisionally. He had led the second expedition against the Tuscaroras, and was, says Ramsay, "a man excellently qualified for being a public leader in a perilous adventure." Arthur Middleton, as President of the Assembly, had led the attack on the Proprietors. He was the second of the name in Carolina settled at Crowfield on Goose Creek.

Besides these there were William Bull, son of Stephen, who built the second house of Ashley Hall, and was beginning a career which was to be of great distinction. Ralph Izard, Colonel Broughton of "Mulberry," Governor Gibbes, Mr. Berresford, all Goose Creek men — the last remembered by his bequest of over six thousand pounds

DRAYTON HALL

as a school fund, called the "Berresford Bounty." The Draytons and Bakers were on Ashley River at "Drayton Hall," "Magnolia," and "Archdale." Fenwicke, Waring, Logan, Harleston, Skrine, Parris, Kinloch, and Othniel Beale are names constantly occurring in councils and commissions. Some Huguenots begin to appear in the same way: De la Conseillière, Le Noble, St. Julien, and Serrurier. Colonel John Barnwell was, next to Rhett, the best soldier of the colony, and with Boone, Yonge, and Lloyd, represented it in England. The second Landgrave, Thomas Smith, had succeeded his father, but the son of the Proprietor, Joseph Blake, was still a minor, his estate admirably administered by his mother, "Madam" or "Lady" Blake ; the first of those managing matrons of Carolina who did so much for the country, of whom we have any knowledge. Their chief seat was "Newington" near the present village of Summerville, a stately brick mansion.

One alone among the families of the original Lords Proprietors ever identified itself with Carolina by residence or name. That of Sir John Colleton, named by Charles II. as one of the grantees of the Province. Sir John himself never came out nor did either of his elder sons ; and the career of the third, Landgrave and Governor James, from whose "nobility" so much had been hoped, was (as already related) most unfortunate. Nevertheless, the family "added house to house and vineyard to vineyard" (and rice field to rice field) until there was hardly a "seated river" from the Cooper to the Broad, on which they had not an estate or a barony. One, just opposite to the town, between the Ashley and Wappoo Creek, called "Waheewah Barony," is supposed to have been the place where Landgrave James built the fine house which he was forced to leave when banished by his enraged subjects. He had another barony, "Wadboo" on the Cooper, with a handsome stone house on it, and a lot of nine acres on the square of his own name in Charles Town, all of which he left to his son.

Those of the family who did not come out (there were several) managed their estates, built houses, etc., by agents, and it was not until 1726 that the Honourable John Colleton, great grandson of the first Sir John, came to reside permanently in the Province at the "Fairlawn

Barony," at the head of navigation of Cooper River, near the present village of Monck's Corner.

Here he built himself a magnificent house, said to have been the largest in the colony. It was burned by the British in the Revolution, lest it should harbour Marion's men who had already annoyed them by lying in ambush among the thick cedars of the avenue. Fifty years ago the plan of the house could still be traced, although it had long served the neighbourhood as a brick quarry.

There was the foundation of a large square central building, with extensive wings which had apparently formed three sides of a courtyard. From one wing the foundation of a wall ran to another heap of ruins, evidently offices ; it was supposed that the wall had been part of a connecting gallery. The site of two artificial fish ponds, which were the fashion of the day, could be distinguished; but the whole place was grown up in oak and cedar, with here and there a ragged box tree or garden plant to tell of what had been.

Here the Honourable John and his wife, Susannah Snell, spent their lives, dying within a few months of each other and being buried at the parish church of St. John's Berkeley (commonly called Biggin Church), the site and glebe for which had been given by the family a few years before.

To this gentleman succeeded his son, who inherited the title from his grandfather and became the third Sir John. Both of these styled themselves "of Fairlawn Barony, in the parish of St. John's Berkeley, in the province of South Carolina." But Fairlawn was only one of their many estates and they were among the wealthiest men of the colony; yet, although naturally of much social importance, they do not appear to have taken any prominent part in public affairs, further than that both were members of his Majesty's Council.

MAGNOLIA GARDENS, ON ASHLEY RIVER

Probably all but two or three of these men were rice planters. Rice had by this time become the chief product of the Province. From little patches planted experimentally by Landgrave Smith, Dr. Woodward, and others (the former in his garden upon the creek which is now Water Street), about twenty-five years before, it grew by 1720 upon every "seated" river, and formed the chief wealth of the Province. Over seventeen thousand barrels were exported in 1724. Indigo came later, and cotton later still, but rice reigned in "the Parishes," and its planters were the dominant class of Charleston, socially and politically, down to 1865.

It should not be forgotten, however, that the planters were likewise citizens, and that they formed a *class* and not a caste. Their ranks were continually recruited from those of the merchants, for like their brethren at home "the Seigneurs of the seas," from whom spring many English nobles, the man who began in trade soon put his money into land and became a country gentleman also.

"Commerce," says Ramsay, "is of noble origin in South Carolina. Its first merchants were the Lords Proprietors of the Province," and during the whole colonial period the merchants formed a wealthy and important element of society. The merchant then owned and sometimes sailed his own ships, sent them according to his own discretion from port to port, he or his son often going as supercargo, saw adventure and life by sea and land, and in order to be successful had to be a man of intelligence, education, and force. Such a one was Othniel Beale, who, having been taken at sea by Barbary pirates, managed to delude the Algerine crew put aboard of him into believing that he was steering for the Barbary coast, when in fact he was making all sail for the Thames! He actually succeeded in getting vessel and crew into port before the rovers guessed his design, and was received and rewarded by the

King. He then returned to Carolina, where he spent the rest of his life, made a fortune, became a member of the Commons and afterward President of the Council. His daughter married the second Lieutenant-governor Bull, but left no children.

Governor Archdale said in 1707, " I am satisfied that a Person with 500 pounds discreetly laid out in old England, and again prudently managed in Carolina, shall in a few years live in as much Plenty, yea more, than a man of 500 pounds *a year* in England."

By this Mr. Archdale evidently meant that English goods, " discreetly " chosen, would indefinitely multiply their value in Charles Town. The " Mazÿck Record " gives the account of just such a successful business as he contemplates. It is a type of the commercial career of the time, and so is given here.

Isaac Mazÿck, the youngest son of a wealthy family of Protestant merchants of La Rochelle, foreseeing the wrath to come, left France before the revocation of the Edict of Nantes, and by so doing was able to take with him " what money he could hastily gather together, about 1500 pounds sterling." He was an educated and rather accomplished man, with some taste and skill in drawing. Some of his sketches and topographical drawings of fortified places in France were long preserved by his descendants. After some stay in Holland, where he laid out his money in goods, he determined to go to Carolina, knowing that he should find there many of his countrymen of his own faith, enjoy liberty of conscience, and be able to " enter into a very extensive trade as a merchant." He arrived, he says, " in December 1686 " and " brought with him a cargo of about 1000 pounds sterling worth of goods merchandise, and immediately settled in Charles Town." He prospered so well that he " carried on an extensive scheme of Trade with England, Portugal, Madeira, the West Indies and

North America," and the better to manage this business, made many voyages to England, the Islands, etc.

He bought for a small price a large body of land (about thirty-five acres) at the west end of Broad Street, then without the walls, which long continued in the possession of his descendants, and other large bodies in the upper part of the town " so that he at one time possessed more land in and about Charles Town than any other person in Carolina or in any town in North America." Unfortunately he sold a great part of this land " which would have been a great estate to his heirs." (He kept enough, however, to make them very wealthy.) He bought also a plantation and sixty negroes on Goose Creek, and his name appears in the list of " Goosecreek men" reckoned as Governor Colleton's chief opponents. His sons were most carefully educated abroad. The eldest, of his own name, was for over fifty years a member of the Commons House, always continuing his father's business, and becoming a large landholder and an assistant judge. The manuscript " Record " — written by his grandson — of the elder Mazÿck, says, " He was in his time the most eminent merchant in Carolina, and made one of the largest estates, with a fair, upright and honourable character ; a sincere Christian, just in his dealings, humane and charitable to all, and a loyal subject of the House of Hanover."

In his Bible is the following, probably written soon after his arrival in America, "God gave me the great blessing of coming out of France, and escaping the cruel persecutions carried on against the Protestants, and to express my thankfulness for so great a blessing I promise, please God, to observe the anniversary of that by a fast."

The story may be said to justify Governor Archdale's opinion as to the advantages of Carolina for a " prudent " man with a small capital.

The Mr. Wragg who had so narrowly escaped the clutches of Blackbeard was another instance of these planter merchants.

He and his brother, for their services in bringing out large numbers of emigrants, were granted twenty-four thousand acres of land ; this estate was long known as the "Wragg Barony." Miss Pinckney, writing in 1766, says : "Miss Wragg shook hands for life with Jack Mathewes last week. They had a mighty jolly wedding of it up at ye Barony." Yet the Wraggs did not give up business, and at the outbreak of the Revolution William Wragg was one of the wealthiest and most respected persons of the town. By the time of the Revolution the merchants took much share in public affairs, as Henry Laurens, Robert Pringle, Gabriel and Peter Manigault, Colonel Shubrick, and others.

All these, planters and merchants, were now looking anxiously for what his Majesty might be pleased to do, and who the next Governor should be. If things had gone adversely for them at home, and the King had held them for rebels, then the fate of the traitor might have been theirs, and their heads not been safe on their shoulders. However, as has been said, their cause had prospered, and in 1721 arrived General Sir Francis Nicholson as Provisional Governor.

Sir Francis was a picturesque person, who had already held similar positions, sometimes with credit, but always with eccentricity. In Virginia, for instance, he had fallen so violently in love that when the lady married another, he threatened to shoot, with his own hands, groom, parson, and magistrate who gave the license!

In Carolina he was to expend his energies on forts and churches. As a good soldier he saw the need for the former, as a devoted churchman he cared for the latter.

He sent Colonel John Barnwell to build a fort on the

Altamaha to keep the Spaniards in check, and made him commander of the southern part of the Province.

For the churches he not only obtained additional assistance from the ever generous S. P. G., but gave liberally from his own pocket. A hundred pounds, for instance, for the new parish just formed to the north, which was, of course, to bear the beloved name "Prince George" Winyah.

There were many difficulties of administration : old debts and paper currency to be adjusted, accounts to be examined, officers to be removed and new ones appointed. It is not to be expected that such changes could be peaceably effected. " The new Governor," says Hewat, "though bred a soldier, and profane, passionate and headstrong himself, was not insensible of the advantages of religion to society, and contributed not a little to its interests in Carolina, both by his public influence and private generosity."

The same was absolutely true of Colonel William Rhett. Of course they quarrelled violently. Rhett, in addition to many other offices, had been made inspector of fortifications. It was alleged that he had neglected his work and abused his position. A new man, Benjamin de la Conseillière, was appointed receiver-general in his stead, and Rhett, proudly conscious of his great services to the State, resented all examination of accounts.

One can easily imagine his haughty sense of injury! The Governor called him (to the Lords trustees) "a haughty, proud, insolent fellow and a cheating scoundrel." Probably, if we had Colonel Rhett's opinion of his Excellency, it would be much the same. The quarrel did not last long, for Rhett died suddenly of an apoplectic fit in 1722, and Sir Francis himself, in announcing his death, asked that some one might be sent to succeed him, " as there are not many persons here qualified." Certainly a tribute to the capacity of his enemy!

Colonel Rhett was buried in the yard of the new, still unfinished church, which had been many years in building. The original wooden St. Philip's had become so decayed that it was thought unsafe, and the new one was placed on the site now occupied by the third of the name, at the head of Church Street. It was just within the city limits,

THE SECOND ST. PHILIP'S CHURCH
From an old print.

the old town wall bounding its yards (east and west) to the north, and also bounding that of the "Old White Meeting," which adjoined its western enclosure; having Fort Carteret and the powder magazine at the northwest corner. To the church Colonel Rhett had given a silver communion service, chalice, paten, and alms-dish, from which the congregation still receives the sacrament, — all marked with the inscription, " The gift of Colonel William Rhett to the Church of St. Philip's, Charles Town, South Carolina."

The Proprietors had liberally given five hundred pounds toward the erection of this church, but now in the spirit of ardent loyalty which possessed the people, they instructed their agents in London " to pray his Majesty to send his picture and arms for a publick building in Charles Town, and also a set of church plate for the church here, which they are to pray may be called ' St. George's Church.' "

There is something irresistibly comic in the idea of his fat Hanoverian Majesty becoming in this roundabout way, a patron saint. Possibly the absurdity occurred to the King's representatives, for the loyal wish was only gratified in part; the plate engraved with the Royal arms was sent, but the name " St. Philip's " was transferred with the congregation to the new edifice. This plate had, many years afterward, a singular escape. Having passed unscathed through the perils of the Revolution, and the fire of 1835, in which the church itself was destroyed, it nearly fell a prey to a burglar ! This man, a " professional " from New York, had committed an immense number of robberies in Charleston, when one morning the family of the church warden, to whose house the service had been taken for safe keeping, found that not so much as a teaspoon remained to them of their own silver, but that all the church plate, removed from its box and carried downstairs, was left placed upon a table. Religious or superstitious feeling can move even a burglar, and the sacred vessels were spared !

The church, which was not opened for worship until 1723, was esteemed, says Burke, the handsomest in America. It had " three aisles, an organ, and a gallery all round. The steeple rises octagonal, with windows

H

in each face of the second course ornamented with ionic
pilasters, whose entablature supports a balustrade, from

St. Michael's Church from Broad Street

this the tower still rises octagonal, with sashed windows
on every other face, till it is terminated by a dome, upon

which stands a lanthorn for the bells, from which rises a vane in the form of a cock."

The church was opened for service in 1723, but the interior was not finished until 1727, the congregation in the meanwhile taking their own chairs with them, there being no seats. In the latter year the pews were put in, and were "granted" to those applying for them. The "grant" following a "benevolence" varying apparently from sixty to one hundred pounds apiece. We have certainly lost much grace and dignity of phrase since 1727. How much better does this sound than "such a pew in —— church was sold at auction for twelve hundred dollars!" The early adoption of the Church of England by many of the Huguenots even of the town, is shown by the fact that Colonel Samuel Prioleau, son of the first Huguenot pastor, Elias Prioleau, Gabriel Manigault, and John Abram Motte, were members of the first vestry of the new church. Probably the very distinct declaration sworn to by each vestryman made this transference easy to them.

"We the vestry and church wardens of the Parish of St. Philip's, Charlestown, who have hereto subscribed our names, do declare that we believe that there is no transubstantiation whatever in the Sacrament of the Lord's Supper, or in the elements of bread and wine, after consecration thereof by any person whatever."

The original church, having become dangerous to bystanders, was pulled down, and the site was presented to the town to build a hall upon, with the curious proviso that the churchyard might still be used for interments. Fancy a city hall in a graveyard! This odd plan was never carried out, and in thirty years more the present St. Michael's was erected on the spot first occupied by the old St. Philip's.

Governor Nicholson had but a stormy administration.

His temper was violent and his language — emphatic.
When the merchants opposed his plans with regard to
the currency, he authorized the Commons to imprison all
the petitioners, and declared that "they will lye most
notoriously in their own interest," and likewise quarrelled
with the Council who sustained the merchants.

But he did his best to encourage education and religion,
and also to pacify the Indians and fortify the Province.
His health was not good, and in three years' time he
returned to England, laying the burthen of government
on the shoulders of Mr. Arthur Middleton, who administered it as "President of the Council" until the death
of Sir Francis in 1729.

The fiery Governor proved the sincerity of his interest
in his friends and in good works by his will, drawn after
his return to England. He first gives most minute instructions about his funeral "immediately after sunrise,"
his grave to be covered with a white marble tombstone
with pillars at the four corners, "thereon expressed my
Travells and the Offices I have borne in Europe, Asia,
Africa and America."   This provided for, he leaves small
legacies and mourning rings to innumerable friends in
England and the Provinces (many in Carolina), "to my
godson Abel Kettelby my silver fringed gloves and my
silver handled sword," and finally gives all his property
to the S. P. G. for the "Encouragement of persons coming from New England, receiving Episcopal Ordination
and going as Missionaries."   It should be said too that
he bore no malice, for rings are left "To Mr. Samuel
Wragg and wife and children, and to the Gentlemen who
now compose his Majesty's Council in South Carolina";
thus forgiving, as a brave soldier does, in death those
with whom in life he has honourably fought.

Mr. Arthur Middleton, a man of firm character and of
much influence in the colony, was yet so embarrassed by

the provisional character of Governor Nicholson's commission under which he acted, that the vexed questions remained vexed.

In 1731, the negotiations between the King and the Proprietors being at last concluded, Robert Johnson was sent out with full authority as first Royal Governor of the Province. Great was the rejoicing of the people. They thoroughly respected Johnson, and appreciated the security which the new government would bring. "Since the Province was taken under the Royal care," says Ramsay, "it was nursed and protected by a rich and powerful nation, its government was stable, private property was secure, and the privileges of the people extensive."

Nevertheless the province lost severely when the division between North and South Carolina was formally made — a vagueness of geographical knowledge as to the true position of the mouth of the "Waggamaw" River costing her thirty miles of sea-coast that should have been hers. Still more did she lose, however, when his "most Gracious Majesty for the better protection of his beloved people of South Carolina," decided to plant another colony to the south to be called Georgia. Here too knowledge was not precise, and by these repeated abscissions the Province was reduced to the odd little triangle of her present boundaries. No uneasiness seems to have been felt, however, and the interest was great when it was known that General Oglethorpe with his colony had arrived at Port Royal. The Assembly was in session, which, Governor Johnson said, alone prevented his going in person to escort the General to his own territory, but he sent Colonel Bull to assist with advice and experience. The Assembly voted money, cattle, and rice, and twenty rangers as a guard to the newcomers. Many gentlemen and ladies sent contributions, lending negroes to help build the new town, and giving provisions, horses, etc., for its support. No such help had the early settlers of Charles Town received. Several gentlemen went with Colonel Bull as assistants, and by way of encouragement, Mr. Hume sent a silver pap boat and spoon to be given to the first child born in Georgia ; which, the narrator adds, " was soon claimed"!

Interest quickened yet more, when Oglethorpe, having started his town of Savannah, arrived in Charles Town to ask further aid, and was received at the wharf with military honours and deputations of Council and Assembly. The Assembly voted him ten thousand pounds for the coming year and (the newly established *Gazette* says) invited the General and staff to a " banquet." The reader must remember that, unless specified, " pounds " do not mean " sterling," but " currency " — about five to one. There was drinking of loyal toasts, the guns in the batteries fired a salute, and the General, not to be outdone, gave not only a dinner, but " a ball and cold supper to the ladies at the Council Chamber, where was the greatest appearance of fashion, that has been known upon such an occasion."

Evidently, therefore, there had been balls before, but for want of a newspaper no mention of them survives. The *Gazette* had only begun in 1721–1722, coming out every Saturday : a queer little grayish sheet, with very black lettering, still to be seen in the Charleston Library.

It was edited by Louis Timothée, a Huguenot, who like many of his race Englished his name and called himself Louis Timothy. He, his widow, their son, and their son's widow, and her son, carried on the paper until 1800, when it was replaced by the *Charleston Courier*, partly owned by a great-grandson.

Not without trouble had permission been obtained for the existence of the paper. Soldiers have never been very fond of the press, and General Sir Francis Nicholson was every inch a soldier. When it was proposed to him to establish a printing-press in order that the laws of South

Carolina, carefully codified by Chief Justice Trott, might be printed, he had thrown every obstacle in the way. He said : "It may be seen how very chargeable it is to have a printer come hither, and if any should come I can't suffer him to exercise his trade without his giving very good security not to print anything without license. And I can't give him any for printing the body of the laws, till his Majesty's will and pleasure be known thereon ; so that in my opinion the money appropriated for a printer may be disposed of for the good of his Majesty's Province." Sir Francis hated Trott, and so did his successor, Mr. Middleton, who speaks of "Mr. Trott's unreasonable proposal to print our laws," and hatred prompted the resistance. The laws were nevertheless printed by special direction and at the King's expense in Charles Town, by "Eleazar Phillips of Boston, first printer to his Majesty." Phillips promptly died of yellow fever ; another unfortunate met the same fate in 1733, and Timothy himself lived only four years. It was the pursuit of journalism under difficulties, but the paper, as has been said, survived.

Before long it had to announce the death of the "good Governor" Robert Johnson, who died in May, 1735. It gives a long account of the funeral services, how he was "decently interred in a vault near the altar in Charles Town Church," and was "attended to the grave" by Council, Assembly, Military, etc., and "by a numerous assemblage of gentlemen and ladies, who came from all parts of the Province to pay their last respects to one, whom they might justly look upon as their common Father." The Assembly erected a monument to him in the church, which was consumed with it one hundred years later.

Governor Johnson when he came from England had brought with him the commission of lieutenant-governor for his brother-in-law, Colonel Broughton — a title not bestowed by the Proprietary government. It was constantly used henceforth, and was always conferred upon a native of the Province, who was addressed as " Your Honour," the Governor being " Your Excellency."

On the death of Governor Johnson the authority accordingly devolved upon Colonel Broughton, who dying in two years, the title was bestowed upon Colonel Bull, who administered until the arrival of James Glen in 1743. These were on the whole peaceful and prosperous years, yet it is easy to see that through them all one increasing purpose runs, the ever strengthening determination of the people to be governed according to their own ideas of constitutional right and liberty. The Assembly, which called itself the Commons, claimed, like its great model, the sole right to lay taxes and originate money bills. But the Royal Council, appointed by the Governor and approved by the Crown, claimed (and claimed legally) that its powers exceeded those of the House of Peers (to which it willingly likened itself) and when it so pleased, altered and added to such bills. This the Commons determined to resist, and the struggle went on from the government of Mr. Middleton in 1724 to that of Lord William Campbell in 1776.

CHAPTER VIII

GREATLY interested was Charles Town when, in the
second year of Governor Bull, General Oglethorpe,
who had repelled an invasion of the Spaniards at Freder-
ika Island on the coast of Georgia, came to confer about
carrying the war into the enemy's country.

The General had, in consideration of his military knowledge and experience, been appointed commander-in-chief
of the forces of both Provinces, and desired to make his
expedition a complete one. The project was the more
agreeable to the Carolinians, because of an insurrection of
the negroes to the southward, which had taken place but
a short time before, and which it was found had been in-
stigated by the Spaniards. They, remembering how
effective their Indian allies had been in harassing the
English, had now formed the fiendish plan of raising up
enemies to them in their own households and inciting the
otherwise peaceful blacks to murder and rapine. The
insurrection had been immediately quelled with the loss of
only twenty-one white and forty negro lives, but the danger had been great. There were thirty-two thousand black
to fourteen thousand white people in the colony; they
were an excitable race, and St. Augustine bribed them to
rebellion.

Yet there was some hesitation at Oglethorpe's proposition, for Moore's disastrous expedition was still fresh in

the minds of the people, and the paper money, which was
its result, rustled like dead leaves in their pockets.   It
was understood, however, that this would be a very different manner of war.   That had been a mere hasty militia
affair.   In this a general trained by Prince Eugene was to
command his own Royal regiment, one of Georgians, and
a body of friendly Indians, while, instead of Moore's poorly
armed schooners, five of his Majesty's warships were to
coöperate.   Warlike counsels prevailed; it was decided
to make more paper money and raise a regiment of four
hundred men to serve as an auxiliary force.   Thirty-two
gentlemen volunteered to form an independent company
and go for the love of adventure, Captain Wright commanding.   Governor Bull appointed a day of humiliation,
fasting, and prayer for the success of the "endeavour
against his Majesty's enemies," and the expedition started
in fine spirits.

'It had been declared by Captain Pearce, commanding
the Royal vessels, "that they ought all to be hung if they
did not take St. Augustine in a very short time."   Nevertheless they did not take it, and failed as or more ignominiously than Moore had done.   Oglethorpe's force
was greater and he had artillery, but the mismanagement
was the same.   The general quarrelled with his own officers, the navy did not coöperate, and, like Braddock many
years afterward, he scorned the advice of mere provincials.   Colonel Nathaniel Barnwell (the son of Tuscarora
Jack), who was serving as volunteer aide, told him that
his father had left the maxim " Never trust a Spaniard or
fear an Indian "; but he did both.   The first deceived and
the second betrayed him.   He must have seen many
sieges of fortified places, but only one shell is known to
have exploded over the fort, and a shot is still shown im-
bedded in the ramparts which *is said* to have been thrown
by his cannon.   The Don sat secure and answered a sum-

mons to surrender by saying that he " should be willing to kiss his Excellency's hands—*in his Castle.*" Weeks passed and summer came. If January and February were the Czar Alexander's best generals, June and July fought as well for the Spaniards. Oglethorpe himself was ill; the soldiers fainted from heat, cooped in a dreadful little fort on Anastasia Island, where Ribault's men had been slaughtered two hundred years before. Even the Indians succumbed. It all ended in a mortifying retreat and painful recriminations.

The story does not belong to Charles Town except as so many of her men were concerned. Most of these were sons of those who had fought under Johnson and Craven. One alone of that generation took part in this war. Colonel Palmer, who had driven the Yemassees as a " stripling," now fell before St. Augustine. There were some new names. Vander Dussen, the colonel, had come recently into the Province, planting on Goose Creek. Of the others—Lieutenant Le Jau was the son of the excellent missionary; Major Colleton, a kinsman of the Landgrave; Captains Bull and Wright were sons of the lieutenant-governor and the chief justice. De Saussure, Maxwell, Bryan, and Blamyer, lieutenants, are names that appear first about this time.

The men of the Proprietary days were passing away. James Moore and William Rhett died within a few months of each other. They had been enemies, but the son of the former married the daughter of the latter and from them the present Rhett family—and many others— are descended. Arthur Middleton too was dead. His son Henry, the creator of the beautiful " Middleton Place," was to become as eminent as his father.

Chief Justice Trott survived all these, not dying until 1740. He had married Colonel Rhett's widow, and his daughter became the wife of her son, but they left no male heirs.

Trott had not resigned his great influence without a struggle. As long as there was the least chance of the return of the Proprietors he plotted and schemed for it. When that hope failed, he tried to persuade the King to restore him to office. Finding this of no avail, he returned to Charles Town, where he died. His obituary makes no mention of his great and useful work of codifying the laws, but says:—

"On the Twenty-first of January last, died Nicholas Trott, Esquire, Doctor of Laws, who for several Years past was Chief Justice of this Province, during the Time the Government was in the Hands of the Lords Proprietors and at several Times had Commission from the Admiralty of England to be Judge of the Court of Vice Admiralty here. Continued in the Office of Chief Justice, till the Lords Proprietors were ousted of the Government. After that he lived private and retir'd from all publick Business, and applied himself wholly to perfect his designed Explication of the Original Hebrew Text of the new Testament; and finish'd one large Vol. in Folio fit for the Press some short Time before his Death. He was born January 19, 1662–3, and died January the 21st, 1739–40, being 76 years of Age." (Saturday, February 2, 1740.)

This commentary does not appear to have been published, and the cool tone of the notice, — not a word of praise, nothing of "genteel interment" or "mourning people," — shows how unpopular the once all-powerful chief justice had become.

It should perhaps have been mentioned before that in Sir Francis Nicholson's time it had been definitely arranged that the Church in South Carolina should be of the jurisdiction of the Bishop of London. The Bishop's delegate was the commissary who held sway over all "ecclesiastical matters in North and South Carolina, Georgia and the Island of New Providence."

In 1740 this important functionary was the Reverend Alexander Garden, always known as "Commissary Garden." Besides his general charge over the religion, morals, and orthodox practices of all the clergy in this wide domain, the good gentleman was rector of St. Philip's, and superintendent of a very large school for the teaching and Christianizing of negroes; a subject to which much attention was now being paid. He was a most excellent man and not illiberal according to the ideas of his time. He gladly welcomed Charles Wesley on his Southern journey, and invited him to preach at St. Philip's, and to attend one of the visitations which he held for his clergy, where views on religious topics were exchanged. Dr. Dalcho says that Wesley described this conversation on "Christ our Righteousness" as such "as he had not heard at any Visitation in England, or on hardly any other occasion." But Wesley still conformed to the usages of the Church.

When the Reverend George Whitfield came, by special invitation of General Oglethorpe, to evangelize Georgia, Dr. Garden received him with equal cordiality. But Whitfield was not to be held within the narrow bounds of rubrics. He was, above all things, a great preacher, and he demanded a great congregation — preferred a big field to a small church, conducted services without prayer-books, and took up collections as willingly in a Meeting House as in St. Philip's itself.

It was very rousing, of course, and probably of permanent benefit to many minds, but it was utterly repugnant to the strictly canonical commissary and he had not the slightest doubt but that it was his duty to stop it. He might as well have tried to stop Niagara. Whitfield positively refused to pause in work for which he felt himself inspired, and the tide of his eloquence swept all before it. If he had only resigned the title of churchman, it would have been well, but he continued to claim the name while violating the laws.

Dr. Garden appealed and enjoined, and finally summoned an ecclesiastical court to try the offender. There could be but little doubt as to the result. Whitfield's breaches of the law had been done in the high places and could not be denied. Mr. Green for the prosecuting Church had his case clear. Mr. Andrew Rutledge, a young lawyer, lately arrived from North Ireland, did all that could be done in denying the powers of the Court. Judgment was of course given for the commissary, and sentence was pronounced. Whitfield was suspended from office, "denounced, declared and published, etc."

A touch of persecution is the breath of an enthusiasm; Whitfield was a martyr and Methodism grew apace. The commissary's own account is interesting. He wrote to a friend: —

"I am also under still further obligation to you, for the favourable Sentiments you are pleased to express of the late Attempts I have been drove into, (under that of old age and other Infirmities) in Defence of what I firmly believe to be the Cause of Truth, against the Franticks gone forth 'mongst us. I could now indeed wish, that my Pen agt w——d had run in somewhat smoother a Stile. But had you been on the Spot, to have seen the Frenzie he excited 'mong the people; The Bitterness and Virulence wherewith he raved against the Clergy of the Chh. of England in general; — and how artfully he laboured to sett the Mobb upon me in particular; — I dare say, you would have thought the Provocacaon enough to ruffle any Temper, and a sufficient Apology for the keenest expressions I have used against him. And as to my putting the Eccles. Laws in Execution against him, my Conscience would give me no Peace

ST. PHILIP'S FROM THE HUGUENOT CHURCHYARD

111

had I neglected so bounden a Duty. I have always executed them on offending Clergymen in this Province, whose offences reached not near the Size and Notoriety of his, and with God's assistance shall continue to do so. When he continued a Presbyter of the Chh. in England, he was Subject to her Laws; now he is cast out they have no further hold.

" As to the State of religion in this Province, it is bad enough, God knows. Rome and the Devil have contrived to crucify her 'twixt two Thieves, Infidelity and Enthusiasm. The former, alas! too much still prevails; but as to the Latter, thanks to God, it is greatly subsided, and even on the point of vanishing away. We had here Trances, Visions and Revelations, both 'mong Blacks and Whites, in abundance. But ever since the famous Hugh Brian, sousing himself into the River Jordan, in order to smite and divide its Waters, had his eyes opened, and saw himself under the Delusion of the Devil, those things have dwindled into Disgrace, and are now no more."

There was good reason to dread the influence of this emotional kind of piety upon half-educated and enthusiastic natures. The unlucky Mr. Bryan alluded to, had as a boy been carried off by the Indians and had remained a long time in captivity. Under the excitement of Whitfield's fervid eloquence he lost his head completely — saw visions and dreamed dreams. At first he only went about denouncing the regular clergy, declaring that the negro insurrection, the failure of the St. Augustine expedition, and the great fire of 1740 were all caused by their sloth and indifference, and glorifying his Apostle.

Later on his mysticism grew wilder. Miss Lucas says, " He imagin'd he was assisted by the Divine Spirit to prophesy Charles Town and the country as far as Pon-Pon bridge " (about twenty miles) " should be destroyed by fire and sword, to be executed by the negroes before the first of next month." Prophecies sometimes work their own fulfilment, and the neighbourhood was justly indignant, though as knowing the importance of showing no fear, people went on quietly on their plantations.

At last the poor man (not until he had roused much attention and excitement in the dangerous class) fancied himself ordered to work miracles, " till at length he came with a wand to divide the waters and predicted that he should die that night. But upon finding both fail, the water continue as it was, and he himself a living instance of the fallacy of his own predictions, was convinced that he was not guided by the Infallible Spirit, but that of delusion, and sent a letter to the Speaker."

Poor Mr. Bryan had gone so deep into the ice-cold water that had not his brother followed and pulled him out, the prophecy of death would have been fulfilled. Whether the ducking or the failure restored his senses cannot be known ; he made submission to Colonel Bull (Speaker of the Commons) and no harm came of it. The whole blame was by the church party laid to Whitfield's account, " He fancied he was supported in his opinions by the sacred oracles and, (as a father of our church observes) so did all the preachers of herrissy in the Primitive Church." On the other hand the Reverend Josiah Smith, son of the Landgrave and minister of the White Meeting (where Whitfield had preached), and other nonconformists, took up his cause warmly, and there was dissension in the little town.

From this time on the *organized* effort to teach and Christianize the negroes continued. There had been much individual effort before, since the year 1702, when the first missionary of the S. P. G., the Reverend Samuel Thomas (who was " so discouraged " at finding that the Indians were addicted to the taking of scalps), perceived

I

that the negroes were more hopeful converts. He set up a school, taught twenty-three to read, and baptized and confirmed several. He lived but a short time, but his successor, Mr. Le Jau, was very zealous. In a few years there were many negro communicants. As early as 1711 the Society's reports mention Mrs. Edwards and Mrs. Haig, Mr. Morris, Lady Moore, Captain Davis, Landgrave and Mrs. Morton, Mrs. Skene, and others as "taking particular pains to instruct their people in religion, reclaim and reform them."

The very first difficulty with the savage native African, the Carolinians were in a measure spared, for those from Barbadoes, the first in the colony, had already received some rudiments of civilization and acted as trainers to the newcomers. To make them wear clothes, speak English, and not murder one another were the first elements of education: all hard to inculcate, especially the first. Any rag of ornament they would gladly put on, but reasonable garments were a burthen, and some men had to be indulged with petticoats, refusing trousers as indignantly as any Highlander. English, of a sort, came more easily, their quickness of ear helping to the sounds; but to prevent their brutal fights was always one of the most troublesome parts of plantation discipline.

In religious teaching the great difficulty was the inherent separateness of religion and morality in the Ethiopian mind. Dr. Garden's plan for his school was to buy two intelligent lads, instruct them carefully in the reading of the Bible and Prayer-book, and set them to teach the others. The scheme worked well for a time, and commended itself to the public. Miss Lucas mentions that she is herself teaching "two little negro girls, who I intend for school-mistresses for the rest of the negro children."

How Dr. Garden's teachers enjoyed it can be under-

EARLY BRICK HOUSES ON TRADD STREET. BUILT BY ROBERT
PRINGLE SOON AFTER THE GREAT FIRE OF 1740

stood by any one who has seen a deacon or a class leader at
an African camp-meeting! The school was supported by
the S. P. G. and by subscribers. The commissary him-

self gave the site for the building, a part of the glebe land left by Mrs. Affra Coming. It went on prosperously for twenty years. Then one "boy" died and the other took to evil ways. Why none of their scholars were put in their places is not known, but the plan was discontinued.

In 1742 there were twelve S. P. G. clergymen in the colony engaged in missionary work.

A blessing in disguise befell Charles Town in the year 1740: a fire, which beginning at the west end of Broad Street swept eastward and consumed every house below the northern side of that street. The houses were of wood and of no great value, but that being the oldest and most populous part of the town, there was much distress. It was hard to provide shelter for the people. Great quantities of goods both for export and import were stored there, and Governor Bull reported to the Lords of Trade that the loss amounted to two hundred and fifty thousand pounds. Even the gun carriages in the fortifications, and some of the bastions which defended the town, were destroyed.

Parliament came to the aid of the colony and sent it twenty thousand pounds. The place was rebuilt of brick. Many of the houses still remaining between Broad and the line of Water streets, all of small, dark brick, date from this time on. That on Tradd Street, between King and Meeting, built by Robert Pringle (first of the name to come to Carolina; a Scotch merchant, and afterward assistant justice), but recently taken down, bore the inscription "R. P. 1742," cut in stone above the door.

CHAPTER IX

FOR eight years there had been no Royal Governor in Charles Town ; and although Lt. Governor Bull was a wise and well-loved ruler, there was natural excitement when James Glenn arrived in 1743. Governors then were received in this wise. The *Gazette* informs us : " Last Saturday arrived here in the Tartar man-of-war his Excellency James Glenn, Governor and Commander-in-Chief of the Province, and Vice-Admiral of the same. Upon a signal of five guns being discharged from Fort Johnson the Charles Town regiment was drawn up under arms upon the Bay ; " — describes the salutes of the forts and " As soon as she " (the *Tartar*) " came to anchor the Clerk of the Council and Master in Chancery, having been first sent on board to wait on his Excellency and show him a proper place of landing, he was received by the Honourable Edward Aitkin and Charles Pinckney, Esq., as members of his Majesty's Council, who conducted his Excellency through the two lines of foot to the Council Chamber, to his Honour the Lieutenant Governor, attended by the rest of the members of the Council.

"His Excellency having then produced His Majesty's commission, he was conducted by them, — the sword of State borne before, — and attended by the Commons House and many officers and other gentlemen of distinction to Granville's Bastion, where the same was published in due form, which was followed by three whirras " (hurrahs ?) a " discharge of cannon at the Bastion and a general volley of the regiment. Then his Excellency attended by all the gentlemen present marched back in like manner to the Council, being saluted as he passed by all

UNDER THE PORTICO. SOUTH CAROLINA SOCIETY HALL, MEETING STREET

the officers of the regiment, and having thus qualified himself by taking the usual oaths, His Excellency walked back again to Shepheard's Tavern, where a handsome entertainment was provided for him, and the numerous company concluded the day with joy, the houses being handsomely illuminated."

It was but a small colony that was doing him honour, but for a Scotch gentleman of no great rank or importance it was a sufficiently agreeable reception ; and Governor Glenn began his administration in a cheerful and friendly spirit, which he maintained throughout.

"To have found Charles Town in ashes" (after the great fire) "and to leave it fair, flourishing and fortified," was, he wrote to the secretary, his earnest wish and expectation. A wish more fully realized than such generally are, for the era of prosperity which had already begun was to continue for many years. The people were busy, industrious, and thriving ; content (except for that ever vexed question of the Commons' rights) and taking thought for improvement of every kind. Many useful institutions began in those years, and societies, both charitable and social. The oldest of these, the South Carolina, which still dwells in its own handsome house in Meeting Street, began in a very small way in 1736. A Huguenot having lost his fortune, some of his friends agreed to hold a meeting at his house once a week, to which each person was to contribute "two bits" or fifteen pence. It was called the "Two bit club." The meetings were very agreeable ; other persons joined, some to practise French, which alone was spoken, others for the pleasant company. Both membership and subscription increased, and the little "Two bit club" became the South Carolina Society. Besides assisting indigent members, and widows and orphans, it established a school for a limited number of boys and girls. Dr. Ramsay, writing in 1808, says that "several hundred children had thus received an excellent plain education." Its invested property then (derived from gifts and legacies) amounted to $137,000, besides the annual subscriptions. Almost every will of those years contains a bequest to the South Carolina Society ; and there used to be a story of one old gentleman who knocked up his lawyer at dead of night to draw a codicil, hoping that it might ease the pains of death if the legacy was duly inserted.

The "St. George's" and "St. Andrew's," English and Scotch, but admitting members of other nations, had the same object as the "South Carolina." The "Friendly" cared for the poor insane, and after the great fire an insurance company was started. That, however, which has been of the most benefit to the people of Charleston was the establishment of the Charles Town Library. Carolinians were always rather a "bookish" people, to use the old phrase, as people who live much in the country are apt to be. When your next neighbour is five miles away, books, through the long winter evenings, take the place of church, visits, theatres, society of all kinds. And so in wills and inventories there are almost always books carefully bequeathed. Landgrave Morton took the pains to direct the distribution carefully.

"To sonn Joseph Morton, Assemblyes Annotations in two volumes, Burges Spiritual refinings, Twise ag't Hord, Cambridge Concordance, Cariles eleven volumes on Job, Burges on Justification, Wodevirs Body Of Divinity, Cole on God's Sovereignty, Pearce his p'percon for Death." "To daughter Deborah Blake Baxter's Everlasting Rest," Baxter's "Call to Repentance," "At the Judgment Day," "Rules for Peace of Conscience," Crooke's "Guide," Flavell' s "Saint Indeed," Watson's "Divine Cordiall," Norcott "Of Baptism." "To my son Joseph the rest of my books." It needs not to remind the reader that Landgrave Morton was the head of the non-conformists. Possibly the "rest of my books" may have been of a less

A Bit of a Typical Charleston Garden

121

severe character. This was in 1685. In 1734 Governor Johnson leaves to his eldest son " all household goods, plate, pictures, furniture, all Books, coach-chaise and chaise horses." No clew to what the books were. The inventory of James de St. Julien, in 1740, mentions, besides much plate and valuable diamond rings, "18 pieces of painting, six plates of Don Quixote in frames, 500 pounds worth of books, and a violin." It is to be supposed that the History of the Don was among the books.

Miss Lucas in 1743 says, " I have a small library well stocked, for my Papa has left me most of his books," and mentions incidentally her Plutarch, Locke, Addison, Pope, etc., also " dictionaries French and English," and speaks of many that she borrows. Virgil, Prince Eugene's Memoirs, Richardson's novels, etc., and promises *not* to read " Father Malbronck."

The taste for literature was evidently already alive when in 1784 a few young men clubbed together their small resources, ordered a few books, and then appealed to the community. Their " advertisement " was so quaint that only its length prevents its being printed here.

It conjures all men to cultivate a knowledge of Literature and Arts ; reminds them that by such knowledge States rise and fall. " How different Great Britain is now from when discovered by Julius Cæsar, think of the fate of Babylon, Egypt and Greece "; how horrible to have one's children sink " to the gross ignorance of the native Indian ! " To prevent this shocking condition, join the members of this Society in " handing down the European arts and manners." " Lieutenant-Governor Bull is President of the Society and a sanguine promoter of its laudable pursuits " — concluding with this last all-powerful argument.

The community took the suggestion kindly. Books, maps, etc., were imported; it became the fashion. The

Governors were its Presidents (except Governor Boone who could not secure election), and at the beginning of the Revolution it had almost seven thousand volumes, many of which were then consumed by fire. It is impossible to overestimate what this library has been and is to the people of Charleston.

The reading of books naturally inspires the desire to discuss them ; and so about this time began one of the first literary societies of the country, — a club, although they did not call it so. It was headed by three clergymen of different denominations : Mr. Clark of St. Philip's, Mr. Hutson of the White Meeting, and an Independent minister, who all met together in peace and harmony twice a month to discuss "some subject or book literary or religious previously agreed upon." The principal laymen were (quoting Dr. Ramsay) "Mr. Laurens, Mr. Gadsden, and Mr. Manigault, merchants, Mr. Crawford and Mr. Rattray, lawyers and learned men, and several others." These gentlemen met at each other's houses alternately, opened each meeting by "a short prayer," discussed the subject, and afterward "other matters not inconsistent with the intention of the meeting." All of which was a great encouragement to young Mr. Robert Wells, who about this same time opened a shop, and began to import the newest books "regularly and early" from England. This shop continued until the Revolution.

Much thought also was then taken for education. Constantly in the wills there are directions "my son must be carefully educated," "the best education in the country," " no cost must be spared on the children's education," and often the direction is that "if possible" or "if my executors see fit" the sons are to be sent "home" to finish their studies in England. The children did not lack for opportunities in Charles Town itself. The advertisements show that schools were numerous. Classical for boys, modern languages and accomplishments for girls. Dancing and fencing are advertised, young ladies are offered "needle-work and embroidery," "painting and musick." Hebrew and Portuguese are attainable, besides, of course, French and Spanish. "High and Low Dutch," and "many in-structive amusements to improve the mind." Sacred music is taught, and "psalmody according to the exact rule." Concerts are much in vogue, — if "accompanied by obliging behaviour they may bring in three or four hundred guineas per annum." Lectures were adminis-tered, "Natural and Moral Philosophy," and electrical experiments shown. There were boarding schools for children whose parents lived in the country, and tutors were in demand to go to plantations. The boys who were sent home found a kind friend in Mr. Corbett who, having kept a school in Charles Town, returned to England, and was made High Bailiff of Westminster. He seems to have exercised a sort of *surveillance* over the whole Caro-linian colony there. The incipient doctors often went to Edinburgh, and the young merchants were sometimes sent to France or to Amsterdam to learn the languages and modes of doing business.

About this time too the curious silence respecting flow-ers is broken, and there is constant mention of gardens. Mrs. Lamboll is said to have been the first person to have one ; it was near the street (then a creek) which still bears her name, and Mrs. Hopton and Mrs. Logan soon followed. Mrs. Logan was the daughter of the gallant Colonel Daniel. Her "Gardeners' Chronicle," written when over seventy, was in great demand formerly, but seems to have utterly perished, the most careful search failing to produce a copy. Many of the landscape gardens of the country seats around the town were made or improved at this time. Mrs. Drayton at Magnolia on the Ashley, Mr. Henry Middleton at Middleton Place, were at work, and many others. Crowfield on Goose Creek was said then to be the most elaborately beautiful place in the Province. It is fully described in the "Life of Eliza Pinckney," already so frequently quoted. In an unpublished letter she, when Miss Lucas, writes inviting a friend to visit her at Wappoo, a letter which shows the fancy of the time.

To Miss Bartlett, Charles Town.

"The majestic pine, which imperceptibly puts on a fresher green, the young myrtle joining its fragrance to that of the Jessamine of golden hue, perfumes all the woods and regales the rural wanderer with its sweets, the daisies, the honeysuckles and a thousand nameless beauties of the woods, invite you to partake the pleasures the country affords.

"You may wonder how I can at this gay season think of planting a cedar grove, which rather reflects an autumnal gloom and solemnity, than the freshness and gayety of spring. I intend to connect in my Grove the solemnity of summer and autumn with the cheerfulness and pleasures of spring, for it shall be filled with all kinds of flowers, as well wild as garden flowers, with seats of cammomile, with here and there a peach tree, orange, plumb, etc."

The taste for gardening and the love of flowers was undoubtedly increased by the presence of Dr. Alexander Garden — not the commissary and indeed no kinsman of his though bearing exactly the same name, but a very charming man, excellent physician, and enthusiastic botanist. That was, it will be remembered, the time of Linnæus, who might almost be said to have invented the science of botany.

Dr. Garden was one of his most enthusiastic pupils, also his friend and correspondent. The woods and swamps of Carolina were to him a happy hunting-ground. He was the popular physician of the town; "our good Dr. Garden" occurs in many a letter, and his conversation, which was remarkably agreeable, naturally often turned on his favourite pursuit.   Linnæus named in his honour the beautiful "Gardenia," and he may be said to have given the first impulse to horticulture in Charles Town.

Governor Glenn thought that the colony was going too fast and acquiring a taste for wealth and luxury beyond its means. He was a Scotchman and looked seriously upon life, doing his best according to his lights.   We may think his lights but dim, when he assured the Lords of Trade that the Indians, of whom he had "been making Sovereigns," were "well pleased with their titles of King but would be better satisfied to be kitchen Boys at Newcastle House." Imagine an Indian "Brave" a contented scullion! He spoke with more knowledge when he wrote of the need of better fortifications, and of the industries and commerce of the place, and of the expense which vexed his thrifty mind.

"I cannot help expressing my surprise and concern to find that there are annually imported into this Province considerable quantities of Fine Flanders Lace, the Finest Dutch Linens, and French Cambricks, Chintz, Hyson Tea and other East India Goods, Silks, Gold and Silver Laces, etc."

"I have endeavoured to restrain and correct the bias of extravagance and luxury, etc, etc."

He then gives a list of the articles of which he says "the quantity is too great and the quality too fine, and ill calculated for the circumstances of an Infant Colony."

The infant was nearly a hundred years old and had bravely outgrown its swaddling clothes, but it certainly does seem to have clad itself richly.   The list begins: —

"The finest Broadcloth. *Shrouds*. Carpets. Cloth of every kind from Cambrick to Osnaburgs. Silks,

British and East Indian. Stockings, Handkerchiefs, gloves and Ribbons.

"Metals. Pewter household utensils. Brass and copper wrought of all sorts. Plate and silver wrought. Watches, gold and silver, Books. China and other earthenware. Chairs and Beds. Fans and other millinery ware. Looking glasses etc. Pictures and Prints. Salad oil. Beer in casks and Bottles. Wine of all sorts, but the kind chiefly drunk here is Madeira imported directly from the place of growth. Coals, etc, etc."

Happily this extravagant importation was justified by the increasing exports which he also chronicled. The colony had a very large trade, for, besides the lumber, naval stores, and furs of its earlier days, rice, favoured by especial acts of Parliament, now amounted to £108,750 sterling, and indigo, lately added by the efforts of Miss Lucas to its other staples, had, by giving the planters a highland crop, nearly doubled the value of their lands. Governor Glenn says that in 1754, ten years after the first little crop was gathered, £26,000 sterling worth was exported. In thirty years this amount was trebled. All this occurring in his administration should have satisfied the Governor somewhat as to the well-being of his Province.

There was certainly a great deal of money spent in plate and jewels. Evidenced not only by the number of handsome things that, surviving the Revolution, still remained forty-five years ago, but by the mention in wills and inventories.

They are enumerated in all those of the gentry and sometimes particular pieces are described. One very attractive one is in the will of Mrs. Sarah Middleton, widow of Hon. Arthur Middleton, first Mrs. Morton and born a Wilkinson. She leaves her stepson, Henry Middleton, a "silver tea kettle, lamp waiter and stand belonging thereto." This is unusual, for the urns and kettles of that day were generally warmed by iron heaters for which a cell was provided. Also to her stepdaughter her " best diamond ring and large silver monteth (?)," besides devising " all her books, silver plate, rings and other jewels not otherwise given " to her cousins Wilkinson.

Governor Johnson leaves " To my daughter Margaret all the cloaths, watches, Rings, Necklaces, Jewells, Linnens, Laces, etc., of my late dear Wife," and all his plate, etc., to his eldest son.

These fine things made the ladies very brilliant when they attended the newly opened theatres in Dock (now Queen) and Church streets. The theatres (" play houses " they were generally called) are described as " temporary " and were probably not much more than barns, but very good acting has been seen in barns, from Shakespeare's time down. There were represented a tragedy called " The Orphan or the Unhappy Marriage," " The London Apprentice or George Barnwell," " Cato, by Mr. Addison with a Prologue by Mr. Pope " and the amusing comedy of " The Recruiting Officer " given " by special desire of the Troop and Foot Companies," all of which were enjoyed with clear consciences by the jolly planters and merchants of the gay little Southern town.

Mrs. Alice Morse Earle, in her very ingenious and entertaining book " Stage Coach and Tavern Days," has given an amusing account of how " Othello " was smuggled into New England in 1762 at the " King's Arms Tavern " at New Port, Rhode Island, as a " Series of Moral Dialogues in Five Parts, Depicting the evil effects of jealousy and other bad Passions, and Proving that happiness can only spring from the pursuit of Virtue," etc.

No such subterfuge was needed in a " Church Colony." Mrs. Pinckney tells us at about the same date, how she dearly loved a play, and tried never to miss seeing Mr. Garrick when in London, and Mrs. Manigault in her diary

The Pringle House, King St.

records the representations of "Douglas," "Mourning Bride," "Romeo and Juliet," "King Lear," and many others.

No amusement, however, was so dear to the people as the races, as was only natural, for horses were bred on every plantation and the children were said "to be born on horseback." Balls, dinners, even the theatre, were in great measure the pleasures of the upper class, but the annual "race week" was a great popular festival shared in by every one, from the Governor and ladies in the Grand Stand to the negroes who sat unmolested on the fence tops.

The whole matter was in the hands of gentlemen who bred and ran their own horses. At first merely those of the country, a strong small breed called "Chickasaw," said to be the descendants of Spanish barbs, which were afterward improved by stock imported from England. The first course, the "York," was too far from the town and the "New Market" was established just outside the limits.

Here were run races commemorated in the "History of the Turf in Carolina," by Dr. John Irving, secretary of the Jockey Club. "Mr. Harleston's colt against Mr. Horrÿ's filly," Mr. Drayton's "Adolphus" against Mr. Nightingale's imported "Shadow," etc. The prizes were pieces of silver, cups, bowls, or salvers "to cost not more than £100 currency." Few were the sideboards in old times that had not one or more of these, all inscribed with the winner's name and "York" or "New Market Course."

The whole low country joined in the sport, as the horses came down with their owners from the different plantations. The schools gave holiday, the law courts closed, the shops were shut, only the sick and the infirm stayed at home. The ladies in their carriages, the gentlemen on their handsomest horses, the boys on their ponies,

K

the "poorer sort" in carts and wagons of every kind, the
negroes in numbers, all thronged from every direction to
the course. It was a gay, open-air jollification, good-
humoured and merry, thoroughly enjoyed by all. For
the members of the Jockey Club and their families was
always given a ball, considered the culmination of the gay
season. These races, interrupted by the Revolution, were
resumed after it and continued in the same fashion down
to 1860.

The Governor endeavoured, he said, by advice and example to inculcate frugality, but he established himself as
became his office, in one of the handsomest houses of the
town, the Hon. Charles Pinckney's, "beyond the Bridge,"
that is, the "Governor's Bridge" which crossed the present
Market Street nearly north of St. Philip's Church. It was
in the new part of the town, just beyond where the old
wall had been a few years before, and had the advantage
of a delightful situation, standing in the middle of a whole
square, on the bay, fronting the water and commanding
a view of the harbour. The house was a fine specimen of
colonial architecture, much resembling that built some
years later by Miles Brewton on King Street, and now
known as the "Pringle House"; surrounded by a lawn
and garden, and with offices, stables, etc., sufficient for
official dignity.

It was occupied by successive Governors, Glenn, Lyttleton, Boone, and Lord Charles Montagu, during the absence
of the owner in Europe, and the long minority and absence
of his son. There was much feasting and good company
in the "commodious mansion house" during those years,
especially in Lord Charles's time — dinners, balls, and easier
and more social intercourse. Dinners were stately and
slow. The tables handsomely set out with the satin-fine
damask cloths and huge napkins, some of which still remain, — old Nankin or East India china and heavy silver

and cut glass. " The manner of living nearly the same as in England, plentiful tables," says Hewat. But modified of course by the climate and by the taste for West Indian dishes brought from the islands. " Turtle with saffron and negro (Cayenne ?) pepper, very delicate for dressing it," terrapins stewed, boiled and baked, and all varieties of fish, flesh, and fowl. On one very important point Hewat and Dr. Milligan, who wrote within five years of each other, bear honourable testimony. The former says, " Where rum is cheap " (brought from West Indies) " the use of it will not be uncommon, especially among the lower classes of people but the gentlemen in general are sober, industrious and temperate." The latter adds " Madeira wine and punch are the common drinks of the inhabitants ; yet few gentlemen have not also claret, port, and other wines."

" The ladies are extremely temperate and generally drink water, which in Charles Town is very unwholesome, the soil not solid enough to strain it sufficiently." This peculiarity of the soil led to the universal building of cisterns. Brick cemented storehouses of rain-water, which, when properly constructed and carefully kept, furnish a singularly pure and healthy water, free from poisonous germs. This " cistern water " is still generally drunk in Charles Town.

That the gentlemen should be " sober, industrious and temperate " was in view of the work they had to do an absolute necessity. It needed every energy and power of head and hand to win from the soil of Carolina the wealth won by these men.

There can be no greater mistake than to suppose that the Carolina planter ever had the easy, luxurious life of his West Indian brother. In the Islands nature is so bountiful, so prolific, that the earth yields her fruits to but little labour and care. In Carolina every step was effort, everything was new, everything was to be learned, — and taught.

The proper arrangement and management of a plantation required the knowledge of many trades, for all was done at home.

The fields must be chosen at the right lay of the land, the water gathered into the reserves, the ditches dug, the banks raised just to the right point so that the rice might never lack and never be overwhelmed by the flood. The science of rice planting is difficult and the execution most laborious. The master then was new to it, and the labourers were untrained savages. To get his work done, and his people not overdone, was his constant care, requiring great judgment.

How the land shall be prepared, when the crop shall be flowed (*i.e.* covered with water), when and in what degree the flow shall be taken off, the exact moment for the harvest, are never-settled questions. Every man answers for himself ; according as he answers wisely or foolishly he is a good or a bad planter.

He must be an engineer too, for his drains and quarter drains, his banks and flood-gates, must be made with an engineer's skill. If a house was to be built, a wagon made, a canoe dug out, the crop to be barrelled, — the master must direct coopers and carpenters. Barns and stables, pigs and sheep, were all in his charge.

His was the whole management of the negroes. He allotted the tasks, enforced obedience, gave orders, settled disputes, heard complaints, redressed grievances, and saw that all were housed and fed and clad in safety and in health. By the beginning of the nineteenth century the people were trained and taught, and there were many who could direct their fellows sensibly and faithfully : the trusted servants of their master. But in 1760 this condition had been attained by but few ; all were to be taught, and from the time that the planter mounted his horse in the early morning, until he had seen his animals stabled at night, mind and muscle had been constantly employed although he might have set his *hand* to nothing. When after supper he sat by his fire or on his piazza, with his Shakespeare or Montaigne for cheer and recreation, he had accomplished an amount of work which none who had not seen it could appreciate.

And the planter's wife — hers too was a busy part. In those days everything was made at home, and she and her maids did all that is now done by hospitals and nurses, clothing stores and canning factories.

All clothing for household and plantation was made under her supervision, spinning-wheel and loom were directed ; all meat was cured, fruits preserved and pickled, poultry yard and garden looked to, larder kept full, and all the wants of a constant and generous hospitality provided. In sickness and trouble the negroes looked to her. She dosed the sick, soothed the dying ; scolded the idle and praised the industrious ; taught the clumsy fingers to work and the savage tongues to speak ; prayed and preached religion and morality ; and often had more influence than the master himself. Then it was as a recent poet says:—

> "De case was mos' like dis,
> De plantation b'longed to Master
> But ole Master b'longed to Miss."

It is no wonder that the good lady and gentleman enjoyed themselves when his legislative duties called him to the Commons or Council: duties which were quite compatible with the theatres, the assembly balls, or the St. Cecilia concerts "performed by gentlemen."

However prosperous a place may be, the elements have to be reckoned with. Ten years before it was a fire; in 1752 it was a dreadful hurricane which ravaged the town. The summer had been unusually hot when in September the

storm came.   The wind and waves rose to extraordinary heights.   "The water poured in on us from the
Gulf Stream," Governor Glenn reports.   The town was
flooded, the water raging before the fury of the wind.
Houses fell, wharves were broken down, the new fortifications gave way.   The creeks which intersected the town
rose until they met across the intervening land.   The
waves passed along Church and down Broad Street until
they fell into the large, partly artificial pond, where the
old drawbridge had been, opposite to St. Michael's, where
the post-office and court house now stand.   Many persons
were drowned, others escaped in boats to take refuge in
the higher part of the town.   Every vessel in the harbour
except the sloop of war *Hornet*, which was saved by cutting away her masts, was cast ashore.   Schooners were
driven up into the streets.   A pilot boat was dashed
against the Governor's residence (the Pinckney House),
her bowsprit knocking a hole into the front wall nearly on
a line with the second-story windows.

When the damage was repaired, a few bricks were
purposely left out as a memento of the great gale, and so
remained until the house itself was destroyed in 1861.

Sullivan's Island, where were many of the townsfolk, had
also been swept, and many drowned.   The rest escaped
among the wooded sand-hills of the eastern end, and half
a dozen floated up Cooper River on the roof of a house.

The people saw with horror that there was no ebb, the
water continuing to rise — another foot would have
drowned the whole place.   But suddenly the wind
dropped, and then "chopping" round, blew with equal
violence from the west.   In a marvellously short time the
waters receded and the town remained — a frightful
wreck.

The work of restoration at once began — first by filling
up the creeks and low places which had greatly added to

COURT HOUSE SQUARE

the trouble. The pond, which had been up to this time a
favourite haunt of wild-ducks, was filled, and in a few

years the State House built on the site. Partly burned during the Revolution, it has been restored and is now the court house. Streets were run from river to river, and Church, Meeting, and King streets extended to South Bay. Roughly speaking, the outlines of the lower part of the present city may be said to have been traced then. Especially does the Battery, the pride of Charleston, owe its origin to this great gale.

The old sea wall from Granville bastion along Vander Horst's creek having been broken down, a new one became necessary, and Mr. de Brahm, surveyor-general of South Carolina and Georgia, came from Savannah to lay out the work. He ran his line from the bastion, southwest to Broughton's Battery near to the present corner of South Bay and Church Street. Thence to a creek opening into Ashley River.

Dr. Milligan, a surgeon who had been for some time in the Province, published on his return to London an account of Charles Town, written after these improvements had been effected. He says : —

"The Bay St. which fronts Cooper River is really handsome and would delight the eye of any stranger who approaches it from the sea." "About eleven hundred dwelling houses in the town built of wood or brick, many of them have a genteel appearance though generally speaking encumbered with balconies and piazzas, and are decently and often elegantly furnished." "Apartments contrived for coolness, a very necessary consideration." He describes the fortifications, churches, etc.; says there are about eight thousand inhabitants, white and black nearly equally divided, and of the former : —

"The inhabitants are of complexion little different to the English, of good stature, well made, lively, agreeable, sensible, spirited, open-hearted, exceed most people in acts of benevolence, hospitality and charity." "The men and women who have a right to the class of gentry (who are more numerous here than in any other colony of North America) dress with elegance and neatness. The personal qualities of the ladies are much to their credit and advantage." "Middling stature, genteel and slender," "fair complexions without the help of art," regular features, etc., etc., "fond of dancing, sing well, play upon harpsichord and guitar," etc. "In short all who have the happiness of their acquaintance will acquit me of partiality, when I say they are excelled by none in the practice of all the social virtues, necessary for the happiness of the other sex as daughters, wives, and mothers."

To all these charming qualities his Excellency proved insensible, for he left the colony a bachelor! He was probably glad to go, for trouble was brewing with the Indians, and indeed his recall reached him when he was a hundred miles from Charles Town on his way to the country of the Cherokees. He immediately returned, leaving the difficulties to his successor, Governor Lyttleton. His rule of twelve years had on the whole been a good one, and his wish was gratified. He left the town "fair, fortified and flourishing."

CHAPTER X

ATTAKULLAKULLA. THE STAMP ACT

GOVERNOR LYTTLETON arrived to find an Indian war upon his hands: a war of wider import than he knew. Cooper and Gilbert Parker have told dramatically how the French, trembling for their American possessions, let loose the Indians upon the "backs of the English Colonys." A dreadful policy already instituted by Spain and followed by England herself in 1812. The tribal outbreaks at various points were more or less involved in these measures, but there were individual grievances as well.

In South Carolina the Cherokees, who lived where Greenville and Spartanburg are now, had a provocation of their own in the encroachments of the settlers by whom the upper part of the Province was now (1756) occupied. These were of many origins. Colonies of Germans and Swiss, one of Huguenots, Scotch and Scotch (Protestant) Irish, and Welsh; besides many people who came generally in small parties drifting down from Virginia and Pennsylvania, coming, as the old people used to say, "by the back door." They had the advantage of settling in a healthy region, less fertile, perhaps, than the low lands of the coast, but better adapted for the labour of white men. They were mostly "plain people," farmers or cattle drovers, called "crackers" from their long, smacking whips; with smaller estates and fewer negroes than the low country planters, with whom they had little in common.

Another difference between the sections was that this

territory, from about eighty or ninety miles from the coast, roughly outlined by the ridge of hills that crossed the Province, never was divided into parishes. Hence the distinction. " The Parishes " expressed the low country ; the oldest, richest, most thickly settled part of the colony, closely connected with Charles Town, and under the influence of the English Church, and English habits of life and thought. But the " Districts " above the ridge were larger, poorer, more sparsely populated, and under no influence save that inspired by the hard conditions of life around them and the sturdy spirit of independence which those conditions bred.

The immediate consequence of this immigration upon the town was, that these settlers coming into contact with the Indians, disputes arose. Disputes with Indians always meant the shedding of blood ; there were murders and outrages which demanded redress, and Governor Lyttleton, promptly taking up the sword which Glenn had dropped, summoned the chiefs to surrender the offenders.

The Indians professed a wish for peace, but asked that their wrongs too should be heard. A deputation of warriors, headed by their great chief Occonostota, passed, painted and feathered, through the streets now unaccustomed to such visitors. The Governor received them in state in the Council Chamber, and the chiefs, entering with great ceremony, laid strings of white beads in proffer of amity at his feet. But the Governor would not take the beads into his hands, or grant the " talk " they had travelled so far to obtain. The lieutenant-governor, who like his father and grandfather was wise in Indian matters, besought him to listen, accept the terms the chiefs proposed, and bind them by important hostages to peace with the frontier men. But Lyttleton was ambitious of military glory, and told the warriors that he would receive submission " in their own country at the points of his bayonets."

He would not allow the delegation to return in their own way, but took them with him almost as prisoners, which they justly thought bad faith, and permitted them to be ill treated on the road. Ordering all the forces possible to meet him at the Congaree River, he set forth with many of the most considerable gentlemen of the province upon his staff. Colonel Bull, Major Hyrne, William Moultrie, and others. It was at this time that the name of Christopher Gadsden first comes into notice.

There being no field artillery in the town, he raised a company since called the Ancient Battalion of Artillery, and having been in the Royal Navy trained the men himself in the use of the guns. This organization, which distinguished itself in the Revolution, still exists for social and charitable purposes, and is affectionately known as "the Old Bats."

Lyttleton soon found that an army so gathered was little better than a mob. But he advanced to the Indian lines, made a brave showing, and announced that he was ready to receive submission and make a treaty. Completely deceived by a wily savage, Attakullakulla or the Little Carpenter, he gave up the hostages whom he had in his hands on the promise of others never delivered. He signed a treaty made to be broken and returned to Charles Town to be hailed as a hero and a statesman, when he had really effected nothing. The military marched out to meet and escort him home, the citizens gave him a banquet, the clergy presented an address of commendation, and the Library Society, which seems to have considered itself a fourth estate (the press had not yet gained that position), made him a speech glorifying his conduct of the bloodless war, and assuring him that he was not only their "Governor and protector, but the patron of Literature and President of the Society, under whose rigorous administration, not only riches and commerce but learning and every branch of polite and useful knowledge must flourish."

Of course the Governor's great personal popularity had much to do with this enthusiastic greeting. His civil administration was good if his Indian was bad, and socially he was much liked. The home government evidently approved, for he was promoted to the governorship of Jamaica, the best gift in the colonial office, and his departure was publicly and privately lamented. Mrs. Pinckney attributes their escape from " an Indian Warr the most dreadful of all warrs " to the " energy and spirit of our Governor " and regrets later that " We lose with this fleet our good Governor Lyttleton; he goes home in the Trent man of war, before going to his new Government of Jamaica." He was the last English Governor whose going was lamented.

Actually before his departure Occonostota and his tribe had risen, thrown themselves upon the settlers, and committed outrages and massacres unnecessary to be related here.

Lieutenant-governor Bull sent in haste to General Amherst, commander-in-chief in America, for help in this emergency. Troops were sent under Colonel Montgomery, and afterward under Colonel Grant. After much hard fighting the red men were conquered and Attakullakulla signed with Lieutenant-governor Bull a treaty of peace which lasted until the Revolution.

This treaty is said to have been signed in the small one-story brick house built by the original Stephen Bull, and still standing at Ashley Hall.

The admiration and respect with which Governor Bull inspired the red men was shown in curious ways. Dr. Maurice Moore, in his " Annals of York," tells the story of the Catawbe Indians, who lived in what is now York County. The chief in 1770 was called " King Hagler," a person of much importance in his tribe. On one occasion he received a party of white men, who went to visit him, with dignity and hospitality, inviting them to dinner.

THE OLD BUILDING AT ASHLEY HALL, STILL STANDING, WHERE
INDIAN TREATY WAS SIGNED

The dinner consisted of venison and sweet potatoes, roasted on coals, and served on bits of bark.

To the surprise of the guests, each piece of meat and each potato was offered on a fresh and separate piece of bark. Hagler explained that he ordered his meal thus, because, when he had been entertained by Governor Bull, he had noticed that a clean platter was used for each dish.

Fenimore Cooper's heroes, the Uncas and Chingach-gook, who were the delight of our youth, are, we now know, but purely imaginary, but Attakullakulla really was a figure for romance. He had all the cunning and treach-ery of the savage of to-day, but he was capable of enthusi-asm for good and evil. Lyttleton he hated and despised, holding him in contempt for having broken the promise of safe conduct made to the chiefs, and hating him for the insults and ill treatment shown to Occonostota and his companions on their homeward journey. It was he who contrived their deliverance from the English, and aided in the uprising that followed so quickly upon Lyttleton's campaign, whereby the "Great Warrior" washed out his disgrace in the blood of the white men. But for two Englishmen he had a real and passionate friendship, for Colonel Bull, whom he esteemed the wisest and truest of his race, as is beautifully expressed in his most pathetic and eloquent speech at the time of the treaty ; and for John Stuart, Indian agent, who had won his affection by personal kindness and talent, and for whom he risked his influence with his own people. Captain Stuart is himself a picturesque and interesting figure. He, more than any other white man, understood and influenced the Indians. His gallant bearing, personal charm, and dominant character impressed them strongly, and to his skilful diplomacy it was mainly due that Bull's treaty was so well observed for fifteen years. A passionate Loyalist, his course in the Revolution made him obnoxious to the people ; but there were long arrears of great service to the Province, to be set against his later actions.

Stuart was at the time of the outbreak in Fort London, a small fortification on the Tennessee River, built by order of Governor Glenn some years before. It was surprised by the savages and most of the garrison were put to the sword. Some few were kept as hostages, and Stuart was carefully secured with a view to making him work the guns which they had captured, in their next fight, under penalty of seeing his fellow-prisoners tortured before his eyes.

As soon as Attakullakulla heard of the event he hastened to the fort and persuaded the men who had Stuart in charge to allow him to have possession of the prize, giving in return his rifle, knife, and all his most valued property. Then, after waiting a day or two to disarm suspicion, he gave out that he and his prisoner were going hunting, and promising a good supply of venison, they left the camp.

For nine days they pushed their way northeastward through the thickest woods and swamps, not daring to go south lest they should meet the Cherokees, and at last fell in with a party of Virginians sent out by Colonel Byrd in search of fugitives from Fort London. To them Attakullakulla surrendered his friend and returned to the fort laden with gifts for himself and with promises of rescue for the unfortunates who still remained there. It was through Stuart's influence and through his confidence in Governor Bull's fair dealing that he at last, but not until after Grant's victory, was persuaded to sue for peace, as already related.

One important result of these campaigns was the training in military skill which many of the Provincials received by serving in company with Montgomery's and Grant's regulars. A regiment commanded by Colonel Thomas Middleton, younger son of President of Council Arthur Middleton, accompanied Grant. In it were Henry Laurens, John and William Moultrie, Francis Marion, Isaac Huger, Andrew Pickens, and others, all to be officers of importance in the coming struggle. As generally happens, the regulars and Provincials did not agree. Colonel Middleton thought his regiment injuriously treated in Colonel Grant's report, and not only wrote a paper in its defence, but according to the custom appealed to the sword, " vindicating the honour of his command."

All these troubles were but precursors of the Revolution, and it is curious to see how men in every walk of life were being prepared to play their parts in that great struggle and how events were tending to bring it about, no man yet dreaming thereof.

Charles Town had perhaps less than any other American city cause for dissatisfaction. Her prosperity was great and increasing. Dr. Ramsay says that George I. and II. were nursing fathers to the favoured colony. Her indigo received a bounty, her rice could be sent anywhere south of Cape Finisterre. The navigation acts which shackled New England troubled her not, and so far from her supply of slaves being limited they were actually forced upon her by England in 1756 (when the colony passed an act to curtail the number imported), lest by so doing " the legitimate business of English merchants and shippers" should be interfered with. The order runs: —

" Whereas acts have been passed in some of our plantations in America for laying duties on the importation and exportation of negroes to the great discouragement of merchants trading thither from the coasts of Africa. It is our pleasure that you do not give your assent to or pass any law imposing duties on negroes imported into our said province of South Carolina, etc., etc."

Still there were some grievances besides that constant one of interference by the Royal Governors with the right of the Assembly to self-taxation, the foreshadowing of the resistance to the Stamp Act. Chief of all was the mortification of seeing their highest offices, especially in the judiciary, filled by men often of poor capacity and evil

L

character, and the conviction which they could not escape, that no matter how fit for dignity or office a Provincial might be, he could never achieve a position of any importance under the government.

The young men sent to England, who came back with the ambitions of educated Englishmen, laid this lesson to heart and it rankled there. The injustice was felt soon after the Royal government began and it increased with time, the first conspicuous instance being the case of Colonel Pinckney, the husband of Mrs. Pinckney so often quoted. He was of the second generation in the Province, his father, Thomas Pinckney, having come from England in 1692. He had been sent to England as a youth and educated there, "bred to the bar," and is said to have been the first Carolinian ever admitted barrister in England. Returning to this country, he became a prominent lawyer and planter and amassed a fortune. He took a leading part in the dispute between the Commons and the Council in Governor Middleton's time, drawing up the statement of the rights and privileges of the House on the tax question, for which he was formally thanked by the Speaker; and was afterward himself a member of the Council. His son, General Charles Cotesworth Pinckney, tells the story not only of his father's case, but of the whole situation, in the following (unpublished) letter: —

[Address lost.] "CHARLESTON, Sept. 18th, 1819.

" The removal of my Father from the Chief Justiceship of this Province carries me near to my first recollection. It was about the year 1752 that the great contest for the Westminster election was decided between Lord Trentham the Ministerial candidate and Sir G. Vandeput the opposition candidate. Mr. Leigh was then an eminent counsellor in England, and High Bailiff of Westminster. He returned Lord Trentham as duly elected when Sir George

Vandeput ought undoubtedly to have been returned as the successful Candidate. The opposition was so exceedingly angry at this return that they began to take serious measures to indite Mr. Leigh for perjury ; to disarm them he offered to vacate the office of High Bailiff, and as our Judges then held their offices not *quam diu se bene gesserint;* but *durante bene placito* of the Crown, my Father's chief Justiceship was taken away from him, and conferred on Mr. Leigh, who held it to his death; and as he was a man of ability and a good lawyer he filled it well. On his death Mr. Simpson, a Scotsman, not a lawyer, was temporarily appointed, and afterwards a Mr. Skinner (an Irishman) still less of a lawyer than Simpson, he was made Chief Justice through the interest of Lord Halifax's Mistress (Lord Halifax being first Lord of Trade.) and held the office till the Stamp Act, when he refusing to do business without stamps the Assembly in the absence of the Governor (   ) prevailed upon Lieutenant Governor Bull, to appoint Mr. Lowndes, Mr. Benjamin Smith and Mr. Doyley, Judges, and they with Mr. Pringle who was a Judge before, opened the court without stamps, and did business as usual. Skinner died soon after and Benjamin Smith resigned, the rest held their offices till about the year 1770 or '71 when (by our circuit court) salaries were given to our Judges. A Secretary of State instead of a Board of Trade being appointed for the Colonies, and Lord Hillsborough (an Irishman) being appointed First Secretary of State in the Colonies, he vacated the existing Commissions and appointed a new set of Judges most of them Irishmen. I do not believe that the system of internal taxation was particularly contemplated by this measure, but as we gave salaries to our puisne Judges by this act, that they might have persons devoted to them and on whom they could depend to fill the places.

(Signed)   "CHARLES COTESWORTH PINCKNEY."

The number of these young aspirants for honours was great, and their position as sons of the most prominent families of the Province made them the more uneasy under the slight. With very few exceptions every man who attained distinction in the Revolution had either been educated abroad, or had travelled enough to perceive the difference between the wide scope offered to talent there, and the narrow limits to which it must be confined in Carolina.

General Pinckney in another letter shows the number of young men at the time present in England.

"September, 1819.

"GENERAL C. C. PINCKNEY,

"My Father carried his family to England for their education in the year 1753. At that time I remember that Mr. McKensie and Mr. Ralph Izard, Senior, John Rutledge and Arthur Middleton were already there. With me went my brother, then about two years old, — I was then about seven — Wm. Henry Drayton, his brother, Dr. Charles Drayton, and Stoutenburgh ; and there afterwards came Thomas Lynch, Paul Trapier, Thomas Heyward, Hugh Rutledge, Harris, Moultrie, Hume, Judge Grimke, Ralph Izard junior, Walter Izard, the Middletons and Stead. After I returned home in the year 1769 Ned Rutledge, General Read, and Major Garden went.

"Of these Hume was the only one who joined the British cause. There may be other Carolinians who were educated in England about the time of the Revolution that I do not at present recollect. I have not named several who were at Edinburgh. Dr. Baron, Dr. Fayssoux, Dr. Chandler and Dr. Harris. If any name should occur to me I will send them to you."

The young doctors generally went to Edinburgh and the merchants sometimes to France or Holland, but the great majority were sent "home." Many of them to Westminster School ; Thomas Lynch to Eton, and then to one of the ancient Universities and to the Law schools. Of course the expense was considerable. In the "Account of the Manigault Family," published in the "Transactions of the Huguenot Society of South Carolina," 1897, it is stated as being about $3000 a year, a large sum for those frugal days. The barrister's gown and " tye wig " alone are said to have cost fifty guineas, or $250. This was for the full costume of a " Templar."

Undoubtedly they enjoyed life as young fellows should; many had relatives and friends who could make things pleasant for them,— the Blakes, Middletons, Izards, etc.; and Mr. Corbett, friend and guardian of most, evidently had it in his power to secure them certain advantages. But they did not go to idle away their time, as rich men's sons are apt to do ; the training was careful and the result showed how well they worked. In a long letter from General Pinckney, written at the request of a teacher in a Charleston school, he details minutely the course at Westminster.

A little boy, expected only to be able to read and write, is admitted to the "Petty Form" and instantly begins with Busby's Latin grammar, and apparently learns nothing else. Through various upper and lower "forms" Busby still clings to him, accompanied by Phædrus, Martial, Ovid, etc., until on arriving at the "lower third" he begins Prosody, scans and writes Latin verses. Latin verses he makes all through his school life. No translations are allowed, the dictionary is his only hope. "The school days are every day of the week except Saints' days, when you go to church and prepare an exercise." On Thursdays and Saturdays, half-holidays, there are also exercises to be prepared. "School hours in summer are from Six in the morning to twelve at noon but are let out generally (a form or two at a time) to go to breakfast." Imagine the poor little hungry wretches who get out last!

" In the afternoon the school hours are from Two to Five o'clock. In the winter the school hours are the same, except that you do not go to school before seven o'clock, and as it is dark before five, each boy has a small wax taper in his hand by which to get his lesson "!

Sometimes they have a half-holiday on Tuesday, if it is " begged by some nobleman or gentleman who has been educated at the school."

In the upper school — through under and upper fourth, fifth, " Shell," and sixth forms, the boy passes, still learning Latin and Greek under the strictest supervision, liable to " corporal punishment " by a " Master," never by an " Usher " — and there is an awful book in which daily a boy's shortcomings are entered. Also, if he has made a very good exercise or behaved uncommonly well the same recording angel makes note of it. These exercises are generally in Latin verse — for instance, " An ode of Horace is set of which the metre is to be changed ; as a Sapphic ode into long and short verse "! On Saturdays there are Bible lessons and " exercises to be done out of school and shown up on Monday morning." The higher the Form the more Greek, until in the last, the seventh Hebrew grammar and some of the psalms come in. There are recitations from Virgil, Homer, and *Milton*, the last the sole recognition of English literature, or indeed, with the exception of the Bible and Catechism, of the English language. There is a Greek play just before Christmas, and Confirmation at " Bartholomewtide," with careful explanation of the Church Catechism. The account concludes, " Latin and Greek and the Rudiments of the Christian Religion are the only things avowedly taught, and it is difficult to go through the school without being a fair Latin and Greek scholar and being able to assign a reason for the faith that is in you."

These extracts have been made to show the ideal of education at that day, — very different from ours. There is one passage, however, showing the greater individuality which the English claim for their system of school education over ours.

"In the Shell (between the fifth and sixth forms) you still go on with Horace and Virgil, construe Sallust, read Homer's Iliad, also Xenophon. Themes and verse exercises as in the fifth, but they are expected to be longer and better composed. It is conjectured you are now so far advanced that, besides the usual school exercises, you have time to do private studies. I remember making a translation of the whole of the 'Castilinarian War' for my private studies while in the Shell. The book containing your private studies is generally called for by the Head Master every three or four weeks, and a boy's reputation is increased or diminished by the pains he has taken with these private studies."

These were the duties of the schoolboys. Much more was expected of them when they addressed themselves to the studies of men.

There is a letter, published in O'Neale's "Bench and Bar of South Carolina," from John Rutledge, who had recently returned from England, to his young brother Edward, who had just gone there in 1769, which shows what these expectations were.

The somewhat authoritative tone is probably due to the fact that the elder had stood in an almost paternal relation to the younger brother for nearly his whole life, their father, Dr. John Rutledge, who had come from the north of Ireland, in 1735, having died before his eldest son was twelve years old. Greatly abridged, it is:—

"The very first thing you should be thoroughly acquainted with is the writing of short hand, which you will find an infinite advantage. Take down notes of everything in Court, even if not worth transcribing, for your time may as well be employed in writing as in hearing." " By no means fall into the too common practice of not attending a place of worship — there is generally a good preacher at the Temple Church." " Be constant in attending the sittings in Chancery, but I should prefer attending the King's Bench and sittings of the Chief Justice of that Court at *Nisi Prius* when they are held. Remember what I hinted to you of attending alternately in the different courts, etc., etc." "You must exert yourself to the utmost to be able by some means or other to attend the House of Commons constantly, or whenever anything of consequence is going on . . . at all events get admittance and make yourself well acquainted with the speakers. Reading lectures upon oratory will never make you an orator. This must be done by hearing and observing those who are allowed to be good speakers. Attend the House of Lords upon every occasion worth it. What I intend is that you may have opportunities of seeing and hearing the best speakers, and of being able on occasion of giving your sentiments upon what you have seen and heard." He must attend Sheridan's lectures, " He reads with propriety though much too stiff, and his voice exceeding bad."

" The Circuit Bill (a bill for establishing circuit courts in the Province which had been opposed by the Government) goes with Lord Charles, and if it is confirmed at Home, you should make yourself acquainted with the mode of doing business upon the circuit in England."

" If you stick to French and converse generally in that language you may soon be master of it," etc. " Whatever you attempt make yourself completely master of ; nothing makes a person so ridiculous as to pretend to things he does not understand. I know nothing more entertaining and more likely to give you a graceful manner of speaking than seeing a good play well acted, Garrick is inimitable . . . mark him well and you will profit by him. You must not neglect the classics . . . get a good private tutor who will point out their beauties to you and make you in six months at your age better acquainted with them than a boy at school generally in seven or eight years. Read Latin authors, the best frequently." He advises making a commonplace-book filled with the finest passages of ancient and modern authors. " Lord Bacon did not think this beneath him, read his apothegms." On cultivating taste and style. "Now is the time to go through a great deal of this, when you begin the practice of law it will be too late." He enlarges on the importance of correct expressions, "a speaker should engage the constant attention of his hearers, command it, and carry immediate conviction along with it," recommends the careful study of English History, and of many law books, discriminating carefully between those practically useful and those rather curious as history.

"And when I say *read* I don't mean run cursorily through it as you would a newspaper, but read carefully and deliberately and transcribe what you find useful in it." " Bacon you know is my favourite." "You will think I have cut out work enough for you while in England, and indeed though it is a long time to look forward " (four years) "if you mind your business you will not have too much time to spare. However I hope you will not fail to do this. Your own reputation is at stake. You must either acquire it when young, or else it will be very difficult to acquire." "One word in regard to your deportment. Let your dress be plain, always in the city and elsewhere, except when it is necessary that it should be otherwise, and your behaviour rather grave." Farewell my dear Brother. Let me hear from you by every opportunity believe me

" Yours affectionately,

" J. RUTLEDGE."

One wonders when the poor young fellow was to find time to eat and sleep, but at least the elder preached only what he had himself recently practised, and the gospel of work had its proper reward of esteem and fame to both.

Such was the training of the sons of Charleston who were to lead her in the new way. A man does not work and study thus, and seek to emulate the great ones of his time, without hope of reward — the reward dear to an ambitious heart of standing foremost among his people, an acknowledged leader of men.

This was perhaps the grievance of a class, unfelt by the people at large, and although the gentlemen were wounded in their pride by these appointments, and expressed themselves strongly on the subject, as Josiah Quincy relates in his journal in 1773, the feeling of loyalty was strong. The Crown had come to the help of the colony when suffering under the misrule of the Proprietors, and the intercourse with the Mother Country was too frequent and too friendly for gratitude and affection to have lost their force.

The accession of the young king, the first English-born king for so many years, was greeted with shouts of joy ; coronation and wedding were celebrated with dinners and balls, and accounts of them were awaited, Mrs. Pinckney says, with " an impatience not to be equalled by any people's within less than four thousand miles."

The opening of St. Michael's, which came about this time, gave pleasure to all. Ten years before it had been decided that more church accommodation was needed, and that a new edifice should be erected on the site of the first St. Philip's, whence we may conclude that scheme of putting the Town Hall into the churchyard had fallen through. In 1752 Governor Glenn, then in office, laid the corner-stone. The ceremonies, without which nothing could be done, — a public dinner with His Majesty's health and salvos of artillery from Granville Bastion, — "concluded a day of peculiar pleasure and satisfaction." That of course was King George II.'s health, but before the church was completed ten years had gone by, and it was the young King for whom the cheers resounded. The bells unfortunately were not up in time to send out a peal of rejoicing for accession or bridal. They did not reach their steeple — the steeple 190 feet high which long served as the guide to mariners along the coast — until 1774. From that day to this the bells of St. Michael's have been the voice of the town. It would be hard to explain to a stranger the strong personal feeling that every Charlestonian has for the sound of these, "The sweetest chimes in all the land." It has spoken to him from his childhood of worship, of terror, of sorrow and joy. Their tone is sacred to his ears, and men who have long dwelt in exile have yearned to hear it once more before they died.

It is hardly necessary to describe this well-known church, said much to resemble some of those built by Sir Christopher Wren, especially "St. Martin's in the Fields." Sir Christopher was certainly not the architect, for he died thirty years before it was begun, and the name of the builder remains uncertain.

It was handsomely furnished, his Excellency Governor Boone (who had but lately arrived) giving the altar plate, which was added to by many citizens. Mr. Fenwicke gave the chancel furnishings of crimson velvet with gold fringe and lace, and Jacob Motte, treasurer of the Province, "fine damask cloths and napkins" and the church books.

Less fortunate than St. Philip's, this plate was all lost — looted in Columbia by General Sherman's army in 1865. The vestry advertised in vain ; but after some years Mr. A. W. Bradford of New York, seeing in a pawnbroker's shop a tankard inscribed, "The gift of His Excellency Thomas Boone Esqr, Governor of this Province, to the Church of St. Michael's Charles Town, South Carolina 1762," bought it and generously presented it to the Church. The cover to one chalice was found in Ohio, and bought by the vestry, but nothing has ever been heard of the rest.

The town was now divided into two parishes — St. Philip's and St. Michael's, divided by Broad Street; the representation, church property, dues and duties being also divided between them; and in order to oblige people to worship in their own parish, no one was allowed to own a pew in both churches unless he also owned a house in both parishes! An odd piece of paternalism. The historian of St. Philip's, Mr. McCrady, has shown that this regulation has caused an unusual separation of family graves — as people had to be interred in their own locality without regard to the natural desire to rest with kindred dust.

All the writers, both of history and of letters, agree in alluding to these years as singularly peaceful and prosperous ones. Crops were good, commerce flourished, and society enjoyed itself.

Governor Boone did indeed make himself very unpopular by attempting to interfere with the right of election, and had odd little difficulties with Mr. Gadsden, Mr. Moultrie, and Sir John Colleton. But the people were used to these quarrels between Governor and Assembly, and troubled themselves but little about them. Only they were glad when he went back to England, leaving Lieutenant-governor Bull once more in command.

Upon them the Stamp Act fell like a bolt from the blue. *Why* it should have made such a commotion is, to people accustomed to bear with equanimity the most enormous taxes, mysterious. It took so little, and so much protection and advantage were given, so many troops guarded the

St. Michael's from Meeting Street

157

frontier, so many ships patrolled the seas, that one really wonders that any objection was made. Still the principle was altogether wrong — the same principle against which they had struggled for so many years, the claim to tax the people without their own consent. The long controversy had so educated the people to political thought that the importance of the measure was at once understood and resented. " No taxation without representation " became the cry. Mr. Pitt and Colonel Barre put it into eloquent words, and America blazed. Proceedings in Charles Town were picturesque if disreputable. The news that stamps were coming and a " distributer " appointed caught the imagination of the lower orders ; Christopher Gadsden harangued the mechanics, St. Michael's bells tolled all day as for a funeral, and Charles Town to her great disgust found herself in the hands of a mob ! Two thousand men paraded the streets, burned the stamp distributer in effigy — a sort of Guy Fawkes affair — broke his windows, and then proceeded to search for the stamps. Taking it into their heads that they were concealed in private houses, they first went to Henry Laurens's. No citizen was more respected than this gentleman. He was of Huguenot descent, had been carefully educated in England and France, had inherited a fortune from his father, and increased it by his own commercial enterprise. He was now a very wealthy man, married to the beautiful Eleanor Ball, with whom it is said he had fallen in love at first sight at her brother's wedding at Coming-tee (Mrs. Affra Coming's plantation on Cooper River). Their house, now much altered, was the large, gambrel-roofed one, still standing upon East Bay opposite the foot of Laurens Street. It was then in the centre of a large square, beautifully laid out as a garden, filled with fine trees and shrubs from every part of the world, under the care of John Watson, an English gardener, brought out to attend to it. Mr.

Laurens had said distinctly that although he disapproved of the Stamp Act he would not approve of the use of force in resisting it; consequently the crowd visited him. In a letter published in Johnson's " Traditions of the American Revolution," he describes how this mob of masked men rushed into his house and put cutlasses to his breast, demanding the stamps. He assured them that he knew nothing of these and ordered them out. They were violent, crying, "Search, search!" and demanding his keys. He " threw them the keys," saying that they were those of his wine cellar and they might help themselves. Mrs. Laurens, who was very unwell at the time, wrung her hands and screamed in terror. But her husband remained cool and dominated the situation, desiring them to do his garden no harm, and not to alarm his wife. They rummaged about for some time, but did very little damage, were careful not to tread on his flower beds, and withdrew, saying " God bless you, Colonel " (he had been lieutenant-colonel of Middleton's regiment in Grant's campaign); " we hope the poor, sick lady will do well." Apparently the mildest-mannered mob that ever broke the law.

They then went to Chief Justice Skinner's — Skinner was a "vulgar and ignorant blackguard." There is a story that, getting very drunk at a ball, he was touched by a gentleman in the dance. Instantly throwing off his coat and wig, he squared his fists, and in the attitude and language of the prize ring declared himself ready for the fight, and dared each and every man to come on ! But he was an Irishman, and had the mother wit of his country. He was ready for the rioters with full bowls of strong punch, and with every appearance of good fellowship drank with them " damnation to the Stamp Act." Thus appeased they went home and did no more that night. In the meanwhile the stamps were all safely locked up in Fort Johnson, where, the Governor informed the people, they were to stay "until his Majesty's pleasure could be known." The gentlemen, Mr. Saxby and Mr. Lloyd, who had been appointed "distributers," showed no desire for martyrdom, and frankly renounced their office, and things gradually quieted down until the inconvenience of doing no business became so great that the Bar remonstrated. The inconvenience was very great. No newspaper, for instance, could be issued, for the editor did not dare to send it out unstamped, and the subscribers would not take it stamped. The various officers of the law courts all declined to risk their positions by defying the Act, and Skinner adjourned the courts from month to month, awaiting further instructions. At last Governor Bull was (as told in General Pinckney's letter) prevailed upon to appoint Rawlins Lowndes, Benjamin Smith, and Daniel D'Oyley associate judges, and they, overruling the chief justice and the Attorney-general, Sir Egerton Leigh, after much delay and many technical difficulties opened the Court on the 4th of March, 1776. The preliminaries of a case were then heard, in which Mr. Bee, Mr. Rutledge, Mr. Manigault, Mr. Parsons, and Mr. Charles Pinckney were all concerned. This day may really be considered the beginning of the Revolution in Charles Town, for it was the first on which orderly and serious opposition was made to an undoubted Act of the British Parliament. The three new judges were laymen, as was also Mr. Robert Pringle, who was on the bench already but had not appeared. Smith, Pringle, and D'Oyley were merchants. Rawlins Lowndes was a planter, but had been for many years provost marshal of the Province, and had much knowledge of the law. The others were, of course, all barristers. Mr. Bee and Mr. Parsons had long been members of the Assembly; Mr. Rutledge has been mentioned already ; Mr. Charles Pinckney was the nephew of Chief Justice Pinckney, and like his sons had been educated in England;

Mr. Manigault was the son of the wealthiest man in the colony, the merchant Gabriel Manigault, son of the Judith already spoken of. He (Peter Manigault) had been for a long time in England, and admitted to the Bar there, and was considered a youth of great promise. Mrs. Pinckney writes of him that "he is to make glad his Mamma's heart by returning to her. . . . I dare assert not only from mine but from better judgments he will make her amends for all her cares, and answer all her hopes." This prediction was truer than such predictions often are. The young man rose rapidly in the esteem of his countrymen, and was at this time Speaker of the Assembly, a position always considered a most honourable one in the colony. Egerton Leigh, attorney-general, and Dougal Campbell, clerk of the Court, were with Skinner the officers opposed to the new judges and the lawyers. Campbell did honestly what he conceived that his official duty required of him, and Leigh also offered opposition. But Leigh, the son of the man who had for a bribe falsified the returns of the election for Westminster, although a "man of parts," was so venal that he commanded no respect. It was told of him that on one occasion a suitor had said despondently to his lawyer, that he knew he had no chance of success because his opponent had given Mr. Leigh twenty pounds. "Run," cried his attorney, "run and give him thirty, he will at once decide for you." Such were the men sent by Great Britain to maintain the law in her colonies.

Governor Bull had still to be reckoned with, and he supported the officers with all his authority. The lawyers appealed to the Assembly and the Assembly supported them ; there was every sign of an endless conflict—the only hope of solution being "at home." In the meanwhile the delegates, Thomas Lynch, Christopher Gadsden, and John Rutledge, sent by the Assembly to the Congress which Massachusetts had called to meet in New York, had come

M

home ; having, Mr. Bancroft says, taken an important and leading part in the deliberations ; "in whatever was done well, her" (South Carolina's) "mind visibly appeared."

The Assembly at home agreed with and adopted the actions of the Congress, all couched in the firmest language of opposition and the most fervent protestations of loyalty. Gadsden did not approve this, he was already a republican; nor did William Wragg, the same who as a little boy had so narrowly escaped the clutches of the pirate Blackbeard. He said that it all meant rebellion, and positively refused to vote for the petition of the Assembly which, suitably engrossed, was sent home by Mr. Speaker Manigault by a fast-sailing ship.

Joy came with the repeal of the obnoxious act in May 1766. The bells which had tolled now rang a joyous peal. Houses were illuminated and bonfires lighted. His Majesty's birthday a few weeks later was joyously and loyally celebrated. His Honour gave a grand dinner at which Council and Assembly, judges and barristers, officers and clergy, all were present and drank loyal toasts with the utmost enthusiasm. The Assembly requested its late delegates, Messrs. Lynch, Gadsden, and Rutledge, to sit for their portraits. They were to be full length and were to be forever preserved in the Assembly Hall, as a memorial of their great services which had aided in bringing about this happy result. Enthusiasm rose to its highest point, however, when Rawlins Lowndes offered the resolution that a marble statue of Mr. Pitt should be ordered and placed in front of the State House as a memento of the gratitude and admiration of the people of Charles Town for his late conduct. William Wragg struck a discordant note by offering an amendment substituting the name of "His Majesty George the 3rd." for that of Mr. Pitt. No one seconded the amendment, and it fell flat. To drink the King's health was one thing, to erect a statue was quite another. The address of thanks, however, was warm and earnest and all that a Sovereign could desire. Mr. Manigault forwarded the "petition" through Mr. Garth, the agent of the colony in London; dating it on the day ten years before the final act of separation was done.

One man did not rejoice.

Christopher Gadsden was even then a genuine republican, believing in and desiring the sovereignty of the people: a doctrine to which the other Charlestonians had by no means come.

His following consisted of the mechanics of the town, some of whom were men of intelligence and character, but naturally not averse to the new doctrine of equality, preached as it was by a man of good birth, and education, an ex-naval officer, and now a wealthy merchant. In Johnson's "Traditions of the Revolution" the author, himself the son of the chief of this party, a highly intelligent and respectable blacksmith, gives an interesting account of Mr. Gadsden's talks with these artisans, sometimes under a great oak on Mr. Mazÿck's lands in Hampstead (the northeastern portion of the city), sometimes at a tavern at the corner of Broad and Church streets, opposite to the present Charleston Library, then the favourite meeting-place for all sorts of gatherings, familiarly called "The Corner." Mr. Speaker Manigault writes to Mr. Gadsden's brother Thomas who was then in London:

"Charles Town, 14th May, 1766.

"Dear Sir, — At last the happy news of the repeal of the Stamp Act arrived, and all was jollity and mirth. Your honest brother was so overcome at hearing it that he almost fainted, and the Corner Club having met on the occasion were attacked by some rascals and got several broken heads," etc.

This was, however, the only discordant voice; with all others the cry was peace and good-will.

CHAPTER XI

THERE is something pathetic in reading of the years before the Revolution. The cloud had passed from the horizon and the world enjoyed itself with no thought of the coming storm. The old order had, it seemed, come back ; the simple confidence in the life which was theirs ; the faith in the Sovereign, in the British Constitution, in the safety which the name of Englishman bestowed upon them, was once more as it had been, as they hoped it would ever be.

The colony was no longer a handful. There were, Henry Laurens told the French Ambassador, sixty thousand white people and eighty thousand negroes. Other estimates made the numbers greater. The larger number of negroes made some persons uneasy. Mr. Timothy wrote of it constantly in his *Gazette*, but the trade was not to be interfered with, and the many servants made domestic life easy.

The new Governor and his bride, Lord and Lady Charles Greville Montagu, a gay young couple, arrived, and were received with equal ceremony and greater enthusiasm than had been the share of Governor Glenn. Lady Charles was the first "Governor's Lady" since Johnson's time, and her coming meant much to society. She was lively and affable, loved a ball or a race meeting, and soon became friendly with the colonial ladies. There are fre-

quent mentions of her in the letters of the day, notes exchanged with friends, *vers de société* (of no great merit), all
in an easy social style. Lord Charles, a younger son of
the Duke of Manchester, was only four-and-twenty, and
was quite willing to take life gayly also. He accepted the
presidency of the library, went to balls and dinners, and
gave a *fête* to the Indian warriors who had been sent to
confirm the treaties.

Travellers who visited the Province then have recorded
its prosperity. Mr. de Brahm, the surveyor-general,
speaks of the improvement of the buildings (he had himself directed the new fortifications), the State House, etc.,
and of the number of sects and churches, which, however,
he says have not " encouraged disorder " because the inhabitants are " renowned for concord, complaisance, courteous-
ness and tenderness towards each other, and more so
towards foreigners, without regard or respect of nature or
religion." De Brahm also says : —

" The hospitality of this province makes travelling
through this country agreeable, pleasant and easy ; for
most of the inhabitants keep a negro at the gate near the
publick road, to invite to refreshments, dinners, *afternoon
teas*, suppers and lodgings. Yea, they will forward them
with chaises, horses and attendance."

Says, they will often send a negro if the road be bad,
to clear the way, row across rivers, guide through forests,
etc.

Those were years of planting and building, of buying
and selling, of marrying and of giving in marriage. Hardly
an old letter remains which does not mention the wedding
of some man soon to be engaged in sterner work. The
Gazettes are full of such notices. Marriages were formal
affairs then, not to be entered into without consultations
of parents and guardians, settlements duly drawn, and
approbation of " the family." The notices are often

quaint and eminently practical. "So-and-so to Miss —— ——, a most amiable young lady with ten thousand pounds to her fortune," was very common. Some are more elaborate.

"Charlestown, Febr. 15. On Thursday last Mr. John Garret, an eminent Merchant of this Town was married to Mrs. Elisabeth Hill, a young, beautiful and genteel lady, with a considerable fortune, eldest daughter of Ch. Hill Esq. deceased. A splendid entertainment in the Evening was prepared for a large Company, who diverted themselves all Night, and in the morning the hearty Wishes of Happiness and Welfare to the new married couple were followed by the firing off the Guns of several vessels in this Harbour."

"On Tuesday last an alliance was completed between two as respectable families as any in this province by the marriage of —— —— Esqr. eldest son of the late Hon. —— —— and Miss —— —— daughter of the Hon. —— ——."

Sometimes the reporter — or if not reporter, the writer — has a more exciting theme, as when he announces the marriage of Lord William Campbell, younger son of the Duke of Argyle, to "Miss Sarah Izard, daughter of Walter Izard, Esqr. an amiable and accomplished young lady, esteemed one of the greatest fortunes of this Province." The dower in this case was fifty thousand pounds, enough in those days to attract any younger son.

These young people needed houses, and many were then built or improved. Mr. Henry Middleton, who in addition to his paternal estates had acquired Middleton Place by his marriage with Miss Williams, gave it, embellished by the terraces and gardens which he had himself made, to his son Arthur upon his marriage with Miss Polly Izard, sister of Lady William. A newcomer to the river was Mr. (soon to be Commodore) Gillon, a Hollander, belonging to an old Dutch family of sailors and merchants. On his voyage to this country he had met the charming

THE RHETT HOUSE, HASEL STREET
One of the First built outside the City Walls.

widow Cripps, who, having been in Europe for the education of her only son, was returning to Charles Town. The voyages of those days gave ample time (if time be needed) for falling in love, and before they reached port the widow had consented to become his wife. They bought the place of Ashley Hill, which they renamed Batavia, adjoining Middleton Place, built a fine house, all the material of which, even the gravel for the terraces, was said to have been brought from Holland, and lived in great style and gayety until the war began, when he became one of the most energetic servants of his adopted country.

There were young wives too at the Drayton places, for Charles, the heir of Magnolia, and William Henry of Drayton Hall, who had been sent as little lads to England with the Pinckneys, had come home now, and married, one a daughter of Mr. Henry Middleton, and the other Miss Golightly, daughter of Culcheth Golightly, one of the wealthiest men of the Province. Her sister " Polly " had made not long before one of the runaway matches that sometimes broke the stated order of things. For choosing to marry Mr. Benjamin Huger, a gallant gentleman, but of no great fortune, and consent refused, she, at a ball one night, caught up a hat lying near, stepped through a window into the garden, and ran off with the " man of her heart." There is a lovely picture of her with the hat — *her trousseau* — hanging on her arm ; another, *Chapeau de paille*.

This was a runaway match, but no *mésalliance*. Such occurred sometimes and were looked upon with horror. One of the darkest stories of the colony is attached to an old ivy-covered ruin of a fine house on one of the adjacent sea islands. Here a young lady, daughter of one of the best families of the Province (now extinct), so forgot her station as to wed her mother's coachman ! The secret was kept for some time, and when discovered, an old servant of the house, furious at the insult to his dead master, stabbed the coachman husband to death. The poor girl (said to have been weak-minded) and her baby (of course there was a baby) survived, sinking to a lower class of society.

At Ashley Hall were no weddings, for Lieutenant-governor Bull, who had married years before the daughter of that bold navigator Othniel Beale, was a childless man. But he did not neglect to embellish this, his hereditary seat, having parks and gardens and a lake with a mound in the centre whereon was a statue of Diana.

The Reverend Josiah Smith, grandson of the Landgrave, the same who had long since supported Whitfield against Commissary Garden, still occupied the old house at Goose Creek, now the home of four generations.   One of the quaintest ghost stories on record is of this house (said to be the oldest in the Province), destroyed by the earthquake of 1886, whence there was a secret passage leading to a graveyard near by, and opening into an apparent vault covered by a properly graven tombstone and thence to the bank of the creek.   The story is that the house being then inhabited by the family of the second Landgrave, an English lady, Mrs. Latham, was employed as governess to the children.   One Sunday, Mrs. Latham sat reading in her room upstairs, *not* Baxter's "Saint's Rest" or the "Sinner's Way to Repentance," as might reasonably have been expected, but a romance, the "Turkish Spy."   She was not too absorbed in her book, however, to hear a slight, very slight sound, at the open door, and looking up, she saw a gentle, sweet-faced old lady, dressed in the quiet style of that household, looking sadly at her.

Rather surprised, but supposing it to be an intimate visitor, she politely invited the lady to enter.   There was no answer, and the guest continued to look at her sadly and shake her head as if in negation.   Mrs. Latham then rose and went toward her ; but as she approached, the visitor noiselessly withdrew, and had disappeared by the time that she reached the door. At dinner-time the English woman went down expecting to see her mute visitor, but she was not at table, and when she asked, was assured that no one had been there. She persisted and described minutely the person of the old lady. At that moment a young brother of her employer, whom she had not yet seen, came in, and Mrs. Latham exclaimed, " There, there is the image of the old lady, as like as a young man can be to an old woman." The family then told her that it was the spirit of their late mother, *née* Mary Hyrne, the widow of the second Landgrave; and that she sometimes appeared to them; her son Benjamin, the youth mentioned, being extremely like her. Mrs. Latham naturally was very much disturbed and wished to leave the house, dreading particularly the sad and disapproving looks of her visitor. Mr. Smith, however, succeeded in convincing her that his mother's gentle shade had come, not in anger, but in sorrow, that she should read so vain and worldly a work as the " Turkish Spy " on the Sabbath Day ; and that only her good was sought by the ghostly monitor. Mrs. Latham took courage, remained, and " became truly pious " under the influence of the most puritanic ghost on record. It is hardly necessary to remind the reader that the Smiths were the head of the Puritan party in the Province.

The many fires which have devastated Charleston have destroyed most of the houses which belonged to the noted men of that time; but some few remain. Miles Brewton, a wealthy merchant, had married Miss Izard and built on King Street the handsome home now known as "the Pringle house," already mentioned. Many historic associations now gather around it. On Meeting Street Mrs. Brewton's sister, Mrs. Daniel Blake of Newington, owned the house now occupied by William E. Huger, Esq., which was also to become famous. Just opposite to it was the house of Governor Bull, which looks curiously like the half of

THE WILLIAM HUGER HOUSE, MEETING STREET

Ashley Hall.   It was probably only one of his residences, for he is frequently mentioned as living on Broad Street. Judge Pringle's brick house in Tradd Street has been already mentioned as one of the first built after the great fire of 1740; Mr. John Rutledge had the house (now much altered) in Broad Street, opposite Orange, now owned by R. G. Rhett, Esq.; and in Church Street, just north of the Baptist Church, is that in which Jacob Motte and his wife Rebecca, sister of Miles Brewton, then lived. At the corner of Tradd and Friend streets lived Mr. George Roupell, the postmaster, and at the other end of the square was John Stuart, the Indian agent, married to Miss Fenwicke, and at that time a most highly esteemed and admired person. Both of these "stood for the King" in the coming struggle, and the square used to be shown to children sixty years ago as "Tory row."

Mrs. Pinckney's eldest son came home about this time, having gone through Westminster and Oxford and become a "barrister of the Temple." He had been, while at college, greatly incensed at the Stamp Act, and his picture, still in the possession of the descendants of his friend, Sir Mathew Ridley, shows him declaiming violently against it. He, it may be supposed, was "ripe for rebellion," but at present his thoughts were of other things, for he was shortly after married to Miss Middleton, daughter of Mr. Henry Middleton. His chief plantation was far to the south, Pinckney Island in Port Royal entrance; his mother having "Belmont," the home place, from which most of her letters are written, for her life. The young people, however, established themselves in the house, on the Bay, so long known as the "Governor's Mansion" (to the inconvenience, it seems, of Lord Charles Montagu, who was absent at the time) and had for neighbours Mr. Laurens, Mr. Gadsden, and Mr. Thomas Lynch, all living upon the Bay above St. Philip's Church, in what was then called Ansonborough, extending from just above the church to Mazÿckboro on the north. The land had been won, it was said, by the admiral and circumnavigator Lord Anson at a game of cards, he having paid frequent visits to Charles

THE STATUE OF PITT

Town while stationed upon the coast.   Anson Street still marks the locality.   Of these Mr. Laurens's house alone remains.   Mr. Lynch's was said to have been of black cypress cut upon his own plantation on· Santee and built by his own carpenters.   So close were the habitations of the men who were soon, as one of them expressed it, to be "all in the same boat, which *must* not sink."

When the statue of Mr. Pitt arrived in May, 1770, it was received with wild enthusiasm.   The vessels in port "dressed" for the occasion, the balls rang out a joyous peal, but were stopped on account of the illness of Mr. Isaac Mazÿck, who was lying desperately ill near the church. The people of all ranks and station flocked to the wharf and drew it by hand, with loud applause, to the Town Hall, where it was to remain until its pedestal should be prepared.   In July it was raised to the place which it long held in the centre of the crossing of Broad and Meeting streets, amid deafening cheers, ringing of bells, waving of flags, and other demonstrations of joy.   Mr. Speaker Manigault read the inscription aloud to the people.   Lord Chatham's health was drunk, and the artillery from Granville Bastion saluted the defender of liberty.

Happy it is for the sons of men that the prophetic vision is not theirs, and that none foresaw the dramatic scene when Chatham, magnificent in flannels, was taken dying from the House of Peers, after spending his last breath in protesting against the dismemberment of the Empire. Even so he had done great good.   He had taught the Americans to know their rights, and when once known, they could defend them alone.

The statue, classically draped, represents Mr. Pitt in the attitude of vehement speech — too vehement for the repose of art, but probably entirely suited to the feelings of those to whom it came.   It had, when erected, St. Michael's, the State House, and the "old beef market,"

where the City Hall now stands, to the north, east, and
south of it. It has shared the fortunes of the town, for in
the siege of 1780, the right arm was carried off by a can-

St. Michael's Churchyard

non shot.   Some time after the Revolution, when the
enthusiasm for Mr. Pitt had subsided, it was found (very
justly) to interfere with the traffic of that crowded thor-
oughfare, and it was removed and stored. Later on it was
again placed upon its pedestal and set up in the Orphan
House grounds (where it was generally supposed by the
children to represent General Washington, as one of them

said "just getting out of bed "), and during the confederate war it lost its head — which, however, was merely cracked off, not broken.

This interesting monument was, about eighteen years ago, rescued from its obscure situation, repaired, and placed in the centre of Marion Square, east of the City Hall, not more than a hundred yards from its original position. The arm, however, has never been restored.

The young men still in England were evidently not so entirely reassured by the repeal of the Stamp Act as were their friends at home, as is shown by a very remarkable letter printed in a Year Book of Charleston, from Thomas Heyward, then a youth of nineteen studying at the Temple. He gives his father a close and accurate account of the debates in Parliament which he had attended, and clearly expresses his apprehensions. He was to sign the Declaration of Independence. For the same reason Thomas Pinckney and James Ladson studied drilling and military tactics.

Four years later, when the Boston Port Bill aroused the indignation of all the colonies and thirty Americans in England petitioned against it, *fifteen* were Carolinians.

This is, however, advancing matters, for the Boston Port Bill was not yet, although affairs in the Northern colonies were by no means as serene as for those few years they were in the South, where the circular letters of the House of Representatives of Massachusetts and of the House of Burgesses of Virginia alone kept alive the irritation which might otherwise have passed away. From Massachusetts there were " petitions " for non-importation, agreements, and other troublous motions ; of all of which the Speakers, Mr. Cushing of Boston and Mr. Peyton Randolph of Virginia, wrote eloquently to Mr. Manigault, who, "by order of the Commons," wrote sympathetic answers, all breathing resistance " to tyranny " — and absolute devotion to his Majesty. Mr. Gadsden and his party drank it all in eagerly and the Commons were stirred. When it came to a mob of mechanics parading the streets with torches and fireworks, huzzaing for " Wilkes and liberty and the non-rescinders of Boston " and claiming to elect their own representatives to the new House, the Governor became alarmed. He addressed the Assembly urgently, warning them of the result of such proceedings, and hoping that their influence would be given against all disloyal and seditious letters and papers received by them. The House answered that nothing could exceed the devotion and loyalty of his Majesty's American subjects, and that *no* seditious letters had ever been received by them ! Lord Charles informed them that the circular letter of the Province of Massachusetts Bay *was* seditious. The House made no reply, but printed the whole correspondence in the *Gazette.* Whereupon the Assembly was promptly dissolved. In all of this Lord Charles appears to great advantage ; he did his duty, kept his temper, was loyal to his King, and wonderfully patient under the diatribes of the Commons. He had suffered much from the climate, and went for a visit to England, followed by the friendship of many, and the esteem of all the people.

Before his return things were yet worse. The rage of " non-importation " had seized the town and made much dissension — mechanics and merchants being at daggers drawn. The " ministerial measure " of quartering troops, not intended for their defence, upon the inhabitants had been violently resisted, and had been defeated by a large majority in Parliament.

The troops had consequently been withdrawn. The questions of taxation were again arising, and on the Governor's return, although Lady Charles and himself were greeted with the utmost warmth, it soon became evident that he had learned in England what to expect and what to do. Instead of his former pleasant and cordial ways he seemed on his return harassed and irritable, declared that he could find no fit house in Charles Town, and took up his lodging across the harbour at Fort Johnson on James Island, where he announced he thought of building "a castle," for the gubernatorial residence.

And so the quarrel went on ; the Assembly protesting against the " Acts," and the Ministers, who deluded his most Excellent Majesty, and the Governor striving to manage the Assembly. He addressed, argued, prorogued, dissolved. The new elections returned much the same members, and the members elected the same Speaker. They continued to pass resolutions, etc. (which seemed from his point of view monstrous), and boldly proclaimed them legal. In short, the Rebellion had (civilly) imperceptibly begun. The harassed young man bethought himself that to change the meeting-place of his unmanageable legislature might do some good, and in that hope informed them that "it would be for his Majesty's service" that they should assemble at the town of Beaufort in Port Royal entrance. His idea probably was that there would be a smaller attendance and greater docility.

Indefatigably, Mr. Speaker and all but five of the members journeyed over abominable roads and watercourses innumerable for seventy-five miles, and were in their seats to greet his Excellency at the appointed hour. Nor had the soft skies of that softest of climes changed the spirit of these obstinate Commons; stiff-necked they had been, and stiff-necked they remained. Lord Charles in three days ordered them all back to their old capital, having received no advantage and much ridicule from the absurd attempt.

Peter Manigault now resigned the speakership. His health was failing fast, and he sailed for England in the

N

hope of recovering it, but died in a few weeks, to the great loss of his country. He had been a member of the Commons House since his twenty-third year, being returned at each election for eighteen years.

Lord Charles gained nothing by exchanging the courteous though firm Mr. Manigault for the rugged strength of Rawlins Lowndes — who was chosen to succeed him as Speaker. Mr. Lowndes was at this time (1773) over fifty years old, and thus much the senior of most of his associates in the Revolutionary contest.

He had made his own in the colony, having come to it as a boy from his birthplace in the Island of St. Christopher (known as St. Kitt's) in the West Indies. Some family influence " at Home " had procured for him the important office of provost marshal, upon which he had entered as soon as of sufficient age. He had there gained much knowledge of the law and of affairs, and was now a man of property, influence, and acknowledged ability. He was of a sturdy, conservative spirit, most reluctant to push things to extremes, but never willing to yield an inch to the undue assumption of power either by " the Ministers " or by his countrymen. Thus as associate justice he had pronounced the first decision against the Stamp Act, and so he was vehemently opposed to the tyranny of the association which tried to terrorize the people into signing the non-importation agreement. Naturally he was always in direct opposition to Christopher Gadsden, who would adopt any means to gain his point. Constantly fighting, they yet had so great a regard for each other, that late in life Mr. Lowndes named one of his younger children for Mr. Gadsden and Mr. Gadsden made Mr. Lowndes one of the executors of his will.

Hardly had he been installed in office when a dispute arose with Lord Charles about the custody of the Commons Journal, in which he stated with great force the rights of the House, the limitations of the Governor, and his own responsibility. The Governor tried yet again the remedy of dissolution. And again the electors returned the same members, and the members chose the same Speaker. His Excellency was weary of the fight; he could do nothing with this "too numerous democracy." Individually and socially he remained to the last a favourite, but politically he was a failure, as any man in his position would then have been. He resigned his office and returned home.

Always courteous and pleasant to his friends he went the night before his expected departure to a St. Cecilia concert to take leave of them. The Journal of Josiah Quincy's visit to Charles Town mentions his presence there.

Mr. Quincy had come from Boston "for his health," but evidently he was anxious to ascertain if the temper of this really loyal people was beginning to fail under repeated trials, and how far they were ready to support the advanced propositions of Massachusetts. He was a close observer and his Journal is most interesting.

He tells of his amazement at the appearance of the harbour, crowded with ships more than any other in America ; of the town, and especially of the fine new Exchange just completed, viewed from the water (we call it the old post office now); of his visit to Charles Town Library, "a handsome, square, spacious room, containing a very valuable collection of books, prints, globes, etc." The Library was housed for over twenty years in rooms lent to it by Mr. Gabriel Manigault, free of rent, he being for much of that time the vice-president,— the Governor generally graciously accepting the office of president. Only Governor Boone was not requested to accept it, neither his politics nor his morals being approved by the community. On every occasion for generous aid one could count upon Mr. Manigault.

Mr. Quincy describes the houses and the people — tells how he went to a dancing assembly where the music was bad and the dancing good, and to a St. Cecilia concert of which he says that it was held in a large and inelegant building withdrawn from the street. Mr. David Deas had, he says, "given him a ticket, on presenting which he was passed from servant to servant and finally ushered in. The music was grand, especially the bass viol and French horns." The first violinist, a Frenchman, played the best solo he had ever heard. His salary was five hundred guineas. Most of the performers were gentlemen amateurs. He comments on the richness of dress of both ladies and gentlemen; says that there were two hundred and fifty ladies present and it was called no great number. The ladies are "in taciturnity during the performance greatly before our ladies; in noise and flirtation after the music is over, pretty much on a par. If our" (Boston) "ladies have any advantage, it is in white and red, vivacity and spirit. The gentlemen many of them dressed with elegance and richness uncommon with us. Many with swords on."

Lord Charles Greville Montagu, the Governor, who was to sail the next day for England, had come to take farewell of his friends, of whom he had many. Mr. Quincy was presented to his Excellency, to the chief justice, etc.

He tells also of a dinner at Miles Brewton's "with a large company, — a most superb house said to have cost him £8000 sterling." A handsome bird, probably a macaw, was in the room during dinner. How handsome and luxurious it all was! The gentlemen held the placemen in contempt. They said, "We none of us can expect the honours of the State; they are all given away to worthless poor sycophants." When politics were talked at dinner, one gentleman, "a hot flaming, sensible Tory," expressed utter distrust of all the Northern states except

St. Michael's Alley
181

Virginia — and especially of Massachusetts, and declared that if ever they renounced the sovereignty of the King, they would have governors sent them from Massachusetts, — a prophecy which it took eighty-four years to fulfil. Mr. Quincy went to the races too. " Spent this day, March 3rd, in viewing horses, riding over the town, and receiving complimentary visits." On March 13 he goes to the races and sees " Flimnap " beat " Little David," who had been the winner in sixteen races. Many are the stories of the deeds of Flimnap the great. On this occasion he ran the first four-mile heat in eight minutes and seventeen seconds ; and two thousand pounds were lost and won on this race. And, says the New England gentleman, " At the races I saw a fine collection of excellent, though very high priced horses and was let a little into the singular art and mystery of the turf."

He tells it all with a curious separateness, a sense of difference, as of looking at a strange people whose traditions and ways were not his — which was absolutely true.

When politics run so high, they inevitably affect social relations. A sad instance of this had already occurred.

Mr. Ralph Izard of "the Elms," Goose creek, had married Miss Delancey of a very distinguished Huguenot family of New York. A lovely and graceful woman as her picture by Copley testifies. In 1766, while the Stamp Act agitation was yet unlaid, her brother came to make them a visit. Miss Pinckney writes to her friend Miss Becky Izard — afterward the wife of Colonel Colin Campbell of the British Army: " We are much obliged for the smart man you have sent us, Mr. Delancey; he is thought handsome here and chose out Miss Golightly (before he saw her) for his flame." The poor fellow was handsome and gay, but he was an ardent loyalist, and unfortunately became involved in a political dispute with a Dr. Haley, " a man of education and influence, patronized by the leaders of the Revolutionary party," and an ardent patriot. They were (Johnson's "Traditions" says) at "a genteel house of entertainment" (probably the South Carolina Coffee House) "in St. Michael's Alley."

The debate soon became angry and passions rose. Delancey gave Haley the lie. Haley instantly challenged him to fight *now* with pistols in an upstairs room, by themselves.

There can have been none but waiters present, for such a duel would never have been allowed. Delancey accepted the terms; they fired both at the same moment, across a table, and Delancey fell dead.

The scandal was horrible. Haley, accused of murder by the Tories, was defended by the Whigs. It became a party question.

The unfortunate man despaired of his escape. To save him from mob violence he was concealed in a dark garret, naturally trying to the nerves. In the darkness he stumbled against a rope stretched across a corner. His inflamed imagination made him accept it as a presage. Hanging would certainly be his fate! Not without trouble was he saved.

The absence of witnesses made the trial one for murder. The best youthful talent at the Bar defended him: Thomas Heyward, C. C. Pinckney, and the Rutledges — all fresh from Europe.

They proved that Delancey had given the offence, had accepted the terms, and (the most effective argument) that he had fired both barrels of his pistol — the balls being found embedded in the wall in front of which Haley had stood, on each side of where his head had been. Haley's acquittal was looked upon as a triumph for the Whigs and as equally a mortification to the Tories. The Izards went abroad, where they remained for some years.

The people hoped, one does not quite see with what reason, that their long-tried and trusted lieutenant-governor would be advanced to the higher dignity, but this was not to be.   Dr. Ramsay and other historians have thought that had he received full power he might have kept the Province for the King.   It seems hardly possible. When the stream comes down in flood, no one boulder can do more than retard its rush.

It is quite unnecessary to describe or even to enumerate all the various acts, bills, etc., which finally precipitated the Revolution.   The proceedings of the patriotic party are, to look back at (be it spoken with all due respect), amusing!   They deluded themselves so completely as to where they were going, and used the words "law" and "British Constitution" with such faith!

The people of Charles Town must have enjoyed an unusual intellectual pleasure at this time : that of having the greatest and most exciting questions constantly debated by the best speakers of the country, without any sense of impending disaster to chill their interest.

The question of the tea, for instance.   The last Congress had said that the tea should not be imported — and here were chests upon chests arriving by every ship.   Even Captain Carling — with whom almost every man had gone passenger to Europe and of whom every passenger was the friend for life — was bringing it in!

Should it be sent back or thrown overboard ?   What would his Honour do ?   His Honour, his sole desire to prevent precipitate action, and, as he believed, the ruin of his countrymen, allowed the collector to store it quietly in the vaults under the Exchange, and let the question of duties rest for the time.

Then came the letter from Boston announcing the famous "Port Bill," and asking all the other Provinces to put themselves in the same position and agree to import nothing while her port remained closed. The response given to this proposal was really wonderful.

In a pecuniary point of view Carolina had now nothing to complain of. Why should she cast in her lot with an almost unknown state, and resign all the advantages that the mother country gave?

Principle alone called, and principle carried the day. The latest — and greatest — historian of South Carolina, Mr. Edward McCrady, says of the Province: " She at least was suffering from no material oppression, what part she took thereafter was in the interest of the commerce and waterfalls of New England and not in her own. She at least was to contend only for abstract truth and abstract liberty."

The response was quick and clear. A public meeting, held as usual at "the corner" of Broad and Church streets, decided at once "to assist their sister colonies in the dangers impending over American liberties." Their assistance was practical, for in an incredibly short time they collected and sent on a subscription of thirty-three hundred pounds in money, and eighty tierces of rice "for the suffering poor of the blockaded Port." Also they called another meeting, which decided to order a general election for five deputies to another Congress, and a committee which should manage things at home. The election of the delegates was a lesson in party machinery. Two men were acceptable to all: Mr. Henry Middleton, who had resigned his seat in the Governor's Council, and Mr. John Rutledge; but the merchants who were opposed to the non-importation plan wished the other three to be Rawlins Lowndes, Miles Brewton, and Charles Pinckney, — all men past their youth, and belonging to the conservative party.

The mechanics, on their part, wanted their great leader, Christopher Gadsden, Thomas Lynch, and Edward Rut-

"The Corner," Broad and Church Streets
Centre of the old walled town.

ledge. Thomas Lynch had been very earnest for non-importation when it had been tried before, having, Governor Bull wrote to Lord Hillsborough, "travelled fifty miles to cast his vote lest the merchants should sell the liberty of his dear country like any other goods." And Edward Rutledge, as advocate, had, with Rawlins Lowndes, as judge, but lately defied the power of the Council and liberated a prisoner whom it had ordered confined. He was understood to be more inclined to the popular party than his brother John.

The merchants foolishly made a show of numbers, going to the polls in a body, with their clerks and dependants ; which, of course, roused the attention of the mechanics. They ran everywhere, calling out their friends, and easily turned the tide, winning the day by a majority (thought very large) of three hundred and ninety-seven.

In the convention a question of great importance had been raised by Rawlins Lowndes. The account of all their proceedings is given in a very animated way by Governor John Drayton, son of William Henry; his materials being taken from his father's voluminous manuscripts. In his " Memoirs of the American Revolution " he says of this that Mr. Rawlins Lowndes, who had been Speaker of the House since the resignation of Mr. Manigault, urged that the delegates should go " with *powers limited!* lest they might be overruled if the more numerous votes of the Northern colonies, especially of New England, should commit the Province to a denial of the superintending power of Parliament, a doctrine which they admit and we deny." Governor Drayton says : " This sentiment from Mr. Lowndes is here brought into view as being from a gentleman of prudence and consideration, and who *at that time* declared the prevailing opinion of the colony."

" It will serve as a point in public opinion for tracing the rapidity with which in a few months later the colony adopted the contrary idea." The sentiment was then so strong that the delegates were sent with power to " con-

cert, agree to, and effectually prosecute such legal measures as in the opinion of those deputies and of the
deputies of the other colonies should be most likely to
obtain a repeal of the late acts of Parliament and a redress
of American grievances." All as subjects of the King !

Governor Drayton might well talk of "rapidity."
Within a few days a general meeting of the people —
so general that every man who chose to come might vote
— chose a "General Committee" of ninety-nine persons,
on which it (the meeting) bestowed practically unlimited
powers. This committee was to consist of fifteen merchants and fifteen mechanics to represent the town, and
sixty-nine planters for the Parishes. "This proceeding," Mr. Drayton gently observes, "was rather unconstitutional ; as the different parishes *did not choose* the
sixty-nine planters who were to represent them. They,
however, acquiesced in the nominations, being sensible it
proceeded from the best intentions and the urgency of the
occasion."

This General Committee appointed sub-committees, one
of which, the "Committee of Observation," superintended
the matter of the tea, when that mild herb once more
roused the indignation of the community. All through
the summer it had continued to come, and the collector
had seized and stored it ; every now and then some especial disturbance being made. At last the committee
ordered that a parcel just arrived should not be allowed
to fall into the collector's hands. The vessel was hauled
out into the stream, and the consignees themselves, publicly, in the light of day, with their own hands broke open
the chests, and, as Mr. Timothy eloquently observed,
"Made oblation to Neptune," by throwing the contents
into Hog Island Channel "in the presence of the Committee of Observation, and of a crowd of citizens who
shouted thrice as each package was emptied into the

Cooper." Moreover, shortly after several hundred pounds of Bohea, which had been smuggled in, was reshipped whence it came, by a very characteristic pride, "to show that the people did not reject dutied tea, simply to use undutied and save the small amount of money." All that which had come first still lay in the vaults, and no one would yet break open the "King's storehouse." But in July, 1776, the "President" of South Carolina applied to have it sold for the public service, and the Legislature (the names had been changed by that time) permitted it to be sold in packages "not exceeding twelve pounds." Think of how the women blessed the new President and the Legislature!

Two things are remarkable in these proceedings : how much the people accepted the leadership of the gentry, and how small was the community.

The artisans and mechanics were eager and active in the cause ; Gadsden having taught and inspired them ; and when it came to choosing delegates, actually carried the election by force of numbers. But they did not select one of their own class, but Gadsden himself, with Rutledge and Lynch, whose views they thought akin to his. As to the size of the community it is really curious. The same names occur over and over again. The members of the General Committee are also the members of the Provincial Congress, and the Provincial Congress and the General Assembly differ only in name. When Governor Bull refuses to recognize the former and a day or two later receives the latter, there is hardly any change except that Mr. President is now Mr. Speaker. And Moultrie records that half the delegation to the Congress were uniformed as military officers.

The tangle of relationships which exists in Charleston to-day had already begun. With some few exceptions, the chief actors in the Revolution belonged to one or two closely connected groups ; and as it is now said that " England is governed from the country houses," so undoubtedly much of the policy was decided in the great houses along the rivers. Legend has it that at Middleton Place were many gatherings. Mr. Henry Middleton, a stately, courteous old gentleman, and his wife, Lady Mary, the daughter of the Jacobite Earl of Cromartie, with his son Arthur, had around them a band of relatives and near friends.

Both were ardent patriots, — the younger perhaps more inclined for decisive measures than any one but Gadsden and his most intimate friend, William Henry Drayton. Many a fiery eager talk must have been held on the long terraces and under the oaks which are noble trees to-day. Gillon would come — no kinsman, but nearest neighbour — and Richard Bohun Baker from the beautiful seat " Archdale," just across the river ; and Charles Drayton from Magnolia, who was Mr. Middleton's son-in-law. William Henry from Drayton Hall was the most brilliant if most erratic man of the time. He in the Stamp Act troubles had been violent against the colonists, speaking and writing eloquently on the side of the ministers. Then he had gone to England, been received at Court, been petted and fêted as the most loyal of subjects, and now on his return he, although the Lieutenant-governor's nephew, and, with his father, a member of his Majesty's Council, had amazed all men by suddenly appearing as the most vehement partisan among the " patriots." Charles Cotesworth Pinckney and Edward Rutledge were sons-in-law of Mr. Middleton also. Rutledge's brother John was Mr. Middleton's colleague in the delegation ; and C. C. Pinckney's first cousin, Charles Pinckney, was soon to be first President of the Provincial Congress. Charles Pinckney's brother-in-law, Miles Brewton, was a member of the Congress and Council of Safety; and Mrs. Brewton, a first cousin of Mrs. Arthur Middleton. Mrs. Middleton's brothers and cousins, the Izards, were also patriots, and Goose Creek was not far off.

From the Cooper many of the soldiers were to come. Mulberry Castle was the great house there, and William Moultrie of Northampton, a connection of the Broughtons by his first marriage to Miss St. Julien, was soon to bear the chief part in the opening scene of the war. Moultrie came of good fighting stock, a descendant of the Multrares, lairds of Seafield and Makinch, who had done homage for their lands to Edward I. and had fallen and fought at Flodden and for Queen Mary. The brothers of his second wife were Isaac and Jacob Motte. The former to be his second in command at Fort Moultrie, the latter the husband of Rebecca Motte, sister of Miles Brewton, one of the heroines of the Revolution. Francis Marion, "the Swamp Fox," lived near at "Chachan." He and Moultrie had been in Thomas Middleton's regiment in Grant's campaign. They were now to be again together. The neighbours gathered and discussed — some for, some against the proposed acts. There was much difference of opinion. This was the Huguenot country, and the Huguenots, grateful to England for much kindness, were, with some distinguished exceptions, slow to join in the quarrel. Not until their hero Marion called them did they come in force, to be remembered in song and story as "Marion's Men."

There was great difference of opinion everywhere; it was the worst of the trouble. In the last great contest in which Carolina staked — and lost — life and fortune, she had the happiness of owning the undivided fealty of her sons. It was not so in 1776. Mr. McCrady has given a list which shows that brother was against brother, and father against son, — hardly a household which was not divided.

This was hardest of all, perhaps, to the stanch old Governor himself. Never man had a harder part to play, and never man played such a part with more honour and credit than Governor Bull. His great-nephew, Governor John Drayton, says of him very truly that "his liberal education and wide experience had enabled him to understand and appreciate the claims of his countrymen, while he also knew the lawful rights of his King whose commis-

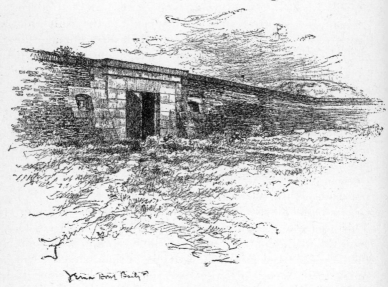

ENTRANCE TO FORT MOULTRIE

sion he bore, and whose commands he felt in honour bound to execute."

It must have been sad in those days at Ashley Hall — and hard for the honest gentleman to differ with his kindred. He had no son to succeed him, and his brothers were against him : Stephen of Sheldon soon to command for the Americans. Of all his friends in the Council, — his two brothers-in-law, Mr. Middleton and Mr. Drayton ; Mr. Bernard Elliott ; his nephew, W. H. Drayton ; and

Daniel Blake — the last alone stood by him. The others dropped off one by one, and the men who remained were venal wretches, like Egerton Leigh whom all despised, or mere placemen sent from England to fill their posts. He had the steady support of William Wragg, of the Roupells, and of many less conspicuous. It would be interesting to know what his own opinions really were ; but as stanch a King's man as Sir Harry Lee of Ditchley, his Majesty's pleasure ruled his actions. He never lost the regard and affection of the people. They always loved and honoured him.

There was some jealousy perhaps of this country-house influence among the townsfolk who had been the first to move. Henry Laurens, who had just come home from Europe, brought back by the threatening state of affairs, wrote to his son John, then in London, " Soon they " (the planters) " will take the reins out of the townsmen's hands ; they are the richest and most numerous, and every one thinks that he knows enough to govern."

Mr. Laurens had come home in a very despairing mind. He gives an account in one of his letters of having had the honour of being consulted by several members of Parliament, and of their ignorance and weakness on American affairs. He had given them the best possible advice ; to let the colonies tax themselves, and trust to their affection for the Crown ; but had made no impression at all. He was evidently thereafter hopeless of reconciliation.

The Continental Congress met. The departure of the delegates being a matter of great interest, the *Gazette* says : —

" Two of our Deputies to the Congress, viz. the Hon. Henry Middleton, for many years a Member of Council, but who had virtue enough to quit it when he found he could no longer be of service to his Country There — and Mr. Edward Rutledge, a young gentleman of most prom-

o

ising talents, bred to the bar and barrister, will embark on Saturday next."

This was the Congress which passed the famous non-importation act, which crippled the colonies more than it injured England, and gave rise to such inconveniences of daily life as Mrs. Pinckney describes when she writes to her daughter that " not a bit of Pavillion gauze " (mosquito net) "was to be found in Town, and that the most necessary and ordinary medicines were not to be had."

A more picturesque effect was produced by the solemn compact to import no mourning goods ! No black stuffs were at that time made in America, and the result was curious. Instead of the long rows of black-clad men and women shrouded in "hoods" and " weepers," and the servants rejoicing in garments of woe, now there appeared relatives, friends, and domestics following the dead in gay raiment of every hue.

The funerals of Mr. Lamboll and Mrs. Prioleau, which were the first to take place under these conditions, were talked of with mingled pride and chagrin for many a day.

Before Congress assembled, in the month of August, the General Assembly had met, — much to its own surprise, for it had fully expected to be again prorogued by way of silencing inconvenient debate. It had been so disposed of several times already, but now the day appointed had come and no inhibition had been received.

Bright and early, at *eight* in the morning instead of at eleven, the usual hour, Mr. Speaker Lowndes called the House to order, and proceeded to business with great rapidity, sending of course in due form to acquaint his Honour with the fact that the faithful Commons were ready to receive any communications which his Honour might see fit to bestow upon them. It may be supposed that Messrs. Heyward and Cattell, the messengers, were not in overhaste on their errand ; for although they returned with the answer that his Honour was pleased to say he would be in the Council Chamber immediately and would send a message to the House, there was time to transact important business. It was in fact *the* business for which the gentlemen had quitted their beds at that hour. Colonel Powell, the chairman of the General Committee, laid before the House an account of the proceedings of the meetings in July last, and of the committee, and the appointment of the delegates to the Congress at Philadelphia, and prayed for an appropriation of fifteen hundred pounds to pay the expenses of the said delegates.

It did not take the Assembly long to understand the report, for most of them were members of the committee, and all had helped to elect the delegates; so the report was promptly received and the appropriations passed. They even had time to talk a little about Indian affairs and send a polite communication on that subject to his Honour, before the good gentleman could get dressed, hurry to the Council Chamber, summon two members of his Council to assist in receiving the Commons, and find a Master in Chancery (the official medium of communication) to summon them.

When the Master arrived with his summons, " Mr. Speaker with the house went to attend the Lt. Governor at the Council Chamber, where his honour was pleased to prorogue the General Assembly until the 6th of September next."

Governor Drayton tells the story of this trick upon his revered uncle, with a chuckle that has come down across a century.

The General Committee decided that it did not consider itself a sufficiently " legal " body for its required duties and powers, and ordered a general election for a better organization. The " legality " is not clearly visible to the ordinary observer, but at least the people had the privi-

lege of choosing their own representatives. These when
elected declared themselves a Provincial Congress, chose
Colonel Charles Pinckney to be their President, waited on
his Honour at his residence in Broad Street, and presented
him with an address. It began: —

" May it please your Honour,

" We, his Majesty's faithful and loyal subjects, the Representatives of all the good people of this Colony, now
met in Provincial Congress," etc., and continued by
giving the Governor much advice, and particularly that he
should call the General Assembly together, and only exercise his " undoubted right of prerogative for the *good of
the people.*"

The Lieutenant-governor answered:

"Gentlemen: — I know no legal representatives of the
good people of this Province but the Commons-House
of Assembly, chosen according to the Election Act, and
met in General Assembly. As gentlemen of respectable
characters and property in this province, I acquaint
you that the General Assembly stands prorogued to the
24th. instant. I have always endeavoured to make the
law of the land my rule of government, in the administration of public affairs; and I shall not omit observing it in
meeting the General Assembly, according to the Proro-
gation. With whom I shall under the guidance of my
duty to the King, and zeal for the service of the Province,
do everything in my power that can contribute to the
public welfare."

The Congress withdrew, recommended the inhabitants
to learn the use of arms and drill once a fortnight, and
appointed " a day of fasting, humiliation and prayer before
Almighty God, devoutly to petition Him to inspire the
King with true wisdom to defend the people of North
America in their just title to freedom and avert the
calamities of civil war." The Congress then adjourned,

leaving the authority in the hands of the Charles Town Committee.

Before adjourning, however, it appointed by its President a *secret* committee, with "authority to procure and distribute such articles as the present insecure state of the interior parts of this colony renders necessary for the better defence and security of the good people of those parts, *and other necessary purposes.*"

"To see that the State take no harm" was hardly more enigmatic — or significant; of course it meant securing the means of defence, for, says Drayton, "in those days words were used in public resolutions, calculated to bear ample constructions for the public service." For this committee Colonel Pinckney (President of the Provincial Congress) appointed Mr. William Henry Drayton, giving him permission to select his associates. Mr. Drayton chose Arthur Middleton, C. C. Pinckney, William Gibbes (a grandson of the former Governor), and Edward Weyman, a very clever young artisan said to have a "peculiar gift for secret and dangerous undertakings"; all of whom were confirmed by the President.

The day of fasting and prayer was very solemn. The Commons House went in procession from the State House to St. Philip's (about four squares), the Speaker in his purple robes and full-bottomed wig, with the silver mace borne before him, walking at their head. The members were, Moultrie (who was among them) says, "Many of them in their military array. On their entering the church the organ began a solemn piece of music, and continued playing until they were seated. It was an affecting scene, as every one knew the occasion, and all joined in fervent prayer to the Lord to support and defend us in our great struggle in the cause of Liberty and our Country." The Reverend Dr. Smith, at the request of the Provincial Congress, delivered an excellent and suitable discourse " on

the occasion which very much animated the men; whilst
the female part of the congregation were affected in quite
a different manner; floods of tears rolled down their
cheeks, from the sad reflection of their nearest and dearest
friends and relations entering into a dreadful civil war,
the worst of wars; and what was most to be lamented, it
could not be avoided."

The emotional nature of woman expresses itself in
tears; but it may be doubted if the great majority of the
women saw the end as clearly as Moultrie did. They
still hoped — *not* desperately. Mrs. Pinckney's letter
on this occasion is quite cheerful, admiring the "good
patriotic Xtian like sermon," and a few days later she
says : —

"The King has promised to receive the petitions . . .
all the Islands and the London merchants are about to
petition. . . . Capt. Turner is also arrived and says there
is a prospect of the Acts being repealed.

"Pray God it may prove true."

In a letter published in the same book, " Eliza Pinckney," a friend of Mrs. Pinckney's, Miss Trapier of Georgetown, writes to her : —

" I see by these preparations of tents, etc., that our soldiers are making ready for the field. I hope there will be
little occasion for them. Heaven interests itself in the
cause of those who have virtue to assist the birthright of
mankind. Divine Liberty ! and Britain surely will shortly
be taught by our successes and continued unanimity, in
spite of all their base acts to disunite us, that America
determines to be free, and that it is beyond the force of
arms to enslave so vast a Continent."

" The blank commissions have come," says another letter ; but where were the arms and munitions of war ? In
the third story of the State House, and in the powder
magazines, all under the guard of his Majesty's keepers !

Clearly this was the business of the "Secret Committee." Accordingly, at dead of night, the five young fellows, and two others, Mr. Benjamin Huger, Mr. Drayton's brother-in-law, and his cousin William Bull, son of the Governor's brother Stephen, having posted sentries and engaged the assistance of some labourers, proceeded to break open the door of the King's armoury. Whereupon there appeared upon the scene, Colonel Pinckney, the President of Congress, the Hon. Henry Laurens, chairman of the General Committee, and Mr. Thomas Lynch, delegate to the Continental Congress.

It was certainly an open secret. The elder gentlemen of course came because they did not choose to leave the younger ones to bear the blame of an act of violence which they themselves had tacitly authorized.

Before daylight they had removed a quantity of muskets, cutlasses, cartouches, belts, etc., and had stored them in the cellars of two houses near the State House, belonging to William Gibbes. At the same time other parties under Christopher Gadsden carried off all the powder in the magazines out of town, and secured that also. This was done without any disguises, but under cover of darkness, in order to avoid "insulting the authority of the Lt. Governor, who was so much respected and beloved, by performing it in open day" — a most peculiar piece of delicacy!

The poor Governor! His only possible proceeding was to lay the matter before his sadly reduced council. That body advised him to send "a mild message to the Commons House then sitting, informing them of what had been done." His Honour, of course, knew perfectly that members of the Commons themselves had done the deed, but he sent the information with due formality, and commended the matter to "the serious investigation and consideration of the General Assembly." The House, fully prepared for the little comedy which was the prelude to so serious a drama, appointed a committee of investigation : Mr. Bee, a lawyer, soon to be a judge, Dr. Olyphant, an eminent physician, Colonel Gaillard and Mr. Izard, planters. They reported to the House that having made all possible inquiry, they had been unable to get *any* information relative to the removal of the arms and gunpowder mentioned in his Honour's message, but " think there is reason to suppose that some of the inhabitants of this colony may have been induced to take so uncommon and extraordinary a step, in consequence of the late alarming reports received from Great Britain," which communication Mr. Speaker forwarded to his Honour with a copy of said reports. These were that Parliament had refused to receive the petitions, had declared Massachusetts in a state of rebellion, and forbade commercial intercourse with the other colonies. Receiving no help from the Commons, the Governor himself examined Mrs. Pratt, the keeper of the State House. But although Mrs. Pratt (who deserves immortality) had seen and heard the whole affair, she had understood nothing ! Not a word of useful information could his Honour get from Mrs. Pratt. Nor was he more successful with the captain of the town watch, stationed at the opposite corner. He had seen a few people in the street ; they had made no disturbance ; he had noticed nothing.

Eight hundred stand of arms, two hundred cutlasses, cartouches, flints, and matches (those were the days of Brown Bess), and eleven hundred pounds of gunpowder had been carried unseen through the public streets, as upon the invisible carpet of the " Arabian Nights " !

It sounds like a tale of the Ku-Klux time, when towns and villages went deaf and blind as wild Justice passed by!

All hope of a peaceful solution was soon at an end.

Again the delegates were summoned to Philadelphia, and sailed, despite of admonitions to caution from Rawlins Lowndes, with assurances from the General Committee that whatever they decided should be sustained. Seldom has more confidence been placed in men. In three days after their departure the fast-sailing brigantine, the *Industry*, outstripping the express rider by four days, brought the news that the war had begun. The battle of Lexington had been fought and " the shot heard round the world " greeted the dawn of a new day.

CHAPTER XII

THE gravity of the situation was apparent to all.   The
General Committee at once summoned the Provincial
Congress, of which (Colonel Charles Pinckney resigning)
Mr. Henry Laurens was elected President.   A committee
of ways and means to put the colony in a state of defence
was first appointed; and then, June 4, 1775, was formed,
not lightly or unadvisedly, but after earnest thought and
debate, that solemn association, signed, immediately after
divine service had been performed before them, by the
President and all of the members.

They pledged themselves " under every tie of Religion
and Honour to associate as a band in the defence of South
Carolina, against every foe. . . .   Solemnly engaging
that whenever our Continental or Provincial Congresses
shall deem it necessary, we will go forth and be ready to
sacrifice our lives and fortunes to secure her freedom and
safety."

It was the first formal declaration of that devotion
which, for weal or woe, the sons of Carolina have ever
given to their State.

The Congress voted to raise two full regiments of foot
and one of horse, and a million of money.   Of this last,
Moultrie says at a little later time: "We talked of millions
and it was next to nothing.   There was one conveniency
in it, a couple of men on horseback with bags could con-

vey a million of dollars from one end of the country to the other in a little time with facility."

It (the Congress), then feeling itself too large and unwieldy a body for prompt action, appointed a Committee of Safety, to be in all respects, in finance, commissions, defences, military organizations, etc., the executive power of the Province, and having done all these things it sent a courteous message to the lieutenant-governor to inform him of the proceedings.

But the moment of William Bull's release had come. The booming of the guns which announced the arrival of H.M.S. *Scorpion*, bringing Lord William Campbell to his new government, spared the gallant old man the pain of receiving and answering the message. He could not, he said, receive any communication when his Excellency was in the colony. The messengers withdrew and the Lieutenant-governor hurried from Ashley Hall to receive his successor.

Lord William probably owed his appointment to his marriage with Miss Izard, which would, it might be presumed, give him some interest and popularity in the colony.

But for this, the ministers would hardly have sent so dull a man to such a post at such a time.

The young people had paid a short visit to Charles Town after their marriage in quieter times, but there had been, legend says, some curiosity to know how they — and particularly " Sally Izard " — would bear her elevation to such a dignity. Would she be natural and agreeable as Lady Charles had been (she, poor thing, had died at Exeter a short time before), or would her title and her dignity turn her head, and " make her airish"? This gossip had been, but times were too serious now.

There was no reason to suppose that the new Governor would bring tidings of any better disposition of the ministers, and it was but a cold welcome which met the young man on the quay. The necessary forms were observed; the militia were arranged in order, " but they made no *feu de joie*, as had ever been their custom; " no prominent gentleman went on board, to meet and escort him to the Council Chamber; only a few placemen, fifteen at most, attended his parade, and when his commission was read before him from the steps of the New Exchange, it was received in sullen silence. It was impossible not to see that the people were angry, and to contrast this with the boisterous enthusiasm of the welcome given to Lord Charles only a few years before.

Standing on the steps of the Exchange to-day, it is impossible to escape a feeling of sympathy for the young man thrust by no fault of his own into so impossible a situation.

Mrs. Blake's Meeting Street house had been chosen as the residence of the new Governor and his lady (her cousin); but it was not quite ready when they arrived, and they were invited to become the guests of another cousin, Mrs. Miles Brewton, in her King Street house. Here they were hospitably and handsomely entertained, and all her old friends called upon the lady. But there could be no ease or comfort in their endeavours to show sympathy or kindliness, while all knew that their husbands and brothers were ranged in direct opposition to all that her husband represented. Her own sister, Mrs. Arthur Middleton, was the wife of one of the leaders of the extreme party; her brothers, Walter and Ralph, were " patriots "; there were but few whose opinions did not agree with them.

No sooner were they arrived than the delegation of the Provincial Congress desired admission. The Congress whose very existence he was bound to deny! The address was brought by ten newly made captains and colonels, only two besides his host, Mr. Brewton, retaining their pacific designations and costumes.

It set forth that they were the humble and loyal subjects of his Majesty, defending themselves against arbitrary impositions and grievances; that "the hands of His Majesty's Ministers having long lain heavy, now press upon us with intolerable weight. . . . No love of innovation, . . . no lust of independence, has had the least effect upon our counsels, . . . solely for the preservation and in defence of our lives, liberties and properties have we taken up arms. . . . We sincerely deplore those slanderous informations, those wicked counsels by which his Majesty has been led into these measures . . . and we wish for nothing more ardently than for a speedy reconciliation with the Mother Country upon Constitutional principles . . . we readily profess our loyal attachment to our Sovereign, his Crown and Dignity . . . our taking up arms is the result of a dire necessity and in compliance with the first law of nature," and much more to the same effect.

One is bound to believe all one's grandfathers ; but although it is undoubtedly perfectly true, that all, except Gadsden and possibly two or three others, would have rejoiced at "a speedy reconciliation upon Constitutional grounds," yet from what terrible wrongs and grievances the people of Carolina were then suffering is beyond the power of this present writer to perceive ! A threat of what would be done if a trifling tax were not paid was so far the worst.

Lord William's reply was dignified and straightforward. He knew, he said, no such body as the Provincial Congress; only the General Assembly as by law appointed. He had not yet had time to study the " unhappy disputes " and make a report of them to his Majesty, but assured them that " no representation shall ever be made by me but what shall be strictly consonant with truth, and with an earnest endeavour to promote the real happiness and prosperity of the Province."

The delegation withdrew, and Lord William was left to study the address. He had not the advantage of Governor Bull's advice, for he had hastened forty miles away from noise and strife to soothe his vexed spirit among his beloved rice fields, at his plantation of Sheldon in Prince William's parish. So carefully did he keep out of the way that Lord William afterward reported that he had only seen him for one day while in Charles Town!

The more his Excellency pondered the address, the less he liked it. He seems honestly, at first, to have desired reconciliation, and the words " we have taken up arms," " we shall take up arms," alarmed him greatly. Such words had not been spoken to any English King since the days of the Stuarts. Was another " Great Rebellion " about to begin?

Mr. Miles Brewton, Lord William's host, was one of the most conservative of the patriotic party, — one of those who, Drayton intimates, acted as balance-wheel to their more impetuous comrades. With him the new Governor talked earnestly and long that evening. He would do much, and could do much, he said, to smooth away difficulties if those words were withdrawn. They amounted to a threat, and who dare threaten a King ? Their immediate effect would be to cause troops to be sent to Charles Town.

His anxiety was so great that he even called Mr. Brewton from his bed in the middle of the night to discuss the matter which had murdered sleep, and entreated him to use his influence with the Committee to substitute some less offensive phrase. Mr. Brewton at last assented and the uneasy young Governor sought his couch.

Mr. Brewton did his best. He consulted with the three of the Committee whom he thought most likely to listen patiently to Lord William's representations. They, however, agreed that no such proposition could be entertained for a moment, and the idea was abandoned.

The Congress adjourned and the Committee of Safety ruled in its stead, Henry Laurens being chairman of the one, as he was President of the other.

Officers were appointed for the two regiments, but there was some hesitation as to how their commission should read, " for the majority of the Committee was not yet prepared for such independent action as issuing them under seal." Moultrie was made colonel of the second regiment, and has left a copy of that given to him, on plain paper with no seal.

" In pursuance of the Resolutions of the Provincial Congress we do certify that William Moultrie Esqr., is Colonel of the 2nd Regiment of the Provincial Congress.

" Dated the 17th June, 1775, and signed by all the Committee of Safety."

The officers fully understood the step they were taking. Moultrie says of this time : —

" Charles Town looked like a garrison town, everything wore the face of war, though not one of us had the least idea of its approach, for we were anxiously looking forward to a reconciliation . . . when on the 19th of April, 1775, war was declared against America by the British troops firing upon the inhabitants of Lexington. . . .

" We were without money, without arms, without ammunition, no generals, no armies, no admirals, no fleets. — This was our situation when the contest began against the country which we had been taught to consider and respect as the finest in the world."

Moultrie had for his lieutenent-colonel his brother-in-law Isaac Motte, grandson of the first Huguenot immigrant of the name, who had long been Royal treasurer of the Province; another brother was one of his captains.

Francis Marion, the favourite Revolutionary hero of South Carolina, was his major. Marion, born of Huguenot parents, came from St. John's parish. In boyhood he had shown a great desire for the sea, and had been allowed to go as a sailor on a trial trip to the West Indies. The trial was short. The schooner was wrecked, the crew took to their boats. That in which Marion with three companions was, drifted about on the ocean for many days before being picked up. The men were saved from starvation by devouring a dog, which had jumped into the boat as they pushed off. A hurricane, a wreck, a burning sea, and raw dog flesh were too much for the would-be seaman, who returned home to become one of the most famous of partisan leaders.

Christopher Gadsden, then in Philadelphia, was made colonel of the 1st, with Isaac Huger (afterward general) for lieutenant-colonel, and Owen Roberts, grandson of the Huguenot pastor " Robert," for his major. The company officers were young men of all the best names of the Province. Moultrie speaks of the eagerness to secure commissions. There might be doubt about political movements, but there was none when it came to military service.

The " Secret Committee " in the meanwhile was at still more dangerous work. Gunpowder was in great demand — a reward was offered to whoever should make it; therefore they resolved to plunder upon the high seas !

It had come to their knowledge that Wright, Royal Governor of Georgia, had ordered an armed schooner to lie in the mouth of the Savannah, to meet and convoy an English vessel which was expected to arrive with a large supply of the precious dust on board.

It was too tempting a prize to be lightly resigned. The committee in turn armed a schooner, got her commissioned by the Congress of Georgia then sitting, and sent her to sea with a crew from both Provinces. Captain John Barnwell and Captain Joyner for South Carolina, Captains Brown and Habersham for Georgia, in command. At sight of them the Governor's schooner took flight, the ship with sixteen thousand pounds of powder was overhauled and had to give up her valuable freight, the powder equitably divided, and the affair kept secret! Evidently, as said before, words were used " with liberal constructions " in those days.

This *escapade* had important results, for an innocent-looking schooner laden with sacks of corn came down from Philadelphia, sent by the delegation, to William Henry Drayton, Arthur Middleton, and C. C. Pinckney. These gentlemen were entreated to send on all the powder possible, for the war had begun in Massachusetts, and the supply there was nearly exhausted. The committee rejoiced that its piratical exploit should have so happy a justification, took the schooner round into North Edisto Inlet, and with the assistance of Georgia loaded her with a liberal supply of powder, covered the casks with rice tierces, and sent her to sea. She arrived safely, "and it was by the arrival of this powder that the American arms penetrated into Canada, and the siege of Boston was continued." Governor Drayton adds, with filial pride, that this enterprise was conducted on the sole authority of these young men, "and had the Revolution not taken place, but Colonial affairs settled down to a Rebellion, there is no doubt but that these distinguished patriots would have been marked out as early victims to private persecution, and British vengeance."

By this time Bunker Hill had been fought, Congress had appointed general officers for an army, and Washington had been made commander-in-chief.

Lord and Lady William now established themselves in their own house, and Moultrie says that his Lordship made himself very agreeable to the younger men, with whom he was on easy and sociable terms, promising commissions and so on. Also the ladies called upon the "Governor's Lady."

P

His Excellency had not yet met the Commons House — the body which he himself had declared to be the lawful representatives of the people; but on the 10th of July it assembled, and he found himself confronted by the same men to whom he had refused to listen, when they appeared as the Provincial Congress. His address was reasonable and well intended, but though he had spoken with the tongues of men and angels, he could have made no effect. Only one thing could have brought peace and that one thing he had no authority to promise. The Commons, by their Speaker, Rawlins Lowndes, answered, deploring the state of affairs, and especially that his Excellency should say "*if* there were any grievances when the whole world resounded with them!" etc. There was no satisfaction to either party. Usually the Governor prorogued the unruly Assembly, but now the Assembly begged to be prorogued. It would do no business, adjourned from day to day, answered his Excellency's exhortations with baffling speeches, and turned the deafest of ears to the subject of appropriations. Lord William declined to prorogue, but despairing of making any impression, bethought himself of the "back country," as everything above fifty miles from the coast was then called. The people of that section were by no means devoted to the patriotic cause, and he soon received promises of help from them. The Executive Committee was anxious about it, too, and was trying to secure its aid.

William Henry Drayton and the Reverend Mr. Tennant, a Congregationalist minister from New England, and a zealous patriot, were sent to inquire into the state of feeling there, and to endeavour to arouse some interest in their cause. They had no success; the few who promised aid under the influence of Drayton's fiery eloquence soon returning to their former ways of thinking;

but they discovered that the Governor was carrying on a secret correspondence with these people, and inciting them to turn their arms against their countrymen. Drayton was so assured of this that he wrote to the Committee of Safety urging them to " take the Governor into custody." The Committee was not prepared for any such decisive measure. The Councils of State were not very energetic just then, for of the leaders of the active party Arthur Middleton alone was present.

Christopher Gadsden, John Rutledge, Henry Middleton, Thomas Lynch, and Edward Rutledge were in Philadelphia, Moultrie and C. C. Pinckney were drilling their newly raised soldiers, and Drayton was in the up-country. The conservative party for once had the power; Laurens, Bee, Brewton, C. Pinckney, speaking generally by Rawlins Lowndes, resisted Middleton's plea for aggressive measures. It is wonderful, considering what very different opinions the members of the Committee held, that they got on without open quarrel. But to the credit of their manners and their self-control there was no collision. Provocation there must have been on both sides. A favourite measure with Drayton and Middleton was the confiscation of the property of those persons who had left the Province, or who refused to sign the association. This Lowndes and his party steadily opposed, and Middleton wrote to Drayton: —

" The matter is not *rejected* only *postponed*. Rawlins *Postponator* declares the resolution not proper to proceed from the committee of South Carolina, and so arbitrary that only the Divan of Constantinople could think of promulgating such a law."

Opposition to such a measure is easily understood. The young men were quite too arbitrary in many ways, as when they punished Mr. Wragg, a consistent Royalist, for refusing to sign the association. First they desired him "to remain within the limits of his 'Barony,'" and then compelled him to take ship for Amsterdam. The ship was wrecked, and Mr. Wragg was drowned. He had escaped the tender mercies of Blackbeard to perish by the injustice of his countrymen. Had he known in death that a monument to his virtues and loyalty would be erected in Westminster Abbey, it *might* have been a consolation.

Governor Drayton tells, with a certain sense of awe, that the Committee even dared to approach his revered great-uncle, the Lieutenant-governor, on the subject of the association. But he, whose good sense and dignity never failed him, answered calmly, that he "wished as well to his country as any man could do," his heart and hand were hers, but holding his Majesty's commission as he still did, "even you gentlemen would look upon me in an odd light were I to subscribe an instrument of this kind." The rebuked visitors held their peace.

The Secret Committee next had recourse to the terrible punishment of tar and feathers!

Three poor wretches, convicted of various malpractices against the Revolutionary party, were by its order "exalted" and paraded through the streets.

The Governor naturally was enraged and alarmed. If he knew, as perhaps he did, that his plots with the up-country had been discovered, it was no wonder that he was so; but being a brave man he met the emergency boldly, and sent a message to the Commons House, expressing his disgust and horror, ending: —

"In a word, gentlemen, you well know that the powers of the Government are wrested out of my hands; I can neither protect nor punish. Therefore with the advice of his Majesty's Council I apply to you, and desire that in this dreadful emergency you will aid me with all the assistance in your power, in protecting his Majesty's servants" (one of the men ill-used had been an English soldier), "and all other peaceable and faithful subjects, in that quiet possession of their lives and property, which every Englishman boasts it is his birthright to enjoy; or you must candidly acknowledge that all law and government is at an end. Sorry I am to add that some particular insults offered to myself make it necessary that I should be assured of the safety of my own family, and that its peace is not in danger of being invaded."

The Royal Governors were certainly badly treated by their home government. About the same time Governor Wright of Georgia wrote to General Gage : —

"I have neither men nor money. The Governors had better be in England than remain in America to see *their* powers executed by Committees and mobs."

In answer to Lord William's complaint, the Commons appointed a committee of inquiry and made Miles Brewton the chairman. The committee after some days reported that they greatly regretted that in the disturbed state of the community violences by mobs could hardly be prevented. That the particular case to which his Lordship referred had taken place under circumstances of peculiar aggravation; that it was really not worse than punishments "frequently inflicted by an English mob upon very petty offenders, surrounded by an active magistracy and even in full view of his Majesty's palace " (alluding to the pillory which long stood near St. James's). " They were very sorry that any particular insults should have been offered to his Excellency, or that he should have any reason to apprehend that the peace and dignity of his family were in danger. They hoped and trusted that his Excellency's wise and prudent conduct would render such apprehensions groundless ; and that on their part every endeavour would be used to promote and inculcate a proper veneration and respect for the character of his Majesty's Representative."

The two men, Lord William and Mr. Brewton, connected by marriage, and on friendly terms, must have both felt to how little such a message amounted.

During these months in Charles Town Lord William had found means of communicating with Fletchall, Cunningham, and other "well-affected" men of the middle country, and had given them liberty to do what they pleased to recapture the Province for the King. A man named Kirkland had managed to elude the vigilance of the different committees, and had had some interviews with his Lordship. This Drayton discovered while with Fletchall; hence his advice to arrest the Governor. The strong opposition of Rawlins Lowndes had spared him that ignominy, but thenceforward he and his household were under surveillance. Captain McDonald, 1st Regiment, disguised himself as a back countryman, and supposed by his Excellency to be a sergeant of Kirkland's company, and empowered by him to carry information to his friends, learned that Lord William had lately received letters from the King, promising that troops should shortly arrive, that the colonies should be subjugated from one end to the other, and that South Carolina would be the seat of war.

Lord William also informed Captain McDonald that although he would send him for safety, as he had already sent Kirkland, aboard the *Tamar* man-of-war, then lying in the harbour, he was as well off in Charles Town, as the militia were ill disposed to the Commons and ready to turn against them.

A man named Floyd also testified that Lord William had said to him, " Tell the people in the back country to do the best they can ; he did not *desire* any effusion of blood, but *whatever they should do*, would meet with his consent."

This was news for an irresolute Council of Safety ! Should the Governor at once be taken into custody ? Mr.

Lowndes again opposing and Mr. Middleton urging the step. They first sent to demand that the Governor should show his despatches, and should deliver to them Moses Kirkland. His Excellency promptly and indignantly refused to do either. Both parties were now on the *qui vive*. The Committee determined to seize Fort Johnson, and gave orders that it should be done the same night, but Lord William was too quick for them. He had been on his way to the waterside when the Committee had met him. After a few hours of consultation with the commander of the *Tamar*, Captain Thornborough, he returned to his house, and early in the night Mr. Innes, his secretary, with a force of the *Tamar's* crew, went to Fort Johnson, dismounted the guns, and withdrew the garrison, before three companies of Colonel Moultrie's regiment, commanded by Lieutenant-colonel Motte, reached the island. Three men surrendered the fort. Luckily the departing force had overthrown but not spiked the guns. They were soon remounted and good as ever.

Lord William now understood that all was over. Taking with him the Great Seal of the Province, the emblem of sovereignty, he entered a small boat on a branch of Vander Horst's Creek, which came up to the back of his garden, and went on board the *Tamar*, riding at anchor in Rebellion Roads. Thence he issued a proclamation dissolving the Commons House of Assembly. This was done on the fifteenth day of September, 1775, and ended the existence of the General Assembly of South Carolina, which had ruled the Province since its first meeting on St. Helena Island in the year 1660 under the government of William Sayle.

Never again was " God save the King " to express the love and fealty of the people.

With no Governor and no Commons, the government was entirely in the hands of the General Committee, which sent a deputation to the *Tamar* requesting his Excellency's return, and assuring him that if he would repeat his declaration to take no active steps against the colony, he should be safe and respected in the town. Lord William replied that he "had made no such declaration which would have been inconsistent with his duty to his King, and that when he returned to Charles Town it would be for the purpose of protecting the loyal inhabitants."

The Committee was by no means happy. The differences of opinion among the people were great. Many who had seemed urgent in the cause were now lukewarm, the militia was insubordinate, the open rupture distressed many who had always expected reconciliation, and the conflicting opinions within the Executive Committee itself prevented any prompt and vigorous measures. Henry Laurens wrote to the delegation in Congress telling all that had occurred and asking direction. He says of the Governor : —

"His Lordship had not only shown a fair face when waited upon, but had in the most condescending terms invited Gentlemen to call on him, in order to give him opportunity for expressing his good wishes to the Colony, while he was at the time privately spiriting up the people of our Frontiers to oppose our Association, and to hold themselves in readiness to act in Arms against the Colony." He relates the circumstances as given, and adds: "We intend to persevere in repairing the Fort" (Johnson) "and will put it in the best posture of defence. We also intend to fortify the Harbour, . . . it is possible the man-of-war may interrupt our proceedings; in such case we shall be under the necessity of attempting to take or destroy her — we are at a loss to know to what lengths each Colony will be warranted by the Voice of America, in opposing and resisting the King's officers in general and the British Marine, tho' such opposition should be necessary for the very existence of the Colony, and support of the Common Cause."

This last seems, remembering what had already happened in Massachusetts, a singular question to ask. But it was one upon which men felt much doubt.

Four months later Stephen Bull of Sheldon, colonel commanding at Port Royal, wrote to ask what should be done against predatory parties, and Laurens after some explanations concludes decidedly : —

" To avoid all mistakes and misconstructions it is our opinion that you ought to fire when you see proper upon the enemy in his advance to rob or annoy you."

To understand the hesitation we must remember that many of these men had once fought as Englishmen ; and not without a pang at heart, even under deepest provocation, do men fire upon the flag which once was theirs.

The delegation wrote to urge that all the cannon should be mounted at the town, and the harbour be defended to the last extremity. But a strange lethargy seemed to pervade the Committee, and little was done until November, when the Provincial Congress met and William Henry Drayton was chosen President. Drayton was at first by no means pleased with his elevation, and declared that he had been made presiding officer " in order to gag him." If his opponents had ever entertained such an idea, it proved that they little knew the man.

Drayton's whole soul was now in the work of defending the country and establishing her independence. Not Gadsden himself had cut more completely loose from all bonds of the past; and instead of Gadsden's rough and turgid though forcible speech, Drayton was an eloquent and graceful orator. No hard and fast parliamentary rules confined him to " putting the question" and keeping order. Every debate was closed by an address from the chair, summing up the arguments and giving his own views with such force, that he became much more effective as President than ever before. His ideas of military and especially of naval matters amused Colonel Moultrie, who declares that he was "neither soldier nor sailor and did not know one rope from another," but at all events he meant that in some way the town should be defended. His first scheme was to block up the channels by sinking hulks, — a plan which has since been tried. It was useless, of course; but it had one effect which he desired, that of provoking the enemy's fleet to open fire.

All the summer the *Tamar* and the *Cherokee* had been lying in and about the harbour; sometimes going to sea for a day or two, sometimes sailing composedly under the guns of Fort Johnson, but never firing a shot.

Now, however, when they saw the channels through which they were accustomed to pass being blocked up, especially that between the shoal which now bears Castle Pinckney and the opposite marsh (known as Hog Island Channel, the same into which the tea had been thrown), they threw half a dozen shots at the hulks to stop proceedings.

The shots fell short, perhaps were not intended to hit, but rather as a protest.

It was, however, quite enough for the gallant President of Congress. He had fitted out a little schooner called the *Defence* with a few small guns, manned her with thirty-five men under Captain Scott of Colonel Moultrie's regiment, as marines, and was on board as commander himself. It was this which excited Moultrie's amusement, but Drayton knew what he meant. Captain Simon Tufts could sail his vessel, and Captain Scott fight his men, but he, and no other, was to give the word when to begin this momentous war.

Accordingly as soon as possible the *Defence* sailed up,

cast anchor, and opened fire on the astonished *Tamar*. Not many shots were exchanged, the turning of the tide separating the antagonists ; but at four next morning the fight was renewed, the *Cherokee* coming to the assistance of her consort. All the time Captain Blake went on diligently sinking his hulks, regardless of the heavy fire. The gunners at Fort Johnson, longing to join in the fray, fired their heavy cannon, but the distance was too great for them to do any damage. Not until the last hulk was sunk did the little *Defence* turn and sail back to the wharf. There she was received with the shouts and cheers of the populace, who had " crowded to East Bay to witness the engagement, or to indulge in the anxious cares which were thereby excited," while Mr. Drayton, who had been on board the whole time, received the congratulations of his friends. The *Defence* had five or six shots in her hull and rigging, the British ships the same, and no one on board any vessel was hurt !

" Anxious cares " were for the moment forgotten. Drayton had done his work, that which he had set himself to do, well; he not only committed the people to his darling policy, but he had excited their enthusiasm. Men's blood boiled with the sound of the guns, and for some time all was activity. A ship in port, the *Prosper*, was seized and armed, the universal Mr. Drayton was promptly commissioned captain (to the amusement of some, as has been said), and everybody concerned in the affair of the *Defence* was formally thanked by Congress, of course after " Divine Service being performed by the Reverend Paul Turquand." They also informed the Council of Safety of Georgia that they intended to attack the men-of-war and asked to borrow some powder. This last declaration disturbed the conservative party greatly. Prepared for defensive measures, they were not yet ready to take the offensive, still clinging to the habits of their lives.

Every "resolution" thus introduced was combated well and strongly by Rawlins Lowndes, and urged with greater vehemence, if not more reason, by Drayton and Middleton. Of these parties Mr. Drayton's son says : —

"It must not be supposed that the persons leading the opposition had any but the purest views. . . . It must not be forgotten that the citizens of South Carolina did not lead, but followed in the Revolution. They had been mildly treated by the Royal Government, and therefore did not easily resign British protection. Hence the public mind weighed how far it should support violent measures against the Ancient Government. . . . Revolutionary principles led them step by step to concede points as proper and patriotic, which a short time before they had thought disloyal and inadvisable."

These gentlemen of the opposition were, he says, "kept in place as eliciting more prudent measures," and "that their conduct in so doing was not disapproved, the high public stations to which many of them were afterwards called during the most critical times of the Revolution will be the best assurance of the public approbation."

Things were going too fast for the moderate party now; the warlike preparations went on, work on the *Prosper* by day and night, etc.; but still reverencing "his Majesty's Representative," it was resolved "that previous to any attack upon the men-of-war in the Roads, the intended attack upon such ships shall be notified to Lord William Campbell if he shall then be on board."

A piece of courtesy worthy of "*Messieurs les gants glacés*," but one of which Lord William, a gallant Scotchman, would never have availed himself.

Having done all this the Congress adjourned, leaving authority to the Council of Safety; but first, with a delicate irony, it requested that the "Hon. Mr. Lowndes shall return the thanks of the House to the Hon. Wm.

Henry Drayton Pres. for the diligence and propriety with which he has discharged the duties, etc., etc."

Mr. Lowndes had fought Mr. Drayton every day of the session, and did not hesitate to say that he was driving to destruction. Nevertheless, with the stately formality of the period, in the most courteous terms he thanked Mr. President for the "integrity of heart, ability of mind, and unwearied attendance which have given the most perfect satisfaction." Those were the days of manners !

The Council of Safety, strengthened by the addition of Henry Middleton and John Rutledge, who had returned from Philadelphia, now seriously took up the question of fortifying the harbour. Another vessel had joined the *Cherokee* and the *Tamar*, the *Scorpion*, Captain Tollemache, which had on board a second fugitive Governor, Joseph Martin, of North Carolina. Lord William and Captain Tollemache wished to open the war themselves by attacking Fort Johnson, but the Captain of the *Tamar* refused, saying that his vessel could not stand the guns. This plan of his Lordship and Captain Tollemache became known in the town, and the excitement was great.

The threat of attack becoming imminent, the misery of " refugeeing " began. People sent their women and children out of harm's way. Mr. Laurens says, " I have just sent Mrs. R. and Miss C. to Mr. Harleston's in St. Johns, Mrs. P. E. and M. have gone as far as Amelia Township, and Mrs. Manigault with vast reluctance will at last be persuaded to go to Silk Hope — but she says that she shall never return." Silk Hope was the plantation on Cooper River where Sir Nathaniel Johnson had formerly raised silk; it had been bought by Mr. Gabriel Manigault.

Mrs. Horrÿ, writing at the same time, gives a lively picture of the situation and of the way in which it was met. She writes to her friend and connection, Miss Trapier, at

Georgetown, the lady whose letter has already been quoted: —

"How distant is the prospect of felicity now ! How uncertain 'tis when we shall meet again! My Mother (Mrs. Pinckney), Daniel (her baby), and myself, intend to go to a little Plantation house at Ashepoo" (a river about twenty miles south of Charleston) "in search of safety, when we can no longer stay here. Think with what reluctance I must leave the place of my Nativity, this poor unhappy Town devoted to the flames, when I leave in it my Husband, Brothers, and every known male relative I have (infants excepted) exposed to every danger that can befall it, were their lives but safe, I think I could bear with some degree of fortitude the Evils of Indigence that stare us in the face, however hard to human nature, and to human Pride.

"Mr. Trapier" (commandant at Georgetown) "will inform you of affairs here, and of the mortifying fact of the number of disaffected in our Province to the American cause. I really believe that the Gaiety and Levity reported of our Sex in Town, is very unjust; I have seen very little of the first and nothing of the second, indeed I think dejection appears at present, the Cloud that hangs over us, ready to burst upon our heads, calls for all our Fortitude to meet the awful event with that decency and resignation becoming a Xtian. . . . Almost all the Women and many hundred *Men* have left Town! In a few days I imagine we shall have hardly a female acquaintance to speak to. . . . My brother (C. C. Pinckney) is at ye Fort. Tom at present recruiting. Mr. Horrÿ goes to ye Fort to-morrow to spend a month."

Women and non-combatants have the hardest fate in war time. While the sister was penning this unhappy letter, the brothers were writing gayly from the fort — that victory is certain — will the ships only come in, and they want for nothing, but "another waist coat and two pairs of socks."

The immediate cause for this alarm was the order issued by William Henry Drayton as President of the Provincial Congress, "To the American officer commanding at Fort Johnson, by every military operation to endeavour to oppose the passage of any British naval armament that might attempt to pass."

Most happily the British ships did *not* attempt to pass. They could have run by easily, and bombarded the town at their leisure, for there was nothing to guard the shores of Sullivan's Island and Haddrell's Point (now Mount Pleasant). But the *Tamar* and the *Cherokee* contented themselves with lying in the roads and looking dangerous. Lord William was still on board; his wife had been sent to a place of safety. After some days both vessels sailed away south, to the relief of the people, it being now determined to fortify the island. The Council sent for Colonel Owen Roberts and put him in charge of the work. The cheapness of war then is a frightful contrast to the military budget of the present.

"Mr. Dewees" (owner of the island two north of Sullivan's, which still bears his name) "is to furnish palmetto logs until further order, not less than ten inches diameter in the middle. One-third are to be eighteen feet long, the other two-thirds twenty feet long. They are to be delivered at such part of Sullivan's Island as shall be directed, and shall be allowed one shilling per foot for all such logs as delivered; in which delivery the utmost expedition must be used."

And this was the beginning of Fort Moultrie, which six months afterward was to withstand the bombardment of a British fleet.

Even before this time the Province had recognized that it was hard put to it for a government. It had no leader;

the Congress and Council were many-headed monsters, and all men felt that delay and vacillation were the inevitable results of the conflicting opinions of so many honest and, possibly, hard-headed men.

The Provincial Congress, finding itself in such a case, asked the advice of the Continental, which had other such questions before it, and it, after deliberation, advised that an election should be held for " a full and free Representation of the People " to compose a body for which should be renewed the name of General Assembly of South Carolina, and that this Assembly should decide upon a form of government which should maintain peace and order " during the continuance of the present dispute between Great Britain and the Colonies."

The Provincial Congress took the advice, with one very important exception. It was itself, it declared, a full and free representation of the people; why hold another election when here were the gentlemen of the country, all devoted to its interests and anxious only for the general good ? This was true enough as regarded the parishes, but the rest of the Province was hardly represented at all. Once more Rawlins Lowndes threw himself into the opposition. He and his party demanded the election, in order that the people might express their wishes more fully on this important point than they could do by a Congress elected so long before when the State affairs had been entirely different. He did not believe, he said, that the present body was vested with powers for this purpose.

The Congress, however, would pass no " self-denying ordinance " and voted to retain its power.

There was a terrible sensation when early in the session Christopher Gadsden, who had been wrecked upon the coast of North Carolina on his voyage from Philadelphia, produced three copies of Tom Paine's " Common Sense," which he had rescued from the waves, and sending one to

Savannah to enlighten the Georgians, presented another to the Congress, boldly advocating the declaration of absolute separation from Great Britain and Independence of America. Tom Paine and his books were, to most decent and law-abiding people then, as the Devil and all his works are to devout Christians to-day. Mr. Lowndes denounced them openly, cursing Paine roundly in full Congress, and John Rutledge rebuked his late colleague, Mr. Gadsden, warmly, declaring that he would himself ride post, day and night, to Philadelphia, to stop so terrible a disaster. These men did not abandon but were driven from their allegiance.

Mr. Gadsden silenced, a committee was appointed, of which Charles Cotesworth Pinckney was chairman, to frame a constitution, to be ready for discussion by the 5th of March.

The report was presented and over every important point debate arose. What the result might have been it is now impossible to say, for while still in progress news came from Savannah that a ship had arrived from England bringing an Act of Parliament passed in December, two months before.

The act declared the colonies to be in actual rebellion, authorized the capture of American vessels, and legalized all seizures of persons and property, and of damages done to the colonies before the passing of the act. It was equal to a declaration of war. There was nothing to be done but to look to themselves, and still hoping for ultimate reconciliation, purchase it by proof of strength and power.

Debate was checked, and in five days the Constitution was adopted. The preamble, written entirely in the handwriting of John Rutledge, differed from that originally proposed, by relating fully the differences between the mother country and the colonies, the desertion of Lord

Q

William Campbell, etc., and wound up with "it is become indispensably necessary that during the present situation of American affairs, and until an accommodation of the unhappy differences between Great Britain and America can be obtained (an event which though traduced and treated as rebels we still earnestly desire), some mode should be established by common consent and for the good of the people, *the origin and end of all government*, for regulating the internal polity of this Colony."

The Constitution as agreed upon provided that the colony should be governed by a President and Vice-president, a Legislative Council and a General Assembly. And the Provincial Congress, having wound up its existence as such by signing this Constitution through its President, Mr. Drayton, in the morning, met again in the afternoon as the General Assembly and proceeded to business.

It first elected the Council — no longer "his Majesty's" but "the Legislative" and then the officers — for President, John Rutledge; Vice-president, Henry Laurens. William Henry Drayton was made chief justice.

The members of the Legislative Council had generally been of the Council of Safety; but Richard Richardson, Le Roy Hammond, and Joseph Kershaw represented the middle of the Province, which had had no representation in the Council before.

This long — it may be feared tedious — account has been given, because this whole affair appears peculiarly characteristic of the people and the race. This great change was made so quietly, — in such accordance with usual custom, changing only that which had to be changed, — that life went on with little jar or confusion. Even when measures were not, as Revolutionary measures can hardly be, strictly legal, they were yet expressed and executed in such terms and forms of law, that the public mind was not shocked; the strongest prejudices were considered, and except in the instance of Gadsden's premature and audacious proposition, which Drayton says "fell like an explosion of thunder" into the House, there was no violence of language.

Contrast this with the French or South American Revolutions!

The choice of John Rutledge, the new President, was somewhat of a compromise brought about by the urgency of the moment. The Conservatives would have preferred Lowndes or Laurens, the Revolutionists Gadsden or Drayton. But in this moment of peril both parties were glad to agree upon a man of intellect and character, not given to extremes, and who had already, by strength of conviction and will, done great service to his country.

Chosen in his twenty-sixth year as a delegate to the Stamp Act Congress of 1766, "the members of the distant Provinces were," says Ramsay, "astonished at the eloquence of the young member from South Carolina."

The impression so made was never effaced. Nine years later, when the first Continental Congress was summoned to meet in Philadelphia, he, with Henry Middleton, was the choice of both parties. When Rawlins Lowndes moved to limit the powers of the delegates, it was he who successfully resisted the resolution. "Oratory was with Mr. Rutledge the vehicle by which sound common sense was given its most fitting and forcible expression." In a powerful speech, he advised the people to choose men in whom they had full confidence, and then to trust them absolutely.

When Mr. Lowndes (who had every reason to fear the superior numbers of the Northern colonies) asked, "What should be done if the Delegates should commit the State to rash action," he replied curtly, "Hang 'em." Plenary powers were bestowed.

Of Henry Laurens, Vice-president, much has already been said. His letters, freely quoted, show the man. He was wise and true in counsel, but slow in action; and saw too clearly all sides of a question to be a prompt or decisive leader. He was to fill great positions before long, and to fill them admirably.

A new selection of delegates for the Continental Congress was necessary.

Mr. Henry Middleton declined reëlection on the score of age and health. Mr. Thomas Lynch was stricken with paralysis in Philadelphia. Colonel Gadsden was to command his regiment, — and Mr. Rutledge the Province. Of the delegation Edward Rutledge alone remained available.

The General Assembly, as the Congress was once more called, reëlected him, chose Mr. Arthur Middleton and Mr. Thomas Lynch in their fathers' places, and Mr. Thomas Heyward to complete the number.

It then adjourned, leaving the President and Legislative Council to direct the preparations for the war which was soon to begin. The change of government was felt. Moultrie, who had suffered from the uncertain policy, says : —

"This new system opened such a scene of regularity, as confounded and astonished the disaffected, and gave great pleasure to the friends of the Revolution."

One would like to know what the women thought of it all. Women are by nature conservative and these Charles Town ladies had no reason to be otherwise. They were well contented with their lot in life ; enjoyed a ball at the Governor's mansion, liked a trip to England, and had small knowledge of the Province of Massachusetts Bay. Moreover they believed in the right divine of Kings (as of everything else in the prayer-book) and that they were made to do justice and judgment, — when not misled by wicked ministers. Women in Carolina were well trained in political thought, and knew the points at issue between the Council and Commons, for instance, as well as their husbands and brothers could do. Too many of them were estate owners and managers for them not to be versed in these matters; but when it came to the Lord's Anointed, it was a comfort to know that most of the clergy were on their side. Not all, indeed, for Mr. Bollman the Assistant at St. Michael's had been dismissed only a little time before for preaching "a most unmannerly discourse" and addressing his respectable congregation as "silly clowns and illiterate mechanics who ought not to censure the conduct of Princes and Governors." This was terrible to them, but when Mr. Smith gave his sermons, "most patriotick and Xtian," before the Congress, although they wept they were happy, for they felt they had the blessing of the church. Mr. Smith was the most distinguished of the clergy of the time, a fellow of Cambridge and a man of piety and talent. He was also very interesting to the fair sex, as being remarkably handsome and the hero of a romantic story. It was said that on his first arrival in Charles Town, as he came up from the wharf, he had been seen from the window by a handsome young lady, who then and there fell in love with him and declared that he, and he only, should be her husband. A beauty and an heiress is apt to have her way, and the attractive young cleric was captured. She — as is proper for a heroine of romance — died early, leaving no children, and he survived to be the husband of two other wives.

When once the war began, the women were, as is generally the case, the most enthusiastic, but in the beginning it was hard. The breaking of old ties, of loyalty that was religion, of kindred and affection — in all the higher class there was hardly a woman's heart that was not thus rent. They bore it as women do bear sacrifices called for by the men they love ; and in the end came peace and healing of wounds, and the pride of the Mothers of the Nation.

CHAPTER XII

BATTLE OF FORT MOULTRIE

THE realities which now faced the people of Charles Town were serious enough, but worse, far worse, were the threats which Dame Rumour diligently spread.

Of these, British instigation of Indian massacres and negro insurrections were the worst. The former report indeed proved that Rumours can, like the Father of Lies himself, sometimes speak truth. The manner in which Great Britain did, through her agents, incite the Indians to slay, torture, and ravage the inhabitants of the back country must always remain a blot on her scutcheon. But she never did emulate the fiendish atrocity of the Spaniards by exciting a servile insurrection. The report had just come in a letter from Arthur Lee, colonial agent; it had died out, revived, grown, and strengthened, until it told severely upon nervous people and timid women. Many persons left the Province in consequence. Among the most conspicuous of these was Miles Brewton, whose wife, a very nervous woman, persuaded him to take her and her children to Philadelphia, where were several members of her family (Izards), in order to escape the worst of dangers. Mr. Brewton, a consistent conservative, seems to have taken the same view of the state of affairs as Henry Laurens, and was probably, like him, glad to put his family in a place of comparative safety, while intending to return himself.

The family tradition is that such was the timidity of Mrs. Brewton that she exacted from her husband, who was part owner of the vessel in which they were to sail, a promise that they should hug the shore and cast anchor every night !

This very classical way of sailing was probably, by doubling the time of the voyage, their destruction. A few days after their departure a frightful storm arose. Their ship was never more heard of. Only the *Gazette* announced that a terrible gale had ravaged the coasts of North Carolina and Virginia, and that many vessels had been lost.

Mr. Brewton's large estate, including a quantity of valuable furniture, silver, china, etc., was divided between his two sisters, Frances, the wife of Colonel Charles Pinckney, President of the Provincial Congress, and Rebecca, wife of Jacob Motte. His house, already so often mentioned, went in the division of the property to Mrs. Motte.

His likeness, by Sir Joshua, still hangs in the drawing-room where Lord William received the Provincial Congress; and an interesting picture of his two little children was unfortunately burned in Mrs. Motte's plantation house, " El Dorado " on the Santee, a few years ago.

It was not rumour but an intercepted letter from the English secretary of war which brought the positive information that Admiral Sir Peter Parker was to sail for the Southern coast and reduce the Southern colonies. Which colony should be first attacked was to be decided later. The fleet was augmented by some of the vessels bringing the army which had just evacuated Boston, Sir Henry Clinton in command. Sir Henry, having stopped at New York, met there Lord William Campbell, who, anxious to return and " protect the loyal people of Charles Town," at once offered to serve as a volunteer on board the admiral's vessel. He accompanied the fleet accordingly. Not until Sir Henry had been some days at Cape Fear did Sir Peter's fleet arrive, and then Charles Town was agreed upon as the point of attack. Washington meanwhile had warned the colonies, and ordered General Charles Lee to the Southern department, with especial orders to " watch Sir Henry Clinton."

Charles Lee, an English soldier of experience and talent, had been appointed by Congress third in command under Washington.

He was brave, brilliant, knew his trade, had fought in half the countries of Europe, and knew perhaps more of the art of war than any other man in America. He had no character, no manners, and an abominable temper, — a difficult man to command a volunteer force.

The situation that he found was this : the town itself had its old bastions, and earthworks were thrown up along East Bay, the warehouses and dwellings being pulled down not to interfere with them. On James Island, the southeastern guard of the harbour, was old Fort Johnson, strengthened, and mounted with heavy guns — a battery on the same island but nearer the town commanded the inner channel. Colonel Gadsden with the First Regiment was here. This fort (Johnson) is not three miles from the southeastern point of the Battery, but Sullivan's Island to the north is farther east and about six miles from it. Sullivan's Island is in shape very like the beak of a " spoon-bill duck," the long part lying along the coast of the main (Christ Church parish) and the western end turning abruptly north toward " Haddrell's Point," the promontory of the shore. A marsh intersected by many creeks, and over a mile wide,. separates the island from the main, and between Haddrell's and the town is the broad mouth of Cooper River. There was no Fort Sumter then, but the shoal on which it has since been built, called " the middle ground," lay between Sullivan's and James islands and did good service. Beyond Sullivan's to the north is Long Island, a narrow channel separating the two, and beyond Long Island, Dewees, whence the palmetto logs for the fort had come.

The fort, ordered in January to be built with "all expedition," was not half done in May when the news of the coming of the fleet was received. At once all was bustle and activity, numbers of mechanics and negroes were sent over to work on it. Soldiers were enlisted and hurried down. All the young men of the *jeunesse dorée* were begging for commissions. Those who had been indifferent or opposed were as one now. "Some persons indeed," says Moultrie, "were incredulous of the good faith of those who were to fight our battles — but the officers who were constantly with them had no such fears." In a few days their regiments were full, they had no longer any difficulty in recruiting.

The approach of the fleet had done more in one week to unite the people than the acts of the ministers or the eloquence of Gadsden had effected in months. Did the government not know that it would be so? Had ever Englishmen yielded to compulsion; and were not these their sons? What thing but one could happen when armed cruisers appeared off Charles Town bar?

Moultrie had command of the fort, and at the other end of the island, facing the inlet which divided it from Long Island (now the Isle of Palms), were two small sand batteries, commanded by Colonel Moses Thompson of Orangeburg (commonly called "Old Danger") with his regiment of rangers, some companies of Colonel Daniel Horrÿ's dragoons, and fifty "Raccoon Riflemen," so called from their coonskin caps, commanded by Captain John Alston, all perfect marksmen.

The flag under which these men were to fight had been

devised by Moultrie himself some time before, and had been hoisted at Fort Johnson, during the attack on the *Tamar* and *Cherokee*. It was a blue field, with a white crescent in the upper right-hand corner, and was, he says, chosen to match the caps of the soldiers, which were blue with silver crescents. The uniform (the description is from Colonel Moultrie's regimental order book), with which every officer was to provide himself, was "a blue coatee, faced and cuffed with scarlet cloth, and lined with scarlet, white buttons and white waistcoat and breeches (a pattern may be seen at Mr. T.'s), also a cap and a black feather."

A miniature of Captain (afterward General) Thomas Pinckney, then of Colonel Gadsden's regiment, dressed in this uniform, is in the possession of the present writer.

On the 31st of May an express galloped in bringing news that the fleet was off Dewees Island only twenty miles away. All was hurry and bustle — the President sending expresses to order down the militia ; militia coming in ; men trying to send their families into the country ; workmen tearing the lead from churches and houses to make musket balls ; soldiers raising barricades across the streets ; and building *flèches* to command the landings. Moultrie and his men were encamped in huts and tents behind the unfinished fort. which was too full of work and workmen to receive them. The fort was a double square pen, built of palmetto logs piled one upon the other, and securely bolted together ; the space between the inner and outer pen was about sixteen feet, and this was filled in with sand ; there were square projections (bastions) at each corner. It was intended to be ten feet high above the gun platforms, but a part was never finished. It was mounted with sixty-two guns, and there were arrangements for protecting the gunners while firing. Moultrie and Thompson had between them twelve hundred men on the island, and ten thousand pounds of powder had been sent by Rutledge for their use. Moultrie says affectionately of the fort, that it was "strong and could hold a thousand men."

But the commanding general was still to come, his arrival expected with very mingled feelings. Drayton says that expresses arrived with the information that troops from Virginia and North Carolina were coming to their assistance, and that Major-general Charles Lee, with Brigadier-general Howe of North Carolina, was posting before them. He adds reflectively : —

"How far the Council of Safety, clogged in its actions by opposition and harangues, would have seized opportunities as they occurred, how far that body as an executive could have harmonized with the high and experienced military officer who was approaching, — and whose singular manners made it necessary for the public good that all unpleasant sensations thence arising should be put down ; are questions upon which so much would have depended, — and from which so much was to be feared, — that it is fortunate for South Carolina, the new government was in operation ; and that a statesman so energetic and so intelligent as Mr. Rutledge, was directing her affairs and condensing her strength."

On the first day of June the British fleet, fifty vessels, arrived off the bar and dropped anchor, showing no sign of entering.

President Rutledge and General Armstrong of Pennsylvania, who had arrived a few weeks before, visited all the fortifications and made every possible arrangement for receiving the enemy. The militia, as they arrived, were assigned to posts and every one knew his duty.

One important arrangement in the town was that in case of fire breaking out in the night-time, "two persons from the main guard shall go to the upper gallery of St.

Michael's steeple, and there hold out a lighted lantern on a pole pointing toward the fire." This device was used to indicate the place of a fire in Charleston, until thirty years ago.

A few days later young Captain Thomas Pinckney wrote to his sister, Mrs. Horrÿ, from the Battery which he commanded on James Island: —

"FORT JOHNSON, Sunday, June 1, 1776.

"I would write more frequently to my dear Mother and Sister had I anything new to inform them ; the only occurrence which has happened since my last is that of the greatest part of the Fleet being got safe over the Bar, one vessel ran aground, and has continued there these three days past, so that I imagine she will never be got off. A flag of truce was sent on Friday by the men of war to Sullivan's Island, but it was fired upon by a sentry and return'd, in consequence of which Mr. F. Huger was sent to the Fleet yesterday in order to apologize; he was very politely received, and his apology admitted. The 50 Gun ship still remains without the Bar. My brother last night recd. a letter from Genl. Howe, dated at Georgetown on Friday. Genl. Lee was there with him, and we imagine they are both now at Sullivan's Island, their Troops were to be at Georgetown today. We are now well prepared for the reception of these Gentry, whenever they shall be hardy enough to attack us. Adieu my dear Sister; keep up your own and my Mother's spirits, there is nobody here who doubts of our success! "

In another letter published in "Life of Thomas Pinckney" he describes General Lee as having "a great deal of the gentleman in his appearance, though homely, and in a split shirt."

The object of the flag of truce, which was sent again

next day, was to bring a proclamation from Sir Henry Clinton, warning the deluded people of the miseries of civil war, and offering a free pardon to all who would lay down their arms and submit. The proclamation was received, but no attention was paid to it, and the day after Sir Henry landed five hundred men on Long Island.

The *Bristol*, Sir Peter's own ship, had some difficulty in getting over the bar, but on the 10th, the tide being high, she scraped in, and the whole fleet lay inside and raked Sullivan's Island with their glasses. "They could see every move we made."

General Lee had reached Haddrell's Point from George-town the day before, and immediately, without visiting Charles Town or consulting the authorities there, crossed to the island, examined the defences, and assumed command. The South Carolina troops had not yet been mustered in as Continentals, and were under the control of their President only ; but on learning of General Lee's action, Mr. Rutledge at once issued an order that General Lee was in command of all the forces, and that his commands must be obeyed. Fortunately he did not give up all authority.

Fortunately, for an important question soon arose; Lee had "hardly looked at the Island when he disliked the task of defending it," declaring (probably any other European officer would have done the same) that the fort was a "mere slaughter pen," and must be abandoned. Haddrell's was the point to be fortified and defended. He proposed this to the President, but he "rejected with indignation, a proposition so humiliating and disheartening to the troops and the people and so advantageous to the views of the enemy."

It is amusing to read the parallel accounts of Drayton and Moultrie from which this story is taken, — the former so provoked and irritated, the second so imperturbably good-natured and easy. Lee returned to the attack and tried to intimidate Moultrie, but failed utterly.

"Do you suppose you can hold the Fort?" "Yes, Sir, I think I can." Others discouraged him also. He tells how "Captain Lemprière, a brave and experienced seaman, and captain of *a very respectable privateer* (!) visited me at the fort after the British ships came over the bar. He said to me, 'Well, Colonel, what do you think of it now?' I answered, 'I think we shall beat them.' 'Sir,' said he, pointing to the ships, 'when those ships come to lay alongside of your Fort they will knock it down in half an hour' (and that was the opinion of all the sailors). 'Then,' said I, 'we will lay behind the ruins and prevent their men from landing.' "

Moultrie's confidence came undoubtedly from his own disposition, but more from his confidence in his officers and soldiers. Men of his own kind, many intimate friends and relatives, all from the town and country at his back, all bound to do or die for the State of their birth.

Again Lee pressed the evacuation upon Rutledge, but " happily," says Garden, " he, confidently relying on Moultrie and his intrepid band, heroically replied to Lee, 'that while a soldier remained to defend it, he would never give his consent to such an order.' He did more, for he wrote to Moultrie: —

" Genl. Lee wishes you to evacuate the Fort, you will not do so without an order from me.

"I will cut off my right hand sooner than write it.

"JOHN RUTLEDGE."

It was probably fortunate, under the circumstances, that neither of the Carolinians was versed in the theory of fortification, or knew how poor their defence was. Lee, baffled in this plan, set himself to fortify Haddrell's, and for this purpose built two batteries near the Point, mounted heavy guns, garrisoned them with the forces he had brought with him, and put General Armstrong in command, ranking him over Moultrie. This would have mattered little if he had not taken more than half of the powder which Rutledge had sent to the fort to supply these batteries at Haddrell's.

From the day of his coming until the fight was won Lee's letters to Moultrie continue distracted and distracting. " Colonel Moultrie's position," said Drayton, " was not of the most agreeable." It was, it must be confessed, in great part his own fault. Having resolved to hold the fort it was his manifest duty to hasten the completion. There was no need to tell him to be " cool," as Rutledge told him, but there was need, desperate need, to urge him to be quick. Unhappily that was what he could not be, nor could he make others so. Lee raged and fumed — showed the weak points. How the fort was so placed at the bend of the beach that if the ships ran past they could enfilade him easily. Ordered *flèches* and other protecting works — ordered the walls raised higher, ordered a bridge built to Haddrell's, for the retreat of which he was ever talking. Moultrie, his admirer has to admit, " was an officer of very easy manners, leaving to others many things which he had better have attended to himself."

Although he had all the force of negroes and mechanics besides his soldiers that he could employ, the fort was not finished except upon the south and east fronts ; the *flèches* and traverse were not built, and there was no bridge for retreat. This Moultrie did not wish to build. Lee, who was very active, energetic, and competent, fretted in vain. He thought worse and worse of the fort, and was " all anxiety for the safety of the troops on the Island, as if they had been placed there merely for the purpose of spiking cannon, blowing up the magazine, and making a soldierly retreat; — not for opposing an enemy." Moultrie knew his own defects and was generous to his tormenting monitor. He was, he says, " brave and energetic, but hearty and rough in his manners which the officers could not at first reconcile themselves to ; yet was thought by many to be worth a thousand men by teaching us not to fear the enemy." He also says quietly: " Genl. Lee did not like my having the command of that important post. He did not doubt my courage, but said I was too easy in command. After the battle he made me his bosom friend."

From the 1st of June to the 28th, the ships lay in the offing, busy landing troops on Long Island. Sir Henry Clinton and Lord Cornwallis, two great English generals, with three thousand English soldiers, were there on that desolate sand-bank, with their tents and the low scrubby oaks and palmettoes as their only shelter. A letter afterward found on the beach told of their suffering from the heat and " the moschetoes, than which no torment can be greater." They were planning how to cross the inlet, but found it deeper than they had expected, and feared to attempt it in the face of Thompson's batteries. The same letter says " the Americans were intrenched to the eyes, had two thousand men, and four heavy guns, — they could have killed us all before we could have landed."

Thompson really had two small guns and seven hundred and eighty men, including two hundred North Carolinians under Colonel Clark.

Moultrie with his usual optimism said, " I had no uneasiness when I found that Sir Henry had not *more* than three thousand men. I never expected any soldiers to reach the fort."

Sir Henry did make an attempt to cross the inlet with a flotilla of boats, floating batteries, armed schooners, but a few discharges of grape-shot drove them back and they abandoned the attempt.

The long suspense of twenty-seven days, most valuable to the workers, was trying to the spirits of the people ; wild rumours possessed the town that contrary orders had been received — that the heart of the King was softened — that there was to be no attack ! Think of the women on the plantations with all the men gone, and only an occasional rider bringing news, generally false !

It seems a special interposition of Providence that the attack was made on the 28th, for on the 27th General Lee informed President Rutledge that he intended to supersede Colonel Moultrie, the next day, if he should find that certain work which he had ordered was not done. Had he done so, it is impossible to say what might have happened, for the soldiers were new to discipline, and Moultrie was their idol.

The work was not done, but the battle was begun.

Early on that morning Moultrie, who had ridden out to visit Thompson's redoubt, looking at the ships which lay off that end of the island, saw that they were loosing their topsails. He galloped back to his fort, sounded the long roll, and served out ammunition.

The men had scarcely time to stand to their guns before the fleet came sailing up, a gallant sight. Confident of victory they came on abreast of the fort, cast anchor, and opened fire. There were eleven, carrying two hundred and seventy guns.

Moultrie had in all sixty-two. The ships lay in double line and poured in their fire. The *Thunder* bomb threw her shells, the fort rocked beneath the blows ; worse than the noise and heat was the awful jar. Moultrie feared it might dismount his guns. Slowly, but with very careful aim, the fort replied, — and then that which seemed almost impossible happened, for the fort sustained comparatively little damage, and the great ships suffered severely. "*Mind* the Admiral, *mind* the fifty-gun ships," was the

R

word passed along the rampart, and the *Bristol* and *Experiment* suffered fearfully. In the fort the shot sank into the soft, spongy palmetto logs, which did not shiver or break, or buried themselves in the sand filling. The heavy shells thrown with great precision fell, many of them, into a little swamp in the middle of the fort and sank harmless. If only they could have kept a rapid fire, but Lee had left them but four thousand pounds of powder, and sent no more. Moultrie had been and was too easy about it ; he should have represented it to Rutledge and secured more in time. Early in the action he said to Motte, his lieutenant-colonel, that he feared they were short of powder. " Write at once for more," said Motte, " and write in the most pressing manner."

" Why," says Drayton, " did he not write the one word ' *Powder* '? That would have been expressive." Instead he wrote to Lee:—

" I think we shall want more powder ; at the rate we go on I think we shall. But you can see for yourself ; — pray send more if you think proper." That was *sang-froid* with a vengeance.

When the note reached town, Lee was at Haddrell's, and it was taken to Rutledge. It did not seem urgent, but the President at once sent all he had, with a note " written on a scrap of paper."

" I send you five hundred pounds of powder, you might be supplied from Haddrell's, you know our collection is not great. Honour and Victory my dear Sir to you and our worthy countrymen with you. Do not make too free with your cannon. Cool, and do mischief."

Lee, who was at Haddrell's where the six thousand pounds of powder taken from Moultrie was, sent none, but a note : " If you should unfortunately expend your ammunition, without driving off the enemy, spike your guns and retreat with all the order you can. I know you will be careful not to expend your ammunition."

If Moultrie did not rage when he received that note, it was not Lee's fault. Had he had his own powder he could have destroyed the fleet !

And so the cannonade went on. They saw that they were doing much damage, but did not know how much. The *Bristol*, the admiral's flagship, suffered most ; at one time Sir Peter himself was the only man left unwounded on the quarter-deck, presently he too was hurt ; — Lord William received a wound in the side, thought slight at first, but which ultimately caused his death.

The captains of the *Bristol* and *Experiment* both died of their wounds. But the ships fought as English ships do fight, and men were sent in small boats from the less injured vessels to supply the loss of wounded and dead. Just before the little supply of powder came the fire was so slow that the British thought the fort was silenced and raised a shout of victory, but then it was resumed more quickly, and the shots told. The cannoneers were good marksmen ; the phrase " the man behind the gun " had not been invented then, but the man was there. The general's coolness communicated itself to the gunners.

In the midst of the fight General Lee came over from Haddrell's and pointed a gun or two. He was impressed by what he saw. The man so quiet and easy at other times was all the soldier now, though suffering sharply from gout. His men were like him, — for use, not for show. " Motte and I were smoking our pipes but we put them away when Lee came down," Moultrie said. Lee stayed only a little while. " You are doing very well, you don't need me here, I shall go back to town," he said, and went.

Sent no powder ! It is hard not to suspect him of treachery, but there is no warrant for it.

When the flagstaff was shot away and the flag fell over the ramparts, the British raised another cheer, for they thought it meant surrender; but Sergeant Jasper leapt down from the wall, seized and tore it from the staff, and climbing back fastened it to a sponge rod and the white crescent rose again.

Then came the greatest danger of all, that which Lee had foretold. The *Acteon*, the *Sphynx*, and the *Syren* ran past the fort to enfilade it from the west. The rampart on that side was not of the proper height and the damage would have been great. But Heaven fought that day for Carolina. As the ships came about, crowded in the narrow channel, they collided, their yards fouled ; they could not manœuvre and ran ashore on the middle "ground," the edge of the shoal on which Fort Sumter now stands.

The *Sphynx* and the *Syren* got off badly damaged and withdrew, but the *Acteon* stuck hard and fast, driven deep in the sand.

A long day it was, and hot beyond words. "To be upon the platform of a fort on the 28th of June, amidst twenty or thirty heavy pieces of cannon, in one continual blaze and roar, and clouds of smoke curling overhead for hours together, is an honourable but a very unpleasant situation," writes the colonel, and then he tells how he never in his life enjoyed anything so much as a glass of "cool grog" from a bucketful, served out to the men after hours of exertion !

All this time the townsfolk were watching the progress of the fight. They could tell nothing of the condition of either the ships or the fort because of the heavy smoke, except occasionally when a gust of wind would clear it away for a moment or two, and then they could see the flag still flying, —and hear the slow response of Moultrie's guns to the brisk cannonade of the ships. Lee's order, "If your ammunition gives out spike your guns and retreat," hung like a threat over the garrison. They *could* not allow themselves to give out. Dark came, and with it a thunderstorm arose. The soldiers, firing slowly through the roar, could not see, but heard their shot strike the vessels. At last the firing ceased on both sides. At eleven o'clock the ships "slipped their cables and quietly without piping" dropped down with the tide to their former anchorage.

Think of the joy in fort and town! By dawn of day the harbour was crowded with boats and small craft of all kinds hurrying to the scene of victory. The fleet had withdrawn to the channel off Morris Island; the fort was practically unhurt, and the *Acteon* was still aground. A few shots fired at her from the fort were promptly returned by her gallant captain, who, throwing out his colours, and leaving his guns shotted, set her on fire and withdrew his crew in small boats. She was boarded by the Americans, but bursting into flames blew up with all her guns, and from her "rose a great column of smoke which soon expanded itself at the top into the appearance of a great Palmetto tree," which was seen by all the garrison.

The loss of life was small, — twelve were killed and twenty-five wounded. The dying cry of one man deserves to be remembered. Sergeant McDonald, killed by a shell, to the men who ran to his assistance, "Fight on, boys, don't let Liberty expire with me to-day."

The flagship alone lost one hundred and four men. The admiral was wounded, the captain killed. The captain of the *Experiment* was killed also, and her loss of men was almost as great. The smaller vessels had suffered less, for the order "Mind the fifty-gun ships," had been obeyed. The *Bristol* had been severely handled, "almost torn to pieces," could not have been got off had not the sea been unusually smooth.

If Moultrie had had powder enough, the ships must have struck their colours or been sunk. They could not have retreated, for wind and tide were against them ; and to have gone up the harbour would have brought them under the guns of Johnson.

This was the service done by General Charles Lee ! He had marred the victory and discouraged the men, yet he received the thanks and praise of Congress !

After the battle Lee was in high good humour. He visited the fort and complimented Moultrie and the garrison upon " a successful defence during a bombardment of seven and a cannonade of eleven hours." On the Fourth of July President Rutledge also visited the fort and congratulated officers and men upon their victory in an eloquent speech, by which, Garden says, " New honours crowned the defenders of the Fort." Taking his own sword from his side he presented it to Sergeant Jasper with warmest praise of his brave exploit.

Nor were (to use the gallant colonel's favourite phrase) " the patriotic Fair " backward in expressing their gratitude. Many were the thanks, tokens, etc., and Mrs. Barnard Elliott, whose husband had so lately been of his Majesty's Council, but who was now captain of the Artillery Battalion, presented the Second Regiment with " an elegant pair of colours, one of red, the other of blue silk, each embroidered with a splendid rattlesnake, coiled, with the motto, ' Don't tread on me.' " This device was suggested by the belief held by the early explorers to whom the rattlesnake was one of the marvels of nature ; and was expressed by Hewat, " One of the most formidable living creatures in the whole universe, he possesses that noble fortitude which is harmless unless when provoked or molested."

The flags were received by Colonel Moultrie, at the head of the regiment, and Lieutenant-colonel Motte, returning thanks, promised that " they should be honourably supported and never tarnished by the 2nd Regt."

It was in rescuing one of these flags that Jasper lost his life at the siege of Savannah. Attempting to repeat his former feat, he was shot as he regained the rampart, and fell dead. He was only a little Irish sergeant, so untaught that he refused the commission that President Rutledge offered him, "because as an officer my comrades would blush for my ignorance." "But still his name sounds stirring," and the boys of Charleston would be surprised and indignant if told that the statue which gazes seaward from East Battery, flag in hand, was not intended for him.

The surprise and anger aroused in England by this victory was great.

John Laurens, writing to his father from London, says that the account of the "Battle of Sullivan's Island (which we now call the Battle of Fort Moultrie), in Wills' *Gazette*, had been copied into all the English papers; but impartial people had been convinced, even from Sir P. Parker's own account, notwithstanding irksome truths had been suppressed, and great pains had been taken by the choice of expressions in relating the matter, to palliate his defeat, that the honour of a very clear victory belonged to our Countrymen." That an English admiral, with a well-appointed fleet of two hundred and seventy guns, should be beaten off by a miserable little half-built fort on an uninhabited sand-bank, was incomprehensible.

"They did not know," Moultrie says, "the resisting quality of our Palmetto Wood."

Clinton's failure to cross the inlet was still more astonishing. Ralph Izard, Jr., then in Europe, says he cannot understand it; cannot imagine how such a general as Clinton can have been a whole month on the island without sounding the passage!

The assertion that the water had suddenly become much deeper provoked great ridicule. Johnson's "Traditions" gives this *jeu d'esprit* from the *St. James Chronicle :* —

A Miracle on Sullivan's Island

By the Red Sea the Hebrew host detained,
Through aid divine the distant shore now gained,
The waters fled, the deep a passage gave;
As God thus wrought a chosen race to save.

But Clinton's troops have shared a different fate;
'Gainst them, poor men, — not chosen sure of Heaven,
The miracle reversed is still as great,
From two feet deep the water rose to seven.

Old Governor Sayle's "iron gate" had once more held fast and baffled the invader!

The thanks sent on the 20th of July were from *the United States of America*, to the officers and soldiers "who with so much valour repulsed the attack which was made on the *State of South Carolina* by the fleet and armies of his Britannic Majesty," and was signed "John Hancock, President of Congress." The Republic had come into being, and the guns of Fort Moultrie had sounded a loud assent to the Declaration, which Thomas Jefferson read in Congress on that same "Carolina" day, a week before the "Liberty Bell" rang out in Philadelphia.

Well might William Henry Drayton say, in summing up the achievements of his people — "We established the first Independent Government. We alone repulsed a British fleet."

CHAPTER XIV

THE battle of Fort Moultrie was fought on a Friday, and the people of Charles Town naturally expected that on the following Sunday the churches would be filled with worshippers, all giving thanks to the God of Battles.

St. Philip's, the White Meeting, the various independent churches were thronged accordingly, but the doors of St. Michael's were closed! The astonished congregation learned with dismay that the vestry had been summoned at seven o'clock that morning, to take action on the refusal of their rector, the Reverend Mr. Cooper, to take the oath to observe the Constitution!

The vestry had for the present only decided "That there be no Divine Service in St. Michael's this day."

This was a very different matter from the dismissal of Mr. Bullman; for the Reverend Mr. Cooper, an Englishman born (as were all the clergy), had been in the town for many years and was much beloved. He had first come out as assistant minister at St. Philip's; but St. Michael's had asked for a rector who should be " of middle age, grave deportment and possess a good audible voice." In return for these reasonable requirements the Church offered a good house and one hundred and thirty pounds sterling a year, besides fees. No suitable clergyman appearing, it had been determined to " call " Mr. Cooper from his subordinate position at St. Philip's.

Mr. Cooper had married in the colony, had made himself extremely popular, and had many and strong friends.

All that could be done to convince and persuade him was done, but he was firm in his convictions and would not part from Church and country. Most sorrowfully and carrying with them the love of many friends, he and his wife left Charles Town.

At home his loyalty was rewarded by the rectory of St. Michael's Cornhill, where he lived for many years, always continuing his Charles Town correspondence.

There were others whose position was much the same. No one was more beloved in the town than Dr. Garden, the physician and botanist; but he too was British born; sympathizing in great degree with American ideas, he drew the line at "bearing arms against the King." He, however, remained in Charles Town, the trusted friend and adviser until its evacuation, and then returned to England, taking with him his Carolinian wife. He had the pain of differing from his only son, Major Garden of the American army, afterward author of the "Anecdotes."

Some true Americans grieved likewise at the parting of the ways. Henry Laurens says that he *wept* when he heard the Declaration read, and it may be suspected that the heart of the Governor was likewise wrung.

Not even yet did some of these men accept fully the final separation. In the flush of victory, for a little while, they were satisfied or even elated, but soon, very soon, came back the thought of the heritage they were renouncing, of the experiment they were trying. They knew, at least many of them knew, that it was not England or the English laws against which they were contending, but only a stupid King and a subservient ministry.

Laurens had spoken truly when he said that their cause was that of the British Empire, — of the constitution itself.

Two years later, Rutledge, who now commended the

battle of Fort Moultrie and welcomed the Declaration of Independence, resigned his office rather than accede to a "permanent constitution" which would render a reconciliation with Great Britain impossible. Arthur Middleton, who had been one of the leaders of the extreme party, when chosen to succeed Rutledge, refused election for the same reason.

They have been reproached with inconsistency, but the charge is unjust. They wanted a free and loyal government, and hoped by force of arms to win it within the Empire itself. That the Provinces should have been for a time a "free and independent league of states," did not make reconciliation impossible. Had not England been once a commonwealth, and was she not again a kingdom? Had not much of liberty been won — and much retained — by the "Great Rebellion," even when "his most gracious Majesty" again ruled his loyal subjects? Might not the sword win for them even from the King himself, — expatriated Englishmen though they were, — the respect and acknowledgment of rights which a large part of the English Parliament was already willing to grant?

It cannot be too clearly understood that with the single exception of Gadsden, the leaders of Carolina were *not* republicans.

They were English Whigs, fighting as Gray and Peel and Russell fought sixty years later, for the reform which was gained the more easily then, because of the lesson taught by the American colonies during the reign of George III.

Yet when forced to choose between rebellion and servile submission, none did more, or suffered more, in the American cause than Laurens, Rutledge, and Middleton.

The Declaration of Independence did not reach Charles Town until the 2d of August, the very day on which the sorely damaged British fleet, somewhat refitted and assisted by transports sent from New York, left the harbour and sailed northward.

Mr. McCrady suggests that the young gentlemen in Philadelphia were in no haste to make a report of the very decisive step which they had just taken. Certainly when sent on, neither they, nor any who sent them, had the least intention of such a proceeding. On the contrary, Gadsden's motion for independence had been indignantly rejected. It may be, as Mr. McCrady supposes, that Edward Rutledge, especially, was in fear of his dominant brother, and that Thomas Lynch, who had been too ill to sign the Declaration, exerted himself to add his name to the letter of the delegates, in order to add his influence to theirs. All such anxiety was needless, now that the State had spoken by the mouths of her guns.

The Declaration was read at the head of the army (as the few regiments were called) to the assembled townsfolk by Captain Barnard Elliott, and the time for opposition being past, all sorts and conditions of men gave enthusiastic applause. Few perhaps realized that their enthusiasm would have to stand the strain of a seven years' war!

For the next three years, however, the war did not touch Charles Town herself — this boon her battle had won her. Men went about their business, sowed and reaped, bought and sold, "rode the circuit," wooed and married.

Trade flourished exceedingly. As one of the few open ports, the wharves were crowded with ships from all neutral countries, and other States got their supplies through her. The British ships cruising along the shore interfered with this commerce as the pirates had done "lang syne," and privateers armed and put out to protect, or to prey, as the nationality might be. A more daring attempt to rid the coast of the invaders resulted unhappily. The State armed some small vessels which it called its

"Navy," they brought in some valuable prizes; but then the Continental frigate, the *Randolph*, having on board a body of South Carolina regulars acting as marines, met in battle the British sixty-gun frigate, the *Yarmouth*, and after a very short fight blew up. All but fourteen of her men were lost. Her captain, Biddle, of Pennsylvania, and Captain Joseph Ioor, of Dorchester, South Carolina, commanding the marines, both went down in her. Captain Ioor was of Dutch descent, one of that Massachusetts colony, almost all of which left Dorchester and went to Liberty County, Georgia, about 1754. With him the name became extinct.

Among the few who escaped this terrible disaster was John Mayrant, of Charles Town, rescued after having floated for two days on the water. He was spared to win reputation fighting with Paul Jones, as lieutenant of the *Serapis*. The story is that when asked for his full name that he might be reported with commendation to the department, he answered that he "did not care particularly about that, but would like to have such a message sent to a certain young lady in South Carolina."

During this comparatively tranquil period several officers obtained leave to increase their knowledge of war by serving under Washington. Colonels C. C. Pinckney and John Laurens had the honour to be received on his staff. Henry Laurens was then President of the Continental Congress. His son John, who had just returned from Europe, thoroughly educated, — "armed at all points" as his father had advised, — brave, talented, handsome, and enthusiastic, was to become the darling of the army. Both gentlemen returned home when they saw their own State threatened.

Several serious fires occurred about this time, evidently of incendiary origin, which proved the truth of Moultrie's declaration that the place was "honeycombed with Tories."

In one of these which swept the lower part of Broad Street and destroyed about one hundred thousand pounds sterling of property, the Charles Town Library, with six or seven thousand books and instruments for astronomical and philosophical experiments, was almost entirely consumed. This loss was acutely felt.

It was in this time also that Major Benjamin Huger rode into town one day with two handsome young Frenchmen by his side: the Marquis de La Fayette and the Baron de Kalb, who had come to offer sword and fortune to the American cause. De Kalb although German by birth was French by adoption, and an officer in King Louis's army.

Not being able to enter the port of Charles Town, they had been put ashore at Mr. Huger's plantation of North Island, near Georgetown, in Winyah Bay. Hospitably entertained, they had unfolded their plan to their host, who had accompanied them to Charles Town, whence they could be escorted to General Washington's headquarters.

Major Huger (formerly the husband of Miss Golightly) was now married again, and was the father by his second wife, Miss Kinloch, of a little three-year-old boy, who sat on M. de La Fayette's knee, and played with his bright buttons and gold-hilted sword. The little fellow was, in years to come, to risk life and liberty to rescue his quondam playmate from the dungeons of Olmütz.

On the meeting of the Assembly in 1778, the increase of Revolutionary feeling was clearly apparent. Resolutions to abolish the Church, to abolish the Council, to abolish the Governor's veto, to adopt a permanent constitution, which, as has been said, would make reconciliation with England impossible, were offered. The first of these motions was postponed, but the republican party held strongly to the others. Rutledge resigned and Middleton declined the governorship, enduring much abuse in consequence ; Rawlins Lowndes accepted office and held it for one year, — having Christopher Gadsden for his Lieutenant-governor. He then resigned, advising the people, in view of the threatening aspect of affairs, to choose a ruler who could direct the military defence of the country — a post for which he knew himself incompetent.

The Assembly politely assured his Excellency that he underestimated his own powers, but immediately elected John Rutledge, who though no soldier had their entire confidence — the greater apparently for his independent course of the year before.

By the new constitution, the President became the Governor, the Legislative Council the Senate, and the Commons the House of Representatives, the whole forming the Legislature, which names are still in use.

Before adjourning the Legislature conferred upon the Governor and his Council the right to exercise sovereign power until its next session.

President Lowndes might well speak of the threatening aspect of affairs. The British under Colonel Archibald Campbell and General Prévost, having gained possession of Savannah, and established themselves there, now began to threaten Carolina.

General Howe had by this time been removed from command, and in answer to requests for assistance sent to Congress and to the commander-in-chief, the State had been told that she must rely for soldiers upon herself alone, but that another general should be sent. Accordingly General Benjamin Lincoln of Massachusetts, a respectable mediocrity, who had been with Gates at the surrender of Burgoyne, was put in command of the Southern department; that is to say, of the Carolinas and Georgia.

Early in 1778 Prévost crossed the Savannah and began his march, first attacking Port Royal. Lincoln was so persuaded that his real object was the town of Augusta, about a hundred miles higher up the river, that he collected as many men as possible at the old Swiss settlement of Purysburg on the Savannah, in readiness to march to its assistance. But Prévost, being in Carolina, and finding only Moultrie with a handful of troops in front of him, advanced rapidly upon Charles Town; Moultrie fighting at every defensible point, in order to gain time; and falling back when overwhelmed by numbers. At last he was driven back into the town itself, Prévost was before the lines, and Lincoln, notwithstanding many messages, was supposed to be still at his "camp of observation" at Purysburg a hundred miles away.

The lines were small earthworks, thrown up from river to river, a little above where Line Street is now. Some skirmishing with the advance guard delayed Prévost's progress. Count Pulaski, one of those gallant Poles whose sympathy in the cause of freedom led them to join their fortunes to those of the Americans, had arrived with a hundred and sixty men of his legion a day or two before. He made a sally with these, but was beaten back, leaving the greater number killed, wounded, or prisoners.

The lines were so weak that the engineers declared them indefensible, but the spirit of the people was high. They remembered all that had been predicted of the " slaughter pen " of Moultrie, and laboured indefatigably to strengthen the works. There is a pathetic story of the aged Gabriel Manigault, who, having lost his only son (Peter, the former Speaker), appeared in the trenches with his grandson, a lad of fifteen, both, musket in hand, prepared to fight for their home.

The British force, said by Colonel Pierce Butler, adjutant-general of the State, to be between seven and eight thousand, though vastly superior in quality, being well-trained regulars, while the garrison had but few Continentals, was not much more than two to one; and despite the opinion of the engineers Moultrie and Laurens were ready and eager to begin the battle, but the Governor would not consent. He said the odds were too great and that they must wait for Lincoln. The same curious division of authority between the civil and military officers which had been seen at the battle of Fort Moultrie still prevailed, and Rutledge was able to keep the soldiers in leash while he parleyed, — offered terms to which the English could not consent. Colonel Prévost, acting for his brother, refused, and again the officers urged instant action. Still the Governor stood firm even against nearly half his Council. He proposed to offer " the *neutrality* of the State during the war." The proceedings of the so-called Privy Council were supposed to be private, but the hot heads among them threw policy to the winds, appealed to the people, and even informed the soldiers in the trenches of the " treachery " of their leaders. These, that is to say the Governor and his party, received " solemn and serious warnings " that their heads should fall if they carried out their purpose. A warning to which these gentlemen paid not the slightest attention.

By military usage the message should have gone by an officer, but the soldiers were furious and refused to carry it. Moultrie with difficulty persuaded Colonel McIntosh to go with Rutledge's brother-in-law, Mr. Roger Smith, a member of the Council, to take the obnoxious proposition to Prévost.

The proposition, it will be observed, was not the *surrender*, but the *neutrality* of the town and State. The State was to be in the position of an independent power ; both Americans and English might use her harbours and profit by her productions. Prévost, with, as he thought, the town an easy conquest before him, would listen to no such offer. He peremptorily refused it ; recognized only the

s

General commanding, and demanded that on the following day he should surrender the town and all its inhabitants as prisoners of war. "Then," says Moultrie, the Governor and Council looked very grave and steadfastly on each other and on him, not knowing what he would say. He said, "I am determined *not* to deliver you as prisoners of war. We will fight it out."

John Laurens jumped up exultant, crying, "Thank God, we are on our legs again."

Mr. Kinloch, General Moultrie's aide, was sent out to say that all conference was at an end.

By all this forty-eight precious hours had been gained.

The night was spent in the final preparations for battle, but when morning dawned, the enemy was gone! Pulaski immediately pursued with his horse, but the English were already across the Ashley River.

The cause of this sudden retreat was an intercepted letter of Lincoln to Moultrie, saying that he would arrive in another day.

Instead of hurrying down, as almost any other man would have done, he came by leisurely stages, "going into camp" *en route*, etc., and instead of coming, wrote to say he *would* come and attempted to send the letter through the enemy's lines. We could have "Burgoyned" them, Moultrie said, but Lincoln was too slow!

To no one was the disappointment so bitter as to the Governor. He alone knew that Lincoln was really in motion, and had made his plan accordingly to take the English in front and rear, and capture or destroy their army. Time only was necessary — time for the tardy, lingering movements of the general, and for time he fought, remaining absolutely silent because in his Council there was no possibility of secrecy. The fact of Lincoln's approach mentioned there would have been at once told in the town, and betrayed to the enemy. Not that the members were not patriotic and devoted, but discretion was wofully lacking (as shown at the siege a year later) ; and yet such was the influence and position of some of the most indiscreet, that he could not afford to offend by excluding them from confidence given to others.

So he played his game, remained silent, bore reproach and threat, and although disappointed in the great hope, gained the forty-eight precious hours, which saved the town the horrors of a storm, and left her another year of life.

For no other act of his career has John Rutledge been so much blamed, and so much praised, as for this. His opponents called him a traitor and a coward. Ramsay praises and Moultrie wonders at his conduct. Mr. Mc-Crady, writing in the light of after time, thinks the proposition of neutrality that of a far-seeing statesmanship. Carolina was, he says, practically abandoned by the Northern states ; the best that could be done both for her and for them was to make her neutral.

Mr. Rutledge made no such claim for himself. The above account is that which he gave to his sons, to whom he said that he "considered it the best thing that he had ever done." He had the proud satisfaction of knowing that the confidence of his countrymen was his. He had differed with his Council, and the next Legislature gave him authority to act without his Council.

It should be noticed that at the siege of Savannah, a few months later, General Prévost made use of the same strategy of parley, to gain time for the approach of his reënforcements, and succeeded.

One most unfortunate consequence of the confusion of authority already mentioned took place early in this affair.

Major Huger had been sent beyond the lines with a small party to complete some earthworks. The general had not been informed, and his orders to fire upon any persons approaching the fortifications by night were obeyed. Major Huger fell dead at the first shot. The distress and anger were great, for Huger was a gallant and excellent officer. Moultrie at once claimed and the Governor agreed that all orders on military matters should henceforth be issued by him alone, while the right of negotiation, parley, etc., remained with the civil authority.

Prévost had gone no farther than to John's Island, a few miles south of Charles Town, whence, after an indecisive skirmish, called the battle of Stono, he returned to Savannah, leaving a wide swath of desolation behind him.

Houses and barns were burned, plantations laid waste, animals killed or driven off ; with an immense amount of silver plate, and a great number of negroes carried away to be sold in the West Indies, to the great emolument of the British officers.

Some horses were quite too valuable to be resigned without an effort. Such were Flimnap and Abdallah, two superb imported animals, of which many tales are told.

Major Garden relates, how the night after the battle, the American army lay upon James, and the English upon John's Island, with only the Stono River between. At dead of night a whisper went through the camp asking for " volunteers for dangerous service." In a few minutes a boat with muffled oars was rowing quietly but swiftly down and across the stream to the John's Island shore. Captain Thomas Shubrick explained to his crew that they were bound for the English camp at Mr. Gibbes's plantation, where were the captured horses. They were on their way to rescue them. The young fellows were delighted, and on reaching the place, crept softly from their boat, found the stable guarded by only one sleeping sentinel, opened the door, and led out the horses.

Instantly two lads were mounted and riding for the

Stono Ferry, which they gained in safety and crossed with their precious booty. The rest of the party had a narrow escape. The horses had neighed upon being led out, and had given the alarm ; but Mr. Gibbes, hearing the stir in the camp behind, called a warning from his window, and the men had time to regain the boat and make off, before the British could get under·arms.

The young men were delighted with their exploit, and presented themselves to General Moultrie the next day, expecting commendation from so great a lover of horse-flesh. To their chagrin the general gave a sharp· reprimand for " unauthorized predatory expeditions." It may be feared that their repentance was slight.

To the student of colonial history the worst of these losses is that of invaluable papers. In this raid of Prévost's the plantations of many of the most important families in the country, those who had played a leading part in early and in recent times, were destroyed : " Beaufort town " and all the places around Port Royal. Those of the Bulls, Barnwells, Heywards, and others were burned, Mrs. Pinckney's house at Ashepoo to which all her husband's books and papers had been sent for safety, Mr. Lowndes's at the Horse Shoe, and many others.

The "torch of Prévost " became a by-word.

In these skirmishes Moultrie had the satisfaction of seeing the gallantry of his officers and men in " field fighting."

The Artillery Battalion (Gadsden's first command) under Major Thomas Grimball, especially distinguished itself. Its two captains were signers of the Declaration, Thomas Heyward and Edward Rutledge, right glad to take the soldier jacket instead of the robe of office.

Heyward was wounded at Port Royal. The reckless daring of John Laurens had nearly cost his own life and that of his detachment in crossing a river under fire. Captain Thomas Shubrick with difficulty rescued the wounded hero, and brought off the men. Major Roberts and Captain Charles Motte, defenders of Fort Moultrie, were killed in this campaign.

It was all but a prelude to the great invasion which was to overwhelm the town and with it the State in 1781,

RELIC OF TAPPY WALL
Erected at time of the Revolution.

when Sir Henry Clinton with a large force brought from New York landed on John's Island at the mouth of the Stono River.

Sir Henry had profited by his experience at Sullivan's

Island three years before, and determined to take the town by the back door. Delayed for a while by storms and other misadventures, he made cautious and elaborate approaches, building batteries at the mouth of Wappoo Cut and on James Island, and sending his supporting fleet under Admiral Arbuthnot to seize the bar. Congress too had sent a fleet, commanded by Commodore Whipple. Unhappily this officer by too great prudence — to give the mildest name — sounded and examined, and came to the conclusion that the wind and tide would endanger his vessels too much if he attempted to defend the entrance to the harbour. He therefore decided to take up his position near the " Middle Ground," on which the *Acteon* had gone ashore, and assist Fort Moultrie in guarding the channel. This plan General Lincoln, after consultation with the pilots and personal examination, agreed to ; and had it been adhered to, it might have been well.

But no sooner had Arbuthnot with his great ships safely crossed the bar without firing a shot than Commodore Whipple's prudence again awoke. He actually persuaded General Lincoln to allow him to bring his fleet up to the town, take out his guns, and sink the ships in Hog Island Channel. How Lincoln could have consented it is impossible to say ; except that although personally brave, he was evidently a very weak man, easily influenced, and was shockingly bullied all through the siege.

The fleet with one hundred and fifty-two guns, nearly three times the number that Moultrie had in 1776, was thrown away by sheer cowardice.

Fortifications had been erected across Charles Town neck, as the narrowest part of the peninsula is called, before Prévost's raid ; these were now strengthened and extended.

They ran from just above the present railway station in Chapel Street, on a creek opening from Cooper River, passing through Inspection (now Citadel) Square, where was a " hornwork," to the Ashley River near the foot of Bull Street. The small piece of " tappy " wall enclosed with an iron railing on Citadel Square is a fragment of this "hornwork," which was itself a fragment of an earlier date.

Had Lincoln been of the same mind as Washington, who, like the Black Douglas, " liked better to hear the lark sing than the mouse cheep," he would have refused to defend the town, and have kept his army in the open. Washington said, both before and afterward, that the defence was a mistake, especially, as he wrote to John Laurens, when the command of the harbour had been given up, " which brings your affairs to a dangerous crisis." He himself had thus spared New York and Philadelphia a siege, and had saved his army.

He had been roundly abused for so doing, and Lincoln was not a Washington. The Charlestonians naturally wanted their town defended, and, as he wrote to Washington, he really thought that such was the desire of Congress, and that he feared to abandon the valuable stores contained therein. The experience of 1776 and 1779 had made the people unduly confident; they hoped for victory. Moultrie describes how such of the ladies as remained in the place would come out to the walls to encourage the workers, and look with perfect composure at the long lines of English marching up and opening their trenches.

Clinton advanced up the west bank of the Ashley. Colonel William Washington, who had lately been sent with a small body of horse from Virginia, and Colonel Tarleton, of the " British Legion," — names with which Carolina was soon to resound, — first met and fought during this advance. Their very first skirmish, Moultrie says, was on Governor Rutledge's own plantation near Rantowles Bridge.

Washington was the son of Bailey Washington, brother to the grandfather of the commander-in-chief, and thus, as he said, his " kinsman."

He was afterward known as " the sword of the army." He soon won the heart of Miss Elliott of Sandy Hill, and was married in the very midst of the war, his wife as courageous and devoted as himself.

John Laurens also dashed himself and a small force against the oncoming wave, but the elder men said these were bravadoes " for honour, not for use."

Heavy batteries along the west bank protected Clinton's passage of the river from Drayton Hall and Bee's Ferry twelve miles above the town, and then from Old Town to Gibbes Farm (now the Grove) only two miles outside of the lines. On their way the usual conduct of invading armies was followed. At Middleton Place, the soldiers were civil to the ladies, but amused themselves by throwing furniture out of windows, mutilating the statues, and cutting the head out of West's picture of Arthur Middleton, as that of a " d——d rebel." The plate had been concealed *en cachette* in a heavy brick chimney, in which were three compartments. Each had its portion of silver, and each was confided to the care of a servant, who thought himself the only trusted person.

The British insisted that plate there must be, and threatened torture. Two of the men yielded, but " Old Moro," the butler, was true to his trust, and one-third was saved.

Carefully the lines were drawn, the trenches dug, and cannon mounted, great guns dragged all the way from Stono. No shot was fired in return to those by which the besieged sought to disturb the workmen, until the 5th of April, when Mr. Tom Horrÿ had the honour of receiving the first ball, and escaped with slight injury.

From that day the siege went on, ever increasing in

energy as more guns were mounted and the trenches pushed nearer and nearer. On their side the besieged worked indefatigably, and two French engineers, Colonels de Lannoy and de Cambray, did all that could be done to strengthen the lines. When Clinton in due form summoned the town to surrender, Lincoln immediately and without hesitation refused. There were in garrison, according to Moultrie, twenty-two hundred Continental troops, and some Virginians under Colonel Woodford arrived during the siege; also an uncertain number of North Carolina militia, possibly thirteen hundred. Of the Continentals, or regulars, eight hundred were South Carolinians, seven hundred North Carolinians, and three hundred Virginians.

In all there were less than four thousand men, and Clinton had thirteen thousand of the best soldiers in America, before any reënforcements came in.

On the 9th Admiral Arbuthnot, having waited for a southerly wind and a flowing tide, crowded on all sail and came up the beach channel. A splendid sight, even to an enemy's eyes! Colonel Charles Cotesworth Pinckney, commanding at Fort Moultrie, opened on them with all his guns, carrying away a topmast or two, and killing (it was afterward learned) some four-and-twenty men.

The ships did not pause to reply, but sailed rapidly past, firing a few shot as they went, which did absolutely no harm. Had Whipple's fleet been in position at the Middle Ground to answer Moultrie's guns, much might have been done, but they were sunk in the mud behind Shute's Folly! It was the difference between the command of Rutledge and Moultrie, and of Lincoln and Whipple!

Before long the shells reached every part of the town. Fortunately the lots were so large and the gardens so many that the casualties were by no means as frequent as if the place had been closely built. Some women were sent out even then by the only way which remained open — a perilous passage by boat, across the Cooper River to " Hobcaw," a place near the mouth of the Wando River. Those who remained were kept (especially after a nurse had been killed with a baby in her arms) in the cellars beneath the houses. And the cellars in Charlestown are particularly damp and disagreeable from the lowness of the land.

A memento of the siege that still remains is the armless figure of Mr. Pitt. The arm was carried away by a shell from a battery on James Island, known as the " Watermelon battery," which did much harm to the lower part of the town. Another, which was destroyed in the great fire of 1861, was a large house in Tradd Street, then belonging to Mr. Ferguson, a member of the Council. A ball from the battery at the mouth of Wappoo passed between two iron balusters of a balcony, bending them outward, and went on its way. The balusters were never straightened, and all children were told the tale.

The horror of the time was greatly increased when the British began throwing red-hot balls and terrible contrivances called " carcasses " from their mortars. A carcass was an iron frame which carried combustibles and burst into blaze as it fell. These things, rising high in air above the low earthworks and falling in every part of the town, spread desolation. So many of the houses were of wood that the effect was terrible. The engineers told General Lincoln that the place must fall.

Lincoln then told the Governor that the town must be given up and advised him to leave, in order that the State might not go with it, — that some government might be preserved. Rutledge indignantly refused; he would not leave the people in their extremity. But Lincoln and the officers and Council persisted, — pointing out the impossibility of saving the town, especially as an officer, General

Duportail, had just arrived, sent by General Washington, to advise, and also to say that no assistance would be sent ; and that Lord Rawdon, with a large reënforcement, was coming to Sir Henry Clinton.

Before the Legislature had adjourned it had delegated:—

" Until ten days after its next session, to the Governor John Rutledge Esqr. and such of his Council as he could conveniently consult, power to do everything necessary for the public good, except taking away the life of a citizen without a legal trial." From this Rutledge was commonly called " the Dictator."

With this individual authority, the officers urged, the Governor might keep alive resistance in the State, perhaps raise new forces; surrendered with the town, all would be lost. It was the right policy, and Rutledge went, taking with him three of his Council. The Lieutenant-governor, Thomas Bee, was at the North attending the Congress, and Christopher Gadsden was appointed to act in his stead: " To satisfy the citizens and explain the circumstances."

Then Lincoln held a council of war and proposed to evacuate the town with the Continentals, and with such of the militia as could go. A debate arose. The general had not the command of his officers and the language was vehement. Colonel C. C. Pinckney, "with less than his usual courtesy," exclaimed : —

" I will not say that if the enemy attempt to carry our lines by storm we shall be able to resist them successfully; but I am convinced that we shall cripple the army before us, that although we may not live to enjoy the benefits ourselves, yet to the United States they will be incalculably great. Considerations of self are out of the question; they cannot influence any member of this council. My voice is for rejecting all terms of capitulation and for continuing hostilities to the last extremity."

Spoken as a gallant young soldier fighting for his

OLD POWDER MAGAZINE, CUMBERLAND STREET
Originally a part of Cortevet Bastion on the City Wall.

hearthstone; but although John Laurens, Colonel Henderson, and others supported him, military policy prevailed, and the evacuation was decided. But they had reckoned without the new Lieutenant-governor — Gadsden had no idea of resigning his own town at the bidding of a military officer. He absolutely refused, and the members of his Council — his particular friends — vehemently supported him, and roused the populace. There was danger of an *émeute!* The mob, called in, told Lincoln that if he attempted to withdraw his forces, they would open the gates to the enemy and cut off his retreat, and Lincoln was not the man to resist a mob. Soldiers say that he should have paid no attention to these proceedings, and have gone his own way, that the civil authority had no place at that moment, and that the general should have asserted his own. But Gadsden, who claimed, mistakenly, to control the militia, was a man of far stronger intellect and will than Lincoln, and, unfortunately in this case, dominated him completely. The passage to Hobcaw was in another week seized and closed; there was no longer any hope of saving the army, — capitulation alone remained.

Even that was postponed, and Clinton's second (more severe) offer of terms again rejected.

What was the object of thus continuing an evidently hopeless struggle it is now impossible to say. Two months of desperate resistance might have satisfied any one that the point of honour was saved, especially when the English flag waved over Fort Moultrie, and Tarleton had fallen upon a body of horse at Biggin Bridge, commanded by General Isaac Huger, and cut it to pieces, thus destroying the last hope of relief to the garrison.

That the condition of things was known in the town is shown by a mortifying circumstance. General Lincoln desiring to communicate with the Governor, it was determined that Mr. Edward Rutledge should make the perilous passage by way of Hobcaw, and endeavour to reach his brother. The passage was perilous because both roads and rivers were in possession of the enemy and capture was more than probable. He was to take a message, *not* a letter; the experience of the year before had shown the danger of captured letters. But Mr. Benjamin Smith, a gentleman of reputation, and a very devoted husband, requested Mr. Rutledge to take a letter to his wife from whom he had long been parted, assuring him that it contained only private family affairs. Mr. Rutledge unwarily consented, not reflecting probably upon the elasticity of the phrase "family affairs."

He and his companion Colonel Malmedy were both taken, and the letter when carried to headquarters was found to be so interesting that it was printed, enclosed in empty shells, and thrown into the town!

There it was quickly and secretly printed and scattered abroad as handbills. It gave a truthful but despairing account of the condition of the defence, and must have been most cheerful reading for Sir Henry Clinton. "Nothing remains to comfort me but the hope of saving my life" — "this letter will run great risque as it will be surrounded on all sides, but I know the person to whose care it is committed, and feel for your uneasy situation, I could not but trust it." "Assure yourself that I shall shortly see you — as nothing prevents Lincoln's surrender but a point of honour of holding out to the last extremity. This is nearly at hand as provisions will soon fail."

Such a confession of impending disaster, written by a prominent gentleman, could but increase the anxiety of the populace — and the confidence of the enemy. The fire the next morning was brisker than ever. The way in which this letter was printed and disseminated, showed that there were many traitors within the walls.

Moultrie's simple and straightforward accounts of this

time are interesting. How the earthworks were topped by sand-bags piled, with interstices between, through which the defenders fired, and they being good shots generally hit their mark whereas the British, " being regulars," fired in platoons, frequently too low or too high, and wasted much powder and shot. How they had to watch, not only the lines, but also all the long water front, where it was so easy to make a landing. How the British, after a time, began throwing numbers of small shot and shells from their mortars, which scattered and were very troublesome. He himself was nearly killed in his bed, for being thoroughly worn out he had lain down to rest for a few hours when hearing a more violent cannonade he jumped up, and while "hurrying on his regimentals" a ball crashed through the roof and on the bed from which he had just arisen.

He never tells of his own gallant acts (but Drayton and Garden say that they were many and that he was always perfectly " cool and unruffled "), but of those of others. How well the cannoneers behaved, standing to their guns under the most frightful fire. How the lads insisted on doing their share, Captain Heyward's young brother of fifteen (Nathaniel) carrying powder for his guns. How John Laurens cut up the rare exotic shrubs in his father's garden to make fascines. How in a sortie his aide Captain Philip Neyle was killed. " Then my poor brother was killed " (Thomas Moultrie). And how, a huge shell bursting within ten feet of the powder magazine in Cumberland Street, they, for fear lest worse might ensue, took out at night ten thousand pounds of powder, and carried it to the vaults of the Exchange in Broad Street, where they bricked it up securely, " and although the Provost was next to it, the British never discovered it, and we found it there when we retook the town."

One wonders if he remembered that other night, when

like a party of mischievous boys they had carried powder through the streets, and hidden it from Governor Bull !

THE OLD EXCHANGE, FOOT OF BROAD STREET

At last the trenches were not more than twenty-five feet from the walls; Clinton had warned them that he would not be responsible for what might happen to a town taken by storm, but they held out. Then came a night of horror.

From one hundred and eighty to two hundred pieces of heavy artillery were fired at the same time, while mortars from both sides threw an immense number of shells. "It was a glorious sight to see the shells like meteors crossing each other, and bursting in the air ; it appeared as if the stars were falling to the earth. The fire was incessant almost the whole night ; cannon balls whizzing and shells bursting continually among the combatants ; ammunition chests and temporary magazines blowing up ; great guns bursting, and wounded men groaning among the lines. It was a dreadful night. It was our last great effort, but it availed us nothing."

Three days before Gadsden had declared that the women would walk unterrified among the shells rather than give up the town, but this night was too much for the nerves of the people. On the 10th the citizens begged to be surrendered ; they could endure no more. Gadsden, who would rather have died, was overruled and Lincoln — bullied to the very last — made what poor terms he could, now that the enemy had so entirely the better of him.

His soldierly demand to be allowed the honours of war was refused ; he was not to march out with drums beating and colours flying, but to pile his arms in humble fashion, and this hurt him sorely. But on the whole the terms, if observed, were not bad. The Continentals were to be prisoners of war, and treated as such. That is, fed and lodged like soldiers, and exchanged as opportunity offered. The militia were to be " allowed to go to their respective homes, and should be regarded as prisoners of war upon parole, which parole, so long as they observed it, should secure them from being molested in their property by the British troops." All civil officers and all persons then in

T

the town, whether they had borne arms or not, were to be prisoners on parole. Lincoln tried to get more liberal terms for the citizens, but was assured that the time for negotiation had gone by ; the last offer was the ultimatum, — made simply "from motives of humanity." There was nothing more to be done.

On the 12th of May the garrison marched to a given point and piled arms.

" Where is your second division ?" asked the officer appointed to receive them of Moultrie, who was in command of this painful ceremony. " There is none," replied Moultrie; " these are all the men we have." The Englishman was surprised. " Sir," he said, " you have made a gallant defence. But you had a great many rascals among you " (naming persons) " who came out at night and gave us information of what was passing in the town." They were very exacting about the militia ; requiring every man however old, sick, or even crippled, to come out — their aim was to include the entire population. " All were good enough to swell a conqueror's list." The Continental officers were sent to Haddrell's Point across the Cooper River, the soldiers were kept in prison-ships in the harbour, the militia disbanded were allowed to go home, and the town lay bound, — a shackled thing in the power of the enemy.

CHAPTER XV

FOR the next three years the part of Charles Town was that of a woman, — the proverbially hard part of a woman in war time.

No more was she to know the excitement, the joy, or the terror of battle ; she had only to watch, and wait, and pray for succour from the deeds of others.

Every male within her walls was a paroled prisoner of war. Many of them were sent as disbanded militia to their homes in the country. The Continental officers were across the river at Haddrell's Point, the soldiers confined in prison hulks in the harbour.

The bewildered citizens tried to recover some sort of position. The consistent royalists — the Roupells, Wraggs, Gardens, etc., — who had suffered because of their loyalty, had a right to rejoice in the triumph ; but there were others, less candid, whose opinions, one writer says, " varied according to the success of the moment," who were anxious to enjoy it also. About two hundred citizens, many of whom had, probably from necessity, been in the patriot ranks, but none of whom were of any special distinction, offered an address, declaring that they had always been well-wishers of the British monarchy ; that they were pleased to find themselves again his Majesty's subjects ; and prayed his protection accordingly.

These " addressers," as they were scornfully called, expressed little more than many others felt, but were ashamed to bring forward at that juncture ; namely, that they would be glad to sit in peace, and did not care particularly whether the peace were assured by King or Congress. The " addressers " were much contemned by their stouter-hearted compatriots, but as time wore on many of these were compelled to do much the same thing.

Further tests and oaths were soon imposed; commissioners of sequestration were appointed; the phrase " shall be protected in person and property," the promise contained in the parole papers, was found to be susceptible of very different interpretations.

The citizens found themselves exposed to troubles of many sorts. The hope of saving some of their effects induced many ladies to remain in town. They were often compelled either to give up their houses, or to share them with British officers and their often very objectionable retinues.

Miles Brewton's house, since his death the property of his sister Mrs. Motte, was at once taken as headquarters by Sir Henry Clinton, and was occupied by successive commanders-in-chief during the rest of the war. Moultrie speaks of being received by Clinton " at Mrs. Motte's house in the drawing room up stairs."

Sir Henry, and after him Lord Rawdon, did not eject Mrs. Motte; on the contrary they " requested " her to remain, insisted upon her taking the head of the table, behaving with perfect courtesy and always speaking of themselves as her " guests." The requests of a conqueror are commands ; the lady from policy played the part of hostess, being often complimented on her admirable housekeeping. She, however, kept her three pretty daughters tight locked in the garret, guarded by a faithful " mauma," who would smuggle them dainties and dessert in her apron. When at last Mrs. Motte obtained permission to retire to her plantation, Rawdon thanked her with scrupulous politeness for her " hospitality," but " regretted that he had not been permitted to make the acquaintance of her family!" Rawdon's reputation was none of the best, and the old lady was quite right.

Lord Cornwallis established himself without the town at Drayton Hall, the owner of which, William Henry Drayton, was then in Philadelphia attending the Congress. He too was courteous to the ladies, but it was said that he

THE "PROVOST"

The Cellar of the Old Exchange used as a Prison during the Revolution.

kept them on very short commons, doling out the scantiest rations to the family and servants.

Drayton Hall, the only house on the right bank of Ashley River which escaped the flames of 1865, still has the letters K. W. cut deep in one of its brick pillars, the work of a Hessian soldier, who supposed those to be the initials of his commander's name, Korn Wallis.

These were the chiefs, who, when they pleased, were courtly gentlemen; others were not so "vastly civil." Many ladies were forcibly ejected, and it was better to be ejected than to be obliged to share a house with odious persons; such as Major Hanger who brought in animals, dogs and monkeys, and vile women to insult the ladies.

Mrs. Izard pleaded to be allowed to remain in her own dwelling on account of the illness of her child, and was driven from it with a dying boy in her arms. Mrs. C. C. Pinckney and her children were turned out, that Colonel Balfour, commandant of the town, might take possession of the house which had so long been the residence of English Governors. Mrs. Heyward, wife of the signer of the Declaration of Independence, left her windows dark when an illumination was ordered in honour of the victory. Her sister was desperately ill at the moment, but the lowest rabble was encouraged to pelt the house with filth and obscene abuse. All these were the wives of Continental officers and had a right to protection. These things were charged to the account of Rawdon.

Tarleton, the dashing sabreur, was more studied in his affronts; the poor lady upon whom he was quartered was only allowed to keep one small room for herself and family. She prayed to be allowed the use of another; but the answer, conveyed in a polite note, was that "reflection convinces me that enemies should not be allowed any convenience."

The chief terror of the town was the "Provost," the damp dark cellar under the Exchange, next to the hiding-place of Moultrie's powder.

In this single room were confined the lowest criminals and malefactors. Men and women together, and any one, however respectable, against whom any complaint might be brought. There they were kept awaiting trial, and trial was often long delayed. The story of two honourable ladies, who were immured in this loathsome dungeon on the most frivolous pretext, is shocking.

Still, on the whole, compared with other conquests, the condition of the conquered was not, at first, so bad. The Continental officers at Haddrell's, although crowded, were well fed and lodged, their families were allowed to visit them, and they had some privileges.

These, however, were curtailed after a dinner given on the Fourth of July, at which the " sentiments " and toasts were too patriotic and too fervently expressed. Moultrie, who as senior officer exercised a sort of protective surveillance over the others, interposed in their behalf, but the rule was made stricter. Still the fact that they could give such a dinner at all argues a certain amount of freedom.

Moultrie apologizes quaintly for his comrades. "It is no wonder they are sometimes quarrelsome and behave badly. They are crowded together and are, some of them, very uncouth gentlemen."

Moultrie himself and Colonel C. C. Pinckney, as field officers (Colonel Laurens was soon exchanged), were quartered at Snee Farm, a place about a mile from Haddrell's. They could sometimes see their friends, and were allowed to have their own servants, to receive letters (which were generally opened), and to have books and papers. The *Gazette*, published by authority, was regularly sent to them, so that they could read every misfortune of their countrymen, and the jeers of the garrison wits at their woes. It is certain that plenty of rebellious news leaked in also, but it was many months before anything occurred that could raise their spirits.

A letter from Colonel Pinckney is given, as showing the way of life and the resolute determination to keep an equal mind under these trying circumstances. Few men would interest themselves so warmly in the education of a nephew of fourteen at any time. It is to his sister Mrs. Horrÿ of Hampton, South Santee.

" MY DEAR HARRIOTT, I enclose you a Letter for your son ; I wish Mr. Horrÿ would purchase Goldsmith's Roman History for him that he may read it this winter at Santee if you carry him there. I see an abridgment of Goldsmith is advertised, I do not mean he should read that, but the work at large in two volumes octavo. Let him read the first Volume which brings down the history to the usurpation of Augustus, over and over again, till he is perfectly master of it, before he begins the History of the Emperors; and when he has finished both, you may then let him read Rollin's Antient History. These with his Latin and French will find him employment during the Winter; but if he should still have any spare time you may teach him Geography, — Guthrie's Geographical Grammar I believe is the best. Exercise him frequently in writing down from his Memory any remarkable event that he has read, attend carefully to his style and language, let him never make use of an ungrammatical expression without amending it for him, and always accustom him to make use of the best and aptest words the language will afford. By no means neglect the making him frequently get by heart select pieces of English Poetry, your own taste will direct you in the choice of them, but be sure to let them be such as he can understand ; and oblige him to repeat them aloud with great distinctness and proper emphasis.

" I am informed my Wife and Children were turned out of my House last Tuesday, pray let me know what is now the pretence for this manœuvre, and whether my Books, Papers and Cloaths are all seized.

" I am very glad we did not know of the wretched fare my Brother had at Camden ; it would have added considerably to my uneasiness for him ; fat pork I apprehend is not the proper diet for a wounded soldier ; we are however

exceedingly obliged to Mrs. Clay and the Ladies at whose house he staid for their care and tenderness to him; Dr. Hay, and the Gentleman of the Faculty [English surgeons] I am informed have shown him the greatest attention, I hope my Mother has recovered of her sick headache and that my dear Sally and Children are well. The failure of the inoculation in my little Charles will I suppose prevent my seeing my Sally as soon as I expected, for as neither Mrs. Moultrie nor any of the People here have had the small pox, he must be free of Infection before she can bring him. I received safe the Blanket and Cloth for Tobey, also a Baskett of Biscuit, for which I am much obliged to my Mother; pray give my duty to her and my love to my dear Sally & Children, my Nephews & Nieces, Mr. & Mrs. A. Middleton, —— Rutledge, Dr. & Mrs. Drayton, Mr. Horrÿ & —— , and be assured that I am
"Your affectionate Brother,
"CHARLES COTESWORTH PINCKNEY."

"I also received a Bottle of Vinegar and Letters from Mrs. Clay & my Brother to my Mother: Now he is in a way of getting proper nourishment, I have no doubt but that he will recover fast. I shall be glad of one ounce more of Bark which I think will secure me from any more Fever this season. I have not had any Fever since the first of September. Both Genl. & Mrs. Moultrie neglect taking Bark, and have now a return of their fever. I return Mrs. Clay's and my Brother's letters; she writes charmingly, — I cannot sufficiently express how much I am obliged to her for the Care of my Brother."

This letter is addressed:
"Mrs. Daniel Horrÿ,
"No. 66 Broad Street.

"By Genl. Moultrie's ⎱
Servant Fortune" ⎰

The passage referring to " my Brother at Camden " relates to Major Tom Pinckney, severely wounded at that battle.

The size of town lots then is shown by the fact that the house at 66 Broad was on the site of the Cathedral, now about 126.

The British had great hopes of persuading the Continental privates confined in the prison hulks to join their army, and at first they were well treated; but severity increased as time went on and they resisted all inducements.

The sick were shockingly neglected in direct violation of the parole conditions.

For a time the thoughts of the people dwelt upon rescue. Would the Governor be able to raise a force to deliver them? Would the Northern States send troops to their assistance? Gradually all expectation failed. Two bodies of troops which the Governor had collected upon leaving town were routed by Tarleton, — and another was also destroyed near the borders of North Carolina; — and then for a time hope seemed dead.

For a little while the country appeared better off than the town. The militia at least were at home, could care for their families, and sow their seed; and although the Continentals were in prison bounds, the women took up the charge and kept things going.

Many a lady sallied forth at daybreak, went the rounds of the stable, barnyard, and field; directed the ploughing of corn and the hoeing of rice, wondering much if husband or son would be at home in time to harvest the crops, springing green in this melancholy May.

This curiously quiescent state endured but for a moment; Clinton, preparing to go North, issued proclamations clearly defining the position of the vanquished. His demands did not probably appear unreasonable to him.

A man must be 'for the King or against him. If for

him, then military service was clearly the duty of the young man ; faithful support, of the old. Such service would be rewarded by " effectual countenance, protection and support," "peace, liberty, and security of property." But if a man were against his Majesty, then his portion was " the most exemplary severity, and confiscation of property."

Not more than might have been expected, but for the parole granted not more than a month before. That parole, it was distinctly stated, was to endure while the war lasted, and by it those who remained at home and observed the conditions should be protected in person and property.

The war was certainly *not* over, and yet these new conditions were imposed. The British expected thus to crush the rebellious spirit, and only roused it to activity.

Many a man who would have sat quiet and listened to the clash of arms far off, when called upon to choose, rode to the American instead of the English camp, and found his attachment to the cause grow as he suffered for it. Even those who having great possessions made obeisance to preserve them, did so under protest more or less public, and, holding that the bad faith of the English commander exonerated them from obligations of sincerity, gave aid and comfort when possible to their countrymen.

The reign of terror began —Tarleton and his " Loyal Legion," a fine colonel and splendid soldiers without a single restraining scruple, traversed the State from the sea to the mountains, slaying and hanging ; Major Wemyss, whose favourite weapon was the torch, Ferguson, and other leaders, were commanding regulars ; many bands of Tories were equally active. Lord Rawdon commanded in the interior. Lord Cornwallis was, after the departure of Sir Henry Clinton, commander-in-chief. Instead of being intimidated the people were infuriated. The old Scotch proverb of " a burnt byre a blazing brand " was fulfilled.

The Tories, zealous in their well-paid devotion to the Crown, and sustained by the power of England, were numerous ; they rose, turned upon their neighbours, and especially in the middle and upper parts of the State, the war assumed the most terrible fratricidal character. What Sir Henry's proclamations had begun, the outrages of his officers enhanced, and then in an evil hour for themselves they burned down the home of Sumter at Claremont, Craven County ; and raided the parish of St. John's Berkeley, the birthplace of Francis Marion.

Sumter and Marion had both been accidentally absent from the siege of Charles Town, but Sumter, hearing that Governor Rutledge was on his way to North Carolina, left home to join him only a few hours before Tarleton (who had nearly captured Rutledge himself) reached his place.

The Sumters had been in great domestic trouble. They had recently lost several children, and Mrs. Sumter, who belonged to the soldierly Cantey family, had been smitten by paralysis. When the British arrived, she and a niece were the only persons in the house ; the only remaining child, a little boy of twelve, having rushed off with the best horse to hide it in a hollow of the hills.

The house, stable, and barn were soon plundered of every desirable thing, and were then set on fire. The young lady appealed to the soldiers to save her utterly helpless aunt, and two of them, lifting her in her invalid chair, carried her into the yard and set her down to watch the blazing house.

Struck with her composure and fortitude one man, more compassionate than his fellows, brought her a ham from her own smoke-house, telling her that he gave it to keep her from starving ; and hid it under the cushions of her chair, lest his comrades should take it away. This was the sole pity shown. The little boy, who had safely concealed his horse, climbed a tree and saw the burning of his home. The place, near the present Stateburg, keeps the name of "The Ruins" to this day.

Sumter, commissioned by the Governor, first as colonel,

THE HOUSE AT THE CORNER OF TRADD AND ORANGE STREETS, FROM WHICH IT IS SAID GENERAL MARION FELL

afterward as general, became, according to Lord Cornwallis, "the greatest plague" of the British in the South. His fiery courage, and willingness to fight against any odds, gained him the sobriquet of the "Game Cock."

It is impossible to estimate the value to the American cause of that broken leg which occasioned Marion's escape from the universal captivity at Charles Town. The habits of that day may be mildly described as convivial, and when a gentleman gave a dinner party, he often turned the key upon his guests until they had done due honour to his Madeira and Port.

Such joviality did not suit Marion, a small, spare man, of sober abstemious habits; and finding himself thus locked in one evening, he tried to escape by letting himself down from a window. Unluckily, — or rather luckily for his country, — he miscalculated the distance, fell and broke his leg. Being thus incapacitated when the siege was about to begin, he was sent home to St. John's to be cured, and so was one of the three Continental officers (the others being General Isaac Huger and Major Thomas Pinckney) who were not surrendered by the capitulation of the town.

The house which used to be shown as the one from which he fell is that built by Captain John Stuart, at the corner of Tradd and Orange streets. General Moultrie says, "the house next Roupell's." Roupell's house, pulled down about thirty years ago, was at the other end of the same square on Friend Street, and it is very probable that there was no dwelling between them at that time, when the lots were still very large.

He too made his way into North Carolina to the Governor, who had gone to confer with General Gates, "the hero of Saratoga," then advancing to meet Lord Rawdon and fight the battle of Camden. Rutledge sent him back with a colonel's commission in his pocket, and orders to collect what men he could and join Gates's army. But Gates would have none of him. He could not imagine that the few score shabby men and boys dressed in any sort of garments, with little black leathern caps, could be of any service to his well-armed and uniformed force. Baron de Kalb, the second in command, the gentleman who had come with La Fayette to fight for America, received him cordially and appreciatively. But Gates, to get rid of the poor-looking party, sent him off with orders to "destroy every boat on the river" (the Wateree River, on which Camden is situated) "by which the British might escape to Charles Town." It was soon no question of the British escaping. Gates's fortune was as bad as his lieutenant Lincoln's had been.

The battle, badly planned and badly fought, was lost; the brave De Kalb was killed; Gates, who had been full of confidence, fled ignominiously, and the American cause was in even worse plight than before.

The loss of De Kalb was much deplored. He had found many friends in the country. His breastplate of polished steel was long preserved at Middleton Place, and the town of Camden keeps his helmet and has erected a monument to his memory.

Marion's shabby jacket had saved him from sharing the calamity.

The deeds of Sumter, as of Pickens and other well-known leaders, were generally performed in the middle or up country, and have only an indirect influence upon the fortunes of Charles Town, but Marion is the hero of the parishes. News of him, of his "Men" and their daring exploits, brought, no one knew how, through the lines, kept hope alive even in the darkest hour of the distressed town.

Distressed it certainly was ; for, the measures already taken for forcing the allegiance of the leading men having failed, Lord Cornwallis determined to remove those whose resolution he could not break, and whose example strengthened the patriotic spirit.

Accordingly one Sunday morning thirty gentlemen were

aroused from their slumbers, arrested, and taken to the
prison of the Exchange, and afterward to an armed vessel
in the harbour.

Among the prisoners were Lieutenant-governor Gadsden, Alexander Moultrie, brother to the general, Thomas
Heyward, and Edward Rutledge, Dr. Ramsay, the future
historian, and other prominent citizens. No reason was
assigned for the arrest, and the prisoners who, having
been taken within the walls of Charles Town, were confess-
edly still on parole, could imagine no reason therefor.
They were enlightened soon enough, however, when they
were informed that " Lord Cornwallis being assured that
by their treasonable correspondence they had promoted
and fermented the late Rebellion in the Country," he had
determined to change their place of residence to St.
Augustine, where they would be transported accordingly.
They sent memorials and remonstrances, of course, but no
answers were vouchsafed. But they were told that those
who considered this proceeding any infringement of the
Articles of Capitulation would be considered as prisoners
of war, and as such be delivered at St. Augustine.

This bribe to acquiescence was skilful, but the prisoners
rejected it. They knew, and Cornwallis knew, that it
was a violation of the terms of capitulation and that he
was simply using the right of the strongest. Moultrie
wrote this bold and sensible letter from his confinement
at Snee Farm : —

"Sir : On perusing the paper of the 29th of August,
of Robertson McDonald and Cameron, published by
authority, to my astonishment I find a paragraph to this
effect 'The following is a correct list of the prisoners
sent on board the Sandwich yesterday morning,' and
underneath the names of the most respectable gentlemen
inhabitants of this State, most of whose characters I am

so well acquainted with, that I cannot believe they would have been guilty of any breach of their parole, or any article of capitulation, or done anything to justify so vigorous a proceeding against them. I therefore think it my duty as the senior Continental officer prisoner under the capitulation, to demand a release of those gentlemen, particularly such as are entitled to the benefit of that act.

"This harsh proceeding demands my particular attention, and I do, therefore, in behalf of the United States of America require that they be admitted immediately to return to their paroles; as their being hurried on board a prison ship (and I fear without being heard) is a violation of the ninth article of the capitulation. If this demand cannot be complied with, I am to request that I may have leave to send an officer to Congress to present this grievance, that they may interpose in behalf of those gentlemen in the manner they may think proper.

"I am etc.

"WILLIAM MOULTRIE."

No direct answer was returned, but Balfour, through a subordinate, informed the general that such letters would not be received; and Moultrie knew that argument was vain with the man who commanded twenty legions.

Not one of these thirty-three men (for ten more were soon added to their number) made the slightest concession of principle. They protested that they had faithfully kept the parole oath, but they made no profession of allegiance to the Crown. Another parole was now required of them with especial reference to St. Augustine. After consultation all the prisoners except Gadsden decided to accept it, but he, with the fiery independence of his nature, positively refused, saying that he would enter into no new contract with men who had once deceived him. The British commanders had disregarded

U

the capitulation of Charles Town and he would trust them no more. " Think better of it," said Colonel Glazier, the English officer who received them on landing, " a second refusal will fix your destiny. A dungeon will be your habitation." " Prepare it," said the brave old man (for he was an old man by this time). " I will give no parole, so help me God." He was accordingly immured in the dark, damp dungeon in the old Spanish castle of San Marco (now most inappropriately called Fort Marion) and remained there for nearly eleven months.

The other prisoners were lodged in the town, were allowed to have their own servants to attend them, and to supply themselves with comforts and even with some luxuries. A silver tea-pot which made the voyage to and returned from St. Augustine is still in the possession of Mr. Edward Rutledge's great granddaughter. The English Governor Tonyn, however, kept a watchful eye upon them, and finding that they had arranged for divine service " according to their rebellious principles " absolutely forbade such a mischievous form of religion, but offered seats in the parish church where they " might suitably pray for his Majesty."

Judging by the following letter such prayers would have brought his luckless Majesty no good. It is from Samuel Prioleau, descendant of the first emigrant Huguenot Pastor Elias Prioleau, and son of the lady whose many-coloured funeral was one of the first evidences of resistance to " Ministerial oppression."

It is to his wife, who had been a Miss Cordes, also a Huguenot. It may be as well to explain that in Southern speech " a pavillion " is a mosquito net.

"St. Augustine, 19th June, 1781.

"Dear Katy: I am well and have recd. yours of the 5th of May, but am glad to find that yr. mother and Katy

Cordes " (a cousin) " are with you and they are well of the small pox.

" I have recd. a Pavillion but no Stockings.

" Nothing has given me greater pleasure than to hear of our Friends behaving in so noble and spirited a manner when they were put on Board the Prison ship, and that my Father and Phil will join them. We that are here I find by Balfour's Letter are also Hostages.

" If anything in that way should happen to me that is to say being hung or shot, which I believe they dare not do, I hope my sons will revenge it when they are able, and never be at peace with Great Britain.

" We hear that the Prisoners familys have been insulted. I beg as a particular favour if any has insulted you or any of my family you will let me know who it was, and what was the insult, as I think I stand a chance of being relieved and may meet them in some part of the world. Beg you will remember me to all Friends. I am Dear Katy

" Afly. yours,
" S. PRIOLEAU, JR."

Address :
" Mrs. Catharine Prioleau.
" In (blot, illegible.)
" S.C."

. It is delightful to come across so frank an expression of the natural man, free from the phrases with which the people of that day usually dressed out their epistles. This stiff-necked Huguenot stands by his cause, wants revenge on his enemies, and says so plainly.

" Phil " was put on board the prison-ship. There is no mention of the father in the printed lists. These hundred and thirty militia officers were arrested and kept in the hulks as hostages for the good treatment of Tories who might fall into the hands of the Americans, and were clearly informed by Balfour that their lives depended on the safety of their enemies.

To their honour be it said that these officers, thus confined, wrote to General Greene, enclosing a copy of Balfour's letter and saying that "should it fall to the lot of any or all of them to be made victims agreeable to the menaces therein contained they had only to regret that their blood could not be disposed of more to the advantage of the glorious cause to which they had adhered."

The next command for Charles Town was that only persons who had taken the oath of allegiance should be allowed to carry on any trade or industry for the support of their families ; or should collect a debt, or require payment for goods or service ; but any one might sue them, and they would have no redress. The Commissioners of Sequestration, of whom John Cruden was the chief, were authorized to seize and sell all property belonging to rebels (even that of Continental Officers, especially protected by the Articles of Capitulation), except a small portion which "from motives of humanity" was to be reserved for wives and children.

This pocket pinch did more than the banishment of the leaders to break the spirit.

Many men submitted and took protection, some to gain liberty to work and save their families from destitution, others, "lords of ancient halls," to save their estates. Perhaps the wonder was that there were not more of these, for many held out obstinately ; and Commissioner Cruden published numerous advertisements of the estates, real and personal, of these indomitable men.

The blow fell very heavily upon the negroes ; for those belonging to rebels were driven down in gangs to the wharves and shipped to the West Indies. And those of "protected men," being more secretly induced to leave their masters, thronged to the British camps, where many died of smallpox, and the rest also found themselves sent to the docks.

The spoil obtained by these measures was immense. Two thousand negroes were shipped, Dr. Ramsay says, at one embarkation ; and Mr. Bancroft puts the value of the property divided by the English and Hessian commissioners at three hundred thousand pounds sterling.

All the time the English were working to persuade the officers and men to leave the Continental for the British army. The former Governor, Lord Charles Montagu, had returned to what he still called "this Province" and was busily engaged in raising a regiment of Americans which should be sent to the West Indies, and thus avoid the odium of fighting against their countrymen. Offers of commissions in this regiment were made to several officers : to Moultrie he offered, in a really affectionate letter, his own position of colonel. He reminded him of their old friendship, and of how natural it is for him to advise, and says : —

"You have now fought bravely in the cause of your country for many years, and in my opinion fulfilled the duty every individual owes to it. You have had your share of hardships and difficulties, and if the contest is still to be continued younger hands should now take the toil from you. You have now a fair opening of quitting that service with honour and reputation to yourself by going to Jamaica with me. The world will readily attribute it to the known friendship which has existed between us, and by quitting this country for a short time you could avoid any disagreeable conversations and might return at your leisure to take possession of your estates for yourself and family." He then offers the colonelcy.

The touch of "avoiding disagreeable conversations" is delightful ! But although the tempter thus showed him the world and the pleasures thereof (and Moultrie was an honest gentleman who loved the pleasures as well as any other man), he rose indignant at the suggestion. His " Memoirs " have fortunately preserved the answer, which is too good to be mutilated, and which having been lately published in McCrady's history is omitted here.

It should be mentioned that before addressing this letter to General Moultrie, Lord Charles had approached his son upon the subject. The young man answered at once " that he did not dare to carry such a proposition to his Father."

Tempting offers were also made to the two Pinckneys, both then prisoners. Their letters are unfortunately lost, but Colonel C. C. Pinckney's daughter has recorded one or two of her father's answers in a little sketch quoted in the " Life of Eliza Pinckney," and therefore not given.

Major Garden says that one of the British officers, a Captain McMahon, told him, after the war, that he had once "attempted to tamper with Col. Pinckney, touching with delicacy upon the possibility of a reconciliation with our government, hinting on the honours that would be his should he declare his approbation of our measures. The result was indeed humiliating to me. I was awed into silence by the superiority of his patriotic virtue, and felt myself degraded by the office I had undertaken."

No pains were spared to corrupt John Laurens. — It need not be said with absolute futility.

These proposals were more easily made because among the British officers were many who had been at school or college with the young Carolinians who were now in the opposing ranks. Sometimes kind offices were exchanged between them, as in the case of the McKenzies. One brother, a naval officer, was captured at sea, on his way to Savannah, and at once asked to be consigned to the care of his old school-fellow, Thomas Pinckney. When Major Pinckney, severely wounded at the battle of Camden, fell into the hands of the enemy, the other brother, an army officer, showed him every attention, and it was owing to his entreaties that the English surgeons interested themselves in the case, and saved the leg, which he had nearly lost.

There was a story of two Francis Kinlochs, cousins and school-fellows, — one on the British, the other on the American side. After some battle they were pursuer and pursued. The latter escaped and the former sent his cousin a message, ."Tell Francis 'tis no wonder he got away, — even at Eton he always could outrun me."

Such good feeling very much mitigated the barbarity of war. Garden, after speaking with great severity of the "cruelties of Cornwallis, Rawdon, Balfour and Moncrieff, the sword of Tarleton, torch of Prévost and Wemyss, rapacity of Cochran, and Prévost," gives a list of honourable exceptions and adds : "The. Lt. Colonels St. George and Fox, Capt. Steward of the Guards, Wynyard, McKensie, Charles Morris, the purveyor, all old Westminsters, were faithful to old friendships." Some of the Loyalists were kind to their oppressed countrymen, and in the low country there were few instances of the terrible *acharnement* between Whigs and Tories, which for three years made the upper districts — to speak mildly — a hell. Mr. Freer, of John's Island, was conspicuous for humanity in this respect ; and Captain Buckel sent two hundred pounds to Johnson at St. Augustine, and offered an unlimited letter of credit for the use of the other prisoners. He was requited at the close of the war by being especially exempted from sequestration and amercement.

In August, twenty-two more exiles were sent to St. Augustine, — among them Arthur Middleton. Thus the three surviving signers of the "Declaration of Independence " (for Thomas Lynch had been lost at sea on his

way to Cuba, where he was going in search of health)
were now prisoners in that little Spanish town.

The leaders safely out of the way, the English imagined
that some restoration of the pleasures of society might
allure their obstinate subjects. Many of the officers were,
as has been said, established in handsome houses; they
now proceeded to give balls and entertain.

They met — one is proud to say — with very little success. No such gay doings as the Mischianza ever took
place in Charlestown. The loyal ladies of course accepted
gladly the invitations of their gallant hosts, but the
"Patriotic Fair," to use Moultrie's favourite name, held
aloof, and it was only almost under compulsion, — when
an invitation equal to a command compelled attendance, that any Whig dame or damsel appeared at these
feasts.

Mr. Gilmore Simms' romantic novel of "Katharine
Walton" gives a vivid impression of this curious society,
where every man and woman was on guard, each striving
to discover what the opinions of the other really were.
The British officers of course were true; but the man
in the brand-new Tory uniform, apparently one of Ferguson's or Fraser's regiment, might be plotting a double
treason, or might be one of Marion's men disguised in
loyal regimentals. He describes a ball given by the
Commandant Balfour in Colonel Pinckney's East Bay
house. It had been the talk of the town for weeks before
it took place, and was talked of for many years by ladies
who had *not* been present.

Balfour, although he could boast of honourable wounds,
was much fonder of wine and women than of war, and
was despised even more than he was hated; but as a host
he spared no pains to make his ball a brilliant affair.
One incident long remembered was the accident of the
chief Royalist belle, Miss Polly Roupell. She was sitting

in the deep recess of the staircase window, which, lacking a button (in those days pulleys were not), was propped on the sword of her partner. The officer, suddenly summoned, hastily withdrew the sword.

The sash fell full on the arm of the lady, who shrieked and fainted from the pain.

The officer, quick in all things, not waiting to find water, seized the bowl which stood near and *douched* the belle with strong rum punch! The shock revived her rapidly, but the arm was broken. A bystander was rude enough to declare that it was "great waste of good liquor," and Major Harry Barry, the wit and *bel esprit* of the garrison, wrote some gallant lines beginning "When fair Roupell a-fainting lay," which it is to be hoped consoled the sufferer.

It was said to have been at a ball given by a Royalist lady, Mrs. Tidyman, in the house which is now No. 2 Ladson Street, that "mad Archy Campbell" laid the wager which went far to justify his nickname.

He was Captain Campbell, a brave, honourable, but terribly erratic and flighty character, easily led into any sort of folly, certainly of unsound mind, but valued for his daring courage and frank speech.

That was the day of wagers. Everything was the subject of a bet, as the old England memoirs show. Men, supposedly sensible, would risk pounds on the chance of which should see the most cows from the window on his side of the chaise when they were going on a journey.

Mad Archy's wager was on a more important matter. He was, in his own wild fashion, deeply in love with Miss Paulina Phelps, a beauty and heiress of a Tory family. The lady was coy and coquettish, and not averse to playing one lover against the other. At Mrs. Tidyman's ball an officer just arrived from Philadelphia devoted himself to Miss Phelps, who accepted his homage with smiling satisfaction.   Captain Campbell felt himself eclipsed, and consequently aggrieved.   His comrades teased him, his rival smiled serene, and he grew furious.   There was talk of a challenge and a duel, but first Mad Archy said he must be married!   To the taunts and jests of his companions he replied by offering a wager.   His beautiful Arab horse to fifty pounds that within three days he would, *with her own consent*, marry Miss Phelps!

The bet was at once taken, but the laughers had not counted upon the weakness of woman.

Captain Campbell invited Miss Phelps to take a drive with him in his fashionable gig, with his fast-trotting horse, to admire the beauties of Goose Creek.   Carlyle somewhere declares that to " keep a gig " is considered a proof of respectability.   Miss Phelps probably thought riding in Captain Campbell's a proof of fashion, for although she knew the distance great for a *tête-à-tête* expedition, and the crack-brained character of her charioteer, she set forth.

Mad Archy's plan was simple.   Two hours of breakneck speed, over banks and ditches, rough roads and pine-wood tracks, all accompanied with the wildest talk, would, he thought, bewilder most people.

Paulina was delicate and silly; she would surely be terrified.   The scheme succeeded; it was a half-fainting, helpless girl, whom he took from the gig, and handed over to the ministrations of Parson Ellington at his rectory, near Goose Creek Church.   Mr. Ellington was as bewildered and almost as helpless as his visitor; for when, the lady being somewhat revived, Campbell announced that they had come to be married, he could only say, " Not without assent."   The terrified girl could say nothing, and the rector's scruples were appeased by a pistol presented at his head, and the assurance that he should be instantly shot if he made further objection.

There was another pistol too, and Paulina probably thought that she herself might be its mark, so in fear and trembling the ceremony was performed, and the triumphant bridegroom bore off his prize to the town — and won his wager!

This marriage so strangely begun did not last long. The bridegroom was killed in less than a year. The bride said afterward that until they arrived at Goose Creek, she had never thought seriously of marrying Captain Campbell, having always supposed his wild talk to be merely "soldierly love-making."

The "Book of Common Prayer" of Mr. Ellington, with his autograph upon the title-page, was discovered lately in a second-hand book-shop in Charlestown, and is now the property of the Goose Creek Church. It is always *en evidence* (*not* in use) on the annual service which is still held in the little old building.

Parson Ellington was one of the Loyalist clergymen in the parishes. The Whigs had of course been dispossessed; but their successors did not sit easy in their seats. They knew well that their "protected" parishioners were, as a general rule, praying with their lips and not with their hearts, keeping carefully to the letter of the law.

The Goose Creek parish was mainly composed of a knot of malcontents, biding their time to resume their arms. It may be supposed that, as they gazed upon the lion and the unicorn above the chancel, they greatly hoped that the Crown might have a fall. On one Sunday, Mr. Ellington in due form and with great fervour uttered the petition " That it may please thee to bless and preserve our Sovereign Lord King George," and waited for the response, " We beseech Thee to hear us." Ominous silence for an appreciable time, and then in sonorous tones from the depths of the Izard pew, " Good Lord deliver us! "

Mr. Izard was warned that mistakes in the order of

the Litany were not permitted, and might be followed by arrest!

There is a hatchment to a Ralph Izard still standing in the Goose Greek Church, but the writer does not know if it is to this Ralph, or to another of his family.

The churches of course felt the troubles of the times; but here the Anglicans had decidedly the advantage. The English necessarily respected their own shrines and but few of the buildings were injured. In most of the States the clergy had stood for the Crown, but in Carolina almost all went with the State. They were dispossessed and some were exiled—notably Mr. Smith, the rector of St. Philip's, who was banished, and his estate sequestrated, but the church property was unmolested. A Mr. Morean was appointed in Mr. Smith's place. At St. Michael's an election was held for clergy and vestry. The pews of the rebellious members of the congregation had been confiscated, but Mr. Commissioner Cruden returned them to the Church, and a loyal vestry with the Reverend Mr. Jenkins for rector, was chosen.

The other denominations suffered. The Presbyterians and Independents seem to have been particularly obnoxious and were abominably treated. So many of their churches were burned, and their clergy so harassed, that Mr. McCrady states that it had much to do with the sudden revolt of the up-country, which was their stronghold. The reluctant militia became ardent volunteers.

Even the Old White Meeting in Charles Town, which was generally regarded with reverence, was turned into a granary. Horses were pastured among the graves of its churchyard, and many of the monuments broken or defaced.

During all this time the women had much to do. The business of estates, of communicating with the authorities, of appeasing the sequestrators, of obtaining small relief of various kinds, was carried on by them.

To effect this they were allowed (always under supervision) some freedom in passing to and between the town and the plantations. Occasionally they were permitted (as Colonel Pinckney's letter shows) to visit their husbands in prison or a friend in distress.

A lady permitted to go on such an errand naturally took something useful with her. Not only the news of the garrison, and intended movements of the troops, — information quickly and widely circulated,— but some tangible, serviceable object. A pair of stout boots was sensible footwear for one about to visit a plantation, but they were often transferred to the legs of one of Marion's troopers by evening, and the lady returned to town in thin slippers which had been an inner *chaussure* in the morning.

One fair damsel so disguised a soldier's uniform cap that it passed for a becoming head-dress, and not to speak of pistols and even swords smuggled under spreading "farthingales," epaulettes for a newly made colonel were on one occasion passed through the lines on the shoulders of an enterprising dame.

Widows were at great advantage ; being responsible for no man's proceedings, they were less severely dealt with than were other women ; and with the danger of no man's life or liberty on their hearts, they could give their favourite weapon — the tongue — full play.

Most of the houses still retained belonged to this privileged class, and little gatherings of friends cheered the weary hours by contriving ways to send help and comforts to the men in the field. The means for these gifts became daily less ; poverty began to be felt. "Two half-worn waistcoats and three handkerchiefs" were things to be thankful for.

One or two Tory ladies who still had kindred or affiliation with the Whigs opened their houses to the garrison, and occasionally a stray patriotic lady or elderly gentleman would find themselves in a truly loyal assemblage. The acquaintance of the officers could not be wholly declined, for business necessarily brought them together, and policy maintained the relation.

One could hardly entreat a man to spare one's house or one's horses in the morning, and cut him in the afternoon; but the men were made to smart for the honour of their conversation. Even the redoubtable Tarleton did not escape their wit, as when having affected to speak scornfully of his most brilliant antagonist, Colonel William Washington, he said that "Washington he heard was an ignorant fellow, and could not write his name."

Mrs. Charles Elliott at once replied, — "At least, Colonel, he can make his mark." Alluding to Tarleton's hand, from which Washington had swept three fingers with his sabre.

The accusation was false, for "The Sword of the Army" had been bred to the Church, and is said to have left it for the same reason that afterward made him decline a seat in the Legislature. He could not, he said, speak in public. Speech or sermon were alike impossible to the hero of a hundred fights.

Once again the commander of the legion was twitted by a lady in behalf of his rival. "I should like to see this fellow of whom people talk so much," he said. "What a pity," said Mrs. Brewton, "that you had not looked behind you at the battle of Cowpens." That being the battle where Washington had chased him from the field.

Tarleton was not insensible to the charm and virtue of woman. When the beautiful Mrs. Shubrick, "a heroine to be proud of," refused to allow him to seize a fugitive who had taken refuge in her room, declaring that he should only enter it over her dead body, he turned away, exclaiming, "If American men equalled the women, the Rebellion would soon be victorious." And to a number of ladies who had taken refuge at Brabant, the plantation of the Reverend Mr. Smith, he showed himself everything that was courteous and considerate.

The wittiest of all the Whig ladies was Mrs. Robert Brewton (afterward Foster). She was the widow of the half-nephew of Miles Brewton, and a great favourite in society; she even dared to tease the dreaded Moncrieff, the commissioner of captures.

He joined her one day as she walked down Broad Street, and as they approached the Governor's house, of which he had taken possession, he carelessly stepped on her dress, and tore from it a long crape fold. He apologized humbly for his awkwardness. " Ah, no," she answered quickly, "'tis just in time for its purpose;" then tying the long strip to the railing of the steps she added, " Where are you, dearest Governor ? Your house mourns for you, and longs for your return as we all do." Banishment was ultimately the fate of this daring lady.

An officer who was going into the country politely offered to take any letters she might wish to send. She thanked him, but declined. She "did not care to have her letters read at the head of Marion's Brigade." The officer really was captured, and believed firmly that she had informed the partisans of his intended visit, — and who can say that she did not ?

Men, even when non-combatants, were allowed less freedom. One veteran patriot, Mr. Tom Singleton, the ancestor of the novelist of Carolina, William Gilmore Simms, was a Virginian by birth, a rich tobacco planter and merchant. It is said that Tobacco Street, in front of the Citadel, takes its name from the large crops brought by wagons from Virginia and stored in the warehouse fronting upon it. This warehouse stood where the Citadel now is, and in front of it was a famous well, the water of which was so much valued for medicinal purposes that people came from far and near to drink of it, and it was bottled and shipped away. When the use of it was discontinued is not known ; it is said to be now covered by the monument of Mr. Calhoun.

The old gentleman owned the entire square, then called " Inspection," but he lived in Church Street, three doors below Tradd ; his house being a great meeting-place for the rebels. Here he harboured and concealed men who stole into the town by night, and forwarded information to the camps. He was bravely aided by his daughter, Mrs. Gates, one of the heroines of the time, who, being very strong and fearless, would often row these secret agents across the river at night, charged with money or information more precious than money, all for "the brigade." Mr. Singleton was as liberal as rich, and lost a great part of his fortune by lending it to the government for revolutionary purposes, and being paid, as was Gabriel Manigault, in depreciated currency. He had, moreover, a caustic tongue, — and used it. Many were his sharp speeches, thinly veiled by civility, aimed at the authorities, especially at Balfour, whom he despised. But his great offence was the uniforming a large pet baboon in an exact reproduction of the commandant's regimentals, and always addressing it by his name and title ! The gibe came to Balfour's ears, and even his great age could not save the old man from being sent to St. Augustine. He lived to return, however, and lies buried with his own people in St. Michael's churchyard.

All sorts of devices were resorted to for the transportation of news. Mrs. Thompson was the wife of Colonel Thompson, of Orangeburg, who had guarded the further end of Sullivan's Island during the battle of Fort Moultrie, and was commonly known as "Old Danger," from "a habit he had of being present at perilous moments." This lady had obtained permission to visit some friends in Charles Town, and came, bringing with her a little six-year-old daughter. She very soon went out, leaving the child alone, with strict orders not to leave the room, but to do anything that a gentleman should tell her. In a little while a gentleman appeared, who put a letter into the bosom of the child's frock, charging her not to show it or speak of it to any one until an officer should ask for it. When he went the mother returned, asked no questions, and they immediately left for the country.

Children in those days must have been singularly obedient and discreet, for not a word crossed the little one's lips, until they reached General Greene's camp. There the general himself asked her if she had anything for him. She said "No."

Then he inquired more directly, if a gentleman had not put something in her frock for him. The little thing gave up her trust, which proved to be an important communication from a disguised well-wisher. Evidently Mrs. Thompson feared being questioned, or even searched, if the paper were in her possession. But who would suspect a mere baby?

It was greatly by means of this secret information constantly forwarded that Marion was enabled to do so much in the early period, when his force was small and untrained, and surprise his great method of warfare.

The phrase "underground railroad" had not been coined then, but the thing existed, and stood the patriots in good stead. Not an expedition left Charles Town, not a convoy set out for the middle country, or a plundering party made ready to start, but some one, man, boy, or even woman, slipped through the lines after dark, now speeding in a canoe, paddling silently along the river-bank, sheltered by the thick marsh, now riding publicly, disguised in a Tory uniform, or slouching along in country homespun, walking by night and hidden by day in some friendly barn

x

or thicket, but all searching for the nearest point where the ubiquitous " Swamp Fox " (Tarleton's name for Marion) might be found.

They would come at last to some spot where a group of lean, hungry-looking men and boys would be lying, all alert and vigilant, with horses lean and wiry as themselves, but like them strong and active, waiting for the least intimation of the enemy.

By 1781 Marion, who had been commissioned by Governor Rutledge, with high praise and encouragement to persevere in his efforts, had collected about him the most adventurous spirits of the parishes. His men were from his own country, between the Waccamaw and the Ashley, and of his own kind. They were planters, farmers, and hunters who knew familiarly every forest path, every river, every creek. Gentlemen rode as privates in his ranks, proud to be known as "Marion's Men," and, this being the heart of the racing country, many a private mounted a blooded horse which had won a cup or bowl for his father or himself. It was said that Marion never demanded arms, clothing, or provisions of the government; the country supplied him. Plantation blacksmiths made swords and pikes from scythes and tires; shot-guns were in every house; the women spun and wove indefatigably, and men who could live on corn-bread and sweet potatoes need not starve.

Not at first attempting pitched battles, for which he knew his force too small and untrained, Marion waged a partisan warfare which may have been the model of De Wet or Cronje. His stronghold was the swamp — the great swamp which borders the Santee for eighty miles from the ocean.

Here, on the low islands in the morass, approachable only by paths known to the woodsmen alone, he mustered and trained his men ; teaching the tactics suited to the country and to themselves, — " Always *surprise* your enemy."

When an attack was to be made, when Tarleton or Ferguson was reported to be on the move, the brigade drew together. An ambush was set, a sudden onslaught, a fierce fight for a few minutes, a column broken or dispersed, a convoy captured, and then off and away, scattering to avoid pursuit and regaining the *rendezvous* by many and devious paths. Or had a party encamped on some plantation, a little boy or a trusty servant would bring a prayer for help from a distressed mistress or old man, and that night a sudden shout, a trampling of horses, a noise of overthrown tents and arms, and before the sleeping men could mount and follow, the fox was off to his earth, — the swamp, — with perhaps a dozen captured soldiers and horses as the fruit of the attack.

It is difficult to realize the condition of the country at this time. The women and children and old men on their plantations ; every able-bodied man away, and hostile camps in every direction. Here a troop of Tarleton's legion, there a detachment of Marion's brigade, — and each in turn chasing each other across their doorsteps. They took it wonderfully quietly. An old journal, published in the " Ravenel Record " by H. E. Ravenel, Esqr., has between such notices as "High wind which blew down the corn " and " Moderate winter and black frost the 2nd, 3rd, and 4th inst." — this, " October 13th. Genl. Stewart with 2000 of the British Troops and Militia Tories, came to Wantoot " (his cousin's place near by) " and remained there until Novr. the 22nd; in which time the Militia was here every day, taking my corn, rice, potatoes, etc." The old gentleman makes no complaint or comment. It was all in the day's work! The widowed mistress of Wantoot, her only son, a lad of seventeen, in " the Brigade," had to endure this long visitation, and was thought to be under obligation for being spared worse things, since " her family are avowedly opposed against us."

Marion had advised the women thus left to take the "Protection," keep the planting going as much as possible, make food for themselves and for him, and send him all the news they could gather. They religiously obeyed. To make rice and corn and potatoes, and to hide it away so as to be able to fill the brigade bags when opportunity offered, to feed and conceal a good horse in the swamp, to remount a husband or a son in case of need, to fatten a pig or steer to be sent to the nearest rebel camp, as a most welcome gift, became the object of every woman's life. Only the sheep was a sacred animal. Mutton was a forbidden food, the wool being sorely needed for the wheels and looms which furnished the scanty supply of clothing attainable.

To hide the food was as necessary as to make it, for the British, and still worse, the Hessians, made close search. One lady was said to have covered her potato cellar with a large slab taken from the family vault, and saved her crop under the shelter of her forebears' names.

To interfere with and prevent this troublesome industry, the British policed the parishes thoroughly, by those "domiciliary visits" which above all things harassed the people. Plantations in Carolina were so large that houses were necessarily far apart. There was no neighbour to call to when Tarleton or Ferguson, with a score or two of troopers, rode up to a lone woman's door and demanded admission! It was worse still if the man of the house had ventured home to spend a night under his own roof. If taken, a prison or perhaps a rope would be his fate. Mr. Peter Sinkler, a wealthy gentleman, thus taken was marched off to the dungeon of the Provost and died there among felons.

It was to retaliate for these captures that Marion (who was besides the least bloodthirsty of men) ordered his soldiers to kill as few and take as many prisoners as possible. They were most valuable to him for exchange. If there was no man to be seized, then plunder was the object of the British. Anything in the house that struck their fancy, and everything useful without. If the stable and barn were not empty when they came, they were clean swept when they left. There was a story of Mrs. Sabina Elliott that when apparently every living thing had been carried off from her place, an old drake came quacking from under the poultry-house. She immediately called a negro boy and told him to "run after the party and give the drake, with her compliments to Colonel ——, she supposed it had been left by *accident!*"

Tarleton sometimes played the fine gentleman on these raids; as when at Mrs. Horrÿ's at Hampton, South Santee (where the fidelity of the servants and the coolness of the mistress alone saved Marion from falling into his hands), he took for his share of the spoil only a fine copy of Milton; his men were less forbearing. Other commanders (Major Fraser for instance) were more frankly brutal. Mrs. Horrÿ tells how he took her watch and a miniature of her friend Mrs. Blake of Newington, which she wore at her neck.

The same manuscript journal tells the story of a widow with three little girls, her sons all in the army, being waked at night by knocks at her door: soldiers demanding admission. She refuses. They threaten to break down the door, to burn the house. The brave woman (Mrs. Ravenel, of Chelsea) answers that they may break in if they please, but she will *not* open. They chop at the door with their swords (the chops may still be seen), but finally they withdraw without admittance.

Feeble old men fared even worse than the women. One gentleman, "old, infirm and lame of leg," had *all* his six sons with Marion, "and consequently his feelings and principles being known to the British and Tories, he was

subjected to great abuse and had his property depredated
upon, etc., etc." This is the tale of many.

The worst outrage of all occurred at the most beautiful
place in the country — at the Fairlawn Barony, the seat of
the Colletons.

The last Sir John Colleton died at the beginning of the
Revolution, having taken no decided part in the dispute.
His widow and some other ladies continued to live in the
stately mansion, when it was visited by a number of soldiers; — it is said unaccompanied by any officer. The
ladies were so shockingly treated that the soldiers were
threatened with severe punishment; but it was only a
threat. The house was burned afterward, because the cedar
avenue had been used for an ambuscade by Marion's men.

Sometimes the tables were turned. The British were
extremely anxious to catch Mr. Ralph Izard, and knowing
that his company of Light Horse was encamped in the
neighbourhood of his plantation of Fair Spring, they
watched for his home-coming and burst into the house
one day when he had just returned. Mrs. Izard, who
was a singularly charming woman (Miss Delancey), met
them at the door, and delayed their entrance by her cool
answers and composure until Mr. Izard had time to conceal himself in a clothes-press. Not finding him anywhere, the marauders withdrew, carrying off much booty.
No sooner had they vanished than Mr. Izard rode off to
the camp of his own men, and brought back a party to
follow the English. He was just in time, for some traitor
had assured them that he was hidden in the house, and
they returned in great anger; broke open the clothes-
press; possessed themselves of the silk and velvet garments, — relics of a gay life at various European courts;
abused Mrs. Izard for deceiving them, and were in the act
of tearing her rings from her fingers, when he and his
troop arrived. The marauders were surrounded, many of

them captured, and the clothes which they had stolen were bestowed upon the rescuing party.

The young men had odd adventures — were often taken, then exchanged, and again in the saddle. If they were particularly obnoxious, they might be kept a long time without being exchanged; sometimes in the dreaded Provost! One young fellow betrayed himself by his appetite. He had taken shelter at Mrs. Motte's place, Fairfield, on South Santee. She rolled him up in a carpet, and pushing it against the wall told him to keep quiet until the enemy had gone, and she could release him. Unluckily he heard through the open window his hostess giving directions to the cook about the chickens which were to be dressed for the dragoons' dinner. He could not bear to be shared out, thrust his head from his carpet chrysalis, and cried, "Keep the giblets for me!" The soldiers heard and he was at once caught and carried off to repent at leisure of his *gourmandise*.

Often the quickness and fidelity of the servants saved their masters from capture.

Daniel Ravenel of Wantoot had gone home for the night when his servant gave the alarm; he sprang up and began to dress. Major Fraser rushed in, sword in hand, and demanded his surrender; the young lad, — he was only seventeen, — half dressed and unarmed, eluded his grasp and ran out into the garden, pursued by the major with his drawn sword. Knowing the ground and being young and active, he got away. His horse was held ready for him at the back gate, and he escaped for the time, only to be taken not long afterward.

The Annalist remarks dryly that peace being restored, Major Fraser walked the streets of Charles Town, and was received like other people, "which Mr. Ravenel did not like, Major Fraser having been a Tory, while he had fought for his country."

Colonel Broughton of Mulberry was saved by the negro patroon (captain) of his rice schooner. The British were nearing the house when he gained the landing at which the vessel lay. The patroon made him throw himself full length on the deck and turned a small boat over him. The schooner was thoroughly searched, but no one thought of looking under the boat.

There are innumerable stories of this kind, but enough have been given to show the nature of the "domiciliary visits," which in the early days of the brigade it was Marion's business to prevent and punish. Later on, when he had gained strength, and the country was aroused, he and his men fought splendidly in many battles : at Georgetown, Fort Motte, Eutaw, etc. But it was as the protector and guardian of their homes that he won the enthusiastic love of the parishes, and made his name a household word forever.

Too much cannot be said of the wonderful elasticity of the spirits of the people through all this trying time. How gay were the men — how brave the women! Visitors to Marion's camp came back amazed at the stories told and the songs sung by the boys on their scanty ration of potatoes; while the mothers and wives at home kept the house, and never talked of fear. The old ladies used to tell with glee, how when the British were supposed to be out of the way, the young fellows would come home to dance *with them*. A message would go to the nearest cousins and friends ; a supper be cooked — it might be but rice and bacon, but it was good to hungry men; the negro fiddlers would come, and then the dance and the feast until the stars grew pale.

Often these merry-makings were disturbed by the enemy; but there was always a negro or two on the watch, and the harsh note of the screech owl, or the cry of the whip-poor-will, would give the alarm. Then "partings in hot haste," a rush for the horses, a sharp scuffle, a hot pursuit, probably a prisoner taken, and for the fortunate, the wild gallop

> "Back to the pathless forest
> Before the peep of day."

CHAPTER XVI

A TERRIBLE event which occurred in Charles Town struck consternation into the whole country.

Among the militiamen disbanded after the capitulation of the town none was more distinguished than Colonel Isaac Hayne of St. Paul's parish, to the southward. He, like his comrades, had accepted the proffered parole, and. gone to his own home — evidently intending to abide by the terms to which he had sworn. The parole being revoked and the question put, — " Will you or will you not become the subject of his Majesty ? " he promptly answered in the negative.

Bribes, and afterward threats, were used; the British being especially anxious to secure his allegiance because of his great influence in his own neighbourhood, and because they knew that the insurgents were equally desirous of his services.

But Hayne was too painfully occupied at home to have any thought beyond his own doors. One child had died, two others were desperately ill, of the smallpox, and his wife's life was despaired of.

In this condition of things he was summoned to Charles Town to appear before the commandant. There he was told that his liberty depended upon his signing a declaration that he acknowledged himself a British subject; but which Colonel Patterson (then commandant) assured him would not commit him to bearing arms against his countrymen. Hayne was most unwilling and uneasy; but if he

314

refused, the Provost would receive him, and he could not abandon his dying wife. He signed the paper and also wrote another, which he left with his friend Dr. Ramsay, declaring that the signature had been "forced on him by hard necessity." "I never will bear arms against my country, my masters can require no service of me but what is enjoined by the old militia law of the Province, which substitutes a fine in lieu of personal service. This I will pay as the price of my protection. If my conduct should be censured by my countrymen, I beg that you will remember this conversation, and bear witness for me that I do not mean to desert the cause of America."

He then returned to his family, and some time after his wife died. What advantage the British hoped to derive from such unwilling service it is hard to imagine, but they again threatened imprisonment unless he joined the army. Indignant at this breach of faith, Hayne considered himself relieved of obligation; accepted the rebel commission which had been pressed upon him; raised a company of his neighbours, and began a vigorous campaign.

There was at the time a certain General Williamson, who had been an American, and then an English officer, and was now in Charles Town, looked upon with some suspicion by both parties, and accused of giving information equally untrustworthy to both.

The Americans were anxious to take him, and hearing that he was living beyond the lines, Hayne made a bold dash and captured him within five miles of Charles Town. The British were furious at the partisan daring to enter their territory, and greatly annoyed at the loss of Williamson, who was cognizant of all their secrets.

A rescuing party was soon in the saddle, with Major Fraser in command, and Mad Archy Campbell leading the foremost troop. Hayne was making for his own camp on the Ashepoo, and had he been well mounted would probably have gained it in safety; but good living during his master's long homestaying had been too much for the fine horse "King Herod," once the pride of the stable. He had grown fat and scant of breath, laboured heavily in the gallop, refused a gate, and finally stumbled and fell at a ditch! Before horse and rider could rise Mad Archy was upon them, and took the colonel prisoner with his own hand.

Williamson was retaken, and the American troop dispersed. Hayne, taken to Charles Town, was confined for some time in the Provost, and as soon as Balfour could obtain the assent of Lord Rawdon (absent from the town at the moment) he was brought to trial as a traitor. Tried by a court-martial arranged by these unscrupulous men, a condemnation was the only thing to be expected; but when it was known that sentence of death had been pronounced, the horror was indescribable. The court had been most irregular; there was reason to suspect that the verdict had been tampered with; every effort was made to change or modify it, but all in vain. What the English really needed was an example!

Many other officers, Hampton, Pickens, etc., had, like Hayne, decided that the compact had been broken by the enemy and that they were at liberty to resume their arms. General Moultrie distinctly states that this view was taken even for the Continentals, by General Greene, Colonel C. C. Pinckney, and himself; and that he should have had no scruple in violating the parole, but that expecting a speedy exchange he thought it best to remain quiet. For the militia there had been at the capitulation no exchange guaranteed; a great difference of position.

The war too was more active in their vicinity. Not Marion only, but Pickens and Harden were making raids into the parishes, coming lower and lower down. Sumter himself was reported to be advancing, and General Greene had ordered Light Horse Harry Lee to "thunder at the gates of Charles Town." To check this growing tide of revolt a warning, and a distinguished one, was necessary.

In after days, when the execution of Hayne was severely censured in England, Rawdon endeavoured to lay the blame on Balfour, who was then dead. There can be no doubt, however, that his was the responsibility. Balfour suggested the plan, but Rawdon, who never *then* declined the title of "Commander-in-chief in South Carolina," had the supreme authority.

No effort was spared to convince the reason and soften the hearts of those two men. Hayne himself sent a manly vindication of his conduct, — denied the fairness of his trial, and demanded another at which he could produce evidence in his favour.

The ladies of Charles Town offered a petition signed by almost all, both Whig and Tory. Numbers of the Loyalist gentlemen interceded for him. His wife's sister, Mrs. Peronneau, and his little children, received in the large drawing-room of the Brewton House, knelt before Rawdon, imploring mercy. Rawdon was for the time the representative of the king, but his "face gave no grace" to the poor little things. Finally Lieutenant-governor Bull, who had lately returned from England, ill and suffering from an agonizing disease, had himself carried in a litter into his Lordship's presence to ask the boon of life.

To each and all Rawdon was obdurate. At, as he specially indicated, the request of Governor Bull, he consented to a short respite that the condemned might take leave of his children. This was the only favour shown. Many of the British officers asked that Hayne should be granted the death of a soldier, not of a spy, — Mad Archy Campbell, who had captured him, declared that he would have slain him with his own hand on the field, had he supposed that such ignominy could be the fate of so gallant an officer.

This also was refused. At the close of the forty-eight hours' reprieve, Hayne, accompanied by several friends, walked from the Provost to the place of execution — what should be the manner of his death he did not know until he had passed the town gates in King Street between George and Liberty. Then the gibbet came in sight. For an instant he paused and coloured, then walked firmly on. A friend exhorted him to die with courage. He said simply, "I will try"; then ascending the cart without assistance, he prayed for a few moments with the clergyman, shook hands with his friends, drew the cap over his face, and himself gave the signal to the hangman. Dying as a gallant gentleman, *sans peur et sans reproche*.

Colonel Henry Lee, who gives this account in his "Memoirs," makes from Corneille the apt quotation: —

"*C'est le crime qui fait la honte, et non pas l'échafaud.*"

One wonders if the clear vision, said to come at the moment of heroic death, showed him his name, as it still stands in the history of his State, — "The Martyr Hayne."

If there had ever been hope of conquering the country, it was over now. Henceforth it was war to the knife. Half the men in the partisan corps were in Hayne's position, and each knew that he fought with a rope round his neck.

The entire body of officers, Continental and partisan, petitioned General Greene to retaliate for the execution of their comrade. They knew, they said, that by doing so they increased their own danger, and were perfectly willing so to do. Greene replied that he would retaliate, not on a Tory, but upon the first British officer who should fall into his hands. Fortunately none of equal rank was captured for some time to come, and men had grown cooler and felt how much such executions would increase the inevitable horrors of war.

The ghastly effect produced on the popular mind by

this tragic event was curiously shown by its giving rise to the only *well-authenticated* ghost story known in Charles Town. The house, which until ten years ago stood at the corner of Meeting and Atlantic streets, a solid brick structure with a beautiful mahogany-panelled drawing-room, belonged at that time to Mrs. Arthur Peronneau, who had been a Miss Hutson, sister to Colonel Hayne's wife. She it was who had gone with his children to plead for their father's life, and her anguish at his approaching death was great. On the day of the execution he passed (the story goes) through Atlantic Street on the way to the gallows, and she, standing at the north window, cried to him in agony, "Return, return to us." He replied, "I will if I can," and walked on.

Ever after, any one standing at the north window after nightfall would hear a ghostly voice in the street below, and steps sounding on the stair and in the hall, as of a man *returning*, — never going down, always up!

He would have been a fearful skeptic who fifty years ago had doubted the truth of the story.

Hayne's execution seems to have been the culminating point of the woes of the time. The tide was on the turn. In the up-country the partisans had done wonders, and General Greene, sent by Washington to take the chief command, combined advantageously the various elements. Governor Rutledge had at last, by the device of using indigo, great amounts of which had been stored in the country, for money, obtained invaluable supplies of clothing, etc. Moultrie says: —

" It was very fortunate the Governor was not made a prisoner in town ; his presence in the country kept everything alive, and it gave great spirits to the people to have a man of such great abilities, firmness, and decision amongst them. He gave commissions, raised new corps, embodied the Militia, and went to Philadelphia to solicit reinforcements ; he returned and joined the army ; he stayed by them ; enforced the laws of the Province ; called the Legislature ; in short he did everything that could be done for the good of the Country."

He was during these years the sole representative of the civil power in the State. It used to be said that the " seat of Government of South Carolina was John Rutledge's carriage ! "

The town had suffered — was still to suffer so much, that it could hardly believe its redemption approaching ; but it was coming, slowly but surely.

Battles were fought at Georgetown, Monck's Corner, and Eutaw, in all of which Marion and his men took gallant part ; and the witty Mrs. Brewton, who had been permitted to make a trip to Camden, could answer when asked by one of her English adorers, — " How does the country look now ? " " Beautiful, everything is *Greene* down to Monck's Corner." Referring, of course, to the general who lay encamped there, not forty miles from Charles Town.

For this and other treasonable speeches Mrs. Brewton was shortly afterward sent to Philadelphia, by special order, it was said, of Major Moncrieff. Her banishment was shared by many other persons, who were exiled by the Commandant Balfour, as being the " wives and families of persons lately exchanged as prisoners of war, who have long chose to reside in the colonies now in rebellion. . . . The weight of which on all accounts is equally impolitick as inconsistent should longer be suffered to rest on the Government now established here and the resources thereof. . . . All such women and children and others above described should leave the town and province on or before the first day of August next ensuing."

This order was levelled not only at the families of the exiles of St. Augustine, but at those of the many Continental officers who had been so long imprisoned at Haddrell's Point, and who were now to be sent on for exchange. Being published on the 27th of June, it gave the unfortunate ladies thus expelled little more than a month to prepare for this involuntary emigration.

How were the distracted ladies to provide funds for such a voyage — they were to go by sea to Philadelphia — and for their support during their sojourn in that place ?

Another order published a few days later forbade them either to sell or let their houses : those were to be given to the "firm friends" of the Government, — *i.e.* to Tories.

Poverty was already pressing hard on the rebellious citizens, every source of income having been cut off. Mrs. Pinckney, in a letter published in her "Life and Letters," gives a curiously minute account of the lack of means at this time : —

" I am sorry I am under a necessity to send this unaccompanied with the amount of my account due to you. It may seem strange that a single woman, accused of no crime, who had a fortune to live Genteelly in any part of the world, that fortune too in different kinds of property, and in four or five different parts of the country, should in so short a time be so entirely deprived of it as not to be able to pay a debt under sixty pound sterling, but such is my singular case. After the many losses I have met with, for the last three or four desolating years from fire and plunder, both in Country and Town, I still had something to subsist upon, but alas the hand of power has deprived me of the greatest part of that, and accident of the rest. Permit me to particularize in part, or you may possibly think me mistaken in what I have now asserted, as a strange concurrence of circumstances must happen before a person situated as I was, should become thus destitute of the means of paying a small debt.

Y

" The labour of slaves I had working at my son Charles
sequestrated Estate by Mr. Cruden's permission " (Mr.
Cruden, Commissioner of Sequestration, was in possession
of Colonel Pinckney's estate, as he also occupied his house
in town) " has not produced one farthing since the fall of
Charles Town.   Between thirty and forty head of tame
cattle, which I had on the same plantation, with the
same permission, was taken last November by Major
Yarborough and his party for the use of the army, for
which I received nothing.

" My house in Ellory Street, which Capt. McMahon
put me in possession of soon after I came to Town, and
which I immediately rented at one hundred per annum
sterling, was in a short time after filled with Hessians, to
the great detriment of the house and annoyance of the
tenant, who would pay me no more for the time he was in
it, than twelve guineas. I applied to a Board of Field
Officers which was appointed to regulate those matters,
they gave it as their opinion that I ought to be paid for
the time it had been, and the time it should be, in the
Service of Government, which it is to this day.   I
applied as directed for payment, but received nothing.
Even a little hovel which in the late great demand for
houses would have been of service to me, was taken from
me, and all my endeavours to get it again proved fruitless.

" My plantation up the path" (namely, the old Indian
path, the precursor of the present State Road, leading up
the country) " which I hired to Mr. Simpson for fifty guineas the last year, and had agreed with him for eighty
guineas for the present year, was taken out of his possession, and I am told Major Fraser now has it for the use
of the Cavalry, and Mr. Simpson does not seem inclined
to pay me for the last half of the year 1781.   To my regret and to the great prejudice of the place, the wood has
also been cut down for the use of the Garrison, for which

I have not got a penny. The negroes I had in town are sometimes impressed on the public works and make the fear of being so a pretence for doing nothing. Two men and two women bring me small wages, but part of that I was robbed of before it reached me.

"I have a right to a third of the rent of two good houses in Town, each of which I could have rented at three hundred pounds per annum sterling, but the government allows but a hundred and fifty pounds sterling for each, so that about two hundred pounds which I received at different times in the course of last year, from Mr. Cruden, or by his order, is all the money I have been possessed of except very trifling sums for two years past."

Still money had to be found, and upon humble petition the poor ladies were allowed to sell their furniture, for what little they could get for it. A forced sale is always a calamitous thing, — to a woman when it is of her household goods terribly so.

There must have been many poor souls whose grief resembled that of Mrs. Tulliver, immortalized by George Eliot in "The Mill on the Floss."

One or two of these prayers for mercy still remain. Mr. McCrady gives one from Mrs. Daniel De Saussure, whose husband was then at St. Augustine. She, after piteous preface, prays "that your Honour will be pleased to grant her indulgence of making sale of the furniture belonging to her dwelling house and kitchen, also a riding chaise ; and to grant her such further indulgence as to your Honour shall seem meet, and your petitioner will ever pray," etc., etc.

So, gathering what they could, over one thousand persons, says Dr. Ramsay, old men, women, and children, were driven forth, most of them sailing in small brigs and schooners for Philadelphia. One party had a strange but happy adventure *en route*, for off the capes of the Delaware they sighted other vessels, also coming from the southward. Soon they were within hail, and imagine the delight when the master of one recognized the voice from the deck of the other and shouted : "Is that you, William Johnson ? I have your wife and children aboard." By an extraordinary coincidence the exiles of St. Augustine and of Charles Town thus met at the entrance to Philadelphia!

The joy of meeting overcame all other feeling for the time, but they had much to endure. The little money which they had brought with them was soon exhausted, and even those who had been rich were in great straits. The present writer has often listened to the stories of an old lady who had as a child been one of these exiles. She was the daughter of Samuel Prioleau, whose letter has been given in the previous chapter, a very wealthy merchant, but her mother was glad to earn bread for her children by making soldiers' shirts at a sixpence apiece. A subscription was made for them, by the efforts of Colonel Bayard, Mr. Hutchinson, and several other gentlemen, who appealed to all the States to assist these sufferers in the common cause. Massachusetts and Pennsylvania responded liberally, Governor Hancock personally subscribing four hundred dollars. The sum raised, however, was to be divided among so many that, except in the case of those who had private friends, the distress was great, — especially from the cold, which to these thinly clad Southerners seemed very severe. The men were better off, for they were quickly exchanged and returned rejoicing to the army. It was well for General Moultrie that Burgoyne was like himself a general, else there might have been difficulty. They "balanced" each other, and both were set at liberty.

At last came the happy night when the cry rang through the streets, remembered well by Mrs. Prioleau's little daughter : —

" Half-past twelve of a stormy night, and Cornwallis has surrendered."

Fancy the joy of the people, and how proud and pleased were the Charles Town ladies when they heard that their own John Laurens had arranged the terms of surrender, and obliged Cornwallis to submit to the same ceremonies which Clinton had imposed upon Lincoln at the fall of Charles Town !

But although the war was now practically at an end in the North, it was by no means the case for the Southern States, and Charles Town, who had been one of the first to open the ball, was to be one of the very last to close it.

The Americans had by January, 1782, regained possession of all but the town, and adjacent coast, which being intersected by rivers and creeks gave easy access to the small vessels of the English. It was thought rather a rash thing, therefore, when in that month Governor Rutledge summoned the Legislature to meet him at Jacksonboro, a little village on the Edisto, about thirty-five miles from Charles Town, within easy reach of the enemy's galleys. Greene, however, undertook to keep good guard, and risk was the order of the day.

Hither came the men who for years had fought and bled for their State, had served her in Council and in Congress, and had never abandoned her. " Good Whigs " all, rejoicing in once more meeting, in comparing their adventures, and telling their battles over again to sympathetic ears.

There was graver work than this, however, for the country was in a lawless and distracted condition, the destitution was frightful, the Tories still threatening. At that time, too, there was no prospect of the end of the war ; the resources of the patriots were exhausted, and funds must be raised for carrying on the struggle. Not a man there but had suffered in purse as well as in person ; they could do no more. As one of them said, "We are squeezed dry; the others must bleed."

"The others" were the Tories and protected men, whose plantations were now in the power of the Americans, as theirs had been in that of the British a few months before.

The "protection" had not been as thorough as they had hoped to receive, but still their places and properties were not devastated as were those of the Whigs, and some of them, by buying up sequestrated estates for a song, had become rich.

It was no wonder then that when the Governor, who was about to resign his office,— which he had already held a year beyond its fixed period because of the impossibility of convening a Legislature to receive his resignation, — addressed them in a fiery and eloquent speech on the subject of these men, they assented willingly.

He told them that the Tories had not "respected the cries of innocence, the charm of the fair sex, the habitations of the widow, the aged and the infirm, or even the temples of the Most High." And all knew that it was true. He reminded them that the terms of capitulation had been cast aside and their property ruthlessly seized, and recommended that the State should indemnify herself by confiscating or amercing the estates of the offenders against patriotism and humanity, and thus provide the means of carrying on the war.

"In the Legislature," says Garden (himself a member), "there were not at the moment of the passing of the Confiscation Act, more than a dozen Members who declared their votes against it. The fact is that the provocation to severity was excessive and the public mind excited beyond control."

Drayton says, "It was supposed that the war would go on a long time yet, and the army had to be subsisted."

The sudden collapse of the war greatly changed this opinion, and Rutledge and his supporters were soundly abused by Judge Ædanus Burke, an Irish politician who wrote an extremely clever pamphlet over the signature of "Cassius," and by others. Rutledge, as usual, went his way; and the people made him judge and chief justice as soon as possible.

Moultrie's account of this much-disputed question is marked by his usual clear good sense and moderation. He says : —

"The Jacksonboro Legislature has been blamed" (for the Confiscation Act), "but the members were most of them soldiers still in the field, the war going on, their wounds yet bleeding, their property destroyed. It was natural for them to be angry with their countrymen, who, having entered into a solemn compact with them to support the cause, were then within British lines, under British protection, sometimes with British commissions in their pockets." To stay quiet and take protection was no great harm, sometimes unavoidable; he had himself advised some persons so to do. "But to take protection, then a commission, and then to treat their countrymen with more rigour than their enemies themselves, was unpardonable."

It is rather hard to see how any one could think differently.

The Jacksonboro Legislature was not always sitting in judgment upon its delinquent fellow-citizens. There was much work to do, for law there was practically none ; and the country, as has been said, was in a distracted condition.

It enacted the necessary statutes ; voted a handsome offering to General Greene for his distinguished services ; thanked its own heroes, Sumter, Marion, Pickens, and others, for gallant conduct ; received the resignation of

Governor Rutledge with the warmest thanks and praise for "unwearied zeal and attention to the real interest of the country," and "satisfaction in the conduct of the executive," and immediately elected him a representative to Congress. It chose his brother-in-law, John Mathews, who had done excellent work in Congress, Governor in his stead, and — amused itself.

The elasticity of the public temper was already, in this brief respite from war and bloodshed, beginning to assert itself, and so many bold soldiers naturally made merry. The horse was in those days as dear and almost as near to the Carolinian as to the Arab, and tales of his prowess and fidelity went freely round.

There is a story of Isaac McPherson (grandson of the lady who had been respected by the Indians because she was "Jimmy's Squaw"), who was commonly called "Dare Devil Mac." He vaunted the qualities of his horse Flimnap (surely it could not have been the same Flimnap which Mr. Quincy had seen in 1773), boasting not only of its speed and endurance, but of its great docility and intelligence. It would obey him like a dog, he said.

Wagers were laid, and the hall doors flung wide. McPherson mounted and rode to the door. Then step by step the proud racer ascended the staircase to the story above. Dare Devil told them to open the window. The men hesitated, declared themselves satisfied, and the wager won; but McPherson insisted. The window was opened, and obedient to hand and voice Flimnap rose to the leap, bounded through the window as if in the hunting field, and darted into space, landing safely, eighteen feet from the house !

A year of desultory fighting along the coast succeeded this Assembly, but all felt that the end was drawing near; and the British knew it too, and were making preparations

to leave, gathering up their ill-gotten gain, especially negroes, of whom they secured many.

Others were resolving to stay and settle in the country.
Even in war time love will find out the way, and there
had been more matches than Mad Archy Campbell's,
between officers and Tory ladies. Mad Archy, by the
way, had been killed in a skirmish at Videau's Bridge,
and the luckless Paulina had died only a month afterward, leaving one daughter. There is no account of
their short married life having been peculiarly unhappy.

Only *one* marriage is recorded, however, between an
officer and a rebel lady, and propinquity and coquetry
are clearly to blame for that.

Mr. John Teasdale, an English, or more probably, from
the name, a Scotch officer, was quartered upon the
Verrees, — a Huguenot family of distinctly "rebellious
principles." The young lady of the house was very
pretty and clever, the stranger susceptible. Of course he
fell in love, and, — a coquettish nature being too strong
for patriotism, — of course she teased him charmingly,
testifying her principles in various ways. One to which
he objected strongly was that her pretty little slippers
were always decorated with rosettes of blue and buff,
and were always full in view of the red-coated lover.
He hated the rosettes, and would beg her to "pull off
those ugly bows." Then they were stuck out further
yet, "but always," the legend says, "in a ladylike way,
not showing more of the ankle than was proper." This
proper little flirt proved so charming that the gentleman
could not tear himself away and "by great perseverance
won her."

He built the house at the head of East Battery.
Its foundations are a part of the old Granville bastion,
most solid and admirable brickwork. An old well lately
discovered near the gate was probably that for the garrison,

and the brickwork extends across the street under the building now used as a hotel.

The house, built about 1779, is still sound and good, with handsome woodwork and Dutch tile chimney-places. In removing some of these tiles from one of the chimneys, a short time ago, a secret chamber was discovered running all around the fireplace, — sides and back. It was not more than nine inches wide and deep, and must have been meant as a place of concealment for money or papers. There was nothing in it when it was discovered, and could only be opened by removing the tiles. To this house Mr. Teasdale took his pretty wife, and in peaceful times became a prosperous Charles Town merchant.

One preparation for departure was extremely obnoxious to the people. Whig and Tory alike were horrified when St. Michael's bells were taken down by order of Major Traille of the Royal Artillery, who claimed them as his "perquisite" in right of his rank as Commander of the Artillery. The vestry applied to Major-general Leslie, then in command, but he did nothing.

It then applied to Sir Guy Carleton at New York and he issued an order for the return of the bells. Unfortunately they had already been shipped to England, where they remained for some time, having been bought by a Mr. Rybenau, formerly a merchant of Charles Town, on speculation.

In this year Charles Town had to mourn the death of her favourite son. John Laurens, the *preux chevalier* of the Revolution, was killed in a petty skirmish, resisting some marauders on the banks of the Combahee. Few men have ever realized the heroic ideal more completely than Laurens. Very handsome, very brave, with the charming combination of fiery zeal and exquisite courtesy he united the romantic virtues of magnanimity and devotion, and the tact and skill of a statesman and a diplomatist.

Having won the admiration of Congress by his gallantry in the field, he declined the high promotion offered him, fearing to wrong his senior officers. When he fought a duel with General Charles Lee, to avenge the insults offered by him to his beloved Washington, his eccentric antagonist declared that he " could have hugged the boy, so much did he admire his conduct." It was he who wrung from the French Court its reluctant assent to the concerted action which enabled Washington to conquer Cornwallis. Then, having retaliated upon the latter the humiliations of the surrender of Charles Town, he rushed back to his native State, where the war still continued, and fell in her defence. She has no prouder name than his.

The death of John Laurens brought to an end the public career of his father. From the beginning of the Revolutionary struggle Henry Laurens had approved, not always the measures, but always the principles, of the patriotic party, and had steadily supported the American cause. He had long been absent from Carolina, having served in Congress four years; the last two as its President. He had been appointed Minister to Holland ; had been captured at sea on his way thither, and taken to the Tower of London on the charge of high treason. His son-in-law, Dr. Ramsay, gives an account of his confinement : always watched by a warder ; not allowed pen and ink ; not permitted to buy himself the most necessary comforts; allowed hardly any exercise ; and continually tormented by gout and other painful maladies.

He was constantly assailed by threats and persuasions to induce him to return to his English allegiance, but he stood firm. When advised "to take time to consider" a proposition made him, he answered " that an honest man required no time to give an answer in a case where his honour was concerned." When John Laurens was sent to France, the English ministers feared his influence there, and urged his father to request him to withdraw, promising that should he comply the father's position would be greatly improved. Mr. Laurens replied: " My son is of age, and has a will of his own; if I should write to him in the terms you request, it would have no effect, he would only conclude that confinement and persuasion had softened me. I know him to be a man of honour. He loves me dearly, and would lay down his life to save mine ; but I am sure that he would not sacrifice his honour or his country to save my life ; and I applaud him."

At last after nearly two years of wearing imprisonment Mr. Laurens was released, being exchanged for Lord Cornwallis. He then went to France and was associated with Dr. Franklin, John Jay, and John Adams in negotiating the treaty of peace and independence of America.

The country was saved, but for the father, " earth was undone by one grave in it."

The treaty was signed in November, 1782, and his son had been killed in August.

He lived ten years more. His fellow-citizens offered him every honour which was theirs to give, but he refused them all. He devoted himself to his children, and his people, and died at his plantation, Mepkin, on Cooper River, in 1792, leaving the singular order that he should be cremated. The order was scrupulously obeyed, and the weird effect of the funeral pile, the still figure in its white wrappings, the torch applied by the son, the flames, and the screams and cries of the terrified negroes, was one of the legends of the river for many a day thereafter.

Peace having been declared, preparations for the departure of the British went slowly on, and negotiations between General Greene and General Leslie, the English commander. There was great anxiety for a peaceful evacuation, and every precaution was taken to avoid a collision between the outgoing and incoming troops. Not only St.

Michael's bells, but also the church books were carried off. The plate was saved by Mr. Lightwood, who took it to Mr. Izard's place, Accabee, several miles from Charles Town, and concealed it there.

Many Tory families decided to go with the fleet. Many soldiers, on the other hand, determined to remain (especially the Hessians) and hid themselves in stables and outhouses until their masters had gone.

At last the joyful day arrived. The American army

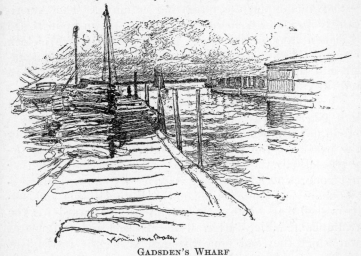

GADSDEN'S WHARF
Scene of embarkation of the British.

had been encamped across the river in St. Andrew's Parish at Ashley Hill, Commodore Gillon's place, and at Middleton Place, which adjoined it. It now crossed the river at Bee's Ferry, twelve miles from town, and marched down as far as Shubrick's Belvidere farm (now occupied by the Country Club) and lay there that night. At daybreak the next morning General Leslie withdrew his troops from the lines, retiring through the city gates (the same through which Hayne had gone to his death) to Gadsden's wharf, at the foot of the present Calhoun Street, and then the embarkation began. Nine thousand citizens and negroes besides the British army were crowded into the fleet — eight hundred of the negroes had been seized by Major Moncrieff alone; forty-eight hundred and twenty-four were sold in Jamaica and Florida.

As the British departed the Americans came in, great care being taken to keep several hundred yards between the advancing and the retreating columns. The American troops under General Wayne were drawn up in Broad Street in front of the State House, and at three o'clock General Greene escorted Governor Mathews and his council into the town. Moultrie who was of the party shall tell the rest.

" I can never forget the happy day when we marched into Charlestown with the American troops: it was a proud day to me, and I felt myself much elated at seeing the balconies, the doors and windows crowded with the patriotick fair, the aged citizens and others congratulating us on our return home, saying ' God bless you, gentlemen,' — ' You are welcome, gentlemen.' Both citizens and soldiers shed tears of joy. It was an ample reward for the triumphant soldiers, after all the hazards and fatigues of war which they had gone through, to be the instrument of releasing his friends and fellow-citizens from captivity and restoring them to their liberties and the possession of their city and country again."

Sixty years ago there were many old people who delighted to talk of the pride and joy of that day. How they had stood, little things in " pinafores and hoods " to see the troops come by. How the Governor had stood on some high steps and bowed to the soldiers and the soldiers had saluted him. How joyous were the ladies who were to get back their homes — no longer to be confined to a closet or an attic; how happy the men who returned to their own!

So far so good, but Moultrie was too honest not to record the omission that marred the scene. General Greene had been ashamed of Marion's shabby jacket when first he met him and years had not taught him wisdom on this subject. The old Continental says: —

" The British evacuated Charles Town. The American Army entered it in triumph ; but our poor partisans were thought too irregular, too ragged of raiment too share the triumph! They were not too ragged to *fight*, only too ragged for *show!* It was a most ungenerous and ungrateful exclusion from the scene of the very men to whom the best part of the grand result was due! They were disbanded here and there in swamp and thicket wherever the moment found them; disbanded without pay or praise, naked, starving, having the world before them, but losing from that moment all their customary guides save Providence."

This unjust exclusion long rankled in the hearts of the partisans, and was bitterly felt by Marion himself, who resented the affront to his men.

Professor Goldwin Smith has recently called attention to an account of the evacuation of Charles Town given in the " History of New York," by Thomas Jones, edited by Floyd de Lancey, 1879. In this it is stated that " the rebels entered the town like so many furies, or rather devils " — that they " seized, bound, dragged to dungeons the unfortunate Loyalists." " Whipped, tarred and feathered, branded and stripped, and to complete the scene a gallows was erected upon which 24 reputable Loyalists were hanged in sight of the British fleet!" " This account I had from a British officer who was upon the spot, *ashore* at the time, and an eye-witness to the whole."

The testimony of this anonymous officer is hardly

worth comment. No allusion to such proceedings is made in any history, English or American, which the present writer has been able to discover, nor is there any legend to that effect.

Most careful compacts had been made by General Leslie for the protection of the Loyalists; nor is it possible that he would have endured such outrage " in sight of a British fleet with an army on board " and guns presumably shotted.

If the Hessians had had any fear of being hanged (a fate which many of them richly deserved), they would never have manœuvred to be left behind.

As a matter of fact, only a day or two before the evacuation, General Marion was advised to attack a party which had been plundering at Lemprière's Point on Cooper River, near the town. He refused, saying that the war was over and that he did not intend to allow the shedding of another drop of blood.

" The war was over."

No other city in America had suffered as Charles Town had done. She lay in ruins, and the old order of things was ruined too.

She had now to build up the new, summoning all her strength and courage to the work.

CHAPTER XVII

RESTORATION. WASHINGTON AND LA FAYETTE

IN 1778 Charles Town had been a thriving, prosperous town, extending from South Bay to the present Calhoun (long called Boundary) Street, and from river to river.

Each house had its own yard and garden, only in the business portion along some part of the east water front was it at all closely built. It had at its back a wealthy and flourishing agricultural district entirely under its control, and a large commerce both of export and import.

In 1783 the town and the parishes were alike in ruins. The incendiary fires, described by General Moultrie, had destroyed a large number of buildings. Hardly a house north of Broad Street had escaped damage by the shells from the lines, and those south of it had been almost equally injured by the batteries on the islands and the guns of the fleet.

Where was the money to rebuild to come from? The plantations were devastated. Moultrie, riding across country from Georgetown to General Greene's camp on the Ashley, after his exchange in Philadelphia, passed through St. John's parish and came to his own plantation, "Northampton." He describes the country: —

"It was the most dull, melancholy, dreary ride that any one could possibly take, of about one hundred miles through the woods of that country, which I had been accustomed to see abound with live-stock and wild fowl of every kind, now destitute of all. It had been so

completely checquered by the different parties that no
one part of it had been left unexplored ; consequently,
not the vestiges of horses, cattle, hogs, or deer, etc., were
to be found. The squirrels and birds of every kind were
totally destroyed. The dragoons told me that on their
scouts no living creature was to be seen except now and then
a few camp scavengers (viz. buzzards), picking the bones
of some unfortunate fellows who had been shot or cut down
and left in the woods above ground. In my visit to General
Greene's camp, as there was some danger from the enemy,
I made a circuitous route to General Marion's camp, then
on Santee River, to get an escort, which he gave me, of
twenty infantry and twenty cavalry ; these, with the volunteers that attended me, made us pretty strong. On my
way from General Marion's to General Greene's camp my
plantation was in the direct road, where I called and
stayed all night. On my entering the place, as soon as
the negroes discovered that I was of the party, there was
immediately a general alarm and an outcry through the
plantation that ' Massa was come, Massa was come ! ' and
they were running from every part with great joy to see
me. I stood in the piazza to receive them. They gazed
at me with astonishment, and every one came and took me
by the hand, saying, ' God bless you, Massa ! I'm glad
to see you, Massa ! ' and every now and then some one or
other would come out with a ' Ky ! ' and the old Africans
joined in a war-song in their own language of ' Welcome
the war home.' It was an affecting meeting between the
slaves and the master. The tears stole from my eyes and
ran down my cheeks. A number of gentlemen that were
with me could not help being affected at the scene. Many
are still alive, and remember the circumstances. I then
possessed about two hundred slaves, and not one of them
left me during the war, although they had had great
offers ; nay, some were carried down to work on the Brit-

ish lines, yet they always contrived to make their escape and return home. My plantation I found to be a desolate place, — stock of every kind taken off, the furniture carried away, and my estate had been under sequestration."

Moultrie was better off than many of his neighbours, for his people remained ; but on most places numbers of negroes had been carried off, and labour was thoroughly disorganized by the abduction of twenty-four thousand from the low country alone. The lands themselves had suffered. The neglected rice fields were overgrown with coarse grass, the embankments were broken down, the reserves run dry. The indigo vats had gone to ruin; the little provision crops for which the women had striven were the only produce of the plantations of the patriots. On many there " was not a horse, not a cow, or a pig, or a chicken to be seen."

How were these places to be restored and brought into cultivation ? Without the fruits of the ground how was commerce to revive ? Without commerce what help for the town ?

Of money there was literally none. While the British occupation continued, there had been coin in circulation, but with their departure that disappeared. The paper money was pronounced valueless, and people bartered one commodity for another, as when the racing stud of Mr. Richardson at the High Hills of Santee, " 43 valuable mares, colts and fillies," were offered in exchange " for prime copper or purple indigo," or produced the little hoards they had kept for extremity. " Plate, rings, keepsakes, old coins, etc., were brought out by those who possessed them, but the great bulk of the people lived without money, or any substitute for it. Buying and selling in great measure ceased. Those who had the necessaries of life freely divided with those who were destitute," — a condition of things which could not last long.

Moreover there were extraordinary complications. The whole fiscal condition was so confused with old, funded debts, paper money, certificates, continental money, etc., that the present writer is utterly incompetent to offer the slightest explanation. It is enough — and correct — to say, that almost every one was bankrupt, for the present, and that every one was looking anxiously for what the morrow might bring forth.

The immediate morrow brought only increase of trouble. Greene's army lay just outside of the town, not under the best of discipline. The soldiers thought that they had done all things, and deserved all things ; and their general encouraged their demands. It was with joy that the citizens saw them depart for Philadelphia, where they were even more unruly.

The disorganized state of the country is shown by a story of how Governor Mathews, wishing to restore the civil government, sent one of the judges to open court in a small town to the southward. The judge set forth in his chaise, but without an escort. The road lay through thick woods. Suddenly from the trees sprang two young gentlemen of condition, who to his utter amazement informed his Honour very politely that they meant him no harm, but that his horses were wanted for the use of the army and must be resigned ! Then unbuckling the traces they made off with the animals.

The furious judge made his way back (how is not stated) to town, and wrote to Governor Mathews. The Governor replied that he was very sorry and would do what he could. He would try to have the horses returned, but thought it best to postpone reopening the courts for some time yet.

With much difficulty he did get the horses restored, but it nearly caused a revolt in the army, which considered itself deprived of its privileges. It shows the disturbed state of the country that two young men of position should have engaged in such a Robin Hood-like scrape!

The unruly soldiers were got rid of, but the carrying out of the act of confiscation and amercement passed by the Jacksonboro assembly was a more abiding trouble.

Had the war continued there would have been little difference of opinion, but the cessation of hostilities modified public feeling. Royalists, Tories, and protected men cried aloud. Their trials, they said, had been greater than they could bear. The fact remained that others *had* borne the same trials to the last.

The Legislature, in which were almost all the men who had voted at Jacksonboro, convened, and after discussion appointed a committee with General Moultrie as chairman to report upon the matter.

It was soon seen that as usual the soldiers, now that the fighting was done, were the most lenient. Marion, ever as gentle a knight as Sidney himself, threw his great influence into the side of mercy ; the Pinckneys and other officers, notably Gadsden, as frank and impulsive in forgiveness as in attack, supported him, and Moultrie gives the result : ". . . after sitting several weeks and giving every one a fair and impartial hearing, a report was made to the Houses in favour of the great majority, and a great part of those whose names were upon the confiscation, banishment or amercement lists were struck off, and after a few years almost all of them had their estates restored to them, and themselves received as fellow-citizens."

Five hundred thousand pounds sterling actually in the hands of the public receiver were, notwithstanding the desperate straits of the treasury, returned to the owners thereof. Complaints were made of cases of hardship and injustice, some of which were probably well founded. But the men of that day were clear-headed, honest gentlemen, and the statements of Moultrie, Drayton, and Garden are of authority.

It did undoubtedly take time for these things to be forgotten, — " he took protection " was a term of reproach for many and many a year. But ten years later Mr. Benjamin Elliott, in an oration delivered before the " '76 Association," after recalling the hardships which his countrymen had endured, says with emphasis: —

" The patriot does not now enjoy one benefit from the Revolution, which has not been extended to the Tory."

In the midst of all this the town declared itself a city! From its foundation to about the beginning of the Revolution it had been styled "Charles Town"; then gradually people wrote "Charlestown." Now, 1783, it definitely dropped the " w " and called itself "Charleston." Nevertheless in its home country the old fashion prevails unto this day, and Charleston is "Town" throughout the parishes.

The first light on the pecuniary question came when the Legislature decided to issue bills of credit (paper money) and lend it in small sums to the inhabitants on mortgages of plate or real estate. The merchants patriotically agreed to receive these bills at par with gold or silver — a beautiful pretence for which they should really be praised. However, it worked well. A gentleman repaired his house on the security of his wife's earrings, or bought a horse and plough with the proceeds of his silver candelabra. It was a small beginning, but it was something. Richer men mortgaged land and could do more. The power of work quickened the spirits of the people.

After the adoption of the Constitution the United States agreed to repay the States for their advances of the Revolution. South Carolina had, contrary to the saying of Holy Writ, gone to war at her own cost. Her advances had been so large that when the accounts were finally made out, one million, four hundred and forty-seven thousand, one hundred and seventy-three dollars were found to be due her. This was called an "immense sum" in those simple days, and went a great way. Banks were founded, trade, commerce, and agriculture revived ; the town was alive again. "Hard Money" reappeared, and as Dr. Ramsay quaintly expressed it, "Gold and silver had a domicile in Charleston."

The rebound was wonderfully rapid. Of course there was much work and hard work to be done, but it was hopeful work. The cultivation of tide-water rice came in then ; that is, flowing the rice with water taken in through flood-gates from the rivers at the top of the tide. This brought into use the great deltas of the rivers, and the swamp-land along their banks, from the head of tide-water to the sea. Tide runs far inland in that level country.

The labour was enormous; the primeval forests of black cypress and gum were to be felled, endless banks built, endless canals dug. It added miles of the most fertile land to the resources of the State, and the sons of energetic planters were made rich by the toils of their fathers.

Literary gentlemen in cool and pleasant libraries are fond of writing of Southern listlessness and indolence. We often think of Tennyson's farmer and his parson : —

"He writes two sermons a week, and I've grubbed Thornaby waste."

Then cotton came in. As early as 1774 Ralph Izard, then in England, wrote to a friend who had charge of his estates : —

"Nothing gives me so much concern as the thought that my people may want for clothes and blankets." And goes on to speak of the possibility of using cotton, "which is produced in such quantities that some of it may be bought." He also says that Mr. Heyward (probably Daniel, the father of Thomas) has as many people as any gentleman in the State, and makes cotton enough to clothe them all. Mrs. Pinckney's overseer writes to her asking for cotton cards, to prepare it for the loom; but its use was extremely limited. In 1784, however, Mr. John Teasdale, the persevering lover of the pretty Miss Verree, sent eight bags of cotton to Liverpool, where it was seized by the custom-house officers, who said that "so much cotton could not possibly be grown in America."

Georgia took the lead with the new industry, followed quickly by South Carolina. It was all-important, for the loss of the British "bounty" on the indigo, and of the exclusive trade, had made its production less profitable; cotton was more easy of cultivation, and less exhausting to the land. The new soon superseded the old high land staple. With good crops of rice and cotton to export, commerce rapidly revived, and by 1793 the trade had trebled itself and prosperity was restored.

Great changes of course had to come.

One very important one was, that the town discovered that she was no longer the State!

For the first four years of the Revolutionary struggle, so great had been the apathy of the middle and up country, that she might well have continued to think herself so; but after the fall of Charleston, when Rawdon and Tarleton ravaged the "districts," things changed.

Sumter, Pickens, Hampton, and other bold riders threw their swords into the scale, and the cause was won by them, not by the crushed and shackled town. Now they asked their reward; let the capital be in the centre of the State, equally accessible to all, not on its extreme edge. It was a blow. Naturally the town did not at once agree. But a little reflection showed the rights of the case and the change was determined. The centre of the State was chosen, and the present city of Columbia begun, thereby "spoiling," the old people used to say, the "best cotton plantation (Colonel Taylor's) in the State." Charleston's reign of one hundred and twenty years was over, when the Legislature met for the first time in its new home in 1790.

There were other changes too to be made to suit the new order of things. The English state had gone, the established church must go with it, and so must primogeniture.

Both of these affected the town peculiarly; it and its parishes were the stronghold of the church. When the support from the treasury and that from the English S. P. G. failed, the whole parochial system went with it. Schools, charities, registers, all were done away with, and were sadly missed. Dr. Ramsay says that the wealthier dissenters had by this time joined the Episcopalians, or rather as he puts it, "the more fashionable Church," and were equally annoyed. When he wrote in 1808, only seven of the twenty-four parishes outside of the town had regular service, although in most of them the churches had been spared by the British. St. Michael's and St. Philip's, thanks to good Mrs. Affra Coming, had their endowments, and pursued the even tenor of their ways.

Mr. Rybenau, the merchant who had speculated in the church bells, reshipped them to Charleston, hoping to make a profit.

The people rushed to the wharf, drew them joyously to the church, and swung them to the steeple. The town had got its voice again, and there was great delight. Mr. Rybenau never enjoyed the fruit of his enterprise, for he died suddenly, his estate was declared bankrupt, and no payment was ever demanded for the bells. It was "a judgment" on sacrilege, of course.

Primogeniture all felt must pass, being absolutely inconsistent with republican institutions. Some of its influences were regretted, peculiarly the loosening of the family tie that came when one of its members ceased to be distinctly the head, and as such responsible for the welfare of the others.

"The aristocracy which had attached itself to some of the old families received a blow," says Ramsay. It would be more correct to say that the great fortunes were broken up.

There was, after a time, as much or more wealth, but it was in more hands.

No great houses like Fairlawn or Newington were built after this. Men usually tried to leave the "home place" to their eldest son, by which arrangement some family seats still remain in the names of their original proprietors; but younger sons and daughters were to receive their share, and although great liberty was allowed to testators, much inequality of bequest soon came to be condemned. Properties were necessarily smaller.

The Duc de Liancourt, travelling in Carolina in 1800, says that there was only one *very* rich man in the State; "a Mr. Blake, who lived in England and had many rice plantations." This was Mr. Daniel Blake, grandson of the Proprietor and Governor, and the ancestor of the present family.

There was great concern about the schools. It was no longer possible or convenient to send so many young men to Europe for education as had been the custom, and where were they to be taught? Something nearer had to be provided.

The question of a college had been mooted some years before, and land and money appropriated for the purpose. Nothing was actually done, however, except obtaining a charter in 1785, until the ever patriotic Dr. Smith (afterward Bishop) took the matter in hand. Dr. Smith was a man of ample means, but such was his anxiety for the youth of the country, that he had collected a number of lads into a school and taught them himself. He now proposed to the trustees of the college fund to make an effort for its establishment, offering sixty scholars of his academy as the first pupils.

The trustees were only too glad to accept the offer. They appealed to the public for aid, improved their char-

CHARLESTON COLLEGE

ter, and repaired the east wing of "the old brick bar-racks" for the college building ; giving it a square for a campus, and surrounding it with a wall. Dr. Smith was made principal, and the first commencement was held in 1794, when four young gentlemen were graduated : one of whom, Mr. Bowen, afterward became Bishop of the Diocese.

All the trustees attended on this interesting occasion. "Judge Bee (former Lt. Govr.), President, Genl. C. C. Pinckney, Vice Pres., Mr. Danl. De Saussure, Chancellor Mathews (former Govr.), Chancellor Hugh Rutledge, Judge Thomas Heyward, General Vander Horst, and Joseph Manigault, Esqr."

All but the last of these had gone through the Revolution with honour and credit in their different stations ; and he, Joseph Manigault, was the little boy who had stood with his grandfather, rifle in hand, in the trenches when Prévost was at the gates.

The present college building, between Greene and George streets, stands partly upon the foundation of "the old brick barracks" held by the troops at the siege of Charleston. Many lads were sent to this college, and many to Princeton, which was for years a favourite place of education with Charleston people. After a time the fame of Dugald Stewart and of Robertson attracted young men to Edinburgh, but only a few went to Oxford or Cambridge.

Education sat heavy upon the hearts of the mothers, who could not bear that their sons should lack the advantages which their fathers had enjoyed. Their admonitions are earnest and well put. Mrs. Pinckney, only a short time before her death, wrote to her grandson at Cambridge (suspected of idleness), offering his uncles as his model, and exclaiming : "An idle man is a burthen to society and to himself. How absurdly connected are the words ' an illiterate gentleman.' "

The following letter from Mrs. Gibbes to her son at Princeton is so good and wise that it is given here. She had been Miss Drayton, and was the wife of the grandson of Governor Gibbes.

"AUGUST 17th, 1788.

" Your last favour to me, my dear Jack, dated July 7th, made your father and myself inexpressibly happy to hear you were so agreeably situated at College; a place where we have so long wished to have you, and where we have a parent's flattering hope of your attaining that knowledge which will at a future day make you not only a credit to your family but also an honour to your country; that you may in the hour of exigency, when your country calls, rise up in her behalf, and be enabled to give your voice unbiassed by party or prejudice. For it too often happens that good men for want of an education to enable them thoroughly to investigate the subject and gain a proper knowledge of affairs; have been under the necessity of forming their ideas from other men's opinions, and be led by them entirely. This is what we may call taking our opinions upon trust.

" In my last to you I requested to know the manner of your employing your time, since when in a letter to your father you have fully satisfied us. It gives me pleasure to know that your thirst for knowledge is so great that it makes the change in your way of life not irksome to you. . . .

" I am glad to find by your letter that you have a dancing and a fencing master. These accomplishments are very necessary for finishing a young gentleman's education. I would have you sacrifice somewhat to the graces, altho' not entirely on Lord Chesterfield's plan. But why have I mentioned that book? It may perhaps rouse a curiosity in you to read it. If you never have pray forbear until you are three or four years older. Your principles will then be fixed: at present it is dangerous reading for a youthful mind. . . . Adieu my dearest son.

> " Your affectionate mother,
>
> "S. Gibbes."

By 1790 Charleston was a pretty place, as all travellers aver. The houses, many of them of wood, were large and airy, and the fashion of piazzas was becoming general. People were adopting the peculiar style of house stretched long to catch the breeze with gable end to the street and long piazzas. It was not as handsome but cooler and better suited to the climate than the square colonial mansion. This manner of house presupposes a garden, for the door upon the street is in truth only a sort of gate, and the true front door opens from the piazza, and gives upon the garden opposite. The curious neglect of flowers, mentioned in the earlier part of this story, had long since passed away, and every residence had its shrubbery garden about it.

The streets indeed were — and are — narrow, in spite of Lord Shaftesbury's admonitions to the contrary ; there being an old-world belief that narrow streets were healthier than wide ones, because they excluded the sun ; — and everybody knew that the sun was a thing to be excluded, " maleficent and dangerous," as they believe in Rome and in Spain to this day. They were generally bordered by good brick walls, for the yards and gardens were the playgrounds of the inhabitants, who took their pleasure privately ; and were planted with the pride-of-India (*Melia Azedarach*), which had the great advantage of harbouring no insects, grew quickly, and gave in summer " dark green layers of shade."

There was no want of varieties of flowers since Watson, the gardener first employed by Henry Laurens, had established his " Nursery and Botanic Garden " in the square above Inspection Street, where railroad workshops are now.

To him succeeded Michaux, sent out by the French

TYPICAL HOUSE IN MEETING STREET

government. He too had a Botanic Garden "up the path," and imported many new things,—the sweet olive,

the tea plant, etc. Some immense camellias on the terrace at Middleton Place were planted by him, and it was said that he had brought the first Roman laurel (degraded by popular speech into the spice tree) from Italy. Michaux wrote a valuable book on the oaks of America. The Drayton gardens at Magnolia were already very beautiful, Mr. Drayton devoting himself, as did his grandson of our day, to his beautiful grounds, and delighting to show the beauty of the native shrubs and flowers.

In the town, behind their high walls, grew oleanders and pomegranates, figs and grapes, and orange trees both sweet and bitter, and bulbs brought from Holland, jonquils, and hyacinths. The air was fragrant with the sweet olive, myrtle, and gardenia. There were old-fashioned roses ! the cinnamon, the York and Lancaster, the little white musk, and the sweet or Damascus. The glossy-leaved Cherokee clothed the walls with its great white disks, and was crowded by jasmine and honeysuckle. The lots were so large, often a square, or a half square, that the yard, stables, and servants' quarters were quite separate from these pleasant places, where according to the fashion of the time there were arbours, in which the gentlemen smoked their pipes, and the ladies took their " dish of tea " of an afternoon.

Captain Basil Hall, who came a few years later, calls the houses " the villas of the wealthy planters, almost hid in the rich foliage," and speaks of the " light oriental style of building, the gorgeous shrubs and flowers, and the tropical aspect of the city."

So renewed and beautified, the little town thought herself well prepared to receive the visit of President Washington, when the Father of his People proposed his Southern tour in 1791.

Travelling then was a matter of preparation and ar-

Vernon Howe Bailey

The Live-Oaks at Otranto

rangement, and Washington, who had a high opinion of what was due his position, was not the man to neglect any detail of equipage.

The President came in his travelling chariot with four horses and outriders. His favourite horse was led behind that he might change the exercise occasionally. His luggage followed in another vehicle, and all the servants were handsomely liveried. As he advanced the people thronged to see him pass, and the gentry of each neighbourhood mounted and escorted him to the next stopping place.

When the cortège reached the Waccamaw River, it stopped for the night at Colonel William Alston's plantation, Clifton. Colonel Alston was one of the largest rice planters in the State and considered a model one. He was an old soldier, having been an officer of Marion's and had lately married as his second wife the beautiful Mary Motte, youngest daughter of Rebecca Motte of Revolutionary fame. She had been a little girl when she was locked up in the garret during Rawdon's tenancy of her mother's house, and was now a lovely young woman with her character written on her face, and made a charming hostess.

Clifton house (since destroyed by fire) stood among fine trees, a little back from the river, with fields spreading wide before it. These fields in early spring were covered with the young rice, springing green from the dark earth and intersected by innumerable ditches, the water gleaming bright in the sunshine. The President was quite unprepared for such perfection of cultivation, and, the passion of his life being agriculture, was delighted. It won from him one of the few enthusiastic remarks reported of him, for he told his hostess that it "looked like fairyland." And afterward in Charleston he said to the Governor, Mr. Charles Pinckney (son of Colonel C. Pinckney, President of the first Provincial Congress), that he had had no idea

that anywhere in America was there such perfection of
cultivation as he had seen on the large rice rivers which
he had crossed.

The next stage was to Georgetown, where he was, of
course, received with all honour, and then to Charleston,
stopping by the way for a late breakfast at Mrs. Horrÿ's
place, Hampton on the South Santee.   Here he saved the
life of a live-oak tree, which had been condemned to the
axe as obscuring the view from the avenue of a fine portico
just erected.

The General's good word saved it, and it still lives to
keep the memory of the visit.

Arrived at Haddrell's, he was met by two handsome
barges prepared for him and the gentlemen who escorted
him.   A committee greeted and accompanied him.   His
own barge was manned by twelve masters of ships then
in port, "volunteers all handsomely dressed at their own
expense."   "Also a flotilla of boats of all sizes filled with
ladies and gentlemen attended him across the river."

At Prioleau's wharf he was received by the Governor,
Mr. Pinckney, the Lieutenant-governor, Mr. Isaac Holmes,
the Intendant, Mr. Vander Horst, the gentlemen of the City
Council, and the Society of the Cincinnati.   These, all
headed by "the mace," walked in procession to the Exchange, where he stood bareheaded on the steps and
received the cheers and homage of the public.   Those
who saw him declared that it always remained one of the
strongest impressions of their lives.   Washington had the
singular good fortune of enjoying his "legend" in his
own time.

He embodied to the people at large, not more than to
those who knew him best, all the virtues which they hoped
for the Republic.   Strength, honour, virtue, courage, justice, truth — all seemed personified in his majestic form.

The house prepared for the honoured guest was that

still standing in the lower part of Church Street, now alas, a bakery. It is a substantial brick building which a few years ago was handsome with fine woodwork.

It then belonged to Thomas Heyward, and was rented and handsomely furnished by the city for the occasion. Here every one that could make an address, made it, — and all were graciously received and answered. How tired he must have been! He visited the fortifications, and confirmed his former opinion that the defence of the city should never have been attempted, but "was noble and honourable."

He went to breakfasts, dinners, and balls, all of which he recorded in his journal.

"Went to a concert where were 400 ladies, the number and appearance of wch. exceeded anything I had ever seen."

"Breakfast with Mrs. Rutledge, lady of Chief Justice, then absent on the Circuit. Dinner with gentlemen of the Cincinnati."

"Was visited about two o'clock by a great number of the most respectable ladies of Charleston, the first honour of the kind I had ever experienced, as flattering as singular."

There was a state dinner at the Exchange, arranged elaborately with decorations, banners, mottoes, etc. But one point puzzled the committee of arrangements, who were honourably anxious that the great man should enjoy himself as much as possible; but how should that be managed? He was, of course, to take in the Governor's lady, that was *de rigueur;* but what other fair dames should have the honour to be his neighbours? Commodore Gillon came to the rescue. Leave it to him and all should go well. So the clever sailor chose Mrs. Richard Shubrick, the most beautiful woman in Charleston, for Washington's *vis-à-vis,* and on his left he seated Miss Claudia

Smith, the wittiest. Eyes and ears were well provided. The plan proved a great success, and is detailed for the benefit of anxious hostesses. Our history is short ; the present writer knew the witty Miss Smith very well. She was a bent old woman, but her eyes were still bright, her wit likewise, — and she had not forgotten the " Washington banquet." She was then Mrs. Henry Izard.

A concert and ball were given at the City Hall, — thronged, of course. The ladies wore scarfs and bandeaux or " fillets " in their hair. White ribbon painted with the President's likeness, and the words " God bless our President " like a wreath around it. These bandeaux were long preserved ; they were more patriotic than pretty, and must have been very trying — but that mattered little, for all eyes were fixed on one object alone.

Sunday was no day of rest. The President went to church in state, attended by the whole City Council and welcomed at the doors by the vestry and wardens. St. Philip's in the morning, St. Michael's in the afternoon.

Finally he went to dine with General Moultrie and the army officers, like any other mortal. Moultrie was a delightful host, could set the table in a roar, and was full of anecdote and pleasantry. If Washington ever unbent anywhere, it was probably at that hospitable board.

The next morning at five the faithful Council were ready to speed the parting guest on his way to Augusta and Savannah. Farewell speeches were exchanged. The Council grateful for the visit, and hoping that he will return — and he thanking them in kindest terms for hospitable attentions and assuring them that it would give him great pleasure to revisit " this very respectable city."

For a lasting remembrance of this event we have the fine portrait of the general for which he sat to Colonel Trumbull at the request of the city, which now hangs in the Council Chamber. Mr. Charles Fraser, himself an artist, says that this picture was said, by persons who knew the original well, to be an excellent likeness. It is certainly a very agreeable one.

Every relic of his presence has been cherished by an adoring people. The plates from which he ate, the tree which he saved, are sacred to their owners. The beautiful dinner table made for his use is a valued possession of the descendants of the Intendant, General Vander Horst; and the pew in which he sat in St. Michael's Church, belonging to the same family, is preserved inviolate as he occupied it.

The Society of the Cincinnati referred to here should have been mentioned before, not only for the great importance then attached to it, but for the extraordinary excitement caused by its establishment. An excitement arising from the suspicious fear of monarchical and aristocratic principles already alluded to, as prevailing in the years that followed the Revolution.

The society began in 1783, when the officers of the American or Continental Army, in cantonment at New Windsor on the Hudson, proposed among themselves that upon parting (they were soon to be disbanded) they should form an association of friendship and brotherhood, in which every officer of good repute should have the right to join, and in which he might be succeeded by his eldest son.

The idea took and expanded. It first appeared on paper in the form of "Proposals" by General Knox, but as Baron von Steuben presided over the meeting called to deliberate upon the scheme, and as his French colleagues took a lively interest in the affair, there can be little doubt that the foreign officers had much to do with its origin and development.

It seemed an excellent and unobjectionable plan. The preamble set forth that

" It having pleased the Supreme Governor of the Universe to give success to the arms of our country, and to establish the United States free and independent, Therefore, gratefully to commemorate this event — to inculcate to the latest ages the duty of laying down in peace, arms assumed for public defence, by forming an Institution which recognizes that most important principle, — to continue the mutual friendships which commenced under the pressure of common danger,— and to effectuate the acts of beneficence, dictated by the spirit of brotherly kindness toward those officers and their families who unfortunately are under the necessity of receiving them; the Officers of the American Army do hereby constitute themselves a Society of Friends ; and possessing the highest veneration for the character of that illustrious Roman, Lucius Quintius Cincinnatus, denominate themselves

' THE SOCIETY OF THE CINCINNATI.' "

What could be more consonant with the spirit of true comradeship ? What more productive of good feeling in every way ?

Far different was the immediate result.

The temper of the time was suspicious of everything that savoured of class, or caste, or rank of any kind, even military. And the provision for succession by the eldest son seemed to many the introduction of an hereditary principle, which they dreaded above all things. This rule of the society was, it was true, derived from the laws of primogeniture, and this the public was quick to discover. " It would form an hereditary aristocracy."

Newspapers denounced it, speeches were delivered, assemblies legislated against the proposed Society. It was even feared that Congress might oppose it, but that danger was averted. The objections raised then seem the merest nonsense now, but were of vital interest at the time.

In Carolina the feeling was bitter. There, where class distinctions died hard, the "too numerous democracy" cried in alarm, while the conservatives entered cordially into the plan.

The officers, however, held to their scheme. Each gave a month's pay as a beginning for a fund; and Washington, after some hesitation, agreed to become the first President-general, thereby giving great strength to the new undertaking. In the Carolinas there was the special complaint that the association was limited to the Continental officers, while the States felt, and felt with pride, that among their partisans there were many, who by service, character, and conduct were deserving of all military position and honour. This exception long rankled, and some officers holding Continental commissions did not become members, disapproving the rule. Marion, however, was a member, his name being on the roll.

The association throve in spite of opposition. The officers of the French contingent took it up with enthusiasm, and this too was an affront to the ultra-democrats, who resented the idea of " an American order being flaunted at a foreign court! " It was arranged that there should be a central " General Society, with officers to meet every three years," and Associate Societies, one in each State; all to be subject to the general authority, but each having power to make minor regulations to suit its own conditions.

The question of the medal or badge of the order was an interesting one. Major L'Enfant of the corps of Engineers offered his assistance and designed the Eagle badge, too well known to need description here.

The chief French military and naval officers who had served in the Revolution were declared members, and were presented with complimentary medals, which were enthu-

THE HOUSE WHERE PRESIDENT WASHINGTON STAYED, IN CHURCH STREET
Now used as a bakery.
361

siastically and gracefully accepted. The Admiral Count de Grasse, in the name of the French navy, sent a beautiful one of gold and enamel, set with diamonds, to General Washington, which is still worn by each successive President-general.

The French officers were said, however, to have been sometimes a little puzzled : orders in France have generally a patron saint,— was this a new one? One gallant soldier asked another: "Can you say where then our American friends have dug up this *Saint Sénatus?* I have looked through *le livre des Saints* and cannot find him!"

The society took itself and its duties seriously, feeling that it was composed of men who had done well for their country and were bound to use their influence for good, or, as Washington said, " of that very respectable body of citizens, the officers of the American Army."

In Charleston, where the Continental influence was socially paramount, and all the most prominent military men belonged to it, it was, the first ferment of resistance over, highly esteemed. General Moultrie was the first State President. The address which he wrote in behalf of his comrades and himself on the occasion of Washington's election in 1787 is admirable in its soldierly warmth and truth ; and the President answers in the same tone. General Thomas Pinckney was the second State President, and Major Garden, so often quoted here, the third.

On the death of Washington, Alexander Hamilton became second President-general, and he was succeeded by the two Pinckneys in turn.

Every Fourth of July the Society went either to St. Philip's or St. Michael's (the original members in their old regimentals) and listened with due decorum to a sermon, "suitable to the occasion." Both the rectors had been in the army. Dr. Smith, chaplain to the First Regiment

(Gadsden's), had shouldered his musket during the siege, and fought for the town. Dr. Purcell had been chaplain and judge advocate in the field. On these occasions the eagle of the Cincinnati shone above the canonicals on their breasts.

Then there was a meeting and an oration which the public was invited to attend, and the day was wound up by a dinner at which the gallant gentlemen enjoyed themselves thoroughly.

So far from endangering the social fabric, the influence of the Cincinnati has always been excellent, keeping alive a kindly and friendly feeling among its widely scattered members, dispensing a delicate charity, and maintaining a high standard of honour and dignity in the conduct of life.

An amusing instance of the hatred of all things English at this time is that among the rules of the Society was one, binding them to have no association with a man in a scarlet coat—meaning, of course, an English officer! Time went on, militia companies were formed in Charleston and decked themselves in many gay colours.

One of these, the " Governor's Guards," a company in which many young gentlemen were enrolled, chose for itself a uniform of red and silver. The Cincinnati always went to its annual meeting with a military escort. On one occasion the " Governor's Guard " courteously offered its services for the purpose.

But the Society, bound by the letter of the law, was forced to reply that, greatly appreciating the offer of the Guard, it was yet obliged to decline, as it was impossible for it to march with a red-coated escort !

In process of time the association declined and in many States dissolved entirely. Before the middle of the last century only seven of the thirteen Societies remained. Of these South Carolina was one. Of late years the prevailing fashion of "patriotic Societies" has caused its revival, and it is now flourishing once more.

Perhaps the most remarkable circumstance of the association is that the South Carolina Society continued unbroken through the war between the States. It held its meetings regularly on the Fourth of July, even when the town was enduring the Federal bombardment; and on one occasion, its secretary, the Hon. James Simons, now the vice-president of the General Society, fulfilled the duties of his office in full Confederate uniform, during a brief furlough from military duty!

In these years of exultation over the success of the Revolution, patriotism seems to have entered into all the common pursuits of life, and to have expressed itself in all sorts of odd ways. That there should have been hundreds of children named George Washington and Thomas Jefferson is natural enough, but "States" given as a name to a thirteenth child by an enthusiastic father (families were enormous then) is odd, but was not infrequent.

Household articles were made to bear witness, not merely cups and platters adorned with heads of distinguished characters, but whole scenes were transferred to china. Cornwallis surrendered on meat dishes, Washington crossed the Delaware on a sugar bowl, and the writer remembers a tall blue jug around which General Putnam's famous steps wound like a spiral staircase, with the hero sitting well on his horse's tail, galloping, sword in hand, into an abyss. Some things were quite elegant. There were decanters of a very graceful shape, said to have been made in Charleston, but more probably only engraved there, with thirteen slender arrows for decoration. Ladies' dresses were embroidered with emblems of the same sort, and the eagle grasping thunderbolts, despite Dr. Franklin's uncivil remarks, was the favourite belt-clasp for years.

Only one year after Washington's visit, in 1792, occurred the horrible massacre of St. Domingo, which converted the Gem of the Antilles into an Inferno of Savagery. The unhappy French, flying for their lives, took refuge chiefly in New Orleans and Charleston. They were, as was natural, received with all possible sympathy and kindness. Not waiting for concerted action the townsfolk threw open their houses and received the fugitives, who proved acceptable guests. Nothing could exceed the courage and cheerfulness of the refugees, who showed the same spirit that was then animating their kinsmen in France. Uncomplaining, gay, and pathetically grateful, they won the esteem and respect of their hosts. No one, it was said, had cause to repent his hospitality. For their assistance the city gave $12,500, besides the proceeds of a concert and many gifts, and the General Government appropriated $1750. This help enabled many of them to begin some occupation; they would take no more than was absolutely necessary, and quickly bestirred themselves for their own support. They were accomplished in music, painting, and the languages, and pupils were soon found. Some of the gentlemen were good musicians, and entered the orchestra of the theatre, which greatly benefited by their skill. Mr. Fraser, whose "Reminiscences" extend from 1785 to 1854, says that thirteen of the best teachers in town were these refugees. Two of the schools established by them were long thought the most fashionable *écoles de demoiselles* that had ever been in Charleston. They were kept by Mademoiselle Daty and her niece Madame Talvande — the latter had been rescued from the massacre as an infant by her faithful nurse. The Charleston *jeune fille*, educated at one of these schools, learned, besides her lessons, a careful demeanour and an absolute submission to the will of her teacher, which would astonish the young people of the present day.

In an inferior class the best bakers, pastry-cooks, dressmakers, hairdressers, and clearstarchers were the St. Domingans or their children, and the beau or belle who had not learned to dance from M. Tastet or M. Foyolle would have been at a sad disadvantage. A few who had some knowledge of business became successful merchants, and more than one was distinguished in medicine. One of these, Dr. Polony, was the most eminent, being a member of learned European societies, and a correspondent of Buffon.

Seven years after their arrival the Duc de Rochefoucault Liancourt visited Charleston and speaks warmly of the gentleness, courtesy, and agreeability of these refugees, and of the untiring kindness and liberality of the citizens. They were well rewarded, for undoubtedly the example of the pretty manners and accomplishments tended to the embellishment of society.

The mother of Joseph Jefferson was one of these refugees. Her piquante face and sweet manners, as a child of eight or ten, attracted the attention of the daughter of General Macpherson, who, finding that the little girl had only a rather careless father to protect her, persuaded him to allow her to take charge of his daughter. The child grew up and was educated in the hospitable home of the Macphersons, until the promise of an unusually fine voice determined her father to educate her for the stage. Most reluctantly her kind friends resigned her, and she was taken to the North for the cultivation of her talent. There she married the elder Jefferson and became the mother of the greatest of American actors. Her son has told the story of her life and its many vicissitudes in his charming autobiography.

This was but one of the ways in which the French Revolution affected the people of Charleston. At first the doctrines of the new dispensation, the rights of the people

and the brotherhood of man, kindled the imaginations of
the men of 1776. They fancied that La Fayette was to
be another Washington, and France regenerate Europe.
They formed Jacobin Clubs, — they, the most conservative
of men ! — and when Citizen Genêt, envoy of the French
Republic, landed in Charleston, he was received with open
arms. The old officers who had fought with the French
auxiliaries took him to their homes and hearts, and
marched with him in processsion to the tune of the
" Marseillaise"!

There were dinners and meetings, much excited talk of
leaguing against England, etc. Washington, who never
lost his head, had at once declared a strict neutrality during
the war; but the Citizen, relying on his own manifest popularity and the loudly expressed sympathy of the people,
paid no attention to the declaration, and proceeded to levy
troops and engage privateers to attack Florida and New
Orleans.

Fortunately Moultrie was then Governor, and was sensible and cool as Washington himself. He issued a proclamation forbidding all enlistment ; refused to permit
the armament of the privateers; ordered out the militia to
enforce his orders, and advised the President to call M.
Genêt to Philadelphia. The belief in the beneficence of
the French Revolution died hard, but was succeeded by
an equally ardent horror when news of the proceedings of
the Revolutionists burst upon the astonished world.

Especially did the banishment of La Fayette shock and
distress America. The people remembered how he had
come as the friend of this country in the hour of her
greatest need ; knew how for years he had laboured to
benefit his own, and resented the ingratitude with which
he was treated. When the news came of his imprisonment by Austria, the indignation was intense ; nowhere
more so than in Charleston, where on his first arrival with

Major Huger, so many years before, his graceful manners and chivalric spirit had made a deep impression. People were proud when they heard that the young son of Major Huger, Francis Kinloch, who as a child had played with the handsome Frenchman at North Island, had risked his life to liberate the prisoner of Olmütz. The attempt had failed, but through no fault of Huger's, who had behaved with singular devotion, giving up his own horse to La Fayette, and being at once himself consigned to the dungeon. The lives of both were constantly threatened, and might be sacrificed at any moment, depending as they did on the whim of an absolute despot. Mr. Huger was, after a time, released and returned home, but La Fayette remained confined despite the entreaties of half the world. The anxiety for his safety was painful, and the people could not understand why Washington did not *demand* the release of the friend of America.

Washington's popularity was sustaining a severe strain at the time (1796–1797) on account of the Jay treaty, the provisions of which were so distasteful to the South and West, that Judge Iredell of North Carolina, associate justice of the Supreme Court, said that "every man south of the Potomac was opposed to it, even stanch Federalists and personal friends of Mr. Jay."

To fasten such a treaty, which conceded almost every demand of Great Britain, upon the country, and to neglect its best friend! Was it possible that the President could mean this! The people stood aghast. Orators and newspapers denounced the pusillanimity of such conduct, addresses and petitions poured in upon the harassed but steadfast man who knew better than any other that a peace at any price with England was imperative, knew the limitations of his own power and the necessity for concealing them. To demand and be refused would be derogatory to the dignity of his young Republic, which could not enforce such demand by arms or influence.

What he could he would do ; but he would not take one step which would lower the prestige with which successful resistance to Great Britain had invested America.

Major Thomas Pinckney was then minister to the Court of St. James, and with him Washington had much correspondence on the subject. Major Pinckney had just returned to England from Spain, where he had successfully concluded a treaty for the free navigation of the Mississippi, and had asked to be allowed to return home, where private affairs demanded his presence. The treaty with Spain (Treaty of San Ildefonso) gave great satisfaction, especially to the West, and somewhat abated the violence of public feeling. The following letters refer to these topics, which were then supremely interesting to Charleston and other Southern cities. A portion of the first has been printed in the " Life of Thomas Pinckney," Houghton, Mifflin & Co., Boston; but not to mutilate the President's epistle, it is reprinted here with the context.

PRESIDENT WASHINGTON TO MAJOR PINCKNEY, MINISTER TO ENGLAND

" PHILADELPHIA, 20th Feb. 1796.

" DEAR SIR: Your letter of the 10th. of October from Madrid has been duly received. With regret I read the request which it contains ; but the footing on which you have placed the matter, forbids opposition, or even persuasion on my part that you would recede from it, altho' the difficulty of supplying your place, to my satisfaction, to the satisfaction of your country or to the Court you will leave will not be found easy.

" Having heard thro' different channels that you had concluded a treaty with Spain, and that the vessel which had it on board had been spoke at sea, we are in daily and anxious expectation of its arrival.

" The information has diffused general pleasure, and
2 B

will be soothing to the inhabitants of the western waters, who were beginning to grow restless and clamorous to obtain the navigation.

"Since the confinement of M. de La Fayette (after the attempt made by Dr. Bollman and Mr. Huger, both of whom are now in this city, to effect his escape) we have heard nothing further respecting him but that his confinement was more rigorous than before. We knew indeed that Madame de La Fayette and his daughter have been at Hamburgh, — that it was reported they were coming to America; — but that instead of doing so they went to Vienna, to try the effect of personal solicitations to obtain his releasement.

"Newspaper accounts go further and say they were permitted to proceed to Olmutz. But how far the latter information is to be depended on, and if true what is or may be the result is altogether unknown to me.

"I need hardly mention how much my sensibility has been hurt by the treatment which this gentleman has met with, or how anxious I am to see him liberated therefrom, but what course to pursue, as most likely and proper to aid that measure is not quite so easy to decide on.

"As President of the United States there might be a commitment of the Government by any interference of mine, and it is no easy matter, in a transaction of *this nature*, for a public character to assume the garb of a private citizen in a case that does not relate to himself. Yet such is my wish to contribute my mite to accomplish this desirable object, that I have no objection to its being made known to the Imperial Ambassador in London (who if he thinks proper may communicate it to his Court) that this event is the ardent wish of the people of the United States, to which I sincerely add mine. The time, the manner and even the measure itself I leave to your discretion, as circumstance and every other matter that concerns this gentleman are better known on that than they are on this side of the Atlantic.

" I shall add no more on this, and but little on any other topic at present. The Gazettes which I presume you receive, will show in what manner the public functionaries are treated here. The abuse however which some of them contain, has excited no reply from me.

" I have a consolation which no earthly power can deprive me of, that of acting from my best judgment, and I shall be very much mistaken if I do not soon find that the public mind is recovering fast from the disquietude into which it has been thrown by the most wilful, artful and malignant misrepresentation that can be imagined. The current is certainly turned, and is beginning to run strong the other way — But I am proceeding further than I had intended, and will therefore conclude with assurances of the esteem and regard with which I am

" Dear Sir
" Your obedt. and affect. Servt.
" G. WASHINGTON."

Copy from original letter, in possession of Captain Thomas Pinckney, Charleston, South Carolina.

PRESIDENT WASHINGTON TO MAJOR PINCKNEY, MINISTER TO ENGLAND

" PHILADELPHIA, 22nd. May, 1796.
"<i>Private.</i></div>

" DEAR SIR: To my letters of the 20th. of Feby. and 5th. of March, I beg to refer you for the disclosure of my sentiments on the subject then mentioned to you.

" Very soon afterwards a long and animated discussion in the House of Representatives relative to the Treaty of Amity, Commerce and Navigation with Great Britain, took place; and continued, in one shape or another, until the last of April, suspending in a manner all other business, and exciting the public mind in a higher degree than it has been at any period since the Revolution, — nothing I believe but the torrent of Petitions and Remonstrances which were pouring in from all the Eastern and Middle States, and were beginning to come pretty freely from that of Virginia requiring the necessary provision for carrying the treaty into effect, would have produced a division (51 to 48) in favour of the appropriation. But as the debates (which I presume will be sent to you from the Department of State,) will give you a view of this business, more in detail than I am able to do I shall refer you to them. The enclosed speech however made by Mr. Ames, at the close of the discussion, I send you, because in the opinion of most that heard it delivered, or have read it since, its reasoning is unanswerable.

" The doubtful issue of the dispute added to the *real* difficulty of finding a character to supply your place, at the court of London has occasioned a longer delay than may be convenient or agreeable to you. But as Mr. King of the Senate " (Rufus King of N. Y.) " who it seems had resolved to quit his seat at that board, has accepted the appointment and will embark as soon as matters can be arranged you will soon be relieved.

" In my letter of the 20th. of Feby. I expressed pretty strongly my sensibility on acct. of the situation of the Marquis De la Fayette. This is increased by the visible distress of his son, who is now with me, and grieves for the unhappy Fate of his parents. This circumstance gives a poignancy to my own feelings on the occasion and has induced me to go a step farther than I did in the letter above mentioned, as you will perceive by the enclosed address (a copy of which is also transmitted for your information) to the Emperor of Germany, to be forwarded by you in such a manner, and under such auspices as in your judgment shall be deemed best, — or to arrest it, if from the evidence before you (derived from former attempts) it shall appear *clear* that it would be of no avail to send it.

" Before I close this letter permit me to request the favour of you to embrace some favourable opportunity to thank Lord Grenville in my behalf, for his politeness in causing a special permit to be sent to Liverpool for the shipment of two sacks of the field peas, and the like quantity of winter vetches, which I had requested our Consul at that place to send to me for seed, but which it seems could not be done without a special order from Government. A circumstance which did not occur to me, or I certainly should not have given it the trouble of issuing one for such a trifle.

" With very great esteem and regard
" I am, dear Sir
" Your obedt. Servant
" G. WASHINGTON."

Copied from original letter in the possession of Captain Thomas Pinckney, Charleston, South Carolina.

The address by Washington to the Emperor of Austria enclosed with this letter is published in the " Life of Thomas Pinckney," and is a model of dignified remonstrance.

The President was careful to supply Major Pinckney with ample funds for the use of Madame de La Fayette, in her unwearied efforts for the release of her husband — a release which did not take place until demanded by Napoleon in 1797, after five years of close imprisonment.

So rapidly did Charleston recover from its " fervour of Jacobinism which did not long agree with federalism," as that acute observer, Mr. Samuel Thomas of Massachusetts, said, that by 1796–1797 the people were eagerly pre-

paring for the war which the insolence of the Directory had
nearly provoked. A meeting was held in St. Michael's
Church and funds were subscribed for fortifications.
" Castle Pinckney," so named in honour of General C. C.
Pinckney, who had just returned from the mission to
France, in which he had curtly refused compliance with the

CASTLE PINCKNEY AT PRESENT TIME

dishonourable demands of Talleyrand and his associates,
was built upon the shoal long known as Shute's Folly.

Great enthusiasm was shown by the mechanics, who volunteered to build a fort by their own unpaid labours.
Accordingly the work was known as " Fort Mechanic,"
and stood on East Battery, where the residence No. 19 is
now. A part of the north wall and the well of the adjoining lot are remains of this fortification. The citizens
also subscribed for a thirty-two gun frigate, which was
built at Pritchard's shipyard on Belvidere town creek, at
the end of the lane on which the Country Club stands

now. She was launched in 1799 and called *John Adams*, in honour of the second President of the United States.

The war being averted, the century was closing, as far as this country was concerned, in "peace and amity." The last years show peaceful occupations. The Orphan House was built after a yellow fever summer which had shown the need of such an institution. An English traveller, who visited it some years after, admired its comfort and management, but adds that such institutions are wrong, since by providing for the offspring of imprudent marriages they encourage overpopulation and its attendant evils! This in North America over a hundred years ago! The Orphan House was built upon the site of the old ramparts, and Mr. Fraser notes that the Intendant, Mr. John Huger, and Mr. Smith, the orator of the day, who stood side by side during the opening ceremonies, both "patriots true and tried," had far different associations with the precinct.

The scourge of fire from which Charleston has suffered more than from war itself visited her again at this time. The conflagration began in an alley near the bay somewhat northeast of St. Philip's Church, and spread as far south as Broad Street, where it consumed the famous "Corner Tavern," which had been the place of public meeting for many years. It was at the northeast corner of Broad and Church streets, opposite to the Charleston Library.

The second Huguenot church was also burned in this fire, and St. Philip's was only saved by the courage of a negro sailor who climbed to the top of the tower and tore off the blazing shingles. Nothing else could have saved the building. The brave fellow received his liberty, a sum of money, and a fishing-boat completely equipped with nets, etc., for his reward. The popular verses which describe this scene as happening at St. Michael's, are erroneous.

Before the end of the century many of the persons mentioned in this rambling story had passed away. The stately old gentleman, Mr. Henry Middleton, first President of the first Continental Congress, had died full of years, and of honours. His wife, Lady Mary MacKenzie, who had paid a short visit to England, died on the return voyage. Mrs. Pinckney, so often quoted here, was also dead. These were all old; but Mr. Arthur Middleton, the son of Henry, and signer of the Declaration of Independence, had gone before his time, aged only forty-five, a victim to the fever of the country. He had been one of the most ardent of patriots, had supported every measure for the good of the State, had advocated them in a series of able articles signed "Andrew Marvell," and had borne the losses of the Revolution with an admirable cheerfulness. It was told that he wore a homespun suit of negro cloth with as much ease and grace as a velvet one, and was always an elegant and accomplished gentleman. His wife (Miss Izard), who was said to have saved General Greene's life by her medical skill when he lay ill of a fever at Middleton Place, long survived him.

For no one, however, was the sorrow of the town and its parishes as great as for Marion. This most remarkable leader of "Irregular Cavalry" died in 1795. His discipline in war was so strict that when an act was introduced into the Legislature offering immunity for any illegal acts committed by the partisans, he rose with indignation. For himself and for his men, he said, he refused such immunity. They had always obeyed the law, and asked only examination into their conduct. If any wrong was proved, they were ready to bear the penalty.

Grave and taciturn while on duty, he was cordial and cheerful among his friends.

Colonel Harry Lee says of him : "Marion was enthusiastically wedded to the cause of liberty; . . . the commonwealth was his sole object; nothing selfish, nothing mercenary, soiled his ermine character."

Children of his own he had none; but Garden says, " Distinguished by integrity in all his dealings, he was the executor of many estates, and the guardian of many children. . . . No man ever lived more beloved, none ever died more universally and justly lamented, than the Huguenot partisan, Francis Marion."

CHAPTER XVIII

CHARACTERISTICS. STRUCTURE OF SOCIETY

LIFE had begun to flow in easy channels by the coming of the nineteenth century. The Revolution, with its subsequent jars and jangles, was a thing of the past; the Republic a settled, working government.

Strangers remarked with surprise how honestly and well men who had grown to manhood under the old *régime*, accepted and helped on the new.

In principle they were Republican; in habit and manners, all that was least so. The impositions of arbitrary power, the sufferings they had endured, had settled their convictions, but could not change their taste. There were many like Mr. Ralph Izard of the Elms, of whom M. de Chastelleux says, in his "Travels," that "with pride and impetuosity he ardently opposed the royal tyranny, without the slightest sympathy with democracy."

The Federalist and Republican parties which now arose differed, not upon Republicanism in creed but in application. "The Federals advocating so strongly centralized a power, as approximated to Monarchy, the Republicans professing such levelling views that the Federals charged them with tending to disorganization. Each" (Dr. Ramsay gently observes) "did injustice to the other."

Political parties are rarely just to their opponents, but it is curious to see how the signification of names has changed. The Republican of to-day represents the Federal of 1800, and it is the Democrat who is charged with Populism, etc.

It used to be said that the adherents of the different factions might be known by costume! The old gentlemen who tied back their powdered hair, wore lace ruffles, diamond buckles, knee breeches, and silk stockings, were Federals — the "Friends of Washington" as they delighted to be called.

The young men, whose locks — undisguised brown, black, or auburn, as nature made them — were cut in a "crop," who had short-waisted, high-collared coats, pudding-bag cravats, and "those slovenly things called pantaloons flapping about their ankles," were Republicans; followers of the brilliant and benevolent Jefferson.

It was almost an affair of generations. The fathers were in one camp, the sons in another; and although the mass of the people went with the sons, it is easy to understand how the unimpaired possession of social predominance consoled the fathers for the loss of political influence. They were mostly elderly men, who had had their share of labour and power, and there was not at that time any especially important measure before the country. Youth was then still deferential, and however it might *think*, expressed itself with modesty in the *presence* of its elders. If the seniors heard of the speeches and rhapsodies poured forth in Republican clubs by their clever boys, why — they "shifted their trumpets and only took snuff." Had they, too, not lost their heads in 1793, — dazzled for the moment by the glare of the period of which the sedate Wordsworth wrote : —

> " Good was it in that dawn to be alive,
> But to be young was very heaven"?

Travellers and natives all agree as to this condition of things. M. de Liancourt, already quoted, says (writing just before Washington's death), "*Society* is altogether Federalist and devoted to the President; the favourite toast is ' Permanency to the Union.' " Had they already any doubt of it ?

Mr. Fraser tells of the cheery meetings of the " Cossack Club."

" If we are told that the poor proscribed Federalists in Charleston, cut off as they were from all the honours and emoluments of office, were in the habit of meeting together *weekly*, it might naturally be supposed that it was for the purpose of interchanging sympathies, or rehearsing their ' *Tristia.*' But not so with the *Cossack Club*, which grew out of the peculiar condition of society at that time ; for a happier and more joyous set never met together to discuss a good dinner and enjoy a glass of old wine, than they did at their *Wednesday meetings*. It had *no rules*, for every member was a law to himself, and that law was never known to vary. *No penalty*, for there was none to enforce it. *No duty* imposed on any one but to contribute to the very extent of his intelligence, whatever might promote their happy and enlightened intercourse, and to pay two dollars for his dinner. This club was remarkable for every quality that had ever characterized the best private society of Charleston. Many of those who composed it had stood high in the service of their country, and brought to the common stock of conversation their varied knowledge and experience as statesmen, diplomatists, soldiers and jurists. Nor was the charm of literary discourse wanting to give interest to their meetings. General Pinckney was a constant member, and always ready to impart information, particularly to the younger members. . . .

" Many of these men were the remnant of a peculiar race of people. Born under a royal government, and early impressed with those exclusive feelings which rank and fortune create, they were characterized by a high and gentlemanly bearing. Most of them had been educated in one or other of the English Universities, and had become familiar with the highest standard of manners in that country. But upon the breaking out of the Revolution, they flocked home to share the fortunes of their country. Such men were, in their proper element, at the head of society — it was theirs to maintain and transmit the ancient character of Charleston for intelligence, refinement and hospitality."

All this goes to show that social life was not much troubled by the intrusion of the Jeffersonian Democracy, except in those inevitable cases where the meddlesome god has his way. It *was* troubled when a fascinating Republican fell in love with some fair Federalist who found the gentleman " vastly agreeable," while lamenting that he differed from " my dear Papa."

There was a story of one young lady who actually eloped from her strong-principled widowed mother, with a handsome young man, objectionable only for heterodoxy of this kind ; who had to fight a duel with an irate brother-in-law before he could establish himself in the affections of the family.

Another lady only got her way after months of friendly intercession by unimpeachable Federals, who assured the father that, although a Republican, the lover was a mild one. Both gentlemen rose to distinction, and as opinions became modified were even considered " respectable "!

There was great uneasiness about the influence that the new order might have upon "the minor morals called manners." Predictions were gloomy: what was to be expected when society should be set to the tune of " the world turned upside down " ?

It is a relief to know that nothing terrible happened, and that good judges declare that if not quite as formal, manners were still as courteous, and in many respects more graceful and refined, than in the preceding century.

Travellers have left us their impressions of place and people in these years, and it is curious to observe that the peculiarities which they describe are those remarked sixty years later. Character and habits had already crystallized into the forms which they were long to maintain.

Of the town itself one gentleman says, "a pretty place though dead level, lying between two noble rivers."

Its appearance, rising from the waves, unlike anything else. The harbour crowded with vessels, generally foreign, and many foreigners in the streets.

The aspect of things is tropical on the shore; alongside are vessels from every part of the world loading and unloading, — from the West Indies in particular. The wharves are covered with bananas, cocoanuts, coffee bags, etc., and rice and cotton to be shipped. The days are bright and sunny, he could fancy himself in equatorial regions again. "The Negroes (notwithstanding their degraded condition) looked bright and happy."

M. de Liancourt describes particularly the gentlemen whom he met. His journey to Charleston was made agreeable by his good fortune in falling in with Mr. John Julius Pringle, a distinguished lawyer, whose conversation he enjoys. He finds the manners of the gentry more European than in the Northern States, and that the ladies are more lively and take a greater share in conversation, but with perfect propriety and modesty.

He does not — sad to say — consider them as handsome as the Philadelphia belles, being too pale and fading early, but they are interesting and agreeable. He is entertained at the Elms by Mr. and Mrs. Izard, whose conversation is delightful. He visits Ashley River, and thinks Drayton Hall the handsomest place he sees. His friend Mr. Pringle is busy building and planting trees at his place near by — then called "Greenfield." Mr. Pringle thinks of calling it "Susan's Villa," in compliment to his wife.

Luckily the attorney-general (whom Mr. Thomas says is " good as great ") determined upon " Runnymede," by which name the beautiful place is still known.

The duke described the abounding hospitality and the too liberal style of housekeeping, the crowd of servants. " In no part of the globe is so much hospitality practised as in America, nor can it anywhere be better exercised than in South Carolina. . . . A Carolinian, though not very opulent, rarely has less than twenty servants in attendance on his table, his stables, and his kitchen . . . and yet things are not neatly kept, and are often shabby. There are few families who do not keep a chaise or a coach, and ladies rarely set foot on the streets."

Mr. Thomas declares that it is "the most aristocratic city in the Union notwithstanding her Jacobinism " and that " Political professions were of Jefferson's school, but practice aristocracy complete."

All of which, with but slight alteration, might have been written in 1860.

One most honourable trait of the period was the attention and deference paid to age, character, and public service. Every man's record was known, and won from his compatriots a respect that wealth was powerless to buy.

A gentleman some years ago told his son that his father, Mr. John Huger, a distinguished patriot, had always been accustomed, as his house had no piazzas, to take his tea, in fine summer weather, on the broad sidewalk in front of his door. The table was brought out and arranged, and passing friends would stop for a cup and a chat.

" How did he manage with the people going by ? " asked the son.

" You surely do not suppose," said the astonished father, " that any one would intrude upon the old gentleman ! Of course when people saw him, if they were not his friends, they crossed the street and walked on the other side, not to annoy him ! "

If a man had been a gallant soldier, his privileges were great. General Peter Horrÿ was Marion's senior colonel and right-hand man, a most highly respected citizen. He, however, had the bad habit of the day which was that of "our army in Flanders." On his annual journey from his plantation near Georgetown to Charleston, he always stopped for a visit at Mrs. Daniel Horrÿ's on South Santee. Mrs. Horrÿ was something of a martinet, and kept even her soldier brothers in order. " Charles, Charles, — you forget, — the girls," would come, if General Pinckney rapped out an oath. But when Cousin Peter arrived, Mrs. Horrÿ endured smilingly, — and if the young ladies bridled and looked down, they were reproved sharply, "Girls — none of that. Peter can swear when and where he chooses."

Had he not been Marion's favourite captain? It was General Peter Horrÿ to whom the ingenious Parson Weems chose to ascribe the honour of having collaborated with him, in the amusing piece of fiction which he called the "Life of Marion." The general vigorously denied any share in what he termed "a pack of d——d lies," and swore if ever Weems dared to set foot in Georgetown County, he himself would break every bone in his body. The ingenious Parson did not enjoy that form of criticism and kept out of his way.

One important change of custom that took place about this time was, that in consequence of the increased unhealthiness of the country the planters spent more time in the city than they had been accustomed to do.

The clearing of the forests, the embankment of the rivers, the flowing of the lowlands, had so added to the virulence of the malarial fever, then known as "the fever of the country," that people who had formerly stayed on their places until August now left them early in May. This brought people together for six months, who had formerly met for only three. By 1800 the system of agriculture was well understood, and both overseers and negroes were expert in their work. The minute supervision of the master was no longer so essential ; and although many went to pinelands or sea islands near at hand, from which they could make frequent visits to the plantations, those who could afford to hire responsible overseers generally came to town.

The year was usually divided in this way. As soon as the first frost had fallen in November, which was supposed to kill the malaria, the family departed for the country. It was often a two days' journey — sixty or seventy miles of sandy road and corduroy causeway. From November to the end of January every one was on the plantation — busy with the thousand duties and many pleasures of that pleasant life. Christmas came in then, and was a great domestic festival for white and black. The Legislature always adjourned, that the members might be at home at the sacred season. If the family consisted of father, mother, and little children, or if it was an elderly household, it remained at home until early in May. But if there were young people, especially grown-up girls, the call of the " gay season " brought them to town again, by the end of January. The St. Cecilias, the Dancing Assemblies, the Philharmonic Concerts, the races, and above all the Jockey Ball, came then.

Race week, the Charleston carnival, brought even the most devoted planter to town for that time at least. He admired the horses, enjoyed the sport, met friends from all over the State, talked with the ladies in the coaches or the Grand Stand, danced at the ball, interviewed his factor, got his crop account (the rice was sold by February), and — it is to be hoped — paid his bills. It was the business, as well as the pleasure appointment for many men, who

2 c

went back to their fields with sentiments akin to those of the Scotchman who, after Sir Walter's annual hunt, told his wife to " let me sleep till next year, for Ailie woman, there's only one day worth living, and that's the day of the Abbotsford hunt."

By the end of March all were back in the country again. The master had gone sooner, for March and April, when all work was going on, and the grain must be sown, were important and delightful months there. All things springing green and the air fragrant with jessamine, dogwood, and magnolia, while mocking and red birds sung on every bough. May — fairest of months elsewhere — has a heavy, sickly beauty in the lowlands of the South; at this time, when the virtues of quinine were imperfectly known, the beauty was deadly. As soon as the streams and ponds looked green and ugly, the ladies were hurried off, and the gentleman followed as soon as the work permitted. He also made occasional visits to the place through the summer ; and too many men lost their lives by exposing themselves at harvest time in the fields, in the deadly months of August and September.

Thus it was that the planters were more than ever as much townsfolk as country gentlemen, and are justly described by Mr. Henry Adams in his history of " Jefferson's Administration," as " the little oligarchy of rice and cotton planters who ruled Charleston."

Their rule was undisputed, for at that time Charleston presented the singular condition of a city with a large trade entirely managed by foreigners ! With the passing of the English the commercial spirit had gone from Carolina ; the land had claimed her sons. They (with the exception of those in the learned professions, most of whom were planters also) were all agriculturists, " the first and best occupation of man."

There were now no more native merchants, enlightened,

wealthy, and influential, such as Henry Laurens, Christopher Gadsden, Gabriel Manigault, and the Shubricks had been.

Their place was taken entirely by strangers, chiefly English and Scotch, who kept to themselves, had their own clubs, and contented with the large fortunes which they accumulated, took no part in public affairs, "nor was there a man among them who took an active interest in politics."

The planters, it must be said, ruled their little dominion well and generously. "They," says Mr. Adams, "were travellers, readers, and scholars." The elder men had been educated abroad, the younger inherited the traditions of their fathers. The advantages which they had enjoyed had taught them to see the needs of others — needs not always recognized by those who lacked. Chief of these was education for the State at large. A plan for a central college had been sketched out, and still exists in the handwriting of John Rutledge, but it had never been put into execution. It was brought up again under the administration of Governor John Drayton (author of the "Memoirs" so often quoted here), and the bill was carried through the Legislature *against* the wishes of the up-country !

Chancellor De Saussure (son of the lady whose petition to Balfour has been given) was only eighteen when thrown into a prison-ship, and sent to St. Augustine. Since then he had studied and graduated at Princeton. He had much to do with carrying through the bill, and says : —

"We of the lower country well knew that the power of the State was thenceforward to be in the upper country, and we desired that *our rulers* should be educated men."

The hardy farmers of the up-country, however, were far

from recognizing their own requirements, and shuddered at the very modest sum which the friends of the measure asked for its execution. Ralph Izard writes to Mr. Jefferson, "A handicraftsman knows that an apprenticeship is necessary to acquaint him with his business, but our back countrymen are of opinion that a politician may be born as well as a poet."

Judge O'Neale, in his "Bench and Bar of South Carolina," adds, "They" (the planters) "forced education upon the up-country, for, strange to say, it was very much opposed to the College."

This feeling, however, soon passed away and the institution has, to a remarkable degree, realized the hope expressed by Governor Drayton that it might prove "a rallying point of union, friendship, and learning for the youth from all parts of the State."

To show what manner of men were these should not be difficult to one who, like the writer, remembers well, in age, many of those who in 1800 were already grown to manhood. Yet to paint the picture of a people is not easy.

Some traits they had in common, traits springing from the creed of their race. They were brave, and truthful, and manly; to be otherwise would be disgrace. They were formal in address, but in society had the courteous ease of manner that comes from generations of assured position, and of living amongst one's peers.

To women they were charmingly and carefully polite; it was always *chapeau-bas* in the presence of ladies. Mothers and wives were queens to sons and husbands; the slightest offence offered to them was cause of battle. The men were, it must be confessed, quick of temper, too prone to resent even a trifling wrong; both proud and passionate, but generous and liberal to a fault; faithful in friendship, but fierce in enmity.

The lodestar of their lives was " the point of honour."

A man's word must be *better* than his bond, because un-guaranteed. A woman's name must never pass his lips except in respect; a promise, however foolish, must be kept. If he had wronged any man, he must offer his life in expiation. He must always be ready to fight for the State or for his lady. This was the unwritten law which made "the chivalry."

These were general characteristics; but there were great *unlikenesses* among them; for that which most marked a planter was his intense individuality, — a certain haughty indifference to conventional usage. The separateness of their lives — each ruling his own world, doing that which seemed good unto himself, forming his own opinions, de-ciding his own problems — caused a certain originality of mind and peculiarity of manner which gave zest and in-terest to society. Their life being far removed from that

> "Where ground in yonder social mill
> We rub each others' angles down
> And merge . . . in form and gloss
> The picturesque of man and man."

"Most planters," says Ramsay, "have respectable libra-ries for their own use." It is hard to tell what, to the good doctor, constituted "a respectable library," but in many country houses there was a "book-room," to use the old word; and if not, at least one or two well-filled book-cases. At Middleton Place, Pinckney Island, and some other plantations there were valuable collections. The favourite books besides the classics (which canonically ranked all others) were the Shakespeare and Montaigne, which dis-puted the honour of being "the Planter's Bible." Conned over and over again in the long winter evenings, they were known by heart. Some men read them every day and spoke in their phrases. "Why do you read that old Montaigne so constantly?" asked a pert young person of fifteen of a gentleman sixty years her senior. "Why, child," was the surprised answer, "there is in this book all that a gentleman needs to think about;" then quickly adding "not a book for little girls." The wives of these gentlemen were "helpmeets" in every sense of the word. Girls were very carefully brought up then. Mrs. Montague, Mrs. Chapone, and Mrs. Hannah More were advising plans for female education, or rather female training, of remarkable good sense and discretion. Their books were studied in Charleston by all the anxious mothers, and the results were not only "elegant females," but useful women, — good housekeepers and good managers as their mothers had been before them; active and busy both by training and by position, as mistresses of many servants, and, generally, mothers of many children. Some were, of course, superior to others in talent and education, — Mrs. Ramsay, the daughter of Henry Laurens, educated in Geneva, remarkably so. Miss Maria Drayton is mentioned as a "scientific botanist"; Mrs. Wilkinson's letters are lively and graphic; and the Duc de Liancourt's testimony to their agreeable and intelligent conversation has already been quoted.

This extract from the letter of one young sister to another, both recently married, shows what might have been found on a girl's private book-shelf. These ladies had been for some time at school in France, which accounts for the predominance of French books. They were Mrs. Francis Kinloch Huger and Mrs. William Lowndes, daughters of General Thomas Pinckney. Mrs. Huger writes, . . . "We spent eight days at El Dorado" (her father's plantation), "and while there I made a division of our books, and packed them up to be sent to town. Your box to be left at Mr. Dart's" (the factor's), "and mine to be sent to Waccamaw" (the river on which her plantation, "Alderley," was). "The only alteration which I made was exchanging with you the eight vols. of Mad. de Sévigné for the eight of Molière."

List of books belonging to Mrs. William Lowndes: —

Dictionnaire Historique, 9 vols.
Elemens d'Histoire de France, 3.
Œuvres de Racine, 3.
Fables de La Fontaine, 2.
Metamorphose d'Ovide, 3.
Dictionnaire de la Fable, 1.
Œuvres de Boileau, 1.
Œuvres de Regna, 4.
Annales de la Vertu, 2.
Leçons d'une Gouvernante, 2.
Télémaque, 2.
Tresors du Parnasse, 5.
Gil Blas, 4.
Drames Sacré, 1.

Recueil Choisi, 1.
Magazin des Enfants, 2.
Trimmer's Introduction, 1.
Adam's Modern Voyages, 2.
Trip to Holland, 1.
Tales of Instruction, 2.
Goldsmith's History of Greece.
Adam's Flowers of History.
Enfield's Speaker.
English Classics abridged.
Reflections for Every Day.
Lettres Mad. de Sévigné, 8.
Some old maps, grammars, etc.

It would be interesting to know what the other half of the books were, but that knowledge is beyond our reach.

As is usually the case after periods of great strain and stress, the world was gay from reaction in the years that followed the Revolution; but it is surprising that, under such very adverse circumstances, the expensive sport of racing should have been so soon revived.

It shows how fixed it was in the habits of the people. The stables had been broken up by the war; the thoroughbreds had been used for troopers — many · had been killed or carried off. One of Tarleton's first exploits had been capturing four hundred horses, "sixty famous ones," of which he tells with natural glee in his memoirs.

Nevertheless by 1789 the racing began again, and Irving's "History of the Turf" gives a long list of imported animals, all of high degree. There were new names on the turf, too; for the middle country entered heartily into the sport, and Colonel Wade Hampton, General Sumter, the Taylors, Richardsons, and others, soon became prominent.

Nothing could exceed the enthusiasm of the negro grooms and jockeys on these occasions. Identifying themselves with their masters, as they always did, it was "my horse" to the trainer and the rider, quite as much as to the owner. There is a story of one little fellow who always rode the mare "Rocksanna." Shortly before an approaching race the boy fell ill. He recovered before the day, but was left with one foot swollen and weak. His master, General McPherson, decided that he was not well enough to ride; another lad must wear the gay jacket. But the boy, terribly distressed, pleaded and entreated, protesting that the mare would never win with another rider, and that his foot "did not count."

The master yielded and the boy rode. The foot did count somewhat, for being swelled, the pressure of the stirrup hurt it, and to relieve the pain he threw his weight too much on the other side. The leather broke, but before the stirrup could fall, the boy caught it, stuck it in his teeth, and brought Rocksanna in ahead, having saved his weight by the stirrup in his mouth! The prize in this race was a large, handsome bowl with race horses embossed around the outside.

The appearance of the course was in one respect gayer than formerly. There were the same fine animals, the same gentlemen in the glossiest of top-boots and white buckskin breeches, but the use of coaches had now become general. There had been some of an earlier date, for a picture of Lady Mary Middleton's with the arms on the panels still remains, and her ladyship died in 1786. In the same year Mrs. Horrÿ ordered from England "that article of luxury, a coach," and sent Messrs. Savage, Bird, and Savage a hundred tierces of rice to pay for it.

These were unusual at the earlier time, and chaises, however handsome, could not make the same imposing effect. They were handsome also, sometimes, as shown by the advertisement of one in 1739 by Mr. Middleton (who was going to England), " To be sold a four-wheeled chaise, neatly carved and gilt, lined with crimson coffroy (?) with iron axletrees, with new set of harness for four horses, at my plantation," etc. The plantation was the beautiful place Crowfield on Goose Creek, mentioned before.

The coaches, though ugly in shape, were very ornamental in colour and gilding; round-bodied, hung high on C-springs, with high box draped with hammer cloth, on which sat an important coachman. Behind was a foot-board on which stood a footman, who clung for dear life to bands which depended from the back, and sprang down to unfold the flight of steps, down which his mistress carefully, with hand on his sleeve, descended to the ground. Hammer-cloth, bands, and liveries all matched, and the doors frequently bore the crests of their owners!

Some of these coaches were wide enough to accommodate three persons on a seat, and they must have been at least four feet from the ground. A few of these unwieldy vehicles were in occasional use as late as 1840–1845. The writer remembers one — a survival — which to her youthful imagination was the prototype of Cinderella's pumpkin. It was round and bright yellow, with a great quantity of gilding, lined with brown velvet ; hammer-cloth and bands to match.

A very old lady, Miss Polly Roupell, the " fair Roupell " of the Revolution, who was said to have gone unmarried all her days for the sake of her English lover killed in the war, used to ride in one of the last of these, long after they had gone out of general use. By that time manners were no longer what they had been in the days of her youth, and there were unmannerly boys. If a group of these urchins, playing on one of the innumerable "greens " which intersected the town, laughed and jeered at the antiquated vehicle, the former belle would put her head out of the window and cry, "You may laugh as much as you like; it *is* old, *but it's paid for*, anyway." Every one respected Miss Polly, Loyalist though she was, and if the boys were caught, they were well cuffed.

Sometimes the races were unprofessional. One of the most noted was between the afterward famous John Randolph of Roanoke and Sir John Nesbit of Dean Hall, Cooper River, each riding his own horse. Randolph won the race, but Sir John won the ladies' hearts, — " they called him the prettier fellow."

Besides the public entertainments there were many private ones, for the houses were quite large enough to accommodate the limited society of the time, and there were persons who made it a point to give a ball every year besides dinners and " carpet dances."

A ball would have been a troublesome matter, there being no caterers or decorators, but for the number of well-trained servants which made things easy. Nothing gave more satisfaction in the servants' hall than the housekeeper's announcement "we'se gwine hab a ball nex' week." Ordinary tasks were dropped and all was joyful preparation.

Rugs or carpets were rolled back and removed, the waxed floors rubbed to still brighter polish; the chandeliers, with their long glittering drops, and the girandoles on the little convex mirrors, were filled with wax candles; the linen slips, with which careful housewives kept their chairs and sofas covered, removed; one or two " nosegays " placed in the tall china or cut-glass jars on the high carved mantelpieces, and all was ready. Many of the rooms were already so handsome, with their panelled walls, carved woodwork, and coved ceilings, long mirrors in gilt frames, and pictures (generally portraits), that they really needed no transient decorations.

People of all ages went to balls and danced, — sedately in a minuet, merrily in a country dance. There was generally some formality in the opening of the ball. A minuet " performed " by two or more important personages began it "high and disposedly."

One of the first balls after the war, says Mr. Fraser, was opened by General Moultrie, who, in full regimentals, danced the minuet with a lady of " suitable age " whom he soon afterward married. As Moultrie was certainly fifty-three at this time, and his proposed bride not too young for him, the dance was probably " stately."

But there was nothing stately about the country dance, in which grandfathers danced with their grandchildren, and mothers with their sons. When the negro fiddlers struck up " hands across and down the middle," young and old joined in, happy as children.

In some respects the manners were formal. The chaperons sat in a row, looking, we are told, " like a Roman Senate," which must have been terrifying to a timid youth. The partner (always in satin breeches and silk stockings, the pantaloon not being yet permitted in the ball-room), approached with profound bows to mother and maid, and bent with hand on heart to ask if he might be permitted the honour of the dance. The damsel courtesied (not too low), looked to her mamma, and replied that she would have the pleasure of dancing with Mr. So-and-So, with proper indifference and reserve of tone. Then by the tips of her fingers he led her to the floor. Yet even this was innovation, for the gentleman would have been expected to write a note to the mamma to solicit the honour, a fortnight before the assembly, in the good old days, —

> " When gallants galloped counties over
>   The ball's fair partner to behold,
>   Thanked for the honour she had done him
>   And humbly hoped she'd caught no cold."

Suppers were elaborate. Boned turkeys, game, terrapin stews (only they called it " cooter stew "), etc. The pastry-cook and her assistants had been at work for a week, making jellies, creams, custards, cakes of all kinds, — all made at home. Sometimes there would be a flight of imagination. Two doves of blanc-mange in a nest of fine, gold-coloured transparent shreds of candied orange peel was thought " sweetly pretty "; and a tall iced cake in the shape of a castle, with the American flag on the tower, and the arms in coloured comfits on the walls, appealed to the patriotic. Greatest of dishes was " a preserve of fowle." Does any one wish the receipt ? It began, " Take all manner of Fowle and bone them all " ; the rest of the precise words are unfortunately lost, but the direction was, to begin with a small dove, into which slip a strip of bacon; put the dove into a partridge, the partridge (quail they are mistakenly called now) into a guinea hen, the guinea hen into a wild duck, the duck into a capon, the capon into a goose, the goose into a turkey (or a peacock if it please you best), — each bird to be well basted and seasoned before inserted, care being taken to place white and dark meat alternately. Roast all until done through, and serve with their own very rich seasoned gravy. The carver cut down, through, and across the birds, and the guests ate — and lived!

There were wines — the old Madeira, that had been warming and ripening many a year in cedar-shingled garrets; Port, and others; and a delicious rum punch made with pineapple, limes, etc., only too fascinating.

The company enjoyed themselves ; but what was their pleasure to that of the darkies, who, for days before, had revelled in the bustle of preparation, and were now gazing with delight at the guests, and expecting the reversion of the feast ? No master in the South could keep his windows clear, on a ball night, of ebony faces and gleaming eyes that took in every detail. It was one of their privileges; and no sooner had the company departed than the musicians adjourned to the servants' hall, the remains of the supper were carried out, and a second fête, even gayer than the first, was stopped only by the rising of the sun.

The costume of the ladies by this time had changed, like that of their partners. No more were the rich brocades and damasks, the plumes and powder; instead, the scantiest and shortest of gowns — bodies at most eight inches long and skirts of two or three breadths, according to width of stuff and size of the wearer, coming barely to the ankles. The stuff was the softest satin, India silk, or muslin, that could be found; the feet clad in heelless slippers, tied with ribbons that crossed about the instep. The hair, descended from the high estate given it by the last and fairest of French queens, hung in loose waves upon the neck, until the awful fashion of wigs came in. When this strange mania prevailed, it was hardly thought decent to wear one's own hair. No matter how long, how thick, how beautiful, the ruthless scissors must clip it close, and a horrible construction by a hair-dresser take its place. It is really grewsome, when one remembers that the hair was especially recommended as " coming from France," — that is, from the guillotine!

The wig fashion did not last long, — only a year or two; then came the Grecian, — bands and plaits, or short curls on the forehead, and next turbans. One sees the turban in many of Sully's early pictures, and they are lovely and becoming; but, then, all Sully's sitters were, apparently, houris!

The following letter is taken from " Our Forefathers," sketches by " The Ancient Lady," Mrs. Poyas of Charleston. It is from Mrs. Logan to her mother, Mrs. Webb, on the marriage of her brother to the daughter of Major

Ladson, a brave Revolutionary officer, whose daughters were remarkable for beauty.

"The first and most interesting piece of intelligence which I have for you, my dear Mother, is that my dear Brother" (Mr. Webb) "is happily united to his Miss Eliza Ladson. . . . The bride looked very genteel and pretty; her style was extremely plain, — nothing but a fine India muslin, trimmed with handsome lace round the neck and sleeves, with a very wide footing let in the front and sleeves.

"She wore a silk cord and tassel round the waist. Her head-dress was two ostrich feathers which was very becoming. The company were sociable and agreeable. . . . Even I managed to dance at the wedding; having no other brother to be married how could I help it?

"I send you some of my new ratifia to drink with the cake," — ratifia of her own making, of course.

The number of servants kept then often causes surprise; but considering the climate, and the conditions of life, it could hardly be otherwise, and it made things delightfully easy.

No one can have comfort or satisfaction who expects to get from negro servants the steady systematic work which enables one or two French or English women to keep a large house in perfect order. But given enough well-trained, obedient, merry, good-natured darkies, a household will run smoothly. By "enough" is meant so many that each can perform his day's duties in half a day, and enjoy the rest of his time in talking, singing, and loitering, — which was for many years the usual condition of things, and is certainly shocking to economic theories.

An average Charleston household of the wealthy class usually had a housekeeper, and her assistant, a mauma, and as many nursery maids as there were children in the house. These were rival potentates, and relations were apt to be a little strained. Each lady had her maid, who was always a sempstress and a clearstarcher. If the cook was a woman, she had a girl in training and a boy scullion to help her ; and there were as many laundresses as the size of the family required. There was a butler and one or more footmen. A gentleman usually had a body-servant, and the coachman had under him as many grooms and stable boys as the horses kept demanded.

It sounds immense and would have been impossible but for the ample supplies brought by boat from the plantations. Also the assistants were generally the children of the elder servants, and were really understudies learning their work. By 1800 there were often three generations of house servants in one establishment, and the unbroken training made them invaluable. Housekeeper, butler, coachman, each was supreme in his or her own department, but " Mauma " was esteemed above all, for she not only ruled " my children " and the nursery maids, but by virtue of experience often also ruled the young mistress, conscious of want of knowledge of those precious first babies.

The confidence was rewarded by the most faithful service to the mistress, and passionate love to her charges. That tie never failed; in the darkest days of Carolina's history " Mauma " was ever true.

A household of this sort which had gone undisturbed for two or three generations was a little world in itself; old people lingered on and were given affectionate tendance; children were born and cared for. It was all one big family. " My servants next to my children," the old ladies used to say. The master and mistress seemed highest of created beings to their servants, who shone in their reflected light, and placed their pride in belonging to " we gran' fambly."

In these first years of the century there passed away many of the most prominent men of the Revolution.

In 1800 died Rawlins Lowndes, and John and Edward Rutledge; in 1801 Bishop Smith. In 1805 Generals Gadsden and Moultrie.

Of these six patriots, three are buried in the eastern churchyard of St. Philip's, Edward Rutledge opposite the south door, and Rawlins Lowndes in a vault near by.

The exact spot of Gadsden's grave is not known. He ordered that it should be levelled and left unmarked, " disliking ostentation of any kind." Bishop Smith rests within the church, near the chancel of which he had been rector forty-two years. It is surprising that the very full inscription on Mr. Edward Rutledge's stone does *not* mention that he signed the Declaration of Independence!

John Rutledge lies in the southern part of St. Michael's churchyard; an upright, gray slab, with only the date and the name " John Rutledge," marks his grave.

Moultrie, the citizens and soldiers having given " this revered and beloved patriot the most honourable and respectable funeral," was interred probably in St. John's, but the spot is not known.

All these men were happy in the esteem, honour, and confidence of their countrymen; but of them all, Gadsden must have felt, in dying, the purest satisfaction. Often rash and indiscreet, but always brave, and true, and absolutely disinterested; the chivalric first leader of the Revolution, the first true Republican of Carolina, lived to see the doctrines which he alone had in the beginning advocated, become the principle and law of the nation. What he had struggled for in youth he still approved in age; declaring his devotion to the American cause unchanged, " believing it to be that of liberty and human nature."

The old men were going day by day, but there was no lack of younger ones, ready and eager to take their part in the battle of life, and especially public life.

The Carolinian then had belonged so long to the governing class that politics seemed his natural career. To that career the law was the stepping-stone, and the best talent of the place went to the Bar.

The Bar was a strong one, and the emoluments great. Mr. Fraser quotes the Duc de Liancourt as saying that four of the elder gentlemen, General C. C. Pinckney, Mr. Edward Rutledge, Mr. J. J. Pringle, and Mr. Holmes, made by their profession from eighteen to twenty-three thousand dollars a year. Mr. Fraser adds that there were eight or ten others whose incomes amounted to eight or ten thousand. This he explains by saying: " The extensive commercial business of Charleston at that time opened a wide field of litigation. Our courts were constantly employed in heavy insurance cases — in questions of charter party, foreign and inland bills of exchange, and in adjusting foreign claims. There was also a good deal of business in admiralty, and, occasionally, a rich prize case. Then again, new questions were continually arising out of the then recent acts of our Legislature. Points now settled were then open to construction, involving considerable amounts of property. Titles of land were not adjusted, or their limits ascertained; and finally, Charleston was then divided into two strongly defined parties, to one or other of which every citizen belonged, that of debtor and creditor."

Of these ambitious young lawyers Mr. (afterward Chancellor) De Saussure, Langdon Cheves, William Drayton, William Crafts, Robert Y. Hayne, Daniel Elliott Huger (afterward Judge), and Hugh S. Legaré were to become the most widely known. The times were quiet enough now, but opportunities for distinction were soon to come.

In 1795, the difficulty of continuing the English Church, while refusing allegiance to its temporal head, being overcome, Charleston had had the satisfaction of receiving

2 D

her first bishop. Mr. Smith was consecrated to that high office in Christ Church, Pennsylvania, in September of that year. This was only the second consecration which had taken place in America. He retained the rectorship of St. Philip's, bringing out the Rev. Thomas Frost as his assistant, and afterward his successor in that church.

The Reverend Mr. Purcell was still rector of St. Michael's, but there, too, were changes. The clerk, who had led the responses, given out the psalms, and been only less important than the parson himself, was given up, and the choir of surpliced boys (the existence of which up to 1807 is proved by the laundress's bill for washing the surplices) discontinued; and that the St. Cecilia band should supplement the organ was now decided to be objectionable!

On one shocking occasion St. Michael's was distinctly *snubbed* by the city! The congregation, being disturbed by the passing of vehicles, prayed that it might be allowed to *stretch chains* across the streets during the hours of divine service! Broad and Meeting are the chief thoroughfares, and the city ungraciously refused to allow their obstruction, but granted a policeman to control the traffic! It was not until 1832 that the vestry resolved to allow no more public meetings to be held in the church. Those were the days of the nullification excitement, and the proceedings were probably too emphatic to be suitable for the sacred precincts. No one can dispute the propriety of the change, but it adds to the historic interest of the building to remember that it was the people's gathering-place for patriotic as well as for sacred purposes.

The Church of Rome first acquired a habitation in Charleston at this time. During the colonial period there had been few Catholics there; for freedom of worship had been granted only to "all Protestants"; but by 1786 there were a good many. At first they held their services in a private house at the corner of Tradd and Orange streets; but in

1801 the first St. Mary's was begun, making the nineteenth place of worship in the town. In this churchyard are many stones to the St. Domingan refugees. Among them a large tomb covers the remains of the Demoiselles de Grasse, the daughters of Admiral Count de Grasse, the commander of the French auxiliary fleet during the Revolution.

The Presbyterians were also a large and very influential body, and there were many other sects, of which the Baptists were the most numerous.

The Huguenot church which had been burned in the great fire of 1796, in which St. Philip's had so narrowly escaped destruction, had been rebuilt, but from the change of language and other causes its congregation had been greatly reduced, most of its members having joined the Episcopal Church.

The people of Charleston at that period have been accused of a want of religious piety and zeal. The accusation is hardly borne out by the letters and private prayers which are sometimes found in old chests and desks; or by the large preponderance of religious books in the old bookcases (most of them, alas, now destroyed by war or by fire). Dr. Ramsay says that the librarian of the Charleston Library informs him (in 1808) that religious books are more in demand than any others.

Perhaps this unfavourable comparison may be owing to the fact that the prevailing form of religion was the Anglican, the language and expressions of which appear reserved and ordered when compared with the fervent utterances of the descendants of the Puritans, or with the enthusiastic speech of the Methodists. Yet " The grave ritual brought from England's shore " satisfies the hearts that love it, more than the most impassioned of extemporaneous prayers : and the man who read his " Holy Living and Dying " should have had a heart as full of love to God, as his who studied " The Saint's Everlasting Rest."

There is little to be said of the science of those days. The Medical Society is called " the only scientific association," but there was no Medical College, or hospital, and the doctors had to go to Edinburgh or Philadelphia for an education.

An impulse had been given to the study of botany by the influence of Dr. Garden. Mr. Stephen Elliott was soon to publish his " Botany of South Carolina," and Mr. Henry Middleton, General C. C. Pinckney, and Dr. Macbride of St. John's are mentioned as "Scientific botanists."

No account of this community of country gentlemen would be complete which did not include the factors, the only gentlemen of native birth except the bankers who did any kind of business.

The factor was well named, for he was the *factotum* of the planter. He furnished the money with which the crop was planted; made all needful purchases for the country family, from plantation supplies to pocket handkerchiefs; received the rice and cotton when sent to market; got the best possible price from the merchant to whom he sold it; kept all the accounts, and tried to make his client understand them; was the general friend, adviser, and confidant; and, as one gentleman said, " Relieved them of the necessity of thinking about disagreeable things."

It would be hard to say to what need " Send to the factor" was not answer sufficient.

Unluckily the planters were too often encouraged, by the ease with which money was thus furnished them, to extravagance and debt; many men hardly looked at their accounts and, without any dishonesty on the part of the agent, estates became involved. How could it be otherwise when it was the common joke against the planters that "they could read Homer and make a speech to explain the Constitution, but couldn't do a sum in vulgar fractions ? "

The offices of the factors and the warehouses of the merchants were upon the bay, and the shopping streets were not far off, — the eastern ends of Broad and Tradd, and Elliott streets. These shops were more varied in their contents than a department store. A planter could buy his Welch Plains and Osnaburghs (for negro clothes) at one counter, his shoes and harness at another, and his groceries at a third; while his wife was choosing satin and laces, or India china, at yet others.

Only the jewellers, of whom there were two, kept their wares apart, and so did Mr. Muirhead, who had " a very respectable book store " in Elliott Street, where there were also a good boarding-house and a bank.

No one would care to live in Elliott Street to-day, nor would any lady be seen there.

The very picturesque country trade, carried on by long, white-topped waggons, with four or six mules or horses harnessed to each, and piled high with cotton bales, was carried on very high up King Street. The waggons were drawn up in yards near the present railway station, and the waggoners slept each on or under his vehicle, with his dog at his feet and his rifle at his side. The cotton unloaded and sold, the list of goods sent down with it was bought and packed, and back they went on their long journey to the very confines of the State, or sometimes beyond them. Everything that was wanted for the year went at one time in these trips, to places remote from the rivers, and large fortunes were made in these yards, before the railroad was built, in the embargo time which was now at hand.

There was not what is now called " a residential portion " of the city. People lived where it pleased them, were often widely scattered and their houses surrounded by large tracts of land. There were many fine houses along the upper part of the bay, where was a fine view of the harbour, and in Ansonborough and in Broad and the streets below it.

There was no East Battery, and Fort Mechanic stood on the last point of solid land; but on South Bay there were some fine houses. The only two that remain are General William Washington's at the corner of Church Street, and the beautiful one supposed to have been built by Mrs. Thomas Smith, granddaughter of Colonel William Rhett, No. 64.

There had been many attempts to build up East Battery, but the walls yielded to every gale, and were totally demolished by the hurricane of 1804. It was then determined to use stone for the construction, and after many difficulties its present limits were attained.

A wharf or pier which projected from South Bay, with a sort of tea-house at the extremity, where people drove of a warm afternoon to enjoy the breeze, and Watson's Botanic Garden, were the only outdoor places of amusement.

It is customary to speak of the "superstitions of our ancestors," — a phrase which often comes strangely from those who eagerly receive every "ism" of the present. It must be confessed, however, that whether they were more or less superstitious than ourselves, their fancies were simpler and more candidly expressed.

Everything was an omen of good or bad luck. You took your life in your hand if you went your way when a rabbit had crossed your path; but if he came from a graveyard, to keep his left hind foot in your pocket preserved you from danger. If the screech owl hooted, death was to be expected; soap could only be boiled, or corn planted, on a waxing moon. A waning one would thin the first, and waste the ears of the second. Calabash (the large

GENERAL WILLIAM WASHINGTON'S HOUSE

Side view.

water gourd) seed must be thrown carelessly on the surface of the ground, to grow where it listed. To sow it in
prepared soil would bring disaster on your family.

The beliefs common to most peoples were held with in-
tensity. He was almost a murderer who should invite his
guests to sit down thirteen at table. A mirror cracking
without cause was as terrifying as to the Lady of Shalott.
A bird flying into a house, or a picture falling from the
wall, made many a cheek turn pale; and to start on a journey, marry a wife, or christen a child on a Friday would
have been thought impious.

There is a certain country road not very far from the
town. Along one part of it, several miles in length, a
big black dog bounds at morning and evening twilight.
He attacks no one, makes no sound, but keeps steadily
at some distance alongside of the wayfarer, within the
trees, until its limit is reached, and then vanishes. Men
have tried to cajole, and to shoot it; but it takes no notice
of the voice, and powder and ball do not harm it; it still
runs steadily on. Why no one ever tried a silver bullet,
is not explained.

Ghosts were not to be trifled with; they haunted many
country and some town houses, and great deference was
paid to dreams.

Two of these dreams were so remarkable and so well
proven that they are worth telling. Both are singularly
straightforward warnings of trouble to come, not fantas-
tic imaginations of excited brains.

A lady of the McPherson family, Mrs. Pringle of " Lau-
rium," Prince William's parish, dreamed one night that
her nursery was burning from a beam ignited beneath
the hearth. She got up instantly and examined, but
there was not the least sign of anything wrong, either
then or through the morning.

In the afternoon, all being well, she went out with her

husband to drive. The avenue was a long one, and as they turned into it from the high road, she saw a servant galloping toward them, who cried out that the house was on fire, smoke bursting out, but that they could not find the fire.

"Go back as fast as you can ride," the lady replied, "carry plenty of water upstairs, take up the nursery hearth, and pour it in; the fire is there."

The order was obeyed, the smoking beams extinguished, and the house, though damaged, was saved. The whole neighbourhood knew the facts.

The other story is still better known.

Mrs. Thomas Shubrick was the wife of the owner of Belvedere, the present home of the Country Club.

One night she started from troubled sleep, and told her husband that she had distinctly seen her brother (who was, they knew, on a homeward voyage from Philadelphia), floating on the sea, on some small object, with a white handkerchief on a stick, for a flag. Her husband succeeded in soothing her, and she soon fell asleep again. But the dream would not let her rest; the same vision returned and again she awoke, — this time much distressed.

Mr. Shubrick used all the arguments that one does use in such cases, and again the obedient wife composed herself to slumber. But when the vision returned for the third time, the sister's feelings became uncontrollable. She insisted, and her husband agreed that he should at once go into town (Belvedere is three miles from the City Hall), hire a pilot-boat and send it to cruise to the northward in the track of incoming vessels. The boat went out and found nothing, nor did she on the second day, but on the third, just as she was turning to abandon the search, a tiny white speck was seen afar off. It proved to be a hencoop on which was a half-dead man, the sole survivor of the wreck three days before!

This lady was the mother of four gallant sailors: Captain Templer Shubrick, who went down in the *Hornet*, when bringing home the treaty with Algiers, made after the conquest of the Barbary pirates; Captain Edward Rutledge Shubrick, who was so beloved that the officers and sailors of his ship, the frigate *Columbia*, asked the privilege of erecting his monument in the eastern cemetery of St. Philip's; Commodore Irvine, and Admiral William Brandford Shubrick, who died not many years since.

The circumstances of this remarkable story were known to the whole town. Hiring a pilot-boat for three days is not a thing done in a closet, and "the Shubrick dream" is one of the faiths of Charleston.

The custom of duelling was by this time recognized as so great an evil, and yet was so entirely a part of the life of the day, that the efforts made through many years to check and to regulate it had but small success. The death of Alexander Hamilton, in July, 1804, aroused great interest in the question. Hamilton was at the time of his death perhaps the most popular man in America, and was reverenced as having been Washington's confidant. He was then President-general of the Society of the Cincinnati, and was known to have expressed himself as strongly opposed to duelling.

A month later General Charles Cotesworth Pinckney, as the President of the Society, addressed a letter to the President of the State Society of New York, in which he said: —

" Is there no way of abolishing throughout the Union this absurd and barbarous custom, to the observance of which he " (General Hamilton) " fell a victim?

" Duelling is no criterion of bravery, for I have seen cowards fight duels, and I am convinced real courage may often be better shown in the refusal than in the acceptance of a challenge. If the Society of the Cincinnati were to declare their abhorrence of this practice, and the determination of all their members to discourage it, as far as they had influence, and on no account either to send or to accept a challenge, it might tend to annul this odious custom, and would be a tribute of respect to the sentiments and memory of our late illustrious chief.

"If the State Society of New York should coincide with me in opinion, I should be glad to have their sentiments how to carry it into execution; whether by submitting it to a meeting of the General Society, at New York, Philadelphia or Baltimore, or by referring the matter at once to the different State Societies for their consideration."

This was followed by an appeal to the clergy and laity "of standing" of South Carolina, requesting their influence in the same cause, and a memorial was presented to the Legislature, asking legislation for the prohibition and punishment of duelling. These papers were signed by C. C. Pinckney, James Kennedy, and William Read, as committee for the Cincinnati, and by David Ramsay, Henry W. De Saussure, William Allen Deas, James Lowndes, and Richard Furman, as committee of the Society of the American Revolution.

It was of no use. Every one of these gentlemen had probably been "out" in his youth (Hamilton had been second to John Laurens, and Pinckney to General Howe), "and now that they are old," the young men said, "they forget the passions of youth and would put bridles upon us." So nothing came of these efforts. Public opinion was yet too strong, and it was impossible to enforce legal penalties.

John Lyde Wilson, once Governor of the State, produced his "Code of Honour," expressly, as he declared, with a view of saving life.

Wilson was not a man of worthy character, and it was

properly objected that to adopt such a Code was to acknowledge and legalize an evil which should not be. Practically it was of use, for its chief point was to insist that there should be no communication between the principals, thus avoiding additional exasperation by letters or interviews, and that all difficulties must be referred to friends, who were in duty bound to use every exertion to prevent a meeting, and to make proper arrangement should it take place. A great improvement upon such shocking affairs as that in which Mr. Delancey was killed at the beginning of the Revolution; or that similar one between Lord Byron and Mr. Chaworth which occurred in London at about the same time. There is no trace in Carolina of those absurd and frivolous duels, common at one time all over Europe, in which men killed each other for a whim, or a trifle. It seems to have been always seriously regarded, almost as "trial by combat," undertaken as vindication or as retribution.

One of the most curious affairs of this sort was proposed by Marion during the Revolution. The story is taken from Sabine's "Duels and Duelling." Marion, it is said, "received a cartel from Major McIlraith of the Royal Army to meet in combat in the open field." (Apparently entirely as public foes.) "Marion in reply expressed himself willing to meet him, with twenty picked men on each side, according to the custom of the days of chivalry! McIlraith assented and agreed upon a spot near an oak tree (which was standing in 1821); but after the parties had been selected and formed for combat he reconsidered the proposals, and withdrew his men without firing a gun."

It is impossible to help wondering what "huge romantic tome" Marion had been reading! Froissart at the very least must have inspired that mediæval proposition!

It should be said that many of these duels were bloodless, for often men who would not refuse a challenge fired in the air, and then it was held scandalous in the other party to fire again. This had been the case with Henry Laurens of the Revolution, who more than once went out, received his adversary's fire, and refused to return it, saying that "a man might have a right to kill him, but could have none to make a murderer of him." There were frequent instances of this, yet valuable lives were sometimes lost.

In the year 1826 the Cincinnati made yet another effort. General Thomas Pinckney had then succeeded his brother as President-general, and Major Garden was at the head of the State Society.

The Society prevailed upon two of its younger members to submit to it (sitting as a "Court of Honour ") what seemed at first an irreconcilable dispute. The story is curious in its development.

The quarrel was between a fiery young sailor and an equally high-spirited planter.

The planter had, it was alleged, called the former a liar and a fool! Naturally the sailor had struck him in the face first, then knocked him down. At this juncture the Society intervened and offered its good offices. The sailor's note of reply remains — "For his part he was content; it was for the other man to say if he wanted more ; if he did, it would afford him, Captain ——, the greatest pleasure to gratify him. He did not see what the Society could do." Nevertheless, little by little, after many sittings, and the examination of many witnesses, it was discovered that the landsman had *not* given the lie, and that none had heard him say "fool " — and the seaman was prevailed on to admit a misunderstanding, and to say that he would not have thrashed the gentleman had he not conceived himself insulted, and he was sorry for the mistake. They then shook hands and declared themselves satisfied, and the Court (General Pinckney, Major Garden, Captain Baker, Major Hamilton, and Dr. Wm. Read, all Revolutionary veterans) rejoiced greatly, and in its report expressed the hope "that the present affair may form a precedent, which may induce not only its own members but the youth of the State generally, to submit their differences to such councils, and thus spare not only life, but the dreadful remorse which torments the survivor in such a conflict."

Evidently the hope failed, and duelling, although it became gradually less frequent, continued a well-established custom until it fell in 1866, with the civilization of which it was a part. The writer can remember but three fatal duels in her own recollection.

The evil was great, but some things can be said in its favour. The knowledge that an account would be required of his words and actions brought constantly to a man's mind, not as a menace but as a principle, the belief that his words were a part of his character and his life. False or cruel speech was to be answered for, as was an evil act; it, therefore, was held *to be* an act, not mere empty breath, as it is too often considered now. "The word" had its true value. Other injuries were thus punished also. An affront to a man's character or family, a wrong or even a discourtesy to a woman or to an absent friend, evoked a challenge, but business difficulties were not cause of battle. Those were settled by courts of law; the duel guarded personal honour, which the law was powerless to defend. One who can remember the exquisite urbanity of the social intercourse of fifty years ago, and contrast it with the careless expressions, the rough give and take, of the present, can but wonder how much the old way had to do with the self-respect and consideration for others of that society which people now call half civilized.

At its worst — and its worst was very grievous — duelling was not so bad as those shocking unregulated encounters which occur now when the passions of men are beyond control, and which cost more lives than were ever sacrificed to the old duello.

CHAPTER XIX

NOT even John Randolph's "deep fosse" of the Atlantic Ocean could secure peace and quiet while the Emperor Napoleon troubled the world. America asked nothing better than to be allowed to cultivate her fields, build up her industries, and sail her ships unmolested. Neither England nor France, now at each other's throats, would permit such profitable neutrality; each demanded the friendship or rather the service of America, while each intimated that it was hardly worth the asking!

Napoleon said scornfully of her ensign that it was not really a flag but only a "piece of striped bunting" which could not defend the ships or goods it carried; and England, less epigrammatic but more aggressive, confiscated her merchantmen and "pressed" her sailors.

President Jefferson's efforts, in the face of such insults, to keep the peace, which he believed to be essential to the "happiness of his countrymen," were pathetic, but humiliating.

Neither of the warring nations respected such forbearance; each insisted that he who was not for was against her.

Neither did his successor, Mr. Madison, desire to risk the combat, and most especially reluctant to do so was the small but still important Federal party. It, looking upon Napoleon as a near and visible Apollyon, was willing to undergo almost any treatment from England rather than weaken her hand against " the Adversary."

The blunder of the English captain of the *Leopard*, who in time of peace attacked the *Chesapeake* and carried off her sailors at the very gate of New York, did much to precipitate hostilities.

The Thirteenth Congress met soon after, filled with eager, patriotic, high-spirited young men. It was evident that the "peace at any price" policy would soon be at an end. In that Congress were Clay of Kentucky, Quincy of Massachusetts, Randolph of Roanoke, and many others whose names were to become famous. Eminent among them were Langdon Cheves, William Lowndes, and John C. Calhoun of South Carolina.

How these men forced the unwilling executive to throw down the glove to England, how the war was fought, are matters of general history.

The enemy, successful at Washington and repulsed at Baltimore, made no attack upon Charleston. Thomas Pinckney, now an old man, commissioned major-general and appointed to command the department of the South, prepared as best he might for the defence of the long stretch of coast from North Carolina to Florida; but there were only two small reconnaissances, easily repulsed.

The fortifications across Charleston Neck, for which the "Patriotic Fair" had with their own hands carried sods, were unassailed.

Pecuniarily the place suffered severely: her commerce was destroyed; there was no importation; her rice and cotton were unsalable. Rich planters needed common necessaries of life, or bought them at enormous profits from clever merchants who made fortunes by their foresight in laying in stocks of goods.

The British fleet patrolled the coast, capturing every little vessel that fell in its way. The loss to individuals was often heavy. One schooner is mentioned as being taken on the passage from the Santee River to Charleston (about sixty miles) with between six and seven thousand dollars' worth of rice on board, all from one plantation.

2 E

There was a story that some officers had even dared to disguise themselves and attend a ball on Sullivan's Island, under the very walls of Moultrie. It was well for them that they were not discovered, for Colonel William Drayton, commandant of the fort, was not a man to be trifled with, and their shrift would have been short. The stoppage of all trade and the high price of commodities told hardly on the poor — their want became great. There was lack of employment, and it was hard to find work for them.

The Ladies' Benevolent Society, founded in 1813, especially for the care of the sick (one of the first societies organized in America for that purpose), even went beyond its original object in efforts of this sort. It advertised for donations of cotton, that poor women might be taught to spin, there being always demand for the yarn for weaving.

The poor would have been badly off then but for this society, which, with judicious wisdom, provided nurses, linen, medicine, and food for the afflicted, in ways and by rules under which, with modifications, it still works to the blessing of the suffering, — ways and rules which have within the last few months received the praise of the highest modern authority on the subject.

Miss Nutting, the head of the Training School for Nurses of the Johns Hopkins Hospital of Baltimore, wrote lately of this society : —

" I have been struck with the wise spirit in which it was founded. The cautious distribution of alms ; the effort to study and understand the needs of the sick and the helpless, and to give the right kind of relief, are characteristic of the most modern 'scientific' methods. It is a little curious to find them suggested anywhere, nearly a hundred years ago."

The good work of this association, especially in and

after times of epidemic, soon made it as popular as the Library Society or the old South Carolina had been. It received legacies and donations, had money in bank, and flourished exceedingly up to the time of the war between the States. Its invested funds were then chiefly destroyed and its means sorely reduced.

One of its most interesting donations was five hundred dollars, given by that sweetest of singers, and of women, Jenny Lind, on her visit to Charleston in 1850.

England and America were both heartily tired of the war before peace was announced in January, 1815; the victory of New Orleans winding it up in a most satisfactory manner to the United States. The gain to the latter was great. She had established her claim to be not merely "a struggling American Republic," but a nation which could hold its own by land and sea with the greatest of powers. Her flag was respected, her rights acknowledged, and all material losses were soon forgotten in the prosperity that set in and continued, with of course the inevitable fluctuations, down to 1861.

One effect of the war upon Charleston was the melting away of the Federal party.

The old gentlemen, of course, kept their faith — in peace time ; but it is seldom that the call to arms does not produce unanimity in South Carolina. The younger men, the rising hope of the party, broke away from it under the impulse of the war, and the elders soon loyally declared for "the country, right or wrong." The address of the members of the Cincinnati to General Pinckney upon his appointment was warm and pathetic in its offers of service.

Conspicuous among these younger men were William Drayton and Daniel Elliott Huger, both lawyers of high standing, who from a sense of duty abandoned their profession and their party to accept commissions in the regular army.

Mr. Drayton was the son of Judge William Drayton, who at the outbreak of the Revolution was chief justice of Florida. He had studied law with and been greatly under the influence of Mr. Edward Rutledge, from whom he had received the strongest Federal principles, and having begun life with nothing, he had now an income of $18,000 a year from his profession. This he renounced for a commission in the regular army, and served until all danger of hostilities was past. He then, refusing all offers of promotion, resigned his commission, returned to the bar, and was afterward member of Congress, and prominent in various ways.

Mr. Huger also had belonged to the old party, but could not agree with its over-prolonged toleration of injustice. He too resigned and entered the army, for the time, then returning to Charleston, where he was to play an important part.

These two gentlemen have been singled out from their fellows, because this was their first appearance in the public affairs of the place, in which they later took great part.

While the war was still in progress a tragedy, unexplained at the time, startled the town. Theodosia, the beautiful daughter of Aaron Burr, was the wife of Governor Joseph Alston, the eldest son of Colonel William Alston, already mentioned as having entertained General Washington, at his plantation "Clifton" on the Waccamaw. The devoted affection between the father and daughter, and her exquisite loveliness and charm, had touched many hearts at Burr's trial for high treason in 1804. The feeling against him after his so-called acquittal, his expatriation and misery, were great sorrow to her; she returned to Carolina a mourning woman. There she was almost idolized by her husband's family; and admired, not only for grace and accomplishment, but for the impression of purity and elevation of character made upon all who knew her. The death of her only child, a handsome and promising boy of fourteen, so preyed upon her health as to cause great anxiety.

Her father had by that time returned to New York, and she was persuaded to go on to join him there. She set sail from Charleston accordingly, and never was heard of more !

For a time her friends hoped against hope — there had been no storm, and the vessel was a stanch one. Had it been taken by an English cruiser news would come sooner or later — after a while that hope failed. The distracted husband made all possible search. The coasts from Carolina to New York were carefully examined, but not the slightest trace of the vessel could be found.

It remained for long a mystery of the sea.

More than thirty years later an old sailor, dying in a village of the North Carolina coast, confessed that he had been one of a pirate crew who had captured the ship and compelled the passengers to walk the plank ! He produced a small picture, which was, he said, the portrait of the lady thus murdered. He had himself taken it from her cabin. The husband and father were spared the ghastly tale, for both were dead before it was told, but persons who had known Mrs. Alston thought that they recognized the likeness.

No dying man would willingly accuse himself falsely of such a crime.

In the first quarter of the century many buildings, both public and private, were erected; many "greens" built over, and low land reclaimed.

The City Hall, built in 1801 for the State Bank, was eighteen years later converted to its present use, and the inside adorned with handsome marble columns brought from Italy. The present Charleston Library was the old

South Carolina Bank, and remained so until 1835 ; the books to that time being kept in the third story of the Court House, to the rebuilding of which it (the Library) had subscribed handsomely.

The architect of the City Hall, the Orphan House Chapel, and the Hall of the South Carolina Society on Meeting Street, was Gabriel, son of Peter Manigault, so long Speaker of the " Commons House of South Carolina." This gentleman, educated in Europe, cultivated architecture rather as a pursuit than as a profession. He built for his brother the house at the corner of Meeting and John streets, and for himself that on Meeting and George. On his removal to Philadelphia he seems to have abandoned the occupation.

The School for Medicine, not called a college for thirty years, was begun by the Medical Society in 1822 ; but the Citadel was only opened in 1833.

In 1816 St. Paul's, the third and largest Episcopal church, was built in the northwest part of the town, on what was then called " the Neck," namely the narrow strip of land between creeks and marshes which connected the city and the country beyond. Everything above Boundary Street (the old lines, now Calhoun Street) was then called " the Neck." The tide found its way through these many winding creeks up to, or even in some places beyond, Rutledge Avenue from the Ashley on the west; and to Meeting Street from the Cooper on the east ; so narrow was the land then. St. Paul's was built on a lot given by Mrs. Radcliffe, the widow of a rich Scotch merchant, who owned so much of the adjacent property that the neighbourhood is named for her Radcliffeborough. It is now one of the most populous parts of the town, but the church when it was built stood almost alone.

The large mills for pounding rice, that is for separating the husk from the grain, and the lumber mills, which were the chief mechanical industry of the place, were built upon the creeks dammed up to make mill ponds. A small part of one may still be seen south of Calhoun Street, which formerly extended from Spring to Bull Street, and considerably east of Rutledge Avenue. It was crossed by a bridge called Cannons-bridge, the whole neighbourhood being named Cannonsborough. Many of the fine houses still to be seen in that part of the city — which has suffered less from war, fire, and earthquake than the eastern — date from the first half of the last century; the colonial town did not come within squares of them.

The old White Meeting, which had suffered greatly in the Revolution, was replaced in 1806 by a handsome building known from its shape as the Circular Church. Many years before the Scotch members of the congregation had withdrawn from the Meeting and established themselves at the corner of Tradd and Meeting streets, ordering themselves strictly according to the Kirk of Scotland, whence their pastors all came. The most remarkable of these came in 1793, when the historian of the church says: "The congregation had the distinguished felicity to obtain the Revd. George Buist of Edinburg as their Pastor." This gentleman, said to have been a fine pulpit orator, soon became president of the College of Charleston. His little church was twice enlarged to accommodate his auditors, but unfortunately he died at forty, in the prime of his usefulness. The present church was not erected for some years, and has been greatly remodelled since the earthquake of 1886.

Meantime the original congregation, notwithstanding this severance, had so increased that another "house of worship" was built in Archdale Street. There were two pastors, who were called "co-pastors," and served indifferently in either church. A singular arrangement was that the "pastors preached the same sermon in both houses the same day," and the two congregations were one corporate body.

This arrangement worked well until, in 1817, it was observed that the sermons of the Reverend Mr. Forster, a young clergyman from North Carolina, who had recently come to the church, were by no means orthodox, although extremely interesting.

Mr. Forster, on being questioned, frankly avowed that by reading and study his views had altered much since he first came to the congregation, that he could no longer subscribe to its Confession of Faith, that in fact he was a Unitarian. The consternation was extreme; especially when it was found that the larger number of his hearers agreed with his opinions. Mr. Forster was much liked and every effort was made to reclaim him; but he was perfectly honest and conscientious and stood firm.

After much deliberation it was decided that the "new idea" should be given full possession of the Archdale Street building, an equitable division being made of the property, debts, etc., of both churches, while the orthodox should remain with the Reverend Dr. Palmer. The separation was effected. Sixty-nine subscribers remained, seventy-five went ; and so was established the Unitarian Church of Charleston.

Not many native Charlestonians joined it, and of those some who had acted hastily and without due consideration returned to the original fold. Mr. Forster's health failed almost immediately, and the congregation had the good fortune to secure in his place the Reverend Samuel Gilman of Boston, — a young man just ordained.

Dr. Gilman, and his accomplished wife (Miss Caroline Howard of Boston), held for years a prominent part in the social as well as in the religious world of the town.

He was not only a scholar and a thinker but a man of the greatest purity and beauty of character, beloved and respected by all.   Mrs. Gilman's tales, sketches, and poems were widely read and admired; and her two stories, "The New England Housekeeper" and "The Southern Matron," are of much value as delineations of manners and customs now almost extinct.

In 1819 Charleston had the pleasure of receiving another President, Mr. Monroe, who came to "inspect the coast defences and make himself acquainted with the people."

Mr. Monroe was an extremely popular President, being reëlected for his second term with but one adverse vote (for J. Q. Adams), — a majority which none other but Washington has ever received.   People admired his conduct in 1812–1814, and his assertion of the rights and authority of the United States.   He, on his part, was very partial to the Carolina statesmen.   Mr. Calhoun was his Secretary of State, and there was hardly a portfolio, or a mission (as embassies were then called), which he had not offered to Mr. William Lowndes, who refused them all, "believing himself to be of most use to the public in the House of Representatives."

Mr. Calhoun travelled with him now, coming, as Washington had done, by the road from Georgetown.   The party included "Mr. Calhoun's lady and family, Maj. General Thos. Pinckney, Mr. Gouverneur, the President's private secretary, and Lt. Monroe, his nephew."

Having spent the night at Colonel Jacob Bond I'on's plantation, about ten miles from the town, the party drove to Clement's ferry, six miles up the river, near the present navy yard, and came thence in a large and handsome barge, "rowed by twenty-five members of the Mariners' Society, steered by their President, Capt. Thos. Jervey; the style very fine."

The entertainments — inspections, reviews, fireworks, presentations of addresses, of societies, dinners, balls, etc., were much the same as those offered to Washington, with but two exceptions. On Friday, having visited the lines, "he breakfasts at the villa of Joel R. Poinsett, Esqr.," and on "Saturday attends a grand concert and ball given in his honour by the St. Cecilia Society." He stayed one week and went, escorted to the Ashley River Bridge, where, declining a salute, he took kindly leave of the citizens; having first promised to sit to Mr. Morse for his full-length portrait, to be hung in the Council Chamber.

This is the *only* occasion (as far as the writer has been able to ascertain) on which a St. Cecilia has ever been given to any one man! Its times and seasons are as fixed as if ordered by the heavenly bodies. Lent alone disturbs its dates! Saturday is unheard of! That would hardly be a real St. Cecilia which did not begin on a Thursday at 9 P.M.

So much has been said of this social organization that it may be as well to give an account of it here. It began (as has been said in a former chapter) in the year 1737, with a concert given upon "Thursday being St. Cecilia's day," being, originally, an amateur concert society. Very soon, however, one or two professionals were engaged as leading performers. Mr. Quincy, in 1773, mentions that the first violin, a Frenchman, received five hundred guineas a year; but amateurs continued to play with them. General C. C. Pinckney and Mr. Ralph Izard were both said to have been performers in their youth; the former playing the violoncello. It was not formally organized until 1762.

There is no mention of any meetings during the captivity of the town from 1781 to 1786. The men were either in prison or riding with Marion; but immediately upon its repossession the Society met again, and continued to do so regularly despite the rivalry of the Philharmonic Club. In 1792 the managers wrote to Major Thomas Pinckney, then Minister to England, to buy and send out for it "one grand pianoforte and twenty pounds' worth of the best modern concert music."

But by 1819, the very year of Mr. Monroe's visit, the musical ardour had declined, and the committee was obliged to report that they could succeed in getting a quintette only for the concert, and proposed giving a ball instead. Evidently for the reception of the President a combination was effected ; but in 1822 the concert was finally abandoned and the ball reigned in its stead.

From that day to this it has held its joyous sway with but little change or variation.

Only in the sixties, as during the Revolution, all the men being in the field, and the city under fire, it was necessarily interrupted.

The singular point of the organization is that with but few written rules to guide, it has remained so steadfast in object and spirit.

The Society elects its members ; names must be offered at the annual meeting by a letter presented by a member. If a man's father or grandfather, or any of his immediate kindred, have belonged before him, there is little doubt that he will be chosen. Nevertheless blackballs (two suffice to exclude) have fallen, when the applicant was a notoriously unworthy scion of his family tree. If a new resident, or of a family recently brought into notice, there will be inquiry, perhaps hesitation, and a good backing will be desirable. But if he be of character and standing calculated to make his membership acceptable to the Society, he will be elected, — unless he has some adversary ; then he may fail. The presenter of such a one will make careful examination into public feeling before subjecting his friend to mortification; and will withhold the letter if in doubt. When a man is elected, the names of the ladies of his household are at once put upon " the list " and remain there forever. Only death or removal from the city erases them, — change of fortune affects them not at all. " To be dropped from the St. Cecilia " is an awful possibility sometimes hinted at, but which (as far as known) has never come to pass.

The members elect the president, vice-president, secretary and treasurer, and board of managers; and have nothing more to do with the conduct of affairs. They are entitled to ask for invitations for visiting strangers. This is a right that *may* be abused; but members are expected not to use it for business purposes, or as a witty woman once said, "not to let the St. Cecilia become a trades-union."

The managers control everything; are entirely independent of feminine suggestion or assistance; get on, it must sadly be confessed, wonderfully well without it; and except that they are more liberal in this matter of invitations than their wives or sisters would be, are above reproach. The managers continue from year to year, vacancies occurring only by death, or rare resignations, — the eldest manager becoming vice and president in due order. An absolute unanimity is supposed to reign in its councils; the board is understood to be as one; if there be rifts, the outside world knows it not.

Three balls are given in the season; the first in January, the second and third in February, carefully arranged to avoid touching upon Lent. Young ladies always come with a chaperon, and the greatest decorum prevails. The latest bride is, of right, taken down to supper by the president, and feels that she has achieved distinction!

One secret of the success of these balls is that unwritten rule, by which every manager holds himself responsible for the pleasure and well-being of the guests. Each has his own special charge: to some the floor, to others the music, the supper, and so on; but each and all have it on their consciences to see that all goes well, — that no guest is overlooked, no lady neglected, no stranger unwelcomed. Such mistake would be a blot upon the scutcheon, by no

means to be allowed.   Before one has time to be annoyed,
a courteous gentleman — with a white ribbon in his but-
tonhole — is at hand, with apparently no object upon earth

JUDGE GRIMKE'S HOUSE

but to devote himself to the entertainment of one's especial
self, no matter who one may be.   For this end no care or
trouble is held too great.

At first the concerts were held in East Tradd Street, but fashion soon deserted that part of the town. For many years before 1860 the balls were given at St. Andrew's Hall, a handsome building in Broad Street, next to the cathedral, which was burned in the great fire of December, 1861.

The Society owned its plate, damask, china, and glass, and a good stock of wine. The suppers, elegantly served, were waited on by every butler and footman in town who could secure a swallow-tailed coat, grinning with delight when he recognized his acquaintances, especially his " own fambly."

Mr. Poinsett and his breakfasts were at that time as marked a feature of society as the St. Cecilia itself. He was of Huguenot descent, the only son of a wealthy physician, and therefore able to follow his own fancies. He studied medicine, and afterward law. His health failed, and he went to Europe in hope of recovering it, but always remained a delicate man, who by sheer force of intelligence and will did whatever he wished. He said of himself many years later, that " despite the doctors, he had managed *comfortably* with only one lung, for over sixty years! "

He travelled over all Europe, was received at many of the courts, gained the friendship and confidence of the Czar Alexander, and slept in the huts of the wild Khans of the Caucasus and the Caspian Sea. The Czar, recognizing his gifts, wished him to remain in Russia, but the new continent was too interesting to be abandoned. He returned home, and was sent on missions to South America, and to Mexico, in the most stormy times of their stormy history. In Chili he commanded an insurgent army, and rescued seven American sailors under sentence of death to the Peruvians. In Mexico, it need hardly be said that he encountered a revolution. The grand Plaza swarmed with armed men while the citizens fled for their lives. A party, including several ladies, rushed into the gates of the American embassy, imploring protection. The only weapon was the American flag! Mr. Poinsett threw it across his doorway and alone defied the ruffians to enter ; — his house was unmolested, the fugitives saved.

On returning he was elected member of Congress, and established himself during the intervals of the sessions in a small cottage with a large garden, surrounded by a grove of stately live-oaks. One or two of the oaks may still be seen on Rutledge Avenue, not far above the present Radcliffe Street, but the grounds have been divided into town lots, and are closely built over.

Next to adventure he loved conversation and flowers, and now that his days of adventure were done, he resolved to enjoy the other tastes.

He had brought plants from Mexico and cultivated them here. The splendid Poinsettia, the red and yellow Mimosa, called " Goat's-beard," and the so-called " Mexican Rose," a species of hibiscus which changes from white to pink and red in a single day, were all introduced and propagated by him.

Once a week he gave a breakfast, at which were collected the best and brightest of the town. Beauty or charm or intelligence in a woman, agreeability in a man, were the things he sought in his guests ; if not possessed, a second invitation was never received. Strangers were always invited, and treated with the utmost consideration and attention.

A small, plain man, with every *disadvantage* of face and figure, he, like Wilkes, " could soon talk himself above the handsomest man in England." His voice was husky always, but cultivation and refinement made it attractive, and he was the most delightful of hosts and best of *raconteurs*. A conversation led by him never flagged ; he could always induce each guest to speak of that of which he spoke best, never allowed any one to prose, and when he took the *parole* himself, avoided with wonderful tact the part of hero of his own stories.   These breakfasts went on for years and were, in all pleasantness, lessons in the art of conversation.

Mr. Poinsett married late in life a handsome and wealthy widow, Mrs. John Julius Pringle (Miss Izard), a daughter-in-law of the attorney-general, — two of whose descendants have received his name in baptism.   He had hitherto taken no active part in the public affairs of the city, but was now to become prominent in them.

Even conservative Charleston was feeling the impulse of the mechanical century.   Steam was soon to be introduced into her mills, and steamboats to her waters. Morse, who was then known only as an artist, was for some time in Charleston, painting many portraits there, and it is said that he perfected his great invention, the telegraph, in a house in Chalmers Street.   Greatest of all, a scheme for a railroad to carry freight and passengers began to be discussed as early as 1813.   The only road then running being a small one for carrying coal from the pits to Newcastle-upon-Tyne.   The scheme remained in the air, however, until 1827, when a charter was granted for this new wonder.   It was proposed to build it to connect the cities of Charleston and Augusta, Georgia, over a hundred miles apart — an extraordinary enterprise for that time.

In the meanwhile the turnpikes were so much improved that by 1820 travelling was no longer the thing of horror that it had been ; stages ran regularly, and with comparative celerity.   Young Dr. Gilman, for instance, when he came to preach his test sermons in the Unitarian Church, was no more than eleven days and nights from Boston to Charleston, whereas it had taken seventeen days to get the

An End of the Drawing-room of the Pringle House

news of the battle of Lexington! People went now to Virginia and the Northern States habitually, as they had formerly gone to Europe — travelling generally in their own vehicles, often with four horses.

Journals of such expeditions remain.

At the Virginia Springs, the men of the earlier period who still survived were to be met. Mr. Jefferson particularly was often there. The following letter to his old friend, Colonel Alston, shows his kindly, affectionate nature: —

"Monticello, Oct. 6, 1818.

"Dear Sir: — While I had the pleasure of being with you at the Warm Springs, I took the liberty of recommending to you some wines of France and Italy, with a note of their prices and of the channels thro' which they may be got; but instead of calling for them on my recommendation only, I have thought it better that you should have samples to direct your choice, for in nothing have the habits of the palate more decisive influence than in our relish of wines. I have therefore made up a box of a couple of doz. bottles among which you will find samples of the wines of White Hermitage, Ledanon, Rousillon (of Riveralto), Bergasse, claret, all of France and of Nice, and Montepulciano of Italy. I now send them to Richmond, to the care of Captain Bernard Peyton, commission merchant of that place, to be forwarded to you by the first vessel to Charleston, some of them I hope will be found to your taste.

"We were much distressed at the springs by the first accounts we received of your fall from your horse; but relieved by subsequent assurances that the injury had been less serious than at first feared, and that you had been able to proceed on your journey. I hope therefore that this finds you in health amidst the comforts of your own

2 f

country. I became seriously affected afterwards by the continuance of the use of the waters, they produced imposthume, eruption with fever, colliquative sweats and extreme debility, these sufferings aggravated by the torment of long and rough roads reduced me to the lowest stage of exhaustion by the time I got home. I have been on the recovery some time, and still am so, but not yet able to sit erect for writing — among my first efforts is that of recalling myself to your recollection, and of expressing the gratification I derived at the springs from your acquaintance and society. However little of life may remain for cherishing a cordiality which it must so soon part with, it will not be the less felt while feeling remains, and in the hope that the tour I recommended of the upper and lower valley of the Blue Ridge may give me, the ensuing autumn the gratification of receiving you at Monticello, I pray you to accept the assurance of my friendly attachment and high respect, and that I may be permitted to place here my respectful compliments for Miss and Mr. Alston, who were the companions of your journey.

"TH. JEFFERSON." [1]

Colonel Alston was at that time considered the type of the home-staying Carolina planter. A very young man at the beginning of the Revolution, he had not had the English education which so many of his class enjoyed, but was thoroughly Carolinian.

He had served under Marion and was one of his most trusted friends. On the conclusion of the war he devoted himself to planting, differing from most of his compatriots in that he eschewed politics. Only once did he consent to allow himself to be sent as senator to the State Legislature, a sacrifice to his friendship for Mr. Jefferson, whose nomination for President was then in jeopardy.

[1] Unpublished letter in the possession of Charles Alston, Esq., Charleston.

He was twice married; first to Miss Ashe, secondly to Miss Motte, by each of whom he had several children. His eldest daughter by the second marriage was the wife of the distinguished Robert Y. Hayne, who wrote of him : —

" It is as a Carolina Planter, — a character associated with the interests and honour and best hopes of the State, — that Col. Alston was chiefly distinguished. Whether we estimate his claims to public consideration by his extraordinary success— the admirable treatment of his slaves, or the progressive improvement of his estates, the result of a wise system of economy and good management. . . .

" It is believed that at the time of his death he was, with perhaps one exception, the largest slaveholder in South Carolina. . . . It was the opinion of Col. Alston that in the management of slaves the true interests of the planter were in exact accordance with the dictates of an enlightened humanity. It was with him a rule through life to treat his slaves with the utmost liberality and kindness, while he never relaxed the reins of a wholesome discipline. His rule was to provide them with dwellings of the best description, and to allow them supplies of every kind on the most liberal scale. The consequence was that his numerous plantations were models of neatness and order, and his slaves always presented an appearance of health and comfort which spoke well for their treatment. They were devotedly attached to their master whose service they would not have exchanged for any other upon earth. . . . . His system was based upon a calculation of practical results. It was not the slaves *only* who were to be made prosperous and happy. If they were among the best treated in the State, his crops were always abundant, and his rice of the finest quality.

*   *   *   *   *   *   *

THE PRINGLE HOUSE

"Until compelled by increasing infirmities to retire from the world, his house was the abode of a refined and elegant hospitality. . . . Courteous in his manners, social in his disposition, surrounded with a large circle of friends and blessed with an ample fortune his tastes and habits were for many years those of 'a Carolina gentleman of the old school.' "

Colonel Alston survived to 1839, dying in his eighty-third year, a consistent member of the Episcopal Church.

His house in King Street, through the marriage of his youngest daughter to Mr. William Bull Pringle, is now known as the Pringle house.

In 1822 occurred the only really serious threat of servile insurrection which had threatened Charleston since that incited by the Spaniards at St. Augustine in 1739.

By this time the disputes consequent upon the admission to the Union of the new States of the Louisiana Purchase were raging.

The abolition party was violent. It was proved that certain negroes who had gone to the North had there become so perverted that upon their return to Charleston, they proposed a plot of insurrection to their friends.

They asserted that in this scheme they had the support of a large and influential body of sympathizers at Boston and elsewhere.

The negroes — or some of them — lent ear. The plot thickened, and the consequences might have been too terrible for words, had not two faithful servants told their masters of the startling tale. These gentlemen at once informed the Intendant, Colonel James Hamilton, and the Governor, Mr. Bennett.

Upon examination it was found that the originator of the scheme was a free mulatto named Denmark Vesey, who had been much in the North in communication with the abolition party, and had brought in and disseminated their publications. His chief colleague was an African called "Gullah Jack, an hereditary conjurer," supposed by the negroes to be immortal and able to work miracles by magic. These and others were the ringleaders. Their chief followers were the mechanics, carpenters, blacksmiths, carters, mill-hands, wheelwrights, etc. Very few were house servants, and it was two of these who had, "for love of their masters," told the story. It is impossible to say how far the field-hands had entered into the conspiracy; but it was known from the Santee to Port Royal.

Their plan was that at midnight on Sunday, June 12, a large body of negroes should cross from the islands to the town, and those from the adjacent country march in. They were to seize the arms in the armouries, particularly those in one known to be carelessly guarded on "the Neck." The Intendant and Governor were to be instantly killed; the town fired in many places; all white men to be massacred, the women kept; all possible booty to be secured. There was much talk of St. Domingo, to which place they were to go with their plunder.

On learning this, the authorities immediately took the necessary measures. There was horrible anxiety and few people slept on the night of the 12th of June; but the guard was doubled, the militia was in readiness, the arms secured. The negroes, seeing the preparations which it was impossible to conceal, kept perfectly quiet. All suspected were arrested. Vesey showed great courage, and could not be brought to confess until confronted with a barber from whom he had ordered a wig made of "white man's hair" as a disguise. Then he broke down.

They were all brought to trial, the trials being conducted with the greatest care by courts of freeholders, men of the first character. It was found that many implicated were too ignorant and stupid to be worthy of punishment; they were dismissed. Of the guilty, twenty-nine were transported and thirty-five executed—twenty-two at one time in the jail yard in the presence of many spectators. Never since the days of the pirates had such a thing been seen.

STOLL'S ALLEY

There was not the least attempt at rescue or even any great excitement on the part of the crowd; but the impression left on many minds was most painful. Henceforth their compatriots might be their foes.

In consequence of the conspiracy the laws for the control and regulation of the negroes were made more stringent. Meetings at night were forbidden; the city guard was doubled; police rules were enforced, which from lapse of time and fancied security had become lax; and free negroes who had gone to the North were forbidden to return. Those employed on coasting vessels or steamboats were not allowed to land. In view of Vesey's performances it was necessary, but extremely troublesome to persons travelling with their servants. The interstate question of the boat-hands threatened to provoke the interference of the general government, in allusion to which Colonel Robert Y. Hayne, then representative in Congress, wrote to C. C. Pinckney, Jr. (youngest son of General Thomas Pinckney) in 1824, recommending patience and moderation. He adds: —

" South Carolina has a character to sustain, and her own dignity requires that no intemperate expression, no threat of forcible resistance to the national government should ever be resorted to. Let us not contemplate or speak of such an event otherwise than in terms of unmingled horror."

This is one of the first notes of danger coming from the South.

On the other hand much was now being done for the religious education of the negro. In 1828, Colonel Hayne's correspondent, Mr. C. C. Pinckney, a man of deep religious feeling, called the attention of a number of gentlemen of the Agricultural Society, and others, to the fact that the number of the negroes was now so great as to be beyond the power of private religious teaching. The ladies, who laboured then as always, might catechize their house servants, but could do nothing with the many hundreds of field-hands.

In this emergency he asked the help of the churches, particularly of the Methodist. The Life of Bishop Capers, of the M. E. Church, by Bishop Wightman, contains the following passage : —

"In 1829 two missions for plantation slaves were established on the Ashley and the Santee rivers. In the preceding year he" (Bishop Capers) "was waited on by the Hon. C. C. Pinckney, to ascertain if a Methodist exhorter could be obtained to oversee his plantation. . . . The Bishop made application to the Missionary Board at the next conference, for a Missionary whose time and efforts should be exclusively directed to the religious instruction and spiritual welfare of the coloured people.

"Soon after Colonel Lewis Morris and Mr. Charles Baring united in a similar request on Pon Pon. These gentlemen took the initiative in a course of missionary operations which may justly be termed the 'Glory of Southern Christianity.' They were all members of the Protestant Episcopal Church, but availed themselves of the peculiar itinerant organization which the Methodist Church afforded."

The gentlemen certainly showed great good sense and knowledge of the race which they desired to benefit. The Methodists worked with admirable zeal; their "riders" went from place to place preaching, praying, and singing, in plain, simple language, but fervent tones, appealing to the imaginative and emotional blacks.

Some planters at first objected, fearing disturbance, but all objections soon gave way, and the exhorters and class leaders were eagerly welcomed. The other churches did their share. The son of Mr. Pinckney, the late Rev. Charles Cotesworth Pinckney, says in his Life of his grandfather : —

"Within a few years" of the correspondence with Bishop Capers "fifty chapels were built by the planters along the sea-board for the religious instruction of their slaves; and fifty thousand negroes were members of Christian churches in South Carolina. . . . At the beginning of the war" (1861) "the Protestant Episcopal coloured communicants alone were two thousand nine hundred and sixty."

Bishop Capers, often called the evangelist of the negroes, was the father of the present beloved Bishop of the Protestant Episcopal Diocese of South Carolina.

In 1825 Charleston, in common with the whole country, went perfectly wild over the coming of La Fayette.

Republics are said to be ungrateful. No such reproach can be made to America in regard to the "Friend of the Nation." No conqueror ever received a more enthusiastic, no benefactor a more heartfelt welcome, than was given to the old soldier who came to gather the laurels won nearly fifty years before. Congress gave him a princely gift, $200,000 and a township of land; but the people gave him the adoration of their hearts, an honour and reverence shared by Washington alone, and La Fayette was a man to appreciate it.

He was said to have been deeply moved as he approached Charleston. He had come to it first as a young, unknown adventurer, and had been received with kindness and confidence. Now his name was on every lip, his praise in every voice.

He came from Camden and Columbia; at the former he had laid the corner-stone of a monument to his friend, the Baron de Kalb, who had been his companion in that first adventurous voyage. De Kalb had fallen at the battle of Camden. "He could have done more than I," La Fayette said, "but Fate took the better man." From fervent rejoicings at Columbia he came to Charleston along the old Indian trail, then the State Road. He was escorted by a troop of handsomely uniformed young men from the middle country, all riding fine white horses, well caparisoned — very unlike the "ragged Continentals" of his youth. The Governor of the State (Governor Manning) sat beside him, and opposite were his own son, George Washington La Fayette, and the son of his first American friend, Major Benjamin Huger, the man who had risked his life to save him from the dungeon of Olmütz. Upon this gentleman, Colonel Francis Kinloch Huger, La Fayette, in the most earnest but delicate manner, pressed a part of the gift which Congress had just given him. " You shared my prison," he said, "now share my wealth. I cannot be rich while you are poor." Colonel Huger, with great feeling, declined. " He had enough for his daughters," he said, "and he had taught his sons to provide for themselves."

Six miles from the town a troop of cavalry and at the lines an infantry escort were ready with an open carriage, drawn by General McPherson's four splendid gray horses. That he might hear his own tongue, the orders for both companies, the Washington Light Infantry and the Fusiliers Française, were given by the captain of the former in French !

Meeting Street was lined by soldiers presenting arms, by the Societies of the Cincinnati and the survivors of the Revolution and others in rank, by the clergy, the school children, etc., all in order, by citizens in carriages, on horseback, and on foot. It was no easy matter for some of the elders who had been slender youths in 1776 to get into their old uniforms now ; and many a sword-belt which had seen good service in its day was punched with new holes, before buckle and tongue could meet.

As he passed, all cheered and wheeled into line. No such procession had ever been seen ; in it was every man in town and hundreds who had come from the country. Windows and doors were thronged with ladies who waved their scarfs and threw flowers in his way.

At the corner of George Street the schoolboys, ranged in order, shouted with glee when they saw the Marquis stop his carriage and alight precipitately. The carriage containing the Generals Pinckney, which had just fallen into line behind, stopped also; and La Fayette, in true French fashion, threw his arms round first one and then the other veteran, kissing each tenderly on both cheeks.

They had been comrades in war and friends in peace, and both brothers had been too much in France to feel embarrassed; but the boys were convulsed with laughter.

He rode along through the burning sunshine with his hat in his hand, unflinching; but the old campaigner knew his trade, and a damp handkerchief was safely tucked into the crown of his curled peruke.

At the City Hall the Intendant, Judge Prioleau, welcomed him, and he stood on the high steps facing the crowd. Only when Washington stood on the steps of the Exchange, and never again, has one figure so entirely filled the thoughts of the people.

If Washington had symbolized to them Strength and Virtue, so La Fayette personified chivalric Generosity, Honour, and Romance.

That was the romantic age; the Charlestonians of 1825 had fed upon the pages of Scott. Courage, daring, self-devotion, love of the good and the true, such as Sir Walter ever taught — were they not embodied in the man before them?

Never had hero-worship a better excuse, never was it more freely offered.

Enthusiasm was sustained by the hero's own evident pleasure in the homage he received, and by the simplicity and warmth with which he expressed his thanks. In every speech (and there were many) there was always some allusion to an event or a friend connected with the subject of the moment all made with the grace of the French *gentilhomme*.

There were endless entertainments of the usual sort — unusually elaborate, perhaps. One new feature was the presence of the first Roman Catholic bishop of Charleston, Bishop England, who came at the head of the " Faculty and Students of the Philosophical and Classical Seminary."

La Fayette presented a standard to the Seventh (militia) Regiment, and paid many private visits — to Mrs. Shaw, the daughter of General Greene; to the widow of General William Washington; to Mrs. Horrÿ, whose son had married his niece; to the daughters of General Pinckney, etc. It need hardly be said that wherever he went he charmed his hostesses by his gracious *bonhommie*.

The grand event of the visit for the public at large was a ball given at the theatre. The theatre then was a large and handsome building, at the corner of Broad and New streets. The pit was floored over and the tiers of boxes arranged for spectators. Of the decorations of the interior it would take too long to tell, they fill a column of the *Gazette*. There was a huge eagle (painted on the ceiling) and portraits of distinguished men, arms of states and cities, inscriptions, sentiments, and mottoes galore. Of the ball itself there remains an account written by a young man but lately come to Charleston, but who was to become one of her leading citizens, the late H. W. Conner, Esq.

His description of the scene and of the ladies is amusing, — where eighteen hundred are gathered together, there must be eccentricities, — but the most valuable part is the simple outpouring of the thoughts inspired by the occasion. He speaks the mind of the community.

The letter is to his mother and sister, and begins with apologies for not describing the entire visit and for referring them to a paper for the account of everything except the Ball, and for the decorations of that.

" From even that description you can form nothing like an adequate idea of the beauty, taste or elegance of the room. The room was 180 to 200 feet long, and on it ranged round on seats rising gradually one above the other, were 1800 ladies as richly and tastefully dressed as the fancy or purse of each one would allow. Many of the dresses were most brilliant as well as costly ; steel seemed to triumph over gold, and silver was quite in the background. Some of the trappings of our Nabobs' daughters must have cost two to three thousand dollars, or perhaps more. The dresses were all white, and in some cases a thin netting of steel or gold or silver gauze was worn over a white muslin dress. The trimmings were either white, pink or blue. Most of them wore something like spencers that fit close to the body of pink or white and all wore rich head-dresses with a profusion of diamonds and jewels of all grades from the common paste up to the diamond of the first water. Some of the finest wore large gold (virgin pure) spriggs or branches, completely encircling the forehead, and all with a rare exception (where the neck was too black or too bony, or the arm knocked-kneed) were bare necked and bare armed or what was very nearly equivalent to it — a long white glove was worn wrinkled up into a purse about the wrist with a little La Fayette stamped on the hand of it, counter checked by one on the band round the waist. What with the beauty of the dresses, (I could not tell which to admire the most) the sight was a terribly grand and beautiful one. I say terrible because as is wont to be the custom here all the artillery of charms and jewels, black eyes, etc., were brought there by their respective owners with the full design of Conquest, and I dare say many a brave heart was laid low upon that memorable occasion.

. . . The General was by arrangement to enter the Ball room at eight o'clock, and his approach announced by the sound of a bugle. When the sound did come, at a quarter after eight, a scene not to be described ensued. The ladies became frantic — with curiosity, I suppose — one hollered, another clapped her hands, a third jumped and skipped, (she was a little French Mademoiselle) and they all rose up by one impulse. The Manager motioned, because if he had spoken no one would have heard him, — he motioned to them to sit down ; he might as well have said to the sea 'cease to rage.' No one saw him, no one heard him, and if they had either seen or heard him, not a mother's daughter of them would have minded him. The men were stationed behind the boxes. Soon after his approach was announced by the sound of the bugle, a most elegant band struck up the air of 'Hail to the Chief, who in triumph advances.' He was ushered in by several venerable relics of the Revolution supporting him on each side. The moment the eye caught a first glimpse there was one universal and continuous burst of applause. It was a motive as pure and holy as love and gratitude could make it that produced it. Here was a man by nature noble, brave, generous, with a form and a face that a soldier would like to look upon, that a philanthropist would dwell upon with rapture, — for his features beam with humanity and gentleness, and upon which the old man and the young could look with admiration and enthusiasm. This man in the pride of his youth when difficulties and dangers thickened around our infancy, and when an overwhelming power was ready to crush us without, and faction ready to consume us within, this man stood forth the champion of our desperate Cause, — was associated with that great apostle of American liberty, our Guardian Angel, Genl. Washington with whom we now identify him — fought and bled not only with him, but with our fathers. Shared the toils of war until peace successfully obtained by the valour and wisdom of our illustrious chief, gave us a rank new placed among the first Nations of the Earth. Here forty years afterwards when the heroes of that day sleep with their fathers, this same Hero after experiencing all the vicissitudes of fortune, but still retaining all the purity of virtue suddenly appears amongst us. He rises as it were from the dead, and the first impulse that his appearance creates is ' Behold the friend of Washington! Our noble advocate and defender, let us honour him. Welcome, La Fayette.' These were my sensations, and I am sure they were general. He was first led round the room, bowing most courteously to every lady he passed, and receiving every demonstration of respect that it was possible to show him. In going around the second time the ladies could not restrain themselves any longer. They seized the old man's hand involuntarily. It was tendered freely to every one, and every one grasped in rapture. . . . I could but exclaim to myself,— was virtue ever more nobly rewarded, — was ever gratitude more fervently expressed, — was there ever a man so purely and so perfectly happy ? My imagination could not suggest to me the possibility of a man being more supremely blessed than the Marquis La Fayette.

"After passing round the room in this way, he was conducted to a kind of Throne prepared for him (see the papers). He met Mrs. Shaw (Genl. Greene's daughter), Mrs. Washington (Col. Washington's lady), the Miss Pinckneys, etc.

"During the time he remained, say from half after eight to ten, there was a general rush to see him, to hear him talk, and shake his hand. Every one by him was received with all the warmth of French manners, and as far as looks and actions could speak he seemed to say, ' Heaven bless the people, — I love you all.'

"The Ball, like all public balls, was a scene of splendid confusion. Forty sets of quadrilles were all going at once. The Marquis is in his form tall and stately, perhaps an inch higher than myself, though not quite so heavy. He is lame a little in one foot, and a good deal infirm from age, though his appearance from the colour of his wig and the brilliancy of his eye is altogether youthful. His features are long and somewhat narrow with a retreating but unusually high forehead. His features, take them together are more expressive of goodness than anything else. His eye is the only remarkably fine feature he has. That is a fine large dark eye, exceedingly quick in its transition from one object to another, and bespeaks great equanimity as well as magnanimity of disposition, tho' it has nothing of that determined and energetic quality, which fits a man for extreme emergency. I think the man's countenance expresses his character as intelligently as language itself could make it." [1]

We smile at such enthusiasm, but at least these good ladies deserved Carlyle's encomium, — they were heroic enough to know a hero when they saw him.

At the end of the week the general left for Savannah, stopping *en route* at Edisto Island, to pay a visit to Mr. William Seabrook, perhaps the largest planter of Sea Island long-staple cotton of his day; a visit that influenced the fate of two persons yet unborn. For when a child came soon after to the hospitable hosts, they named it, girl though it was, for their distinguished guest, "La Fayette Seabrook." When years after the Conte Ferdinand de Lasteyrie travelled in America, he came with letters from the General to the Seabrook family, and the fair La Fayette became Mme. de Lasteyrie! so preordained, we may fancy, by her name.

[1] From unpublished letter in possession of Miss Conner, Charleston.

2 G

This was the last time that the two Pinckneys ever appeared in public. General Charles Cotesworth died in the same year, aged eighty-one. General Thomas survived scarcely three years, dying at seventy-eight.

Their deaths, it was said, marked the end of an era. They were the last conspicuous examples of the old *régime* to survive in Charleston. They were buried with all possible civil and military honours, the one in St. Michael's, the other in St. Philip's churchyard.

No political event, not the Revolution itself, ever (before 1860) produced in Charleston the excitement that was caused by the Nullification movement of 1832–1833. It may not be generally remembered that in 1832 the tariff on all coarse woollen and cotton goods; on iron, salt, and other commodities, all essential to the South for the use of her negroes, was trebled—raised from 25 to 75 per cent. The duties on articles of luxury, such as tea, coffee, silk, etc.,—not produced in New England, was reduced. The motive was plain, the manufacturing interest was governing the country. The South, which had cheerfully agreed to a moderate duty for the protection of infant industries, proposed in 1816 by her own statesmen, Lowndes and Calhoun, resented the increase.

The Legislature of South Carolina protested and petitioned all to no avail. It then appointed a committee to consider the remedy for these evils. The committee replied that it considered "Nullification" the remedy and recommended that a convention of the people should be called to apply it. By nullification is meant (I observe for the benefit of non-political readers), not the right of secession which had been so forcibly stated by Massachusetts in 1812, but the right of a State, peaceably and within the Union, to annul any act of Congress, which her own courts should pronounce unconstitutional.

This right had been asserted in the famous "Kentucky Resolutions" of 1787.

Hitherto the people of the State had been unanimous ; all detested the tariff, all called it a grievous wrong. " England had done nothing equal to this! " But when it came to pitting one small State against all others, men paused.

They split into parties. None would be anything but a State Rights man, but they bore their names with a difference. Colonel Robert Y. Hayne (then Governor), General James Hamilton, Mr. McDuffie, Mr. Turnbull (known as " Brutus "), Colonel Preston, and their friends, were " Free Trade and State Rights." But their ordinary appellation was " Nullifyers," and their enemies added " Fire-eaters." Their great leader was Mr. Calhoun, but he, though the apostle of their creed, in practice advocated patience and self-control.

The other party, Colonel William Drayton, Mr. Poinsett, Judge Huger, Mr. Henry Middleton, Mr. James R. Pringle, Mr. Petigru, etc., were " Union State Rights " or " Unionists " — also taunted as " Submissionists."

Disraeli, who knew politics, said that the first essential for a good campaign was a good " cry." Each of these parties was well provided.

Nothing could exceed the warmth of feeling and the painful division of friends and families. Households even were divided against themselves; the closest bonds were snapped. There were speeches, processions, pamphlets. The Nullifyers were sarcastic at the expense of men who, having vehemently declaimed against the tariff, were now for " basely submitting." The Unionists were equally scornful when they asked if the veriest Fire-eater really supposed that Government would allow itself to be defied by one small State. " We can die for our rights," cried the Nullifyer. " You will die and not get your rights," said the Unionist. Such remarks were not pleasant at the dinner or tea table, — and yet social life went on.

The Legislature summoned a convention and the convention met. It was known that the great majority were Nullifyers, and many must have felt as did the young lady, Mrs. X, to whose husband — a naval officer then at sea — the following letter is addressed: —

" The Convention has met and began its sitting yesterday, it is said will continue for a fortnight, though why that should be, when all its members are of one opinion and have only to pass their vote, I cannot conceive.

"My two uncles and Mr. Turnbull (Brutus) have gone. By way of giving ardour to their deliberations, your friend S. has a place, and to give the sanction and respectability of age old Capt. Richard Bohun Baker, and Major Hamilton" (two of the last remaining veterans of the Revolution) "have been dragged from their firesides to partake of the uncomfortable honour. . . . I suppose that the debates will be published and although a hater of politics, I shall read them, for I think we are about to try a noble but hazardous experiment, and though I advocate the measure, I tremble at its approach."

This lady was a *mild* Nullifyer; her own family being extreme ones, — her husband's strong Unionists.

At the same time the sister of the young officer writes in great provocation. The two letters are given to show the wide divergence of opinion in one family.

" No one can be more anxious to see the nullifying law passed than I am, though well convinced that it must end in defeat and danger, I wish to see the end of it, and what measures Congress will pursue. As to taking off the tariff in consequence of our nullifying, there is not a Nullifyer fool enough to affirm much less to believe it. . . . I must tell you of a trick of a brickbat that will amuse you. The two parties met the other night after a supper ; the Nullifyers began to throw stones " (the wife says " The Union men became violent, but Col. Drayton restrained them."), "— one of them hit Mr. Petigru on the shoulder and rebounding flew into B. B.'s face, giving him a terrible blow on the cheek. A. M. tells the story very pathetically, but it was impossible not to laugh. Had the blow been aimed at *him* we should have been sorry, but its coming back at him from Mr. Petigru made it delightful ! There was wit in that brickbat. . . . You are sailing away from the United States, that you may return safe and well to the *United* States is my earnest hope and prayer."

The ladies were as enthusiastic and as well informed as the men. One of the best explanations of the doctrine of State Rights is " The Quintessence of Long Speeches or a Catechism of State Rights," by Miss Maria H. Pinckney, eldest daughter of General C. C. Pinckney.

Neither party had long to wait. In one week the convention passed the ordinance nullifying the act increasing the tariff, and ordered that no duties should be paid after the 1st of February, 1833, — little more than six weeks off.

The Nullifyers were delighted. Mrs. X wrote, " A. M. is in a perfect ecstasy. Says successful or not it will form a noble page in history. As for the other party they are *Submissionists.*"

The " *Submissionist* " theory did not last long. The President then was General Jackson, a South Carolinian by birth, a Democrat in politics, but a soldier above all things, and as prone to use the strong hand as any man alive. Almost by return of mail came his proclamation : " If the duties were not paid, the State should be reduced by force." The Governor, Robert Y. Hayne, a man of the finest character and intellect, with a singular power of influencing men, replied in another proclamation, maintaining the rights of the people and their determination to defend them. To count the cost has never been a characteristic of Carolinians. The threat greatly increased the number and the ardour of the Nullifyers. Offers of service poured in upon the Governor. Men armed and drilled, subscribed money, and raised companies. The State spent a large sum for arms. General Jackson, advised by Mr. Poinsett, who remembered revolts in South America, sent troops commanded by General Scott, and a fleet under Commodore Elliott. Nothing can be more curious than Jackson's letters to his intimate friend, Mr. Poinsett, published in the Life of the latter. Beginning with kind expressions of "my native State," "our State," he lashes himself into fury before he gets to the end. What the State owed to Judge Huger and Colonel Drayton can hardly be overestimated. They, knowing well their own people, persuaded Jackson to hold his hand and strike no blow until some "overt act" was committed. It is curious that in spite of the wild excitement of both men and women there *was* no overt act. The people were ripe for war, and the President equally so. He swore that "he would make blue cockades as scarce as blue roses in South Carolina." The leaders on each side held them back, for the leaders of the Nullifyers did *not* desire disunion.

Mrs. X writes on the 30th of January: "In spite of all these signs of warfare I cannot yet imagine the possibility of such a thing. War if it does come will be a terrible calamity, but with all its horrors I do not dread it as much as I do the dissolution of our glorious Union. I am sorry to say *that* is sometimes spoken of seriously and coolly, and as matter rather for rejoicing than grief by many persons, and I fear very much that even if the obnoxious laws should be repealed, and the Constitution restored to its former purity, the two sections of the country will never return to their former harmony. End how it may, we shall be no longer brothers, but rivals."

So the troops and the navy were treated with the utmost politeness, and the commodore in particular, a kindly old gentleman, became a great favourite with the ladies.

Both sides waited breathlessly for the other to act, both waited for February, when the refusal to pay the duties should be made.

Most happily Mr. Clay stepped in with his compromise bill for reducing the tariff gradually for nine years, the reduction to begin at once. Mr. Calhoun and the congressional delegation instantly supported the bill, and the situation was saved. The convention again summoned, after listening to the eloquence of Benjamin Watkins Leigh, sent from Virginia to counsel conciliatory measures, passed another ordinance annulling the first, and the cloud cleared away. All were satisfied except the extremists on both sides, who would have been glad had things been pushed to the worst.

Both sides claimed the victory: the one party because the duties were paid, the other because the tariff was reduced, and the pride of both was satisfied.

The same lady wrote again (her letters are given as showing the *popular* ideas of the State Rights party): —

" We Carolinians are a lucky people, we have had the satisfaction of taking the lead in a most honourable resistance, and of displaying great courage in a threatened danger; and now we have the still greater of seeing that danger quietly disappear. . . . Mr. Clay's bill which has passed in the Senate pacifies our constitutional scruples, though not our just demands."

It is odd, but it is human nature after all, to find people amusing themselves under such circumstances, but they certainly did.

" There has been much gayety. A masquerade, the St. Cecilia's, the Race Ball, but not many private parties.

A subscription ball given under the especial patronage of the Count de Choiseul for poor old M. Fayolle, who has lost his all in a shipwreck." A ball was a very appropriate method of assisting M. Fayolle, for he was the old St. Domingan master, who had taught half Charleston to dance. The Count de Choiseul, then and for many years French consul at Charleston, was a most interesting person. A nobleman of the old *régime*, he had absolutely refused submission to the new order; had defended Malta under the *drapeau blanc* until he could hold out no longer. And had then taken refuge in England, where he married. The influence of friends at home procured him the position of consul at Charleston, where he was an important figure for more than thirty years.

His eldest son fell fighting gallantly as captain of the Louisiana Zouaves in the war between the States. His second has now succeeded to the title of Marquis de Choiseul, in France.

Before the fleet sailed, however, one private ball was given in its honour. The mother-in-law of Mrs. X wrote to her son, telling him how many of his naval friends and particularly his old commander, Commodore Elliott, had " asked after you and sung your praises." She therefore determined to show them some attention. This was in March, when things had quieted down.

She writes with satisfaction : —

" So I sent out invitations" (for a ball), "and got a list from Duncan Ingraham, who said I should invite *all* the wardroom. I did so, and many came, and as I was the mother of a naval officer all came in full uniform, which they have not appeared in elsewhere, as they said party spirit ran so high. However, I asked them as friends of my son, and it was *my* business, and there were State Rights and Union people, and it all went off very well."

Grief unites people more than joy, and when a great

man dies, all is forgotten except his great qualities. No one in Charleston stood higher or was more admired than Robert J. Turnbull. He was a political writer of much power. His pamphlets, signed "Brutus," are still prized. When he died in April in the strength of his manhood, it was a shock to all.

Colonel William Drayton and himself had been for years as brothers, Mrs. Turnbull having been a mother to the former when his own parent had died leaving him an infant in Florida. Now politics had severed them. Mrs. X writes: —

"Mr. Turnbull's funeral was immense, guns were fired in his honour, his party met and determined to wear mourning for him, and to appoint some fit person to pronounce his eulogy. In the meantime many *unfit* persons have volunteered to be his eulogists, and the papers have been filled with pieces in his praise. Most of his opponents forgot their party animosity at his death, and joined with his friends in following him to the grave. Colonel Drayton looked very sad, and my uncle shed tears. They were both formerly his intimate friends."

So passions calmed down, the people grew together again, and the storm was averted for thirty years.

CHAPTER XX

SOCIAL TOPICS. MEXICAN WAR

IN the light of after events it is hard to believe how calm and confident those thirty years were. The great questions of the day were vehemently discussed in Congress and in the State legislatures, but the people at large never dreamed of the disruption of the Union, still less of the possibility of war. Many of the Union men had, after the nullification compromise, been sent to Congress or appointed to office at home, and the result was harmony. The State had to lament the loss of Colonel William Drayton. He thought himself coldly looked upon by his townfolk, and sensitive and high-spirited, willingly accepted the presidency of the moribund United States Bank, and removed to Philadelphia. He is the father of the present Drayton family of that city.

At home the chief interest was in the new things which were changing the ways of the world. " The steam packet about which we are all agape, which now (1833) runs regularly from this place to New York," and the railroad, which three years before had actually reached the Savannah River at Augusta, one hundred and thirty-six miles away ! When the engine, the " Best Friend," the first locomotive used in America, was put upon the track, and drew a car which could carry twenty-five passengers at the " daring and dangerous pace of twelve miles an hour," and was even trusted to transport the mail, the world stood amazed!

By the late thirties travelling became, as the railroad

system extended, *comparatively* easy, and some families
went regularly to Newport or Saratoga for the summer.
In the winter visitors from Boston, New York, etc., often
coming in search of health, were frequent. To make
these journeys one left Charleston by a steamboat for Wil-
mington, North Carolina. Then bits of railroad with connecting links of stages, thumped and bumped along through
North Carolina and Virginia. Passengers for the North
generally went by Norfolk and the bay boats to Baltimore.
The bay boat was a haven of rest to the weary body which
had endured those stages and those pristine cars, — worse
than second or third class now! Their suppers, too, were
famous, while the eating-houses along the track were of a
badness unspeakable. Passengers for Richmond or Washington knew no such solace ; — until they reached a small
boat on Acquia Creek their discomfort remained, but the
shortness of time silenced all complaints.

There was then nothing that could properly be called a
hotel. There were taverns, inns, and boarding-houses.
The tavern was the lowest of these places of entertainment;
inns were " vastly more genteel," to use that obsolete form
of commendation. In Charleston these were often kept
somewhat as English lodgings are now.

The owners lived in the background; cooked, and took
the orders of the guests as to what they would be pleased
to have for dinner, if they occupied private rooms, or served
them themselves if they preferred the *table d'hôte*. Two of
these houses were admirably kept by free coloured people,
who were quite characters. The first, Jones's, is described
by the traveller Hamilton (already quoted) as being the
best inn of the place, kept by " Jones, a negro, with silver
forks, clean tablecloths and all the luxuries of the table;
. . . iced claret to convert Diogenes into a *gourmet*."
" Charleston realizes the English idea of a *city*." A
valuable manuscript narrative by Mr. J. Francis Fisher,

of Philadelphia, who married Miss Eliza Middleton, also mentions Jones's. Later than Jones's was Eliza Lee's, — the house now called the Mansion House in Broad

The Mansion House — "Eliza Lee's"

Street. Both Jones and Lee were in great subjection to their wives, who were excellent cooks, and as excellent cooks are apt to be, great termagants as well.

Their tempers were chiefly expended upon their husbands, and did not affect the guests, except that the latter were sometimes amused by glimpses, through an open door, of a cuff or a slap, with a dishcloth, bestowed in the pantry by his angry spouse upon the pompous butler of the dining room. Both women were mulattoes, cleverer than their dark husbands, and so oppressed them; but they kept good clean houses with attentive and well-managed servants, owned by themselves.

The first hotel was the Planters' — now a ruinous old building opposite to the Huguenot church, at the corner of Queen Street. "A merry place it was in time of yore," when the wealthy men of the middle country, Hamptons, Mannings, Richardsons, Singletons, Canteys, etc., would come down with their families, and retinues of horses, carriages, and servants, for two or three weeks of "the season," for the races, of course. General Cantey was one of the last of those gentlemen, who, objecting to run his horses for money, yet dearly loved a race.

He satisfied his conscience, says "The History of the Turf," by never putting his winnings into his own pocket, but giving them to one of the Camden charities or to the Orphan House.

Returning travellers vivified and brightened society. Especially was this the case when Mr. Henry Middleton, who, after being member of Congress, Governor in 1812, etc., had been appointed Minister to Russia, came home permanently. Mrs. Middleton was Miss Herring, an English lady; and their children had grown up during their father's long stay of eight years at St. Petersburg. Mr. Middleton had been greatly esteemed by the Czar Nicholas, who upon his departure presented him with beautiful portraits of himself and the Czarina — an especial mark of favour, granted, it is said, to only two other diplomatists. These pictures of the handsomest of the Romanoffs, which still remain, were brought home to Middleton Place when Mr. Middleton, withdrawing from public life, established himself there with his unusually agreeable and cultivated family. The young people were full of the accomplish-

The Old Planters' Hotel

ments and animation springing from wide and varied associations. The eldest daughter, Miss Maria Middleton, afterward Mrs. Edward Pringle, was peculiarly distinguished; an excellent musician and brilliant talker, she drew and painted with taste and skill, and was graceful and charming in all social arts and scenes. Her youngest

sister, who married Mr. J. Francis Fisher of Philadelphia,
greatly resembled her.

Mr. Henry Middleton's younger brother, John Izard,
came back also for a time to Carolina. His life had been
romantic and picturesque. Inheriting a large fortune
from his mother he had been able to indulge his artistic
talent and fancy and had for many years wandered over
Europe, studying and painting, chiefly in Italy and Greece.
He was really an archæologist. Professor Charles Eliot
Norton of Harvard, in a memoir lately published, calls
him the first American archæologist, and dwells on the
accuracy and excellence of the drawings reproduced in
his chief work — a folio published in London in the year
1818, entitled "Grecian remains in Italy, a description
of Cyclopean walls and of Roman antiquities with topographical and picturesque views of ancient Latium by
J. J. Middleton." Many beautiful water-colour drawings
by this gentleman are still in possession of the family.
They are generally scenes or buildings of Greece and Italy,
the works of an artist, not an amateur; but apparently
his ample fortune, variety of talent, and social success combined to make him careless of the reputation which he
might have won had necessity or ambition spurred him
on. Life was too easy and pleasant for laborious days.
In Paris he enjoyed the intimate friendship of Madame
de Staël and of Madame Récamier.

Madame de Staël paid him the doubtful compliment of
saying that the languid hero of "Corinne," Lord Nelvil,
was drawn from him — a compliment which he did not
highly prize.

For Madame Récamier he had a warm and sincere admiration and esteem. A beautiful copy on porcelain of
Gérard's well-known portrait of this lady, still at Middleton Place, is said to have been given by her to Mr.
Middleton.

He married Mademoiselle de Falconet, the daughter of a great Swiss banker living at Naples, and some time later brought his wife to Charleston. They established themselves in a large house, at the corner of Meeting Street and South Bay, which had belonged to his mother's family, the Izards, intending to reside there permanently. Unfortunately they lingered too long one spring at Middleton Place, where their only child, a little girl, contracted the fever of the country and died. It was too much for the poor mother: her child's face was ever before her; she sank into a melancholy and died a few years later.

A portrait of this lady still remains; it is very beautiful: the face of a Muse with long, straight, noble features, magnificent eyes, and graceful, majestic figure.

It may easily be imagined how the coming of such spirits as these would quicken and animate a society in which there was already so much intellect and cultivation as in that of Charleston. Hospitality and gayety remained as great, but took on a lighter, more modern fashion. "They brought us into touch with the last European thought and custom," was said of the Middletons, years after, by a near and dear friend of many years' standing.

Never since the years immediately preceding the Revolution was Charleston so prosperous, so cheerful, so full of advance of every sort, as in those between 1840 and 1860. By this time the commerce of the place had regained its proper position.

No longer abandoned to strangers, there were now important mercantile houses of her own people. Her cotton and rice were carried in ships owned at home, her importations came direct from Europe.

Her wharves were filled with vessels flying the American flag. The old Exchange, by this time called the Custom House, bristled with eager merchants and captains. The office of Collector of the Port was one of

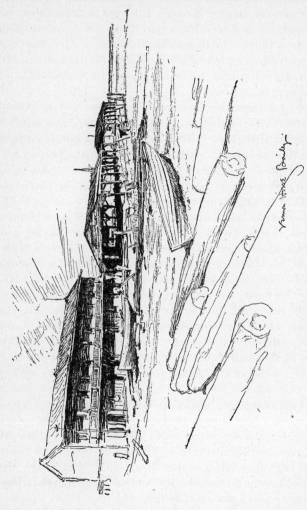

OLD WHARVES ALONG THE HARBOUR FRONT

importance. It was considered of much consequence that
the incumbent should be acceptable to the business men
of the town. In 1845, President Polk proposed to nomi-
nate a new one. On this subject Mr. Poinsett, who then
resided chiefly on his Peedee plantation, wrote to Mr.
William Bull Pringle, his connection. After speaking of
other offices he says: —

" I did *not* sign the memorial in favour of Mr. X's appointment. I refused to do so on the ground that the
Collectorship of the Port was one of peculiar interest
to the Merchants and citizens of Charleston with which a
non-resident ought not to interfere."

Other things were beginning. In addition to the old
Charleston Library another society was founded, called
the Apprentices' Library; the idea being that the books
collected should be more especially adapted to the needs
of young tradesmen and mechanics. The society built a
good hall in Meeting Street, which was used for lectures,
etc., the library and reading-room being below. Here
Glidden lectured on Ancient Egypt, Agassiz on Zoölogy
and the Glaciers, Thackeray on the Georges, etc., and
Macready, declaring himself too old to *act* " Hamlet," read
it to an enthralled audience. Here there were for several
winters loan exhibitions of paintings, the moving spirit
being Mr. Fraser, who never during his long life relaxed
his devotion to art.

The paintings exhibited were generally portraits —
three or four by Romney, as many by Sir Joshua, a dozen
or so of Copley's, and more by Stuart, Trumbull, Peale,
Morse, etc., with many lovely Sullys.

Washington Allston's " Bloody Hand " was at one time
exhibited here, and possibly others of his pictures. Sully
and Allston were native Carolinians.

One very beautiful picture shown here had a peculiar
story. One of the " characters " of the place in the earlier

part of the century was Miss Van Rhyn, a very clever old
Dutch woman, of whose past life absolutely nothing was
known. Her education and mother-wit were quite beyond
her station, which was that of a small shopkeeper. Her
wares were always good ; for fine Holland linen, Flanders
lace, Dutch Delft ware, etc., people always went to Miss
Van Rhyn. Her manners were odd and abrupt but not
common, and the good ladies, her patrons, enjoyed a talk
with her and her humorous, caustic remarks.

She had received particular kindness from Miss Lynch
Bowman, granddaughter of Thomas Lynch of the Revolution, and at her death left her this picture, which had, she
said, been painted by Van Dyck! The picture was lovely
enough to have been attributed to any artist. It was
"Charity," a beautiful woman of large and generous pro-
portions with an infant at the breast and exquisite little
children clinging round her knees. There was the noble
poise of the head, and the hands with which all Van Dyck's
creations are blessed; but there was much incredulity as
to a painting by Van Dyck being in the old lady's possession. When, however, it was found that Van Dyck's
favourite pupil was named Van Rhyn, and that he was
known to have done much work on his master's canvases,
the mystery received a possible solution. This painting
received so much injury during the Confederate War
that its restoration was impossible.

There were many exquisite miniatures by Malbone, who
spent some time in Charleston about 1800, and many of
Mr. Fraser's own. These form a gallery of almost every
Charlestonian distinguished in any way from 1800 to 1850.
He excelled in likeness and expression, and although his
painting lacks the delicacy of Malbone's, it is still good.
This is but an inadequate account of these exhibitions,
which did much to stimulate the taste for art. They
increased in interest as time went on, and many new
paintings were brought from Europe.

The theatre then was in Meeting Street, near the site of the present Gibbes Art Gallery. It was large for those days and handsome, built in the old way with a pit, in which none but men sat, two tiers of boxes and a gallery above all. There was always a good stock company, and stars came frequently. Fanny Ellsler danced there, Jenny Lind sang, and Rachel acted Adrienne Lecouvreur ; to name only three of the many artists who trod those boards.

To give an account of the many households, or of the still more numerous individuals, who together formed the vanished society of that time would be impossible, but some few may be mentioned to give an idea of the people and their life.

Each family was generally characterized by some especial taste or interest, but in all the manner of life was, broadly speaking, the same.

In the Middleton household, as has been said, the artistic prevailed; there was a certain foreign tone, also, from long residence abroad and several European marriages.

At Judge Huger's, the house in Meeting Street from which Lord and Lady William Campbell had fled at the beginning of the Revolution, politics held chief part.

The Judge himself was one of the striking figures of the day. When in Congress he was frequently called the typical Southern Conservative, but his standing among his fellow-citizens was due to a fine high-mindedness which commanded their respect, and reconciled them to his proud and masterful temper. This was so marked that he was said to have replied to some suggestions, sent to him in Congress from his constituents at home : "They think so-and-so, do they? They have no right to think at all; *here* I am to think for them." Yet his high temper was under control. When insulted in the Senate, he remarked with deadly coolness, " *This* is not the place for personal altercation," continued his speech unmoved, and — challenged his accuser that night. The latter apologized, both to him and to the chamber, extolling the conduct of the Carolinian.

Earlier in life he had shown his disinterestedness when, being a circuit judge, he had advised the diminution of the salary of that office. The salary was diminished accordingly, with the proviso that the men then on the bench should hold theirs intact. Judge Huger immediately resigned, resuming the position at the reduced rate.

So in 1845 he voluntarily withdrew from the Senate, in order to make room for Mr. Calhoun, whose presence, it was felt, was necessary for the welfare of the State, and afterward took no active part in public life. His many sons and daughters were now grown up, and his house was gay with a delightful family.

The eldest daughter, Miss Emma Huger, handsome, high-bred, and witty, was said to be the greatest belle ever known in Charleston. No one knew the number of her suitors, but no one was surprised when she chose, from among them all, a man marked by personal distinction, Mr. Joseph Allen Smith — who assumed his mother's name of Izard — once an officer of the army, but then a planter on Savannah River. This remarkable couple, known and admired in this country and in Europe, made the brilliancy of the house.

The Judge's dinners were famous; the legal element, of course, prevailing, but not lawyers only — every one who took an interest in public affairs, or was important in the State or city. Mr. Petigru, Judge King, Mr. Legaré, and Mr. Alfred Huger were among the most remarkable.

Mr. Petigru, the acknowledged leader of the bar, famous for his luminous expositions of the philosophy and reason of the law, as well as for his irresistible humour and pathos when addressing a jury, was also the fortune of a dinner party, — full of witty anecdote, with a voice and expression that gave zest to every *bon mot*.

THE SIMONTON GATEWAY, LEGARÉ STREET

He had in years to come the great sorrow of differing upon the most vital points from the great majority of his countrymen, and of seeing them adopt a course which to

him presaged only disaster. But he had also the great
consolation of knowing that such difference never lost him
their high esteem and consideration; a tribute paid by the
public to character and consistency.

Hugh Swinton Legaré was perhaps the best scholar and
finest speaker there: a great jurist, a classical scholar,
and an orator. He had been much away from home, having been for a long time *chargé d'affaires* at Brussels.
This was once used as the pretext to twit him with an indifference to his own State. His friend, Mr. Pringle, told
of the animation with which he sprang up, exclaiming,
"Sir, he who is indifferent to his native State must be
wanting *here* or *here*," touching head and heart as he
spoke.

Mr. Legaré was slightly lame, but his head was fine,
his eyes luminous, and his voice an organ of many stops.
He loved to read poetry aloud, and nothing could be finer
than his tones in Manfred's soliloquy, or Dryden's "long-
resounding line." He was appointed Attorney-general
of the United States, and died in middle life in Boston,
where he had gone to deliver a Bunker Hill oration.

Mr. Alfred Huger — called in his later years "the last
of the Barons" — was the most striking figure of all. His
tall, erect form, leonine head, deep eyes, shaggy brows, and
sonorous voice harmonized perfectly with the rugged
strength of his character, which was of the highest quality.
Taking no active share in public life, he yet thought
deeply upon political questions, as his letters attest. Personal interest never influenced him; not a rich man, he
was always a most generous one, and having no children
of his own, he was a father to many orphans. He was
honoured in public estimation for many things, for none
more than for his conduct in Nullification times. The
postmaster was the venerable Peter Bacot, who had
been appointed to his office by General Washington him-

self. An appointee of Washington was a sacred character then, and no one dreamed of disturbing the old gentleman (who was an excellent officer), until President Jackson and the spoils doctrine came in together. Even then he would have been unmolested had he not been a Nullifyer. Jackson thereupon determined to remove him, and offered the position to Mr. Alfred Huger, a Unionist. The place would at that time have been of great consequence to Mr. Huger, but he unhesitatingly declined it. " Nothing," he said, " would induce him to supplant so excellent a man and officer as Mr. Bacot upon merely political grounds ! " No persuasion could move him from his purpose, and Jackson then conferred the appointment upon his own nephew, Mr. Hayes, who had married Miss Frances Middleton (cousin of Mr. Henry Middleton).

Mr. Hayes came down with his commission in his pocket, but after being a short time in the town, and learning the warmth of public feeling on the matter, he informed his uncle that he too declined the appointment, destroyed the commission in the presence of Mr. Bacot, and left the city. The old gentleman held the situation until his death, and it was then conferred upon Mr. Huger, who held it until the outbreak of the war between the States, so that for seventy years there were but two postmasters in Charleston. Mr. Huger survived the war and died, unshaken by misfortune, almost the last of his generation.

At these dinners every public question was ably discussed by men who were, or who had been, in political life themselves; and the younger men, the Judge's sons, sons-in-law, and their friends, learned and carried on the faiths of their fathers.

It would be a great omission not to mention, in an account of this house, that important personage, Jack, the butler. Jack disputed with another old man, Harry, the butler of Mrs. Henry Izard, the reputation of being the best and most thoroughly trained servant in the town. From the judging of the wines to the arrangement of a salt spoon there was nothing which these withered brown potentates did not decide and maintain. Nothing would have astonished either more than that master or mistress should dissent from his verdict.

Jack was intolerant of anything which he considered a breach of the etiquette of the table. Nothing could have induced him to serve a gentleman before a lady, or a younger before an elder brother. To place fruit and wine on a table-cloth instead of upon the mahogany was to him a falling from grace. On one occasion he was much annoyed when a senator from the up-country twice asked for rice with his fish ! To the first request he simply remained deaf; at the second he bent down and whispered into the senatorial ear. The genial gentleman nodded and suppressed a laugh ; but when the servants had left the room, he burst into a roar, and cried — " Judge, you have a treasure. Jack has saved me from disgrace, from exposing my ignorance ; he whispered, 'That wouldn't do, sir; *we* never eats rice with fish ! ' "

Of all the gentlemen here described none was perhaps more remarkable than Judge King. Having come as a very young man from Scotland to the most conservative of cities, without especial introductions, he had made himself by force of intellect, learning, and character one of the most prominent and valued citizens ; had been long upon the Bench, had acquired a large fortune, and for many years owned and occupied the handsome house at the corner of Meeting and George streets, now the High School.

Here, surrounded by his large and cultivated family, he entertained with the most genial kindliness, perhaps more constantly than any other gentleman. For over twenty years Mrs. King's ball took place on Tuesday in Race week, as regularly as the Jockey Ball on Friday. The Judge's dinners were many and most agreeable. Conversation under his guidance was never trivial or personal. The topics were literature, travel, important events, questions of the day, — all illustrated with the anecdote and experience of a rich, well-stored mind. His voice was deep and melodious ; it was an event to hear him read Burns, with just enough accent to give the true flavour to the lines. He lived long enough to see the world crumbling around him, dying toward the close of the War between the States.

All these gentlemen were members of a rather remarkable literary club, which, formed somewhere in the twenties, it is said chiefly at the instigation of Judge Prioleau, held its last meetings in 1860.

For all those years this club met once a fortnight from October to May at the house of one or other member. The host of the evening was expected to prepare a paper on whatever subject he might choose. The subject was always announced at the previous meeting, that the members might not be unacquainted with the matter. The reading ended, the other gentlemen present took it up, asked questions or discussed the subject. The topic was dropped when supper was announced, punctually at eleven o'clock, and general conversation wound up the evening.

Strangers were always cordially invited, and often the host would prevail on one of them to take his place as speaker of the evening, thus adding the zest of variety to the entertainment. Literature, science, foreign affairs, art and social questions were the subjects for discussion, religion and American politics being barred.

Mr. Fraser's " Reminiscences," so often quoted, were written to be read here, and some other essays — for such they really were — were long remembered ; as when

Hugh Swinton Legaré spoke on Greek Republics, Mr. Poinsett on South American ones, Maury on the Hydrography of the Seas, or Agassiz on the Coal Measures.

The leading planters, lawyers, doctors, clergymen, and merchants all belonged to the club. In later years Sir Charles Lyell, Professors Agassiz, Nicholls (Astronomer Royal), and Bache, Mr. Everett, Commodore Maury, and others, too many to mention, have all addressed it. It may safely be said that from somewhere in the twenties until 1860 few strangers of any note visited Charleston without being entertained at this most agreeable of societies.

But little has yet been said of the ladies of this time; not that there were not many worthy of all praise and admiration, but in deference to that reserve which was their honourable and distinctive trait. In that day and in that class, ladies shunned all public exercise or display of talent or beauty. Their letters were admirable, but they did not write books. They charmed drawing-rooms with their voices or music, but never appeared on a stage. They talked delightfully, but did not make speeches; and although they captivated men with their beauty and charm they were not professional beauties.

The few who have been named here have been chosen because each was preëminent in her own way, and because neither has left a daughter to continue her tradition.

There was, however, one household in which the guiding spirit was so distinctly a lady, and that lady so essentially a Charlestonian of the Charlestonians, that the writer departs from this reserve in order to complete the study of the life of the town by the observations of travellers.

This was the old colonial home, in Tradd Street, of Mrs. Frederick Rutledge, granddaughter of Eliza Pinckney, and widow of the second son of Governor John Rutledge.

The animating spirit was her daughter, Harriott Pinckney, wife of the eminent naturalist, Dr. John Edwards Holbrook. Here were no politics; science and literature reigned supreme. Dr. Holbrook, a Carolinian by birth, and with a Carolinian mother, was, on the father's side, of a Massachusetts family. He was Professor of Anatomy in the Medical College of Charleston, and was, says Professor Agassiz, the first native-born American to receive recognition and esteem among the zoölogists of Europe, — his first work, "The Herpetology of North America," having procured him that distinction.

He had an immense foreign correspondence, and received innumerable letters of introduction from Europe and the North. A silent man, with a talent for making others talk, he enjoyed society almost as much as did his brilliant wife.

She, sympathizing thoroughly in her husband's pursuits, had her own interests as well. Mrs. Rutledge gladly opened her doors to her daughter's friends, and few societies were more agreeable and intellectual than that gathered in the old house which still bore the mark of Clinton's shell.

From Friday afternoon to Monday morning during the winter, and for the month of April, when the exercises of the college were at an end, Dr. and Mrs. Holbrook were usually to be found at a pretty cottage built on the site of Mrs. Pinckney's pre-Revolutionary home, Belmont, about four miles from town. Belmont house had been burned by the British, and its woods destroyed, as Mrs. Pinckney laments in her letters ; but sixty years had done much to repair the waste. Of this place and its inmates, Mrs. Agassiz, the wife of the great professor, writes in the Life of her husband. After speaking of his lectures and work generally, she says of Agassiz, his wife and family, using Mrs. Holbrook's pet name for her country home : —

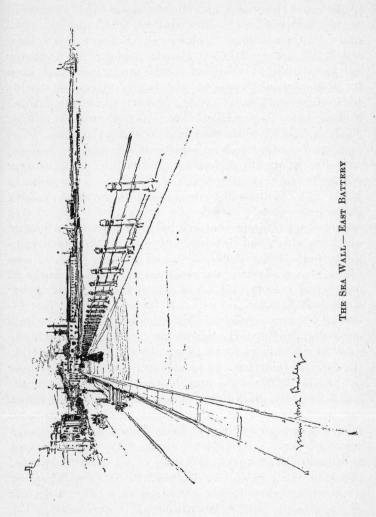

The Sea Wall — East Battery

"Their holidays and occasional vacations were passed at the house of Dr. John E. Holbrook, the 'Hollow Tree'" (properly "Belmont"—the "Hollow Tree" was only a pet name for the old family place of the Pinckneys'), "an exquisitely pretty and picturesque country place in the neighbourhood of Charleston. Here Agassiz had been received almost as one of the family on his first visit to Charleston, shortly after his arrival in the United States. Dr. Holbrook's name, as the author of the 'Herpetology of South Carolina'" (North America), "had long been familiar to him, and he now found a congenial and affectionate friend in the colleague and fellow-worker whose personal acquaintance he had been anxious to make. Dr. Holbrook's wife, a direct descendant of John Rutledge, of our revolutionary history, not only shared her husband's intellectual life, but had herself rare mental qualities, which had been developed by an unusually complete and efficient education. The wide and various range of her reading, the accuracy of her knowledge in matters of history and literature, and the charm of her conversation, made her a delightful companion. She exercised the most beneficent influence upon her large circle of young people, and without any effort to attract, she drew to herself whatever was most bright and clever in the society about her. The 'Hollow Tree,' presided over by its hospitable host and hostess, was, therefore, the centre of a stimulating and cultivated social intercourse, free from all *gêne* or formality. Here Agassiz and his family spent many happy days during their southern sojourn of 1852. The woods were yellow with jessamine, and the low, deep piazza was shut in by vines and roses; the open windows and the soft air full of sweet, out-of-door fragrance made one forget, spite of the wood fire on the hearth, that it was winter by the calendar. The days, passed almost wholly in the woods or on the veranda, closed with evenings spent not infrequently in discussions upon the scientific ideas and theories of the day, carried often beyond the region of demonstrated facts into that of speculative thought."

The Swedish novelist, Miss Brémer, is also enthusiastic in her description of Belmont and its mistress, "that *thinker*, inspiring and sympathetic, with whom she passed an entire day *tête-à-tête*, with ever increasing pleasure and admiration and no weariness."

Mr. J. Francis Fisher, whose MS. has already been quoted, after speaking of Mrs. Rutledge and her mother Mrs. Horrÿ (Mrs. Pinckney's daughter), says: "Mrs. Holbrook was the dear friend of my wife and our almost annual guest from the year of our marriage. . . . In Europe they" (Dr. and Mrs. Holbrook) "joined us at Schwalbach — Mrs. H. brought up by the accomplished ladies I have just mentioned was the most thoroughly informed and agreeable talker I ever knew — without the slightest pedantry or conceit. Her conversation had more in it than that of any other woman I ever met. She seemed to be informed on every topic, and willing to be led to every subject. For whole days we have been together when her fund of pleasant things never seemed to run dry. Without being a wit everything took a bright turn with her, and she had some anecdote or illustration to give emphasis and interest to any subject. She would discuss the most serious subjects in a tone which was the very opposite of that of an *esprit fort*, while it exhibited the candour, independence and vigour of a remarkable mind."

This lady, whose large and loving nature was as remarkable as her intellectual qualities, died toward the close of the Confederate war, broken-hearted at the ruin of her country.

If it takes all sorts of people to make a world, so is it

also with that little world which we call society. Besides
the life which has been described, there was another, gay,
bright, *insouciante* as the spirit of youth could make it.
A world where happy young folks mingled with tranquil
old ones, and the girls and boys danced and flirted while
the elders looked on and talked of their own youth. It
was the day of small and easy parties, meeting about
eight o'clock for tea; then talk, music, games, perhaps a
little dance — ice-cream and cake, a glass of wine for the
men, lemonade for the ladies, and by twelve every one
at home again ; — no trouble, no display, no *gêne!*

The athletic outdoor games of the present day did
not exist — even croquet was not ; but there were
bowling parties, and some archery, and boating, and
every one rode — long, delightful rides through the shady
lanes and thick odorous woods that then surrounded the
town — all swept away now.

The Battery was a cool and cheerful walk and drive,
and the large gardens had arbours where tea-tables were
set, or gentlemen smoked the tobacco then forbidden in
drawing-rooms.

There was one figure of that time so entirely unique
that it should not be omitted here. The widow of an
Englishman, Mrs. Holland was a connection of the
Robert J. Turnbull family, and was, like Mr. Turnbull
himself, partly of Greek descent. She was, even in middle
life, extremely handsome, of a tall, full form, with beautiful arms and hands, oval face, soft, lustrous dark eyes,
and a complexion of that perfect whiteness that sometimes
goes with black hair.

Her dress was peculiar, — always of soft-flowing white,
of no particular fashion that could be discovered, except
that the full folds seemed rather to drape than to dress
her, and that the wide sleeves, in falling back, showed the
arms to the elbow, or drawn down, covered the hand.

The East Battery

She never, by any chance, put on a bonnet, hat, or cap, wearing instead a large white lace veil which covered head, shoulders, and arms. In winter a white cashmere shawl with a narrow palm-leaf border (the only coloured thing ever seen about her) was added for warmth. Her black, closely braided hair was bound by a "fillet" — a slender gold chain with a large jewel in the centre, worn just where the part of the hair begins on the brow. It was popularly reported that she slept in this; at least, no one ever saw her without it.

This picturesquely garbed lady was one of the most charming of women. She had a delightful voice, both in speaking and singing; was very fond of society, and in great request.

But, although in very narrow circumstances, her pride as well as her inclination made it imperative for her to return the invitations which she received, and this she did with the most perfect taste and simplicity. She lived in two small rooms in the house of a friend. One of these, her bedroom, became for these very frequent occasions a second *salon*. A couple of shawls converted the small bed into a couch; wardrobe and toilet table were disposed of. Here came eagerly every one invited, the very flower of the town. Mrs. Holland's charming manner of receiving her guests, the attention paid to each, set every one at ease. She played upon the guitar and sang delightfully sweet songs, English, Italian, and Greek — that all could appreciate and enjoy; sometimes asking one or another visitor to accompany her.

Her conversation was as varied as her music: grave, gay, or pathetic, but always gentle, dignified, and easy. Men and women loved to talk with her. Only once was there a contretemps, when some blunderer drew out a door pushed back against a wall, and the lady's robes, hung behind it, swung out into the room! Not in the

2 i

least embarrassed or annoyed, Mrs. Holland smilingly apologized for "the intrusion of her garments," begged the gentleman to replace the door, and — sang another song.

The refreshments were the simplest possible. Lemonade or claret-sanger, and sweet wafers, made crisp and fresh at the moment by her own maid; — nothing more. Yet so great was the charm of the *réunions* that gentlemen and ladies would leave the handsomest parties to go to them. When the guests were so many that chairs failed, benches were brought in, sometimes even boxes — no one cared. There was a story of one very accomplished gentleman lately returned from Italy, who was asked by another as they left the house, "Do you know on what you have been sitting?" "No." "On the edge of a packing box with 'soap' branded on the bottom." "My dear sir, I would sit on St. Laurence's gridiron to have the pleasure of spending the evening with Mrs. Holland."

This charming lady died leaving no family.

The story of the events of these years has been postponed in order not to interrupt the sketch of that society which was so soon to pass away. The events were not many, and at the time few perceived their political significance, but the burning of old St. Philip's went to every heart.

It has already been told how it had once been saved from the flames by a sailor climbing to the steeple. It is hard to believe that this example could be forgotten, but the extract of a contemporaneous letter shows that it was so.

"But St. Philip's! the least exertion would have saved it, one good head might have saved that noble building. Nothing was done, however, they stood and saw it burn to ashes. The steeple caught first, one wet blanket could have extinguished it, but though there were hundreds of sailors in port nobody thought of sending a few up to the

THE SOUTH PORTAL AND GATES, ST. PHILIP'S CHURCH

roof to smother the one spot of flame. That one spot
spread, wreathed slowly round, and finally burnt the
church to the ground without one single effort having

been made to save it. It seems to have been the direct will of Heaven that it should have perished by the stupefaction of everybody who looked on. Poor Mr. Gadsden" (the Rector, afterward Bishop) "fainted when he saw it; but on the former occasion Mr. Frost" (then Rector) "offered a great reward, and it was saved. . . . Subscriptions are flying about for rebuilding."

The paper on the following day gives much the same account. Only one of the monuments was saved — a statue of Grief! A mural tablet to Colonel Daniel, of the first attack on St. Augustine, after being lost for sixty years, has lately been discovered used as a well-curb, and has been placed on the wall of the present, the third, St. Philip's. The subscriptions for this were liberal. The new edifice soon arose, larger, in some respects handsomer, than the old, but its *prestige* was lost; St. Michael's is now the historic church of the city.

The outbreak of the Mexican war, long foreshadowed as it was, caused much excitement throughout the Southern States.

Mr. Calhoun's earnest opposition surprised many who did not follow his line of thought to the ultimate results.

The war was extremely popular with the people at large, who saw in it the opportunity for military distinction, and increase of territory for the South.

The young men marched off gayly to win honour in the "Palmetto Regiment," under the command of General Scott, on almost every field from Vera Cruz to the City of Mexico. Almost all of the higher officers afterward distinguished in the war between the States had won their spurs in Mexico.

In March, 1850, came the great blow — the death of Mr. Calhoun, following close upon the Mexican War. It is impossible to express the grief, one might say the consternation, of the people; to give any idea of the sense of

St. Philip's Church

lost leadership which men endured. When his remains were brought home, every house was hung with mourning, every sleeve wore a band of black ; as the stately pageant of his funeral swept through the streets, sobs were heard on every side and strong men's eyes were full of tears,— their Prince had fallen.

The city begged that, though not of her sons, he might yet rest within her walls ; and his children granted the request, feeling that it was fitting that the greatest of Carolinians should lie with the great men of past times. His tomb stands in the centre of St. Philip's western churchyard, — "one green *Magnolia* for all sentinel."

For ten years more the town lived its normal, pleasant life, as has been shown. It was a city of happy homes and cheerful intercourse. Relationships were many, friendships strong. A stranger who had lived among them for eighteen years said, " They were a high-minded, noble, generous people, confiding and confided in. . . . It was only for one man to ask a favour of another to have it granted, and granted in such a manner that he did not feel it to be a favour. There was no stopping to calculate the loss or gain by the granting or withholding of it."

The fears of politicians, the debates in Congress, the threats of enemies, disturbed them but little. All trusted to the Constitution, hoped for a peaceful solution of the difficulties, and dreamed of happy days to come.

The awakening came in eighteen hundred and sixty.

CHAPTER XXI

CONFEDERATE CHARLESTON. THE END

IN order to finish the story of Charleston, some mention of the war in which her old life ended must be made, briefly as possible.

This is not the place for a detailed account of the causes or of the conduct of that war. The one would demand the pen of a statesman, the other that of a soldier. Either would say that the trouble had begun in the early days, even at the adoption of the Constitution itself.

But, popularly speaking, it was not until the abolition movement of the twenties — already alluded to — that any real difficulty was apprehended by the people at large.

Soon after Mr. Calhoun's death the disputes about the newly acquired territories, and whether they should abide by the agreements of the Missouri Compromise, became bitter. The action of the " Free-soil Party " and of the legislatures of many of the Northern States, in sending petitions to Congress for the abolition or restriction of slavery, contrary to the Southern reading of the provisions of the Constitution, irritated and alarmed the people.

A convention was called in South Carolina to consider the dangers to the rights of the States. In this convention the question was put whether the State should decide to secede from the Union, either singly or in coöperation with her sister States. After much debate, the convention, by a majority of 136 to 19, adopted a resolution offered by the Honourable Langdon Cheves, affirming the right of secession, but declaring it inexpedient to use the right at that time.

The matter thus settled, the people were content for the moment. The Secession party was then so small that it had not attracted much attention except in political circles.

It was very different, however, when in 1859 the John Brown raid outraged the South. The prompt action of the Federal Government prevented further disorders, but the feeling evinced by the North filled the South with horror and indignation : much as loyal Spain might feel to-day if England should extol and canonize the would-be assassin of King Alphonso and his bride !

For the first time the Southern people thoroughly understood how they were regarded, and when the split in the Democratic party assured the election of Mr. Lincoln, they prepared for the worst.

South Carolina took the lead — not unnaturally, for her political faith had been taught by her great statesman and her creed was clear.

The Legislature, called to await the result of the Presidential election, on hearing that Mr. Lincoln was chosen, at once summoned a convention of the people. It met at Columbia on the 17th of December, 1860, and immediately adjourned to Charleston.

St. Andrew's Hall, in Broad Street, the scene of so many joyous entertainments, was the place of meeting. The delegates occupied the gilt, velvet-covered chairs sacred to the chaperons of the St. Cecilia ; and the president, Mr. Jamison of Barnwell, stood on the dais below the beautiful picture of the young Victoria, in her coronation robes, painted from life by Sully for the faithful Scotchmen.

The time was too grave for thought of these accessories.

On the 20th of December the Convention passed unanimously the Ordinance of Secession, and the State stood alone !

By dark that evening every one knew that the die was

cast. The excitement was intense but quiet; there was no tumult, no huzzaing, no shouting. One or two persons illuminated their houses, many wept as they saw the rejoicing.

It was all too grave, too serious, for levity.

Great as was the majority for Secession, there were still many who disapproved.

Some grieved that the house their fathers had built should be destroyed, some mourned the possible severance of relatives and friends, some thought the moment inexpedient, but none doubted the *right*. Even Mr. Petigru said, "The State is Sov'ran. Who can put a hook in the nose of Leviathan?" To all her sons Carolina had always been their sovereign lady and mistress, and when she had once spoken, all obeyed.

These were days of breathless anxiety. What would the other States do? What would the Government at Washington do!

When the guns sounded the secession of Florida, it was sweet music to the ear.

So strong was still the belief in the controlling power of the Constitution that many, even of the politicians, really thought that there would be no war, no attempt at coercion. It is hard to understand now how this opinion could have been held. The whole movement was based upon the fact that the Constitution was being violated, and that yet greater violations were approaching; and yet it was confidently asserted that in this case it would have power to stay the hand of the majority. It is a curious proof of the influence that the study of the Constitution and the trust in its authority had over the men of that day, for the belief prevailed among those best versed in its provisions, and the theories thereon. Travellers, and business men, better acquainted with the thought and temper of the Northern people, had no such

FORT SUMTER

illusions. Their anxiety was intense. This belief, long
continued in many quarters, had an unfortunate effect in
preventing or delaying preparations and measures most
necessary at the time.

On the 25th of December, Major Anderson, commanding at Fort Moultrie, moved his whole force under cover
of night to Fort Sumter, entirely unperceived. The
women and children of the garrison, whom he sent up to
town, requesting that they should be sent North, brought
the news.

Fort Sumter, standing grim and terrible sixty feet
above the waves in the centre of the harbour, mounted
one hundred and forty guns, many of which seemed to
look directly into the front windows of the Battery houses.

Doubt and delay were done. Then came the call to
arms. Quick and bright was the answer, — the State
knew her sons.

All was life and animation, — every man volunteered.
Some were officers, more were privates — the private
everywhere the favourite. The militia companies grew
sixty to a hundred strong in a day. New companies
were formed; the old ones split into first and second
corps, their recruits were so many.

In the country it was the same thing, the whole State
sprang to arms. The other forts, Moultrie, Johnson, and
Pinckney, were garrisoned; earthworks were begun at
many points. Events followed too quickly to relate.
A vessel, *The Star of the West*, with troops and provisions,
attempted to reach Fort Sumter, was fired upon by a
small battery upon Morris Island, and withdrew. It was
afterward believed that this was a stratagem to "fire the
Northern heart" by the affront to the flag. It certainly
fired the Southern; it was the beginning of coercion.
More States seceded and a government was formed at
Montgomery, Alabama.

There were embassies to and from Washington, "peaceful envoys" sent to Major Anderson, — really to plan the reënforcement of the fort, — ostensibly to arrange the "statu quo." It must be confessed that in those many interviews the Southern envoys showed more good faith than discernment. Major Anderson was to send to market freely, have fresh vegetables, groceries, etc.

No restrictions were put on the communications with market woman, grocer, or butcher!

When General Beauregard arrived to take command, that brilliant officer, who had learned strategy along with other military knowledge, limited the shopping, and put the purchasers under strict surveillance.

Under General Beauregard's direction the most intelligent activity prevailed. In his Life is recorded his surprise at the spirit which he found. Planters laboured at the earthworks by the side of their slaves, no work was too hard or too disagreeable for the enthusiasm of these white-handed gentlemen! Every man had an "infallible" plan for reducing Fort Sumter, and murmured only at the incomprehensible delay. The greatest goodhumour and gayety prevailed, and the Palmetto banner waved proudly over all.

What was in truth much more remarkable than any enthusiasm on the part of the gentry, "the slaveholding aristocracy," as they used to be called, was the enthusiasm of the lower classes.

It was only natural that gentlemen should do all, and dare all, for the faith and the order of their lives. But that from little store, from workshop, and from field the men should come with equal ardour, was astonishing. They had nothing to gain, no slaves to keep, — but they had their State to defend, and they came. It was a splendid exhibition of loyalty and it never failed.

Batteries of many sorts were erected at every available

point along Sullivan's, Morris, and James islands, so that Sumter stood in a semicircle of guns.

Two of these batteries were remarkable as being the first of those ironclad defences afterward so much used. The one was the invention of a civilian, Mr., afterward General, Clement H. Stevens, who was killed in the Atlanta campaign under Joseph E. Johnston.

It was "made of heavy timbers overlaid with railroad iron, so fitted together as to present a smooth inclined surface, to be profusely greased when ready for action. Three heavy guns were fired through embrasures fitted with thick iron shutters." The other very ingenious work was a floating battery, built in somewhat the same way, of rough logs and plated with iron. It was the device of a gallant ex-officer of the United States Navy, Captain John Randolph Hamilton (the son of Governor Hamilton of Nullification), who had perfected it against much discouragement, until Beauregard arrived and pronounced it "good." When the long-postponed day of battle came, " Captain Jack," as the very popular sailor was universally called, commanded his own battery, and did good service against that western side of the fort which no land gun could reach.

January, February, and March were so full of crowded life that they seemed an eternity, and yet one dreaded lest eternity should end. End it did when one night at eleven o'clock seven guns thundered out over the town and every man sprang up, seized his rifle, and ran to the wharves. It was the signal that the relieving fleet was on its way South, and that the whole reserve must hurry to the islands.

Several days passed; the work was ready, soldiers were pouring from the up-country into the town. Half the gentlemen of the State, whose regiments were not yet organized, were serving as volunteer aides on the staff of

General Beauregard or General Ripley; their wives were at the Mills House or the Charleston Hotel, where Governor and Mrs. Pickens had their apartments. The town looked like a place *en fête*. The excitement was too great for alarm. Mothers parted from sons, wives from husbands, girls from lovers, dry-eyed though with trembling lips. There was no thought of defeat, victory was on every lip; yet — what might be the cost?

At ten o'clock on the night of the 11th of April the signal was given that the bombardment was to begin on the morrow!

At day dawn on the twelfth a shell rose, screaming, from Coming's Point, into the pale amber sky, and arched its way to Sumter, bursting directly above the fort. In five minutes the Battery swarmed with people, — soon the houses, the wharves, even the housetops were crowded. The roadway was so blocked with carriages that boys crossed from the pavement to the sea-wall jumping from one roof to another rather than risk a passage among the horse hoofs. When a country regiment marched down, it was impossible to make room. It had to turn back to the Battery Garden.

For two hours the shelling went steadily on with no response from Sumter. Even the flag did not go up until the sun rose; then with military precision it slowly ascended the staff and floated out to the breeze. Major Anderson was saving ammunition, and his men were having breakfast, he afterward explained. At seven the fort began firing and kept on steadily though slowly all day. It was said to be the first battle on record between two forts firing at each other, as Moultrie and Sumter hurled their shot across the channel.

The anxiety was awful; those batteries were filled with the men of the town. Everything from eighteen to sixty was there. The first blaze of excitement was over,

OLD WAREHOUSES NEAR EAST BAY

and as the hours went on a silent, mute dread took possession, — all were keyed to too high a pitch for audible
emotion.   Not a woman looking on but had her heart on

one of those islands. "Have you any relative there?" asked a stranger of one young girl. "My five brothers," she answered, — white, but calm. The old men moved about restlessly; one or two muttered something about the War of 1812!

At last, at four in the afternoon, word came that "no one was hurt" — then rang out a "shout that shook the towers!" Some women burst into tears, — one or two fainted.

How such a miracle came to pass has never been explained. Shot and shell, admirably aimed, had been flying to and fro for twelve hours. Guns had been dismounted, walls breached, batteries damaged, but no blood had been shed on either fort or islands! All that night and next day the cannonade went on. By twelve o'clock a smoke was seen to rise from the fort — it had been fired by red-hot shot. Boats put out, and after much parley, Major Anderson accepted General Beauregard's generous terms of surrender, saluted his flag, and was conveyed with all the honours of war, by the steamer *Isabel*, to the fleet, which had for hours lain, inexplicably idle, in the offing.

Victory was ours ; the enemy had gone, the harbour was at rest, and the new flag, the " Stars and Bars " which Beauregard said " began to look well," floated beside the Palmetto from the battered walls of Sumter.

The joy and exultation, the hope of speedy recognition of independence, of peace, were delightful but short-lived.

The immediate result was the uprising of the North.

As in the Revolution, the seat of war, after one brilliant exploit in Charleston harbour, shifted north, — to Virginia, for the defence of which troops were hurried on. Before Beauregard went he insisted strongly on the importance of the Charleston and Savannah Railroad, and the intricate waterways by which it could be approached.

It was accordingly well guarded for the next four years.

At home, men and women settled down to the stern reality of war, — of a war for which the most necessary material was scant or wanting, and for which almost everything had to be supplied by individual effort and sacrifice. From the moment when our troops took possession of the scarred and battered Sumter the work of rebuilding, of fortification, of drilling, of collecting supplies, began and went on ceaselessly. *Men* were at first the only necessaries of which there were enough ; more offered than could be armed and clothed. Gentlemen came forward and raised companies, equipping them entirely at their own expense. The supplies in the arsenals were soon exhausted and arms had to run the blockade, now established along the coast. One devoted Carolinian, over sixty, and with no military experience, having thus equipped a company, got the command of it given to his younger brother and served in it himself as a private.

Every woman worked. Ladies sat day by day among their maids, sewing shirts and trousers for the soldiers. The plantation tailors were brought out to help make the jean coats; knapsacks were fashioned of every conceivable thing, and people knitted as they breathed.

Victory and joy came yet again in July, when Manassas was won. Joy alloyed by grief when the bodies of her heroes, Bee and Johnson, were brought back to the town, and lay in state in the City Hall, at the foot of the great white statue of Calhoun, with a mourning people round them.

These were general and colonel, and so entitled to the honours of the stately burial accorded them. But

> " Not the chiefs who dying see
> Their flags in front of victory . . .

> Claim from their monumental beds
> The bitterest tears a nation sheds."

Then began that long list of the wounded and dead of those splendid privates who made the glory of the Confederacy.

The best of Carolina lay dead in their gray jackets, unmarked by band or star; but they fell for their country. "Grief was pride," and even their mothers said, "It is well."

This is not the story of the Confederate war, or even of the defence of Charleston harbour ; the man who had a chief share in making that defence possible has already written its history so as to win the admiration of all military readers. This is only a little record of the life of the city, and of how she bore herself under these strange conditions. Of how on a beautiful November day the people thronged to the water front south and west and listened to the booming of far-off guns.

It was the first defeat, foreseen and inevitable, but nevertheless defeat.

Beauregard had warned that the magnificence of Port Royal was its weakness ; and now the great ships had floated up the entrance on a sea of glass, and the best harbour of the South was lost. From sixty miles away the sound came soft but distinct through the hazy autumn air.

In December of the same eventful year a fire swept the town in a great swath from northeast to southwest, as it had done when St. Philip's was burned. This time the extent laid waste was far greater. It began upon a wharf on Cooper River above the market, where negroes *en route* for the up-country were cooking their supper. It was a windy night, their fires got away from them, and a hay store on the wharf caught. All hope of checking it was soon over, for the wind, rising, drove great beams flaming through the air, so that the conflagration spread by leaps

LOOKING OVER THE CITY TOWARD THE COOPER RIVER

St. Philip's Church at left, the Custom House in middle distance.

and bounds. There were no men, the fire department was broken up, all were in service or at the camps of preparation upon the race-course or in St. Andrew's parish. Passing just north of the new St. Philip's, the fire consumed the Circular Church, just west of it, and burned across to the Ashley. By daybreak all was a wilderness of smoky ruin. Men rushed down from the race-course, General Ripley took command, and by blowing up houses at last stopped the devastation. Many important public buildings were destroyed: the new Agricultural Hall, the largest building in Charleston, the theatre, St. Andrew's Hall in Broad Street, the cathedral, St. Peter's Church, the large rice mills far out in Ashley River, many shops, and many private residences. Two old colonial houses often mentioned here, the Pinckney house on East Bay and Mrs. Rutledge's on Tradd Street, were among those burned.

Many valuable stores and much public and private property were consumed.

It made it easier for people to take the advice of the general then commanding (General Pemberton) and leave the city.

Those who were thus made homeless, and many of the families of the officers and men enlisted "for the war," removed to what were supposed to be safer places. The weary work of "refugeeing" began in that spring of 1862.

General Lee, who was in Charleston for a short time then, answered a gentleman who said that "it was difficult for so many men to abandon their business for the war," "Believe me, sir, the business of this generation *is* the war." All the talk of "ninety days," or of "one year levies," was over now. Comprehension of the magnitude and probable duration of the struggle had come.

Women whose houses had been spared, or whose hus-

2 K

bands or sons were in service on the coast, remained at home, and listened with what composure they might to the quick, sharp rattle of musketry fire mingling with the deeper sound of guns, when, on the 16th of June, the enemy, having effected a landing at the same Stono Inlet by which Sir Henry Clinton had some eighty years before, attacked a small earthwork thrown across the centre of James Island, at a place called Secessionville. The Ashley River between the south front of Charleston and James Island is not a mile and a half wide. There were no defences there. The works upon the island itself were the only safeguard, and now these were attacked by General Benham, U.S.A., with 7000 men, and were defended by Colonel Lamar of South Carolina with 750 men and five small guns. Every cannon shot, every rattle of musketry, was plainly heard in the city. Four times the Federalists charged the works. Hagood with three South Carolina Regiments reënforced Lamar, and the enemy withdrew, having lost, he said, 685 men ; 204 of ours had fallen. This repulse saved the town, but neglect of the "back door" had nearly lost it then.

"When so outnumbered did you not think of retreat?" asked a lady of a young officer with a bullet through his leg. "Where could we have run to?" replied the soldier; "the bottom of Ashley River would have been the only refuge. Had we crossed to the town you would have beaten us out with your broomsticks."

There was a sort of pause in that autumn of 1862. The blockading squadron gathered more closely along the coast, and the land forces worked quietly at the mouth of Stono, which they always held; but there was no attack. For a brief interval a curious gayety prevailed, when parties of merry girls went down at night to Sumter, garrisoned by the First South Carolina Regulars (Artillery) under Colonel Alfred Rhett, and danced on the parade-ground, charmed with the bright trappings and gallant bearing of their young hosts. Beauregard came back from the West to the great joy of the citizens, bringing with him dashing Creole aides. An entertainment was even given, feverishly enjoyed and long remembered as the "Beauregard ball," where every man who danced was in uniform, with his "leave" in his pocket — and his heart on his sleeve. And maids were kind, — for who could tell if ever those men should dance again; were not the battlements of Sumter, the casemates of Wagner, awaiting them?

They did not wait long. In April the ironclads began the bombardment of the fort; in July the land forces on Morris Island took it up. How the Federal army and navy invested Charleston; how neither ships, men, nor money were spared in the attempt to force old Governor Sayle's "Iron Gate"; and how all failed, is a tale that has been often told. Battery Wagner, the defence of the northern end of Morris Island, being taken after eight weeks of stubborn resistance, the heavy siege guns joining with those of the fleet bore on the devoted fort. Crumbled to pieces after a time; a mere heap of ruins, no longer tenable by artillery men, with every gun dismounted but held indomitably by Stephen Elliott with his riflemen, Sumter rose by the skill and energy of her chief engineer, Major Johnson (now Rector of St. Philip's), to be a fort again, a fine earthwork mounted with guns. Under Elliott, and after him Miles, Mitchell, and Huguenin, she stood for two years at bay. In those two years great deeds of arms were wrought. Ironclad rams hurled themselves against men-of-war; torpedo boats assailed ironclads. Again and again the fort repelled attacks.

Blockade runners stole in and out, bringing, at immense risk, invaluable supplies and news of the outside world. The city never lost heart; not even when on the twenty-second of August, at half after one A.M., a screaming shell flew over the sleeping town, and burst in a yard beyond the Battery. In a moment the town awoke; another and another! The alarm and horror were indescribable, for at first people thought the city was taken. The negroes were panic-stricken.

A young staff officer sleeping in the upper part of the town, tired after a long day's service, described himself roused by a negro servant, "The General send for you, sah!" "What?" "The General send for you, sah! *Something* da, fly over the house. *I* run for de stable." Most people observed the same prudent policy, for as the young man rode down the whole length of the town to headquarters, he passed through rows of brilliantly lighted houses, but no one was in the streets. Some persons were forced to go out. On East Battery a boy, brought home from camp, was lying desperately ill. The shells fell about the house. An ambulance was sent for, the lad's sister got in and took his head on her lap. A gentleman rode ahead to seek a refuge. They drove at a foot's pace — their way lighted by the bursting bombs, until out of range. There a kind friend took them in; the boy died next day. There were cases of women in dire distress.

It proved that General Gilmore, commanding the Union forces, having established a gun (afterward known as the "Swamp Angel") on a point in the marsh between the end of Morris and James islands, sent an *unsigned* note addressed to General Beauregard, *not* to that officer's headquarters, but to Battery Wagner, five miles off across the bay.

This note demanded "the immediate evacuation of Morris Island and Fort Sumter by the Confederate forces. . . . Should you refuse compliance with this demand, or should I receive no answer thereto *within four hours* after it is delivered into the hands of your subordinate at Fort Wagner, I shall open fire on the city of Charleston, from batteries already established within easy and effective range of the heart of the city."

This letter did not reach town until half after ten that night. General Beauregard had not yet returned from inspecting some works on one of the islands. His staff officer returned it at once for signature. General Gilmore opened fire at half after one, and returned his note of warning at nine next morning, signed eight hours *after* he had begun shelling.

It need hardly be said that this proceeding did not advance by one hour the progress of the siege or the fall of the city. There was at the moment much individual suffering. A few unhappy women and new-born infants died of it. This was the sole advantage gained by the Federal commander.

There was, in point of fact, but the one gun then "established within easy and effective range of the heart of the city," and that burst at the thirty-sixth shot. When the great bombardment began, which went on "spasmodically" from the fall of Battery Wagner until the surrender of the city, February, 1865, people simply moved up-town or into the country, and suffered inconvenience to which they soon became accustomed.

By that time hearts were so tempered by trial, so bound to "the Cause," that loss of property troubled but little. "Fight on, conquer in the end, and never count the cost," was the universal cry.

As long as possible the churches were kept open, but the steeples were used as targets, and they were greatly damaged. At St. Philip's the rector, Mr. (afterward Bishop) Howe, was in the middle of his sermon, when a shell passed over the roof and burst in the western churchyard. The congregation remained seated until the service reached its proper close, and after a peculiarly

fervent blessing dispersed quietly. The Episcopalians left
in the town united, after that, for worship in St. Paul's,

GATEWAY, ST. MICHAEL'S CHURCHYARD

Radcliffeborough, the rectors taking it by turns to offi-
ciate.   Other denominations made similar arrangements.
  Ten shells passed through St. Philip's, its chancel was
wrecked, its organ demolished ; St. Michael's suffered in

the same way, the other churches likewise; many tomb-
stones were shattered by falling shells.

There were wonderfully few casualties; as in the
British siege of 1781, the large lots and gardens saved
many lives. Some few men, who insisted upon living
among the dilapidated houses, were injured by falling
buildings, and one old ground-nut cake mauma was
literally knocked to pieces in the market.

Officers stationed in the town would amuse themselves
by going down at night to the Battery to see the burning
fuses coming across the water. Headquarters were
moved to Governor Aiken's house, Hampstead, and all
military offices were above the line of fire.

Through all this time there was one comfort which
seldom failed. Generations of kind treatment and wise
training bore fruit; the negroes behaved admirably.
Few, indeed, were the instances where this was not so.
At first, some — generally mechanics — went off to the
enemy; but of house servants and plantation hands by
far the greater number kept their own way, faithful,
steady, and kind. A man leaving wife and children, perhaps forever, would say to his butler, "Scipio, keep the
house straight and the boys in order; help your mistress,
and don't let the people trouble her." And Scipio, a
trifle more consequential than usual, assumed the trust.
To "Mauma" it was not necessary to speak; she guarded
her charges (including her mistress) with fierce devotion.
The instances are innumerable. The field-hands worked
steadily, and made the crops, with a boy of sixteen or
man of seventy as sole overseer. Servants who went to
the army with officers behaved most faithfully. Many
brought home the bodies of their dead masters; others
came back with horses whose riders would need them
no more. All performed prodigies of ingenious cooking
and catering. Yet when General Sherman passed through

the country, many of these same people abandoned their homes, beguiled by the vision of wealth, and wandered off, many to die by the roadside of want and hardship.

Others, however, remained trusted friends and servants, faithful and affectionate, to the end of life.

By 1864 the town presented the most extraordinary appearance. The whole life and business of the place were crowded into the few squares above Calhoun Street, and along the Ashley, where the hospitals and the prisoners were and the shells did not reach. There were shops, selling the poorest wares at the most fabulous prices ; — had they not been brought at risk of death or imprisonment through the blockade? A tin cup, painted red, holding about a gill, cost ten dollars. The coarse brown sugar put into it to make a Christmas gift for a child — the same.

People were coming and going ; men to their work, women to the hospitals. Almost all the women were in mourning, and their strained, anxious eyes belied their smiling lips. But by this time to doubt would have been treason; all were cheerful and confident, busy and helpful, doing little kindnesses and sharing every comfort. "Come and dine, we have a bit of fresh meat to-day." "Your wife is sick ? I will send her ' a draw ' of tea." "We have got some flour and butter from the country, — I will make some fresh biscuits for the boys in the Fort." "I have not cut up all my curtains yet. I will send one for frocks for the baby." No one can tell what those war-time babies and their mothers endured. Some were born under fire ; some by the roadside ; — it was awfully biblical! Although some died, many survived and are healthy men and women to-day.

At the railroad shops and along the water front there was great activity. The men and materials needed for the relief of the garrisons and for the constant rebuilding of Sumter were being prepared at one place ; boats of various devices at another. Experiments were going on with torpedoes, with rams, with booms, with defences of every description. Great ingenuity was shown in making military engines of the most unexpected and hopeless materials — old river boats became rams, copper gutters were melted up for torpedoes, St. Philip's bells had long ago been converted into guns. St. Michael's bells, it should have been said, were taken down and sent to Columbia for safe keeping. Thus thrown directly into General Sherman's way, they shared the destruction of that place ; were burned and broken to pieces. The fragments being afterwards gathered up, they were sent to England to the same foundry where they had originally been cast. There, with English permanence, the old moulds were preserved. They were recast, returned to Charleston, and ring to-day the same tone as when they pealed for the birthday of his Majesty; having five times crossed the Atlantic.

To pass from this bustling, crowded scene to the lower part of the town was like going from life to death. Early in December the present writer drove during a short truce for the exchange of prisoners from Calhoun Street to the Battery, and saw but *two* human beings : men who crept out of yards wondering at the sound of wheels.

Everything was overgrown with rank, untrimmed vegetation. Not grass merely, but bushes, grew in the streets. The gardens looked as if the Sleeping Beauty might be within. The houses were indescribable : the gable was out of one, the chimneys fallen from the next ; here a roof was shattered, there a piazza half gone ; not a window remained. The streets looked as if piled with diamonds, the glass lay shivered so thick on the ground.

On the Battery the three great guns gazed seaward, and the red-collared artillerymen, who were playing ball to keep themselves warm, ran up to greet the visitors. The forts were silent, but the flags flew defiant. A small steamer with a white ensign steamed slowly across the harbour. It was a strange scene.

It was almost the end.

In less than two months General Hardee, then in command, was ordered to evacuate the forts and city and withdraw his small force of fourteen thousand men to North Carolina, where a last stand might still be made. All who could went out ahead of the army — in trains, in carriages, in carts — and their flight was in the winter!

General Sherman, marching from Savannah with seventy thousand men, burning as he came, having destroyed all but one of the great houses of Ashley River, sent a corps to occupy the city. It was surrendered by the municipal authorities. They also sent a boat to inform Admiral Dahlgren, commanding the fleet, that the forts were empty and could now be safely occupied.

The Federal ironclads then first entered Charleston harbour, after a siege of five hundred and sixty-seven days.

The iron gate had held fast, but the defence was ended.

Of what that defence was a Charleston woman cannot speak. An English officer who saw it all — Colonel Henry W. Fielden, of H.B.M. army — said, writing to its historian: —

" Though five and twenty years have elapsed since the close of the operations around the city of Charleston, the lessons to be derived from their study are as important as ever. We find a large commercial city at the commencement of a great war, defended by nearly obsolete works, and with several unguarded approaches, rendered impregnable in a short time by the skill and genius of the general in command, supported by the indomitable valour, devotion, and tenacity of its defenders, and by the unflinching spirit of all ages and both sexes of the community."

With the fall of the city and of the Confederacy went out the old life of Charleston.

What that life was has already been told.

If the new is, or shall be, better, purer, braver, or higher, it will be well.   This is the tale of the old, and it is done.

INDEX

509

Printed in the United States of America.

NEW ORLEANS:
THE PLACE AND THE PEOPLE

By GRACE KING

Author of " Jean Baptiste Le Moyne, Sieur de Bienville,"
" Balcony Stories," etc.

Illustrated by FRANCES E. JONES

Cloth   12mo $ 2.50

" It is a delightful book, and is beautifully illustrated with a great host of effective pictures, by pencil and camera. . . . Few people could have done the work so well, none could have done it better than Miss King." — *New Orleans Picayune.*

" It is neither a history nor a guide-book, but it is likely to be more entertaining than either to most readers, and many will be stimulated to carry their study of the subject further. Miss King knows her New Orleans thoroughly and has given us a most fascinating book." — *Springfield Republican.*

" Miss King's book is rich in attractiveness, and it ought to attain a wide circulation among the people whose history it tells so accurately and so charmingly. The book is handsomely printed and the illustrations are a creditable and striking feature." — *New Orleans States.*

" ' New Orleans: the Place and the People ' is a work which will appeal to Northern as well as Southern readers, and for this excellent work too high praise cannot be given." — *Chicago Evening Post.*

" One of the most readable books that has appeared for years. . . . This is a triumph of literary art, and when it is added that the pictures are as clever as the text, it will be seen that the book is noteworthy." — *San Francisco Chronicle.*

PHILADELPHIA:
THE PLACE AND THE PEOPLE

By AGNES REPPLIER

With many Illustrations by ERNEST C. PEIXOTTO

Cloth   Crown 8vo $ 2.50

" Miss Repplier has written *con amore.* She knows her material thoroughly, and has very sympathetic feeling for her city, although she is not blind to its faults as revealed in its history, nor to its defects of taste as disclosed by its architecture. . . . This volume will take its place among those foot-notes on history which are as interesting as the history itself." — *The Outlook.*

" The plan is not that of systematic history, but the freedom of the method employed, combined with Miss Repplier's brisk manner and her unfailing sense of humor, which in no way impairs her loving loyalty, makes the resulting volume the more entertaining, and it will interest and inform very many readers whom the more sober-minded historians have failed to reach." — *Philadelphia Times.*

THE MACMILLAN COMPANY
64-66 FIFTH AVENUE, NEW YORK

BOSTON:
THE PLACE AND THE PEOPLE

By M. A. DE WOLFE HOWE

Illustrated by LOUIS HOLMAN

Cloth   **8vo**   **$ 2.50**

Its modern human interest is the distinctive quality of Mr. Howe's richly illustrated description of Boston. It is to the nineteeth century that the city owes the most, yet almost every account of its history has hitherto given the greater space to the revolutionary or earlier times.

Its illustrations include portraits of distinguished Bostonians, from old prints, paintings, miniatures, daguerreotypes, and photographs, many of them hitherto unpublished; pictures of homes and birthplaces of famous persons; queer old broadsides, significant for their information and admirable for their typography; monuments and statues; mural paintings and old buildings; general views, ancient and modern; quaint and artistic relics from the collections of the Bostonian Society; and coats-of-arms, medals, coins, and seals hitherto relatively unknown.

OLD QUEBEC:
THE FORTRESS OF NEW FRANCE

By SIR GILBERT PARKER

Author of "The Right of Way," " Pierre and his People," etc.

With more than One Hundred Illustrations

Cloth   **Demy 8vo**

In this delightful book the author of "The Right of Way" has told sympathetically the story of his chosen city from the earliest times to the present day. It is a picturesque and honorable chronicle. Americans who make even a brief sojourn in that most individual of Canadian cities feel the effective and potent spell which it casts on all who have lived within its curious limits. Many of the episodes and incidents in its history are dramatically effective; and through good use of these episodes in its founding, in its struggles, and in its intimate connection with the most stirring period in the history of the continent, the author has been enabled to write a charming book. The humor and tragedy of Canadian life have long been Sir Gilbert Parker's especial field. No better writer could have been chosen to describe a city with so romantic a history as Quebec. No one knows its people better than he.

THE MACMILLAN COMPANY

64-66 FIFTH AVENUE, NEW YORK